O9-ABH-961

UNSTUCK
IN TIME

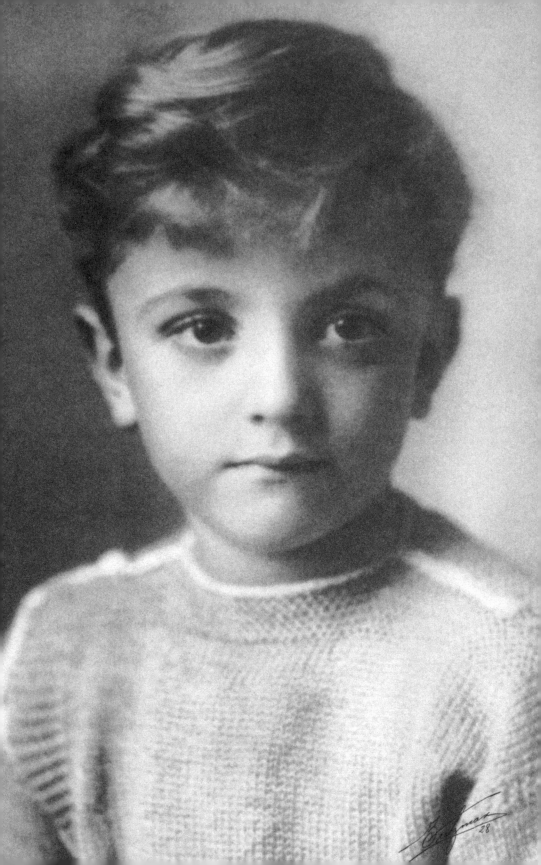

UNSTUCK IN TIME

*A Journey Through Kurt Vonnegut's
Life and Novels*

GREGORY D. SUMNER

7

SEVEN STORIES PRESS
New York

Copyright © 2011 by Gregory D. Sumner

A Seven Stories Press First Edition

Seven Stories Press
140 Watts Street
New York, NY 10013
www.sevenstories.com

College professors may order examination copies of Seven Stories Press titles for a free six-month trial period. To order, visit www.sevenstories.com/textbook or send a fax on school letterhead to (212) 226-1411.

Book design by Jon Gilbert

Library of Congress Cataloging-in-Publication Data
Sumner, Gregory D.
 Unstuck in time : a journey through Kurt Vonnegut's life and novels / by Gregory D. Sumner. -- 1st ed.
     p. cm.
 Includes bibliographical references and index.
 ISBN 978-1-60980-349-0 (hardcover : alk. paper)
 1. Vonnegut, Kurt. 2. Vonnegut, Kurt--Criticism and interpretation. 3. Vonnegut, Kurt--Characters. 4. Autobiography in literature. 5. Self in literature. 6. American Dream in literature. 7. America--In literature. I. Title. II. Title: Kurt Vonnegut's life and novels.
 PS3572.O5Z863 2011
 813'.54--dc22

                              2011032265

9 8 7 6 5 4 3 2 1

Printed in the USA.

Contents

List of Illustrations

Frontis: Kurt Vonnegut, circa 1928. *Courtesy of Nanny Vonnegut*

Page 20: Newlyweds Kurt and Jane Vonnegut, 1951. *Courtesy of Nanny Vonnegut*

Page 38: Kurt and Nanny Vonnegut, 1958. *Courtesy of Nanny Vonnegut*

Page 59: Kurt Vonnegut, 1965. *Bob Doeppers/The Indianapolis Star*

Page 80: Left to right: Nanny Vonnegut, Kurt Adams, Steve Adams, Edith Vonnegut, Kurt Vonnegut at Niagara Falls, 1965. *Courtesy of Nanny Vonnegut*

Page 102: At a press luncheon at the 21 Club, circa 1967, for CBS Films's *Virtues,* are the picture's producers and five of its eight writers. Producers (standing, left to right): Si Litvinoff, Francis Ford Coppola, and Raymond Wagner. Writers (seated left to right): Jack Gelber, Bruce Jay Friedman, Paul Krassner, and Kurt Vonnegut. *The Film Daily*

Page 122: Kurt Vonnegut at his home in Barnstable, Cape Cod, 1969. *Israel Shenker/Getty*

Page 146: Kurt Vonnegut, 1971. *Fred W. McDarrah/Getty*

Page 170: Kurt Vonnegut, 1975. *Bernard Gotfryd/Getty*

Page 188: Kurt Vonnegut in New York, 1979. *Mary Reichenthal/AP Photo*

Page 212: Kurt Vonnegut at Manchester University, 1983. *Kevin Cummins/Getty*

Page 238: Kurt Vonnegut at his home, 1985. *Oliver Morris/Getty*

Page 260: Kurt Vonnegut with Jill Krementz and Lilly, 1987. *Allen Ginsberg/CORBIS*

Page 286: Kurt Vonnegut, 1990. *Ron Galella/Getty*

Page 310: Kurt Vonnegut attends NY Film Festival premier, 1999. *Gregory Pace/CORBIS*

Page 322: Editorial cartoon by John Sherffius, April 12, 2007. © *2007 by John Sherffius. Used by permission of John Sherffius and Creators Syndicate, Inc.*

Preface

Kurt Vonnegut was generous in our correspondence more than a decade ago, when I broached a fledgling aspiration to write about his life. He wrote back telling me that he liked my study of the muckraking New York critic Dwight Macdonald, an "exemplar of perfect political decency" he knew a little and admired, along with Orwell, as a figure from "the golden age of romantic anti-fascism." With a teacher's gentle hand he cautioned that the biography I imagined undertaking would not be an easy thing to accomplish. "You would find yourself trying to tell a story with only one character, with no supporting cast, no gang," Mr. Vonnegut explained. He continued, with typical humility and even embarrassment:

> I was once hired to write a scenario based on *The French Lieutenant's Woman*. I had to give up, because everything was in people's heads. In the world of the senses, absolutely nothing happened. My life has been pretty much like that.[1]

So I decided to tell Kurt Vonnegut's story by walking across the foundation stones of his legacy, his fourteen novels. Written under dramatically changing personal circumstances, against the backdrop of seismic shifts in our country's historical circumstances, they read together as a kind of diary, an impassioned and sometimes brokenhearted meditation on the American Dream. I hope he would forgive me the conceit of trying to explain his art, and that this companion to his life and books is in some measure faithful to Vonnegut's spirit, which continues to inspire so many readers of all ages.

When I find a well-drawn character in fiction or biography, I generally take a warm personal interest in him, for the reason that I have known him before—met him on the river.[1]

—MARK TWAIN

The function of an artist is to respond to his own time.[2]

—KURT VONNEGUT

Storyteller

Kurt Vonnegut and the American Dream

*America is the interplay of three hundred million
Rube Goldberg contraptions invented only yesterday.*
—from *Timequake*

Breakfast of Champions, Kurt Vonnegut's guided tour through the wasteland of early-1970s America, opens with a disclaimer. Acknowledging the title as a registered trademark, deployed in the book as slang for a dry martini, the author dutifully cautions that its use "is not intended to indicate an association with or sponsorship by General Mills, nor is it intended to disparage their fine products." While there are no imperatives, legal or otherwise, for doing so here, it seems appropriate to begin this journey across Vonnegut's novels with my own caveat: the use of "American Dream" as an organizing principle in no way implies a neat or settled interpretation of what that expression means. At its broadest level it is a *story*—about perpetual reinvention, boundless opportunities on an endless frontier, rags-to-riches success.

Kurt Vonnegut was a lifelong student of stories—how they worked and what made them compelling to readers. He had the good fortune to grow up in a house full of books in a city with free public libraries, visits to which

1

he recalled as treasure hunts, magical excursions where a child's imagination could feast. At home he absorbed the conversation of uncles and aunts and neighbors, and, like millions of others during the Great Depression, lost himself nightly in front of the radio and once a week in the darkness of Saturday movie matinees. To get attention as the baby brother, Kurt picked up on the nuances and timing of the jokes that filled the air around the family dinner table, bite-sized offerings of solace aimed at making bearable unpleasant everyday realities.

Influenced by the artisanal ethics of his architect father and grandfather, and the literary aspirations of his mother, Kurt displayed early on a talent for making people laugh and for translating his observations into writing. As a schoolboy journalist at Shortridge High he learned to produce material to deadline, his method polished by the immediate, unfiltered feedback of peers (rather than teachers). At Cornell he continued his apprenticeship, spending late nights at the campus newspaper office, playing hooky from his chemistry studies. Before he knew it, Vonnegut found himself swept into his own unlikely adventures as a soldier and POW during the Second World War, a bit player far from home in an epic struggle of good versus evil. Upon return to civilian life, with its own very different pressures, he was driven to find a way to convey the stories he had witnessed amid the chaos of the war's last stages. It was a survivor's task he would, in time, accomplish admirably, with a lot of grit and determination and luck, the sharp eye of a reporter, and the sensitivity of a poet.

Vonnegut's next stop was the University of Chicago, where (like another budding writer, Saul Bellow) he was a GI Bill graduate student in the department of anthropology. His research there, cataloging the shapes of stories across cultures, confirmed a long-held suspicion that creation myths, folk tales, and religions all amounted to, more or less, intricate gadgets—Rube Goldberg contraptions—custom-designed to provide cohesion and purpose to communal life in its various forms. On his own he came to the insight expressed by his friend the evolutionary biologist Stephen J. Gould, that what distinguishes human beings from other primates is the use of their big brains to tell stories. Conceiving and adapting the stories to changing circumstances and passing them on to others seemed a universal impulse.

By 1950 Vonnegut had begun to practice the craft of writing for money, at first in his spare time, supplying short stories to the slick weekly magazines in that golden age before the hegemony of television. Vonnegut would impart his ideas about the mechanics of storytelling to his students at the Iowa Writers' Workshop in the mid-1960s, and later at Harvard and the City University of New York. All the way into the twenty-first century he would graph story trajectories in front of full-house audiences on the lecture circuit. Americans, he would point out, prefer their narratives to trend dramatically *upward* in the last act, *Cinderella*-fashion—even though real life often does not work out that way.

In his short fiction and essays and speeches, and above all his books, spanning half a century, Vonnegut would come to be recognized as a master storyteller himself. When I look beneath the simplicity of style for which he is so well known, the sardonic wit, fanciful plots, and star-crossed characters, what I find at the heart of his fourteen novels, from *Player Piano* (1952) to *Timequake* (1997), is a profound engagement with the national story, the rags-to-riches American Dream he took in as a boy. In those works he resists the muscular version, the harsh social Darwinist narrative that celebrates grandiose ambition and unbridled power, "winners" at the expense of "losers."

Readers respond to Vonnegut's unique voice with laughter, outrage, and tears. We share his identification with those who struggle under the ethos of survival of the fittest, his concern about the price we pay for all of our machines and footloose mobility. We fall in love with each character he presents to us, develop a warm personal interest in their fortunes. They are familiar—we feel we have "met him on the river," to use the author's favorite quotation from Mark Twain. We stick with the ride, however harrowing and convoluted it may be, recalling the punch line of Vonnegut's favorite dirty joke, a woman's advice to her lover as they are about to engage in sex: "Keep your hat on, we could end up miles from here." We understand at a deep level what he means when he concludes that, for so many, America has proven to be "an impossibly tough-minded experiment in loneliness." Vonnegut's art is a record of the ways in which the experiment has gone terribly wrong, how language and mythology, dreams and stories, conceal injustices and great crimes.[1]

Throughout his life, Vonnegut remained devoted to an alternative version of the American Dream story. Even at his most pessimistic he never gave up on its more noble possibilities. "It still seems utterly workable to me," Vonnegut told an interviewer on the subject of the U.S. Constitution during the Watergate crisis, one of its most embattled moments. "I keep thinking of ways to fix it, to see what the hell went wrong, to see if we can get the thing to really run right."

The embrace of *Cat's Cradle* and other experimental novels by an emerging youth counterculture, and the publication of *Slaughterhouse-Five*, the book that made Kurt Vonnegut a household name in 1969, in the midst of the Vietnam trauma, were events tied to the 1960s insurrection. But like his entire body of work, those artifacts transcend the moment of their first appearance: They are more complex, and more subversive, than commonly remembered. They are about something more enduring than the earliest readers might have suspected. To borrow a line from his most famous book, they deserve to be *unstuck in time*.

Restless boomers were, along with science fiction fans, the backbone of Vonnegut's initial audience. Before his works were enshrined in the canon of officially assigned readings, college students took a clandestine thrill in his magician's bag of tricks—the demystification of the creative process, the irreverent tone, the episodic, rule-breaking narratives, the time-travel and flights to extraterrestrial venues like the planet Tralfamadore. They adopted to the point of cliché the gallows humor of *Slaughterhouse-Five's* signature phrase, ". . . so it goes." Along with *Catch-22*, the 1961 novel by fellow World War II veteran Joseph Heller, Vonnegut's work bookended the sixties with an absurdist debunking of "Good War" and victory culture fantasies of national innocence. It struck just the right chord for a generation questioning their country's shallow materialism, nuclear madness, and Cold War misadventures.

In the character Edgar Derby, however, the middle-aged schoolteacher in *Slaughterhouse-Five* who tries to act responsibly in horrific circumstances, we find an almost corny faith in the very civic virtues that seemed to be disintegrating at the end of that decade. The book owes its power and moral urgency to sources far removed from the ideological wars of its time. When read within the larger arc of Vonnegut's career, we can see it as a meditation on the dignity, courage, and shattered dreams of the parents of its young fans, the children of the Great Depression. "Poor old Edgar Derby," quaint symbol of decency, fair play, and moderation, took his country's ideals in audacious good faith, as a way to find meaning in the hopelessness of the POW experience. The squarest, most unlikely hero of the 1960s, Derby is as much the author's alter ego as the wan, waif-like Billy Pilgrim.

It is true that Kurt Vonnegut was a critic of the American experiment, an outsider of sorts, a man of the Left, broadly speaking. He loved the socialism of his German American forebears and the labor militancy of fellow Hoosiers Eugene Debs and Powers Hapgood. Anarchists Sacco and Vanzetti were martyred heroes to him when he was growing up, as was John Dillinger, who waged war against the bankers until his betrayal in front of a Chicago movie theatre. Vonnegut understood in his bones the wages of the Ponzi-schemed, predatory capitalism that had wrecked so many lives in the years after 1929, including those of his mother and father.

He was freethinking and pacifist by inclination, inspired by the "Merchants of Death" antimilitarism widespread in the heartland as Europe lurched toward another war in the late 1930s. He found knee-jerk nationalism in any form repellent. In the 1960s Vonnegut used his notoriety to condemn the folly of the Vietnam War and the shredding of the Constitution that went along with it. His critique of abuses of power would continue from Lyndon Johnson and Richard Nixon to the George W. Bush years that troubled him so deeply at the end of his life. He was a communitarian in politics and approved of many aspects of the sixties' youth revolt to which he was an elder statesman—civil rights, women's equality, environmentalism.

But through it all Vonnegut remained a *patriot,* if I may use that word with its baggage, of a kind that was quite unfashionable when his famous war novel first appeared. For him, Franklin Roosevelt was a great president and World War II was still a "Good War," despite the many atrocities (the firebombing of Dresden among them) perpetrated by the winning side. Had he been of age, Vonnegut once remarked, he probably would have volunteered for service in Vietnam, as wrongheaded as he knew that enterprise to be. It was the patriotic thing to do.[2]

As a man and as a writer, Kurt Vonnegut was an exemplar of the kind of *connected criticism* political philosopher Michael Walzer has identified, a lover of his country even as he rails against its shortcomings and anguishes about its failed promises. He was a brokenhearted American Dreamer, not a bull-in-a-china-shop revolutionist. Like James Baldwin he believed in keeping at the project of a more just society, of *achieving our country*, no matter how daunting the setbacks. The gloom that famously pervades his books is always relieved by moments of transcendence, small gestures of kindness, friendship, love, and dignity—we think of Edgar Derby here—that keep alive for us another way of living, another sort of human utopia.[3]

These grace notes, delivered with poignancy and lyric beauty, in an unmistakably native idiom, are the reason we return still to Vonnegut's novels. They point a way to imagining how to redeem the story, how to integrate the most rational and humane elements of our shared American Dream into the expansive ethic of "planetary citizenship" he knew was so urgently needed in our time.

Impossible Dreams

A Writer's Education, 1922–1952

It is hard to adapt to chaos, but it can be done.
I am living proof of that: It can be done.
—from *Breakfast of Champions*

At a bookstore event in lower Manhattan in 1996, Kurt Vonnegut confessed to the audience that his childhood had been, essentially, a *happy* one. "Which," he added with calculated sheepishness, "is no way for a writer to begin." Indeed, his was a privileged life from the earliest years, and even the difficult times that would come had their compensations. Vonnegut declared often that even with their heartaches he would not have traded the experience of coming of age during the Great Depression and the Second World War for anything. Those twin crises affected everything like massive weather systems, prolonged and uncertain in resolution, and they taught lessons about courage, endurance, citizenship, and community—about being part of something larger than oneself—that could not have been learned in more sedate times.[1]

As a boy, "K" drank deeply of the sunniest, most inspirational versions of the American Dream, and to an astonishing degree he went on to live out its grandest promises. But loss, dislocation, and chaos were also familiar motifs. Vonnegut understood the fragility of the human condition, the paradoxes of the success story at the center of our culture. He saw firsthand the underside of the dream, the destruction its dynamism can leave in its wake. "I wrote out of my life," he told the bookstore crowd that evening, and the painful knowledge that was part of his education colored everything he ever created, most especially his fourteen novels. The identification with the underdog that runs through them, the tenderness for misfits, castoffs, and losers in a country of ambitious strivers, was a perspective forged in his youth, the product of close observation.

Kurt Vonnegut Jr. was born into the fourth generation of a spectacularly prosperous German American family. They were farmers, merchants, and artisans, skilled and ambitious, who, beginning with great-grandfather Clemens Vonnegut in 1848, settled in the middle of the country in the bustling frontier capital and transportation hub, Indianapolis. The author devotes the opening pages of *Palm Sunday*, his 1981 "autobiographical collage," to a genealogy assembled by his "uncle" John Rauch (actually the husband of his father's first cousin, a Harvard graduate, attorney, and family griot related to the author by marriage rather than blood). It describes the bounty these men and women encountered after their arrival in the New World:

> The immigrants had been literally starved—materially and socially—in the Nineteenth Century of Western Europe. When they came here and found the rich table of the Midwest, they gorged themselves. And who can blame them? In the process they created an Empire by the hardest work and exercise of their inherent and varied talents.[2]

These "guilt-free people of the German tide," Vonnegut added to his uncle's narrative, had not been involved in "the genocides and ethnic cleansing which had made this for them a virgin continent." In short order they established businesses and social clubs interwoven with those arising at the same time in Milwaukee and Chicago, Cincinnati and Detroit. The author's paternal ancestors built a dry goods concern that would grow, by the twentieth century, into the Vonnegut Hardware chain, an institution to generations of Hoosiers. On this foundation they became civic leaders, a kind of local aristocracy admired even beyond their very intact ethnic world.

Vonnegut sons and daughters traveled widely, bringing back elements of their vibrant old-world *Kultur*—libraries, museums, a symphony orchestra—to uplift what otherwise might have been just another dull and dusty provincial outpost in the farm belt. The young men attended Ivy League schools and then complied with the expectation they return home to start a family and pursue a career in the professions. Grandfather Bernard Vonnegut and his son, the author's father, Kurt Sr., became architects, responsible for some of the most distinguished structures of their city— office buildings, department stores, theatres, and the German American club downtown, a baroque gem known as Das Deutsche Haus. In 1913 Kurt Sr. married Edith Lieber, quite a catch as the "richest girl in town," heiress to a brewery fortune. Edith was beautiful and intelligent, broadened by her own Grand Tours and her suitably elite (if only "ornamental") education. According to Uncle John, the wedding party at the swank new Claypool Hotel on Washington Street was the social event of the season, an extravaganza "long remembered in Indianapolis."[3]

But the next year brought the first in a succession of blows to the Vonnegut-Lieber family fortunes, and "the curtain fell on a glorious scene—never to be witnessed again." From the perspective of middle age, Kurt Jr. would remark that the benevolent "planet" his parents loved and understood was destroyed by the First World War. Xenophobic furies "lobotomized" German American communities across the nation as citizens mobilized against the evil Huns of propaganda caricature. In Indianapolis vigilantes splashed Das Deutsche Haus with yellow paint. (The building was quietly renamed the Atheneum, and endures to the present day.)[4]

Afflicted by a mixture of fear and weltschmerz for their lost prewar world, Kurt and Edith did not pass along much German language or culture to their children, overtly at least. By the time their third child arrived, on November 11, 1922—the anniversary of the Armistice ending the Great War crusade—memories of the hate campaign were still fresh, and dwelling on the past brought more pain than was comfortable to endure. "They volunteered to make me ignorant and rootless as proof of their patriotism," the author lamented. So separated did he feel from his ancestral heritage, he once observed, that the German soldiers who captured him in the next war, during the Battle of the Bulge, "might as well have been Bolivians or Tibetans for all they meant to me."[5]

The unraveling of the extended family and its resources, built up over decades, did not happen overnight. The Lieber Brewery, famous locally for the gold medal its signature beer once earned in Paris, was forced to shut down due to Prohibition, but otherwise finances held up well enough and prospects for the future still seemed bright. There were aunts and uncles and other relatives around to nurture a young boy's imagination and provide a sense of security, as well as the irreverent company of older siblings Bernard and Alice. Annual summer idylls at the cottage on Lake Maxinkuckee in northern Indiana seemed as though they would continue forever.

Then came the shock waves of the stock market crash of 1929. The reverberations reached deep into the Vonnegut household. There were no missed meals at the elegant brick house on North Illinois Street, designed and built by his father, no trips to the neighborhood soup kitchen or church bread line. But creditors had to be juggled, crystal and china sold off, and his parents acquired a reputation around town as "charge-account deadbeats."[6]

In *Fates Worse Than Death* Vonnegut considered the mind of Kurt Sr. during this slow-motion slide. Design commissions dried up and he had to close his office, scratching from home for the occasional freelance project—"jobs so uninteresting, I now understand," his son wrote, "that they would have been soporific to a high school drafting class." A gentle man with a dreamily artistic temperament, Vonnegut's father had almost no work worthy of his talents for sixteen years. He was like a character from "a particularly lugubrious fairy tale," a Sleeping Beauty who turned into Rip Van Winkle. But he never allowed his children to know how demoralizing the situation had become. "I now perceive his deception," Vonnegut reflected, "as having been a high order of gallantry."

> While my two siblings and I were growing up, he gave us the illusion that our father was jauntily concerned with his professional past and excited about all the tough but amusing challenges still to come. The truth was that the Great Depression and then World War II, during which almost all building stopped, came close to gutting him as an architect.[7]

When young Kurt brought friends by the house after school they pronounced his father a specimen "as exotic as a unicorn," in both appearance and manner. "In an era when men of his class wore dark suits and white shirts and monochromatic neckties," Kurt Sr., known to all as "Doc," outfitted himself in thrift store garb. The loud colors and textures, so seemingly haphazard, had actually been selected with a careful eye, his son would realize only much later, "juxtaposed so as to be interesting and, finally, beautiful."

> While other fathers were speaking gloomily of coal and iron and grain and lumber and cement and so on, and yes, of Hitler and Mussolini, too, my father was urging friends and startled strangers alike to pay attention to some object close at hand, whether natural or manmade, and to celebrate it as a masterpiece. When I took up the clarinet, he declared the instrument, black studded with silver, to be a masterpiece. Never mind whether it could make music or not.

Kurt Sr. was an esthete, as well as "the first planetary citizen my new friends had ever seen," Vonnegut concluded, "and possibly the last one, too. He was no more a respecter of politics and national boundaries than (that image again) a unicorn. Beauty could be found or created anywhere on this planet, and that was that."[8]

In contrast to his father's wondrous strangeness, Vonnegut paints a darker portrait of his mother, Edith, who never reconciled herself to the family's diminished circumstances. She did transmit to her children a sense of ambition and a love for the written word. "Sons try to make their mothers' impossible dreams come true," Kurt Jr. once declared, and in this case it would actually, in time, happen. In the 1930s he watched as she tried to craft stories for mass circulation magazines as a way to supplement the household income. But she lacked the common touch—the "vulgarity," to put it another way—to adhere to a formula that would sell. "Fortunately," Vonnegut tells us, in an arch reference to *his* eventual success in the marketplace, "I was loaded with vulgarity."[9]

Edith struggled to maintain appearances, but an air of madness and doom enveloped her more and more with each passing year. "Late at night, and always in the privacy of our own home ..." Vonnegut remembered in *Fates Worse Than Death*, "she expressed hatred for Father as corrosive as hydrofluoric acid." These harrowing domestic episodes help us understand the struggle to understand women that plays out in Vonnegut's novels. Edith's problems had their origins in an unhappy childhood and economic humiliation as an adult. Combined with a perhaps inherited tendency toward depression and a toxic mix of alcohol and barbiturates, the latter prescribed to relieve her insomnia, these burdens would prove more than she could overcome.[10]

There were many good things going on in the Vonnegut household amid the economic gloom. Classical literature, music, and art were available in abundance, right alongside magazines, comic books, and radio comedians. Kurt Sr. and Edith, steeped in the freethinking skepticism of their ancestors, promoted curiosity and reason in their children, inoculating them against the fundamentalist intolerance that was part of the local mores. "I am grateful that I learned from them," Vonnegut once commented, "that organized religion is anti-Christian and that racial prejudices are stupid and cruel." He credited Ida Young, the "humane and wise" black woman who worked in the house as a cook, for having a large role in raising him, encouraging the development of the most "compassionate, forgiving aspects" of his nature. He was fortunate to have such good teachers at a time when Indianapolis was as divided by jim crow segregation as any southern city.[11]

The transfer from private to public school, made necessary by financial exigencies, was, in retrospect, a lucky break. It forced Kurt Jr. to mix at a tender age with children of the Hoosier "yeomanry" that he otherwise would not have encountered so intimately. And he took in the democratic education offered by his teachers, like the contents of the neighborhood library, as a precious gift. "Everything I believe I was taught in junior civics during the Great Depression—at School 43 in Indianapolis, with full approval of the school board."

> America was an idealistic, pacifistic nation at that time. I was taught in the sixth grade to be proud that we had a standing Army of just over a hundred thousand men and that the generals had nothing to say about what was done in Washington. I was taught to be proud of that and to pity Europe for having more than a million men and tanks. I simply never unlearned junior civics. I still believe in it. I got a very good grade.[12]

Kurt Jr.'s progressive politics took root in like manner, a reflection of early influences. He breathed in the socialism of his forbears and read about the exploits of Eugene Debs and other heroic figures of the Left at the prodding of Uncle Alex, his father's younger brother, a Harvard-educated life insurance agent in Indianapolis who liked to debate "radical" ideas even though he himself was staunchly conservative. The author frequently paid tribute to Alex's ability to notice beauty and the simple pleasures of life. "We could be drinking lemonade in the shade of an apple tree in the summertime," Vonnegut reminisced in 1999, "and Uncle Alex would interrupt the conversation to say, 'If this isn't nice, what is?'"[13]

What young Kurt learned in books about the inequities of capitalism, the nobility of the labor movement, and the crimes of the armaments profiteers resonated with the pain he saw all around him as people tried to hang on in the flood. Cheered by the rhetoric of Franklin Roosevelt, he stayed true to the immigrant belief in America as a utopia, a flawed but open experiment in human possibility. He grew up worshipping the civic religion of the Bill of Rights and the Gettysburg Address, and, like most young people of the time, committed the words of secular prophets Abraham Lincoln, Carl Sandburg, and Mark Twain to memory. "I was raised," Vonnegut remembered, "to be bughouse about the Constitution."[14]

By his own account Kurt Jr. cut an awkward figure in his teenage years— tall, skinny, and insecure with girls. But along with the marching band, he found a niche where his talents were recognized and applauded. For hours every afternoon Vonnegut could be found working on the *Shortridge Daily Echo*, the only daily high school newspaper in the country. There he developed his voice and began to harbor ideas about a career in journalism. The routine of deadlines and feedback from fellow students was invaluable and exciting as he practiced the Hemingway-inspired principles that would define his mature style: tell only what you know, in the leanest possible prose, readily transparent to the reader.

By graduation day an apprenticeship was waiting for him at the *Indianapolis Times*, the city's liberal afternoon paper. But writers, then as now, lived a precarious existence, and the idea was vetoed by his father and brother. He would follow the example of Bernard, who earned his PhD in physical chemistry at MIT in 1939, and go east to pursue a degree in the sciences. Thus, in 1940 the eighteen-year-old Kurt Vonnegut Jr. left home, for good as it turns out, another fragment in a larger family diaspora. He would always wonder what might have happened if he had not gone away. Maybe he would have risen from cub reporter to swashbuckling local journalist, or found his way to a partnership with his father, designing beautiful buildings once the patrons got well again. It was, for an exile, a bittersweet, impossible dream, pleasant to revisit from time to time.

Vonnegut's years as a student at Cornell amounted to a "boozy dream," he recalled in a "Self-Interview" for the *Paris Review* in 1977. He felt ill-suited for the disciplines of chemistry and biology, and claimed to have devoted more energy to fraternity pranks than attending class. But exposure to a way of thinking outside the humanities, as an architect's son and then as a prospective scientist, surely helped to make Kurt Vonnegut the "aggressively unconventional storyteller" he was on his way to becoming. He would use sci-fi techniques in his fiction, of course, and would come to refer to his jokes and stories as machines, gadgets—carefully assembled "mousetraps." He would speculate in a number of his books about how our behavior might simply be the playing out of chemical and mechanical processes (*Breakfast of Champions*) or the cold logic of evolutionary imperatives (*Galápagos*). By training and temperament he was comfortable on both sides of what novelist C.P. Snow called "two cultures," the scientific and the humanistic. What made him different from most writers he knew, Vonnegut once quipped, was that he knew how his refrigerator worked.[15]

In college he found a way to continue his journalistic passions, gravitating naturally to the offices of the *Cornell Sun*. He spent many satisfying ink-stained nights putting the newspaper together, crafting pieces that were, in the period leading up to Pearl Harbor, fiercely isolationist in tone. In his new memoir no less a figure than Robert Jay Lifton, then an undergrad himself barely eighteen years old, recalls the atmosphere at the *Sun*. "I also wrote a few humor columns, inspired by the formidable presence of Kurt Vonnegut, just before he went off to war," Lifton writes. "Vonnegut was a charismatic figure at the paper (I always thought of him as editor in chief though he was actually associate editor), even then notable for his mordant satire." Sharing similar misgivings about the dehumanizing potential of bureaucratic organization and technology, Lifton and Vonnegut would become lifelong friends, appearing together beginning in the 1960s as celebrity spokesmen protesting America's involvement in Vietnam and the dangers of the nuclear arms race. "He taught me much about combining passion with a sense of absurdity," Lifton explains, "but everything began with that glancing encounter at Cornell."[16]

Like other draft-age undergraduates Vonnegut participated in the campus ROTC program. In 1943, after being hospitalized with pneumonia and flunking most of his courses, Vonnegut lost his draft deferment and enlisted in the U.S. Army. By that stage in the wartime mobilization there was a marked oversupply of junior officers, and his cohort of recruits was informed from the start that they had no chance of promotion. It was a situation common to other foot soldiers who went on to writing careers, such as James Jones, Nelson Algren, Norman Mailer, and Joseph Heller. After boot camp Private Vonnegut was sent to Carnegie Tech and the University of Tennessee for classes in mechanical engineering, along the way learning the operation of the 240-millimeter Howitzer, the largest mobile field piece used by the artillery.[17]

In early 1944 Vonnegut found himself at Camp Atterbury, an hour south of Indianapolis. It was there that he met his partner in the "buddy system," Bernard V. O'Hare, a lifelong friend who would figure in the pages of *Mother Night* and *Slaughterhouse-Five*. The 106th Infantry to which they were attached was short on riflemen, "bodies of the lowest grade," Vonnegut recalled, and the busloads of incoming college kids would be made to fill the need. O'Hare and Vonnegut were converted into an unlikely Mutt and Jeff pair of battalion scouts. As they awaited deployment Kurt Jr. took advantage of proximity to his family, sleeping in his old room and enjoying the use of the family car on weekend visits home. "But mother died on one of those," he reported in *Fates Worse Than Death*. In the last act of her spiraling despair, Edith Lieber Vonnegut took a fatal overdose of sleeping pills on Mother's Day, 1944.[18]

"So our fucked-up division finally went overseas," Vonnegut wrote of the ensuing months, in the aftermath of D-day, "and wound up defending seventy-five miles of front in a snowstorm against the last big German attack of the war." Amid the chaos of the Bulge, he and his companions found themselves wandering in circles in the endless fields and woods of Luxembourg or Belgium without proper camouflage or weaponry or combat boots. As he described it later, "I imitated various war movies I'd seen." Attempts to locate friendly lines were in vain—they had all been overrun by Nazi tanks.[19]

On December 19 Vonnegut and O'Hare crouched in a gully with a number of other exhausted GIs, their bayonets drawn in terror. Shell bursts cut through the treetops above, leaving no choice but to comply with the loud-speaker instructions to surrender. Before long they stood shivering in crowded boxcars for a journey of indeterminate destination and length— "Christmas was in there somewhere." Royal Air Force mosquito bombers targeted their train at night, and a car full of higher-ranking soldiers from the battalion took a direct hit. "Every time I say I hate officers, which I still do fairly frequently," Vonnegut mused in 1977, "I have to remind myself that practically none of the officers I served under survived."[20]

In a letter written in a Red Cross Club in Le Havre, France, just after the war, published posthumously in the collection *Armageddon in Retrospect,* Vonnegut gave his family a picture of his life in captivity. For sixty miles "the supermen marched us, without food, water or sleep," he recounted, his outrage still fresh. Many prisoners died from exposure in the cattle cars, or from the shock of the scalding showers through which they were herded on New Year's Day, 1945. About one hundred and fifty Americans were dispatched to Dresden to work as contract labor in a factory that made vitamin-enhanced syrup for pregnant women. "I was their leader by virtue of the little German I spoke," Vonnegut continued, referring to the bits of the ancestral tongue he had picked up around the house as a child. It was a thankless duty, made more difficult by the poor diet and physical demands they all endured, the lack of medical care, the justice exacted by "sadistic and fanatical guards" for the most petty infractions.[21]

"It was the first fancy city I'd ever seen," the architect's son tells us of Dresden. Crammed with refugee civilians, its ornate structures largely untouched even this late in the war, Dresden was a magical Oz for the men as they passed in ragged formation through its streets. Long known as "the Florence of the Elbe," it was "about as sinister as a wedding cake," Vonnegut later observed. A concrete hog-barn complex would serve as their not-too-disagreeable quarters.[22]

On the night of February 13, emergency alarms sounded, a common occurrence. With their guards, teenagers and men well past fighting trim, the prisoners absentmindedly repaired to the meat locker two levels below ground. It proved to be the best bomb shelter in town.

"When we came up, the city was gone," Vonnegut remembered in the Red Cross letter to his family. A massive Anglo-American incendiary raid had destroyed the central district, killing thousands in the process. "But not me," he added, with a mixture of puzzlement and relief.

> After that we were put to work carrying corpses from Air-Raid shelters; women, children, old men; dead from concussion, fire or suffocation. Civilians cursed us and threw rocks as we carried bodies to huge funeral pyres in the city.[23]

For all of his reservations about violence, Vonnegut considered the Second World War a just cause, something in which he was proud to have participated. But the Allies' destruction of Dresden went too far, he believed. Whatever dubious strategic advantage might have been achieved—"the railroads were knocked out for roughly two days"—paled when balanced against the human cost. The exercise made no sense to him except as a product of inertia, or, in the case of the British especially, an act of revenge. His involvement in the grisly clean-up operations gave him a view into the darkness usually obscured by "Good War" romantic narratives. "Not many know," Vonnegut once recalled, "how tough America got."[24]

As the Red Army made its final advance from the east just weeks after the Dresden firebombing, the Germans evacuated their charges to a camp somewhere near the Czech border. One day in early May the guards melted away and the gates to freedom swung open. With a few other abandoned prisoners, Vonnegut and O'Hare commandeered a horse-drawn wagon and "traveled and looted [their] way through Sudetenland and Saxony for eight days, living like kings," before being absorbed into the vast machinery of repatriation. The panorama of refugees they encountered in that extraordinary moment after the fighting stopped is depicted in the last pages of Vonnegut's 1987 novel, *Bluebeard*.[25]

Kurt Vonnegut's name will forever be linked to the Dresden firebombing, and the account of the experience in *Slaughterhouse-Five* remains his best-known achievement. He sometimes tried to evade the power of the experience, as in his comment to *Playboy* in 1973 that the most remarkable thing about his period of captivity was the physical privation. Like other POWs he lost a lot of weight in a short time, and the memory was indelible. "Hunger is a normal experience for a human being," he explained, "but not for a middle-class American human being. I was phenomenally hungry for about six months." But the impact of seeing a city destroyed before his eyes eclipsed even the trauma of artillery fire and cold and near-starvation, and it would stay with him at the deepest level.[26]

After shipping home, Vonnegut spent time in the library scanning back newspapers for more than a token mention of the "astonishing" event he had witnessed—he found almost nothing. This conspiracy of silence came as a shock. O'Hare, who would go on to a law practice in Pennsylvania after the war, noticed the same news blackout, and shared with his buddy the lesson to be learned: their government could never be fully trusted again.[27]

Kurt Vonnegut's "war story" would have to wait to be told, germinating for years until he could arrive at a form and language to convey what he saw in all its surreality. For now, like other returning veterans, this twenty-two-year-old brevet corporal was preoccupied with the headlong rush into readjustment and making up for lost time. On September 1, 1945, Vonnegut married Jane Marie Cox, his childhood sweetheart, a Phi Beta Kappa graduate of Swarthmore. With his veterans' benefits he enrolled in the department of anthropology at the University of Chicago. He moonlighted during this time as a police reporter for the Chicago City News Bureau, producing accounts of an endless stream of fires, accidents, murders, and other daily ephemera.

Vonnegut's academic work reinforced the detached, otherworldly eye that he had developed as a child encouraged to be skeptical of received truths, and honed as a coping mechanism during the war. At the University of Chicago, he remembered, religions "were exhibited and studied as the Rube Goldberg inventions I'd always thought they were." Of particular impact were lectures by Professor Robert Redfield, whose studies of traditional folk societies—enclaves of like-minded extended families—seemed to him the key to understanding the ills of modern life. One can see Redfield's influence in a speech Vonnegut delivered decades later to a gathering of the American Psychiatric Association, urging that patients be advised to join churches or social clubs of any kind—less for their content than for the companionship they offered. He had known this kind of extended family twice in his life, first growing up in the Vonnegut clan and then as a soldier, and he understood its life-sustaining nourishment. "Human beings," he told his audience, "have almost always been supported and comforted and disciplined and amused by stable lattices of many relatives and friends, until the Great American Experiment, which is an experiment not only with liberty but with rootlessness, mobility, and impossibly tough-minded loneliness."[28]

Vonnegut proposed an MA thesis comparing story trajectories across premodern and industrial cultures, to be titled "Fluctuations between Good and Evil in Simple Tales." It violated the paradigms of the time, and his committee rejected the idea as "unprofessional." He left Chicago without a degree, moving with Jane and infant son Mark to take a job in public relations at General Electric headquarters in Schenectady, New York, arranged through his brother Bernard, an acclaimed climate scientist at its research lab. At GE Vonnegut observed the culture of scientists and marveled at their innovations, some beyond the wildest dreams of his youth. With Jane he immersed himself in the life of the hamlet of Alplaus, where they are remembered still for their down-to-earth acts of good citizenship. In memory of Dresden, Vonnegut volunteered for the fire department, an experience that would inspire the 1965 novel *God Bless You, Mr. Rosewater.* But he was miserable as a corporate "flak," writing ad copy amid the claustrophobia of a company town. With an eye to escape, he devoted his spare time to crafting short stories that he hoped to sell to the mass-circulation magazines so hungry for material with their weekly production schedules.

The breakthrough for Vonnegut occurred when *Collier's* editor Knox Burger, a Cornell acquaintance, bought "Report on the Barnhouse Effect," which was published in February 1950. There was more product in the pipeline, and at the going piece rate—$750 each, minus agent's commission, a considerable sum in those days—it seemed that Vonnegut was on the verge of achieving in his own life his mother's impossible dream of becoming a writer. In 1951 he "quit this goddamn nightmare job," as he put it to his father, vowing to "never take another one so long as I live, so help me God," and relocated again with his family to the rustic quiet of Cape Cod. Anything approaching reliable commercial success, let alone critical acceptance, was, alas, still far in the distant future.[29]

Player Piano

Progress Is Our Most Important Product
—General Electric publicity slogan

What are people for?
—The Shah of Bratpuhr

Twenty years after his first novel, Kurt Vonnegut reflected on the intimate, overlapping dialogue he had created between his life and his writing. "I want to be a character in all my works," he said in the preface to *Between Time and Timbuktu,* a 1972 teleplay for public television.

> I don't mean that I am a glorious character. I simply mean that, for better or for worse, I have always rigged my stories so as to include myself, and I can't stop now.

Vonnegut inserted himself more or less "slyly," he explained, in ways that were not overt until *Slaughterhouse-Five* and the books that followed. But as we enter the landscape of his imaginative universe, this journey across his fourteen novels, autobiographical elements are there to be found in abundance, embedded even in his earliest efforts.[1]

Vonnegut's debut novel, *Player Piano* (1952), features the style and themes associated with his later work. From the start we can hear the author's voice, playful and ironic, in its jokes, digressions, and language games (vernacular speech, sound effects, lists, and song lyrics). We are introduced to issues that would obsess him throughout his career: the identity crisis of people reduced to uselessness, the search for purpose and community in a world of chaos, the complexity of relations between the sexes, the longing for satisfying rites of passage.

Player Piano is a commentary on the scientifically engineered future Vonnegut saw being born every day at the GE lab, surrounded by innovative technology, paid to celebrate its virtues. He admired the design behind the turbines, insulators, and water wheels being produced there with ever-greater speed and efficiency. "The world needed these things, and General Electric was good at it," he recalled of his attitude in an interview with National Public Radio in 2007, just before his death. "After the Second World War, the whole world had been knocked down, and we were going to have to rebuild it." But he worried about the impact in human terms of the "progress" that was supposed to be his company's most important product. "Machines frequently got the best of it, as machines will," he explained later—a pattern with troubling implications.[2]

"Automation," a concept that had not yet been coined at the time he was writing, was not in itself evil in most cases, Vonnegut recognized. It "wasn't a vicious thing to do," but simply the result of an innate human drive to solve problems and improve efficiency. The germ of *Player Piano,* the story of a young man's rebellion against the mechanization of society, occurred to him one day while he was touring the GE complex, taking in the latest advances spurred by the war.

> I saw a milling machine for cutting the rotors on jet engines, gas turbines. This was a very expensive thing for a machinist to do, to cut what is essentially one of those Brancusi forms. So they had a computer-operated milling machine built to cut the blades, and I was fascinated by that. This was in 1949 and the guys who were working on it were foreseeing all sorts of machines being run by little boxes and punched cards.

For his novel the author chose the quaint artifact of the player piano to symbolize how readily people accepted machines to displace and improve upon the human factor, how casually they embraced the process of their own obsolescence.[3]

As he wrote at night and on weekends, Vonnegut embellished only slightly what he was witnessing during his days at work. The result was taken as fantasy, even though he thought of himself as a journalist talking about contemporary reality. "There was no avoiding it," Vonnegut said in an interview, "since the General Electric Company *was* science fiction." For its earliest readers *Player Piano* was easy to digest as yet another genre piece, the kind of refracted social criticism they were accustomed to encountering in the chill of the McCarthy period and the Korean War. But Vonnegut was reaching for something deeper and more personal.[4]

Those familiar only with his later work might be surprised at this novel's dense prose, earnest tone, and relatively conventional structure, which follows in the dystopian lineage of Edward Bellamy, Aldous Huxley, and George Orwell. Vonnegut knew well the tradition in which he was laboring and had no problem acknowledging his debts. "I cheerfully ripped off the plot of *Brave New World,* whose plot had been cheerfully ripped off from Eugene Zamiatin's *We,*" he admitted.[5]

Player Piano fits its time, too, as an exposé of the organizational life from which Vonnegut was recoiling, the pressures for conformity that were a popular subject for writers of the period. "Accurately and spiritually a vision borne of the frustration of the fifties," in the eyes of his friend Dan Wakefield, it conveys the free-floating restlessness and disappointment many veterans felt after the war, even amid economic miracles. As they commuted between office jobs and suburban tract developments, it was normal for them to wonder if the sacrifices they made had been worth it.[6]

Vonnegut's sensitivity about people reduced to interchangeable, disposable parts was heightened by his experiences as a GI and confirmed by what he saw happen to his father after the war. "When prosperity, but not his children, returned to Indianapolis," Vonnegut would recall decades later, "Father became a partner of much younger men in a new architectural firm. His reputation was still excellent, and he was one of the most universally loved men in town." But when the phone company decided to add floors to a skyscraper he had designed years earlier, they hired somebody else to do it. "An architect was an architect. Bell got the job done and it looked OK." His father did not complain, but the son knew the effects of the blow.[7]

Vonnegut's own history was also at play in this novel, and is the reason it emerged as it did, when it did. After his return from Europe he married and, with so many other discharged soldiers, went back to school. The University of Chicago's department of anthropology seemed another welcoming extended family when he first arrived in the fall of 1945. It was the gateway to an esteemed profession, promising work that was stimulating and full of creative possibilities. He left two years later, disillusioned and without a degree, having had several proposals for a master's thesis rejected by his graduate committee.

The next stop for Kurt and Jane was upstate New York, into the arms of a corporate family that offered the security of a regular if unspectacular paycheck ($92 a week). The steady work and predictable income was important as the first of their children arrived, Mark (named after Mark Twain) in 1947, and then Edith (after her paternal grandmother) in 1949. The Vonneguts enjoyed socializing with the young scientists and their wives at GE, many close-knit friendships developed, but the tedium of the work and the regimentation of life in and around the "Electric City" was too much to endure.

Vonnegut found relief from the claustrophobia on his regular trips into Manhattan, and as he had done in college, he turned to his writing talents to let off steam. He began to craft short fiction and embarked on what Jerome Klinkowitz calls his "get even" novel, chronicling the contradictions of life at GE.[8]

In 1951, with several stories published and a contract in hand for *Player Piano*, Vonnegut quit his job and "lit out for the territories," as Twain might say, moving his family to Cape Cod—first to Provincetown and then to the rustic village of West Barnstable. He kept food on the table with tales custom-built to appeal to the middlebrow readers of *Collier's* and *Ladies' Home Journal*. He often derided his output from this period as hack work, but the stories hold up not just for their workmanlike construction but for their sincerity and warm empathy. He connected with his audience because he knew their world and longed, on some level, to remain part of it.

Looking back, Vonnegut called leaving GE "an alarming thing to do," and so it was, especially for a child of the Great Depression, for whom stable employment was sacred. There were no guarantees in his new life, little to fall back on at thirty years old with only a high school diploma. So, beyond the issues of the machine and the pressures of corporate conformity, *Player Piano* is about what it was like to take this leap into the unknown, to walk away from a standard career path in pursuit of ill-defined freedom and integrity. Like his protagonist in this story Vonnegut is torn between a desire to be *inside* and *outside,* between a hunger for the safety and respectability valued by his parents and the drive to leave home, to go his own way.[9]

The protagonist of *Player Piano* is Dr. Paul Proteus, an executive at the sprawling factory complex north of the Iroquois River that divides the upstate New York town of Ilium, a thinly veiled version of Schenectady. He is heir to an empire fashioned by his late father, the nation's industrial czar in the recent world war whose powers had come to eclipse even those of the president. "Production without manpower," Fordism taken to its logical conclusion, was the new mantra, and it proved critical to victory over the foreign enemy.

Ten years later—"after the riots had been put down, after thousands had been jailed under the antisabotage laws"—Paul finds himself a troubled prince, ripe for the transformation suggested by his surname, a reference to a mythological figure who could change his shape at will. Facing the prospect of an even loftier position in the hierarchy, Paul's evolution as he contemplates leaving the system, his ambiguities, moments of vacillation, and efforts to balance divided loyalties, mirrors Vonnegut's experience as he pondered his exit from GE and forms the lynchpin of the story.

Gazing from his office window at the anonymous structures stretching into the horizon, Paul daydreams, imagining the bones and arrowheads over which the buildings had been erected, remnants from a time in the valley when Mohawk and Algonquin guerrillas engaged each other in mortal combat. Now, on the same ground, "the machines hummed and whirred and clicked, and made parts for baby carriages and bottle caps, motorcycles and refrigerators, television sets and tricycles—the fruits of peace." Paul's disaffection has been leaking of late, causing some in the organization to question whether he really has what it takes for leadership. Shepherd, his lieutenant, a scheming little brother, whispers about the shaky nerves of his boss.

Paul retreats from time to time to Building 58 of the Ilium Works, home of Edison's original 1886 workshop, a museum of a human-scaled world that, like that of the native warriors, vanished long ago. As much as Paul, like Vonnegut, is infatuated by the smooth ballet of today's machines, he pines for the rough-hewn people who used to inhabit the place, their initials carved like hieroglyphics on the brick walls of the workshop. A photograph of these antique men hangs over Paul's desk, a group of beaming farm boys pressed together shoulder-to-shoulder. From sweeper to foreman, they exuded the pride of a sacred lost camaraderie.

Vonnegut spoke often of his identification with the artisanal past that Paul romanticizes here, whether in his ancestral Europe, on the American frontier, or in other preindustrial cultures around the world. With the churches of the Middle Ages, for example, "no one signed his work," he observed with admiration, "every member of the community set glass or carved stone or wood or whatever for the glory of God, and for the glory of the community. That would satisfy me." In this ambition Kurt Jr. was honoring the ethos of his forebears.

> When I went into the arts it was sort of like taking over the family Sunoco station. . . . My father was an architect, painter, and a potter, and he celebrated people who worked with their hands. So when I heard this sociologist say the age of the Cathedrals was a good time to live, when he described it as honest people doing simple work with simple tools, well, I was ready to agree that that was for me.[10]

Back at the office, Paul mouths the company line, that the old ways were costly and grossly inefficient. "You can imagine what the scrap heap looked like," he tells his secretary. "Every kind of human trouble was likely to show up in a product one way or another." But his nostalgia, the aching sense of something missing, will not go away.

Paul's discontent finds focus with the return of Ed Finnerty, an engineer who, with Shepherd, came up with him at the Works as a true believer in the early days of the war. Finnerty's contempt for authority, his calculated affronts to the decorum of the managers, made him a clandestine hero to

Paul, who has so far limited his iconoclasm to driving a dilapidated old Plymouth. Now, back in town after abandoning his post in Washington, the mercurial big brother arrives unannounced at the Proteus residence. The potential for mischief, for distraction from a single-minded focus on his promotion to head engineer at the Pittsburgh plant, does not escape the watchful eye of Paul's wife.

Anita Proteus is the archetypal ambitious helpmate of postwar culture. She may reflect the acidic side of Vonnegut's mother, as well as the ambivalence the men of his generation felt toward the demands and frustrations of domesticity. Jane Vonnegut was not the social climber of this portrait, but there were plenty of other models in Schenectady from which to draw a caricature.

Vonnegut sometimes insisted that women were not a strong suit in his work, blaming the problem, at least in part, on the difficulties of identification. He *performed* as he wrote, he explained, assuming the attitudes and points of view of his characters, and, he observed, "I don't make a very good female impersonator." But the tensions between Paul and Anita in *Player Piano* reflect vividly the emotional landscape married couples across social classes face in building their lives together, something Kurt and Jane understood well. "You know there *were* these shattered realities in my life," Vonnegut remembered of the early years of their marriage. He was the head of a young family, a novice author needing privacy and burdened by the pressures of being a breadwinner, while Jane attended to the housekeeping and the children. "I'm working in a houseful of diapers and my wife wanting money and there not being enough and so forth. I was angry at my wife for the same reason everybody is angry with his wife."[11]

Vonnegut's women were always more richly complex than he allowed. Anita shows her wounds later in this novel, for example. Beatrice Rumfoord in *Sirens of Titan* learns through her hardships how to love, and Eliot Rosewater's wife Sylvia in *God Bless You, Mr. Rosewater* earns our sympathy as she tries to understand her spouse's bizarre, perhaps insane behavior. Memorably heroic female figures appeared with even more frequency as Vonnegut's craft progressed and he moved toward acceptance (if not resolution) in his own relationships. From real life we think of Mary O'Hare (Bernard's wife), inspiration for the anti-romantic quality of *Slaughterhouse-Five*, the childhood influences Ida Young and Phoebe Hurty (a brash widow from his childhood, to whom he dedicated *Breakfast of Champions*), and of course sister Alice, to whom *Slapstick* is so passionately dedicated. Then there are the tragic creations Mary Kathleen O'Looney in *Jailbird* and Celia Hoover in *Deadeye Dick*, the resourceful Mary Hepburn in *Galápagos*, and the formidable Circe Berman and Marilee Kemp in *Bluebeard*. A sensitivity to the challenges faced by women, an acknowledgment of their power and resiliency in the face of those challenges, runs through them all.

Anita Proteus burned to transcend her roots on the wrong side of the river. Once Paul's secretary, she seems to have duped him into matrimony with a false alarm about pregnancy. Anita "had the mechanics of marriage down pat, even to the subtlest conventions," Vonnegut writes, and was able to "turn out a creditable counterfeit of warmth" for her husband on cue. But the punctuation mark to their exchanges—"I love you, Paul. I love *you,* Anita."—grates on the reader, and seems more hollow with each repetition.

Anita welcomes her husband home with his usual cocktail. "Successfully combin[ing] the weapons of sex, taste, and an aura of masculine competence," she is prepared for the company dinner party that evening. Paul likes to think he is in charge, that Anita's strengths are merely a reflection of *his* status, but he submits without complaint to her nagging, "bordering on baby talk, as though he were a lazy little boy."

Upstairs, Paul finds the rumpled Finnerty, who explains what brought him back to Ilium. "When I got this year's invitation to the Meadows," Finnerty confides, "something snapped. I realized I couldn't face another session up there. And then I looked around me and found out I couldn't face anything about the system any more, I walked out, and here I am." It is a dramatic version of Vonnegut's departure from GE—an *alarming thing to do,* and something he dreamed about long before actually taking the step.

At the country club Paul makes his way through a crowd of young men "identical in their crew cuts and the tailoring of their tuxedos." His boss, Kroner, waits for him at the bar—a man with "the priceless quality of believing in the system, and of making others believe in it, too." Kroner's style was a doting paternalism, attentive to the vulnerabilities of every employee. One wanted to please him, to win and maintain his respect. As they clasped hands, Paul, "in spite of himself, felt docile, and loving, and childlike," as though "in the enervating, emasculating presence of his father again."

Proteus hits the mark with his after-dinner speech, a boilerplate testimonial to the benefits of the machine. But the consensus is spoiled by the entrance of Finnerty, swaggering with drink, who points out the costs of the golden age everyone else is celebrating. As vacuum tubes increased, so too, he pointed out, did rates of suicide, divorce, and juvenile delinquency. In the spirit of the intramural competitions encouraged by the company, Paul faces off against Checker Charley, a game-playing computer, which overheats and bursts into flame. Is it sabotage?

In bed Paul reviews the events of the evening, still in the flush of victory. "Anita's hammering at the subject of Pittsburgh had tended to make him curl up tighter and tighter. Now he felt himself relaxing somewhat, straightening out like a man."

Paul's belief in his father's mechanized utopia is undermined by furtive visits south of the Iroquois, to the district of Homestead (another nod to the past by the author, invoking the labor battles at Carnegie Steel in 1892). On a mission to purchase a bottle of whiskey for the Irishman Finnerty (Vonnegut is not immune to stereotypes), he passes work crews repairing a road, members of the Reeks and Wrecks—the Reconstruction and Reclamation Corps—along with the army, the destination for those scoring poorly on the National General Classification Tests.

In a saloon at the end of the bridge, he encounters men too old for such service, each in turn recalling how they had become obsolete. One of these old men, Rudy Hertz, gives Paul a noisy, familiar welcome. With Finnerty and Shepherd, Paul once taped Rudy's movements so that his job could be automated, and the man's unbroken pride in his machinist skills now makes Proteus uncomfortable. Rudy insists on music to celebrate the reunion, and a coin deposited into the bar's player piano produces a stilted but recognizable version of "Alexander's Ragtime Band." The only thing missing is the dancing fingers of a human being. "Makes you feel kind of creepy, don't it, Doctor, watching them keys go up and down," Rudy comments, without malice. "You can almost see a ghost sitting there playing his heart out."

The next day at work Paul commiserates with Bud, an engineer who has just invented himself out of a job. P-128s are no longer needed, the young man complains, oblivious to his part in the process. Bud was a compulsive gadgeteer in the American tradition, and had even designed the proverbial better mousetrap to replace the cats that once patrolled the Works. Paul can do nothing to help—punch cards had the final say on employment matters, and the graph on Bud's Achievement and Aptitude Profile had already classified him as redundant. The next stop, if he was lucky, was project supervisor for the Reeks and Wrecks.

That evening Finnerty convinces his friend to join him for a drink across the bridge, back in forbidden Homestead. As he prepares for another border violation Paul slips into his battered leather jacket—"perhaps a swat at my old man," he imagines, "who never went anywhere without a Homburg and a double-breasted suit." The streets are filled with people on parade in the costumes of the lodges and fraternal orders that have sprung up on this side of Ilium, a dash of color and common purpose amid the otherwise drab surroundings.

As drinks flow, Finnerty talks about his loneliness, the abiding sense of not belonging that only intensified for him when he was promoted to headquarters. Washington is far worse than Ilium, he declares, a collection of "stupid, arrogant, self-congratulatory, unimaginative, humorless men," driven by their parasitic wives. Paul finds the openness bracing.

The Reverend James J. Lasher, R-127, SS-55, once, like the author, a student of anthropology, inserts himself into the conversation. No one was interested anymore in the message he used to peddle to his congregations, he complained, the old faiths no longer worked. Vonnegut observed this kind of demoralization during the Depression, and it will be a recurrent motif in his novels. "What do you expect?" Lasher insists as he looks at the patrons hiding behind their boisterous bravado, drowning their pain in alcohol. "For generations they've been built up to worship competition and the market, productivity and economic usefulness . . . and boom! It's all yanked from under them."

Homesteaders, the Reverend concludes, were hungry for a fresh religion, a mythic narrative to counter the one of technological progress embraced by the engineers. From the look of the revelers it is clear to him that the right messiah could lead them into class warfare, and he relishes the idea. "Sooner or later someone is going to catch the imagination of these people with some new magic," Lasher declares. "At the bottom of it will be a promise of regaining the feeling of participation, the feeling of being needed on earth—hell, *dignity.*"

Paul's opinion of the denizens of Homestead has already been evolving beyond the clichés of the managers. He recalls the Reeks and Wrecks man who improvised a roadside repair on his jalopy, and now he studies a pool hustler who wins bets identifying musical numbers on the television above the bar with the volume turned off. "This was *real,* this side of the river," Paul thinks to himself, a place where people struggled and adapted and used their wits to survive.

Like Paul, Kurt Vonnegut was born a prince of sorts, spending his first years in a bubble of privilege. He ventured out too, awakening at an early age to the virtues of people beyond that world. After being pulled out of private school, he remembered, his friends suddenly became "the children of mechanics and clerks and mailmen"—the Reeks and Wrecks of his home town, Indianapolis. Kurt Jr. liked the fact that fathers got their hands dirty and mothers cooked and cleaned without the benefit of servants. "Peer pressure, which is the most powerful force in the universe," he concluded, "made me a scorner of my parents' class."

These values would be reinforced in the army, where Vonnegut, the erstwhile college boy, learned to dislike officers and rubbed shoulders with those, like himself, in the lower orders. It was the outlook of the people he knew best at GE, and of those with whom he now identified in his life as a writer struggling to support his family, the carpenters and plumbers and salesmen whose livelihoods depended on serving the Cape's population of moneyed families.

Overcome with excitement, Paul scales the tavern booth to issue a proclamation. "Friends, my friends! We must meet in the middle of the bridge!" He has a messianic streak, longing to be a mediator like Freder in Fritz Lang's *Metropolis,* but he couldn't pull it off. With a crash the table collapses, then blackness. Finnerty remains awake throughout the night, however, jawing with Reverend Lasher and improvising on the player piano, wresting control with raw human feeling.

Alternating with the education of Paul Proteus, Vonnegut introduces the story of a visiting potentate, the Shah of Bratpuhr, leader of six million members of the Kolhouri sect. He is on a goodwill tour studying the American way of life, escorted by Ewing J. Halyard, a self-regarding State

Department official burdened by yet another assignment baby-sitting undistinguished dignitaries from small countries. In *Player Piano* the Shah is comic relief and provides the wise outsider perspective Vonnegut would later express through Tralfamadorians and other extraterrestrial devices.

His Highness blurts impolitic observations about what he sees, horrifying his guide at every turn. He refers to a detail of Reeks and Wrecks as *Takaru*—"slaves," in his native tongue. The same confusion occurs in a review of the army. And the unveiling of the latest in the nation's EPICAC series of super-computers, so big it is housed in Carlsbad Caverns, provides yet another opportunity for misunderstanding. The Shah drops to his knees and poses a koan-like riddle to the glowing tubes before him. As Peter Reed has noted, EPICAC, like Checker Charley, is one of a family of humanized machines inhabiting Vonnegut stories, designed to "plan and play, write poetry, fall in love, commit suicide." (Later examples include Salo in *Sirens of Titan*, Mandarax in *Galápagos*, and Griot in *Hocus Pocus*.) Built to solve problems from atomic weapons to "the number of cigarettes and Cocoanut Mound Bars and Silver Stars required to support a high-morale air force," the behemoth is stumped, then dismissed by the little man as *Baku!*—a false god.

We follow Paul Proteus each step of the way as he is drawn into the plans for rebellion hatched by Finnerty and Lasher. They know he is vulnerable to persuasion—Paul wants something beyond Shepherd's office politics and the home remodeling, soap opera preoccupations of Anita. An overture by Kroner to declare once and for all his loyalties pushes the protagonist's always-cautious hand. He buys a broken-down farm and embarks on a crash program to reeducate his wife to the "new values" he is discovering. The dream of escape to a rural arcadia is a reference to the author's move off the grid to the ramshackle circumstances of the Cape Cod marshlands.

But there is no time for Paul to avoid the Meadows, the island retreat mandatory for Ilium managers every summer. Vonnegut's model was "Association Island," a GE property on which morale-building activities of the sort depicted here—solemn speeches, team sports, an open bar late into the evening—actually took place. The highlight at the Meadows is the appearance of a bronze-painted actor who inducts young "braves" by the light of a bonfire into oaths of brotherhood.

"It's a cheesy little religion which is satisfactory for a week or so," Vonnegut remembered of Association Island. Some were reluctant to tell their wives what had happened at the retreat, but "it's a very clean operation," he insisted. "I think the book would have sold a great deal better if I had intimated that there were party girls flown in and so forth, but there are not."[12]

Still unsure about when to make his break, Paul, like so many Vonnegut protagonists to come, is swept forward by machinations larger than himself. At the Meadows council house Kroner and the other chiefs are gathered in an emergency session. An antimachine conspiracy calling itself the Ghost Shirt Society presents an imminent threat to the system. They ask Paul to become a double agent, and the meeting adjourns before he has a chance to object.

Once Paul is ashore, Anita announces that she is making her own break—she and Shepherd are in league together. A more sympathetic character now, Anita cries real tears, admitting to the disease of the age, a feeling of uselessness. "I'm sick of being treated like a machine!" As she and Paul part she offers an embrace of unusual tenderness, shared, "out of all things, the goodness of her heart."

Paul lapses into his unaffiliated life without direction. The farm, with its hardships, was a passing fancy and is quickly forgotten. At the police station he registers as required as a "potential saboteur," and is shocked to see there his Meadows tent-mate, a consummate company man, being roughly handled and charged with vandalism. Paul wanders across the bridge to the tavern.

"You're on our side now!" Finnerty tells the woozy hostage as he awakens from the effects of his spiked drink. Reverend Lasher appears, expounding on the Ghost Shirts, a spiritual movement that swept through the tribes West of the Mississippi at the end of the nineteenth century. Rather than submitting to a fate as "second-rate White men," a few decided to make "one last fight for the old values," and shamans promised that magic shirts would repel enemy bullets as they rode into battle. The example could be used now to inspire a similar crusade for human dignity, this time against the machines.

It is no accident that both sides in *Player Piano* resort to the imagery of native warriors to marshal their forces. A longing to transcend over-civilization pervades Cold War books and movies generally, and explains the popularity of the frontier genre in the early days of television. Vonnegut knew the terrain well, having proposed a master's thesis at Chicago (that was rejected) comparing the Plains Indians to the cubist painters in France, who imagined their revolution in style as a struggle against the incursions of the camera.

Paul has no choice but to cooperate with the insurgency. "You don't matter," Finnerty tells him firmly. "You belong to History now." Also present at the meeting in the old air-raid shelter is Ludwig von Neumann, formerly a political science professor at the local college. (His name seems to be a reference by the author to the father of mathematical "game theory," then in its infancy.) Von Neumann reads aloud the manifesto he has drafted, a broadside against "the divine right of machines, efficiency, and organization" that had been a byproduct of the World Wars.

If we go by the principle that Kurt Vonnegut always "rigged" his stories so that he was present as a character, we can find him in this novel in each of the principal Ghost Shirt leaders. Von Neumann is the detached theorist, Lasher the moralist and myth maker, a precursor to Winston Niles Rumfoord in *Sirens of Titan* and Bokonon in *Cat's Cradle*. Finnerty is the firebrand, the freebooting man of action the author secretly longed to be. His comment that "out on the edge you can see all kinds of things you can't see from the center" would become a signature Vonnegut aphorism. Paul, meanwhile, is the reluctant hero, well meaning but clumsy and self absorbed, slow to grasp what is happening to him. He is a child, not sure exactly how to become a man.

"Through all his adventures he had been a derelict," Vonnegut writes of Paul Proteus, "tossed this way and that." But now arrives the chance for his protagonist to seize his destiny—to *become a character,* to anticipate a phrase from *Slaughterhouse-Five.* After being seized in a police raid, Paul considers the man in the next cell and experiences a solidarity he never thought possible. "For the first time in the whole of his orderly life he was sharing profound misfortune with another human being." Vonnegut experienced this type of community during his time as a POW.

Kroner and Anita pay a visit, still believing Paul to be on their side. Who, the older man wants to know, is the leader of the conspiracy? "I am," Paul responds. "And I wish to God I were a better one." At his televised trial, Paul is the voice of the rebels. The prosecution dismisses him as a "spiteful boy," and he does not deny it. "Sordid things, for the most part, are what make human beings, my father included, move," he says, looking into the cameras. "I'm no good, you're no good, we're no good because we're human." A rock through the courthouse window initiates the liberation of the people's messiah.

The Shah's itinerary, meanwhile, includes time with an average man living in prefab hell in his M-17 unit in Proteus Park, Chicago, "a postwar development of three thousand dream houses for three thousand families with presumably identical dreams." Levittowns on this model were springing up outside cities across the country as Vonnegut was writing. Infantry veteran Edgar Hagstrohm's gruff defiance in the presence of his VIP guests, his admitted affair with a deceased friend's widow, his wife Wanda's sense of uselessness amid her labor-saving devices ("Supper will be ready in twenty-eight seconds") all subvert the message of contentment meant to be conveyed, and touch even the Shah. He leaves them with the exhortation *Brahouna!* ("Live!")

As the motorcade reaches the Homestead side of the bridge back in Ilium, Halyard offers the Shah a gift on behalf of his government. "At no expense whatsoever to you," he announces with condescending self-assurance, "America will send engineers and managers, skilled in all fields, to study your resources, blueprint your modernization, get it started, test and classify your people, arrange credit, set up the machinery." The visitor shakes his head in disbelief. "Before we take this first step," he asks through his interpreter, "please, would you ask EPICAC what people are for?"

Bombs detonate, buildings are ablaze. "To the Works!" a man cries as Dr. Proteus is carried aloft from the courthouse. "The dull thunder of explosions walked about the city like the steps of drunken giants, and afternoon turned to twilight under a curtain of smoke." It is the first of many apocalyptic episodes we will encounter in Vonnegut novels, all told through the prism of his real-life experiences in war, his memories of Dresden. The leitmotif of giants "walking" above us recalls the muffled sound of the bombs he and his companions heard that February night from the their subterranean meat locker.

In the saloon command post Finnerty pleads for restraint, but museums, bakeries, the local sewage disposal plant all burn in the indiscriminate destruction. Word arrives of "victories" in Oakland and Salt Lake, but they are isolated and easily reversed. The second guessing and recriminations begin. Touring a landscape of bodies and destroyed machines, it is clear that the motivations of the leaders, the "sordid things" that drew them together, interfered badly with their judgment. Von Neumann thought of the rebellion as an academic exercise. For Finnerty it was "a chance to give a savage blow to a close little society that made no comfortable place for him." And for Lasher, "a lifelong trafficker in symbols," it was an opportunity to fight in a holy cause, and now to die as a martyr.

Longing for purpose, Paul allowed himself to be used in their scheme. There is a sense here of the failure of Vonnegut's still-young generation of men, torn between nostalgia and the allure of the future, thwarted in their efforts to build a new world. Though tested in war, their development was stunted, they lacked the vision and discipline to achieve the values for which they had once fought. The defeat may not be permanent, however. Maybe others will learn from their mistakes.

Kurt Vonnegut was hardly an overnight success. Despite his years in the wilderness, however, the stacks of rejection letters and the indifference of the reading public, he felt blessed in many ways during his long apprenticeship. "It was an era of romantic anarchy in publishing," he recalled of the writing business in the 1950s, "which gave us money and mentors, willy-nilly, when we were young—while we learned our craft." *Collier's* editor Knox Burger and agents Kenneth Littauer and Max Wilkinson became Vonnegut's friends and recognized his unique talents from the beginning. They took the time to teach him how to shape stories for the market. Littauer, a World War I flying ace, accommodated his client's wish to aim high with his debut novel. "Is there any particular publisher you want?" Vonnegut remembered him asking when it was time to shop *Player Piano*. Scribner's was the naïve reply, the house of Hemingway and Fitzgerald. Promoted as a tale of "America in the Coming Age of Electronics," the book failed to find an audience, in what Klinkowitz describes as the first "in a frustrating series of campaigns" to introduce the promising emerging author.[13]

The book did better as a Bantam paperback, published in 1954 under the title *Utopia-14*. But this adjustment in marketing strategy only accentuated the temptation among many to pigeonhole Vonnegut's work and dismiss his larger aims. "I was classified as a science-fiction writer because I included machinery, and all I'd done was write about Schenectady in 1948!" he later protested. The label would plague him for years, synonymous as it was with quickly written work and lurid packaging. It was certainly a badge of inferiority to critics squeamish about technology, typically products of humanities programs, Vonnegut complained, who felt that "anyone who knew how a refrigerator works can't be an artist too." An encounter with a member of the literary elect at a cocktail party during the lean years stuck in his mind. "When we were introduced, he thought a minute, then said, 'Science fiction,' turned, and walked off. He just had to place me, that's all."[14]

Though he disliked the routines of corporate life, Vonnegut remembered GE during his years there as an exemplary enterprise in many respects, and it bothered him when it fell short of its civic responsibilities—part of what he saw as a more general decline in ethics in favor of blind pursuit of profits. As guest of honor at an alumni banquet in the mid-1980s, he drew applause from old friends when he declared "the General Electric Company that loaded up the Hudson River with PCBs sure as hell wasn't the company that I worked for."[15]

Most of the initial sales of *Player Piano* were in Schenectady, Vonnegut believed, among employees anxious to decode who-was-who in the roman à clef. After its release, management abruptly terminated the retreats at Association Island. "So," he quipped, "you can't say my writing hasn't made *any* contribution to Western civilization."[16]

The Sirens of Titan

You, young man. In your pocket is the culmination of all Earthling history.
—Winston Niles Rumfoord, to Chrono

You finally fell in love, I see.
—Salo, to Malachi

Sirens of Titan (1959) posits a world in which all human endeavors turn out to have been engineered by remote intelligences, toward the most mundane end imaginable. The protagonist, a wealthy and profligate lost soul named Malachi Constant, is led across the solar system on the way to finding his purpose in life. The allegory is a reflection on the path traveled by Vonnegut and his generation of young men. "Malachi's adventures parallel the experiences of many Americans of Vonnegut's age," Jerome Klinkowitz has noted—"an adolescence free of responsibilities, then military service, followed by a heroic attempt to keep together a family amidst the centripetal forces of modern life."[1]

Indeed this work, couched in the form of a Sputnik-era space opera, can be read as a hero's journey in the mythic tradition identified by Joseph Campbell. It is an odyssey from chaos to exile, and then to home—which turns out to be a state of mind and a way of relating to others, rather than a destination. The lead character discovers that the free will he has always taken for granted is an illusion, that he has been used in an ambitious stage drama aimed at that most speculative and elusive of aspirations, the betterment of humanity. Amid concentric circles of manipulation and competing narratives designed to make sense of it all—and the flying saucers and mind-control devices and Martian sleeper agents that Vonnegut throws at us in quick succession in this wildly convoluted tale, comic book trappings we never take seriously—Malachi Constant embraces the truths that reside *within*. He comes to understand that heroism lies not in dramatic, macho gestures or the mastery of ultimate principles, but in making peace with our tragic limitations, acting with decency, and caring for those around us. With him we learn that there is something irreducibly beautiful about human beings, and that we *do* have choices, even in an absurd, largely determined existence. For all of our delusions and blind grasping, we remain capable always of dignity, self-sacrifice, and love.[2]

Vonnegut wrote this second novel after a hiatus of several years from long-form fiction. During that time he began and abandoned work on *Upstairs and Downstairs,* an account of a downwardly mobile Indianapolis family not unlike his own during the Great Depression. He scratched out a living on the Cape producing short stories for the "slicks," popular magazines like *Collier's,* the *Saturday Evening Post, Cosmopolitan,* and *Ladies' Home Journal,* as well as sci-fi vehicles like *Galaxy* and *Fantasy.* Sometimes the words flowed with ease and the house was filled with an atmosphere of carefree abundance; sometimes pages came from the typewriter only with great difficulty. Vonnegut supplemented his income, meanwhile, with a series of temporary jobs—teaching English at the Hopefield School for disturbed children, writing copy for an ad agency and, very briefly, for *Sports Illustrated,* and trying his hand at managing a business, as one of the first licensed Saab dealers in the United States.

Mark Vonnegut helps us understand why, aside from deficiencies in product quality, his father was so unsuccessful in the latter endeavor. "He usually did the test drive. I tried to tell him not to go around corners so fast, especially if the customers were middle-aged or older, but he thought it was the best way to explain front-wheel drive. Some of them were shaken and green. He didn't sell a lot of cars." Vonnegut joked later that his failure as a

Saab salesman cost him an invitation to Stockholm to receive the Nobel Prize for literature.[3]

There were big changes in Vonnegut's family life during these years. In 1957 a third child, Nanette, was born, and his father, Kurt Sr., succumbed to cancer at his secluded cottage in the hills of southern Indiana. The next year Vonnegut's sister, Alice, died of the same disease—a loss whose impact he would address later in the novel *Slapstick*. In the hospital Allie took her last breath less than twenty-four hours after her husband, Jim, perished in a railway accident—his New Jersey commuter train, "The Brokers' Special," plunged off an open drawbridge. It was a bizarre turn of events that must have confirmed for Vonnegut the random cruelty of the universe. He and Jane adopted his sister's three eldest boys, James, Steven, and Kurt. (Vonnegut tells us in *Palm Sunday* that a fourth nephew, the infant Peter, was adopted by paternal relatives in Alabama.) It was a generous and admirable act, done without hesitation, but finances now became even tighter.

Vonnegut recalled the genesis of *Sirens of Titan*. "Write me a book!" Knox Burger demanded at a cocktail party, challenging his friend to get back into the game. "I had an idea; he liked it. I went home and very cheerfully and very quickly produced it. Almost automatic."[4]

"Everyone now knows how to find the meaning of life within himself," a narrator from the indeterminate future begins. "But mankind wasn't always so lucky." A century earlier, in the "Nightmare Ages" between the Second World War and the Third Great Depression, people still looked beyond for direction and spiritual nourishment. "Gimcrack religions were big business."

Ever in need of new frontiers, the United States "flung its advance agents ever outward, ever outward" from the home planet. In a cornpone speech asserting his country's determination even in the face of setbacks, the president reminds us of Lyndon Johnson, a NASA enthusiast in the U.S. Senate in the 1950s. "It isn't the American way," Vonnegut's fictional chief executive declares, "to take no for an answer where progerse [sic] is concerned." Thought necessary to keep citizens entertained and engaged in common purpose, the enterprise was itself a kind of officially sanctioned "gimcrack religion"—and doomed, of course, to failure.

These unhappy agents found what had already been found in abundance on Earth—a nightmare of meaninglessness without end. The bounties of space, of infinite outwardness, were three: empty heroics, low comedy, and pointless death.

Kurt Vonnegut witnessed a moon launch in person in the early 1970s, and he admitted in the *New York Times Magazine* the visceral, almost sexual excitement he and the other spectators felt as the engines engaged and the behemoth rumbled skyward. It was a triumph of engineering and a bold expression of romantic ambition. "John F. Kennedy was largely responsible for it," he told *Playboy,* describing the mythological dimensions of the space race. "He was a tough, joyful athlete and he loved to win. And it wasn't a bad guess, really, that this might cheer Americans up and make us more energetic."[5]

But given the urgency of the problems on Earth, the crash program was also obscenely expensive, a made-for-TV "vaudeville stunt," in Vonnegut's estimation. "The sort of dreams that I would have," the author told CBS when he declined an invitation to be a commentator on the *Apollo 11* mission, "would be a habitable New York City," the money better spent trying to "get this colony in class A shape." He worried that fantasies of escape to other planets encouraged the dangerous notion that Earth, so precious and fragile a Garden of Eden for humankind, was disposable and easily replaced.[6]

Vonnegut found it encouraging that the public became bored so quickly with manned space flight. "There was nothing they wanted on the moon," he observed, applauding the common sense behind this loss of interest. "A third grader knows there's no atmosphere there." The regions beyond our home world—the immediate neighborhood, anyway—offered only "empty heroics, low comedy, and pointless death." This was reinforced by the ballyhooed comet Kahoutek, which "was to make us look upward, to impress us with the paltriness of our troubles, to cleanse our souls with cosmic awe." When it fizzled, he told a commencement audience in 1974, the message seemed to be that only *we* can solve our terrestrial problems. "Help is not on the way. Repeat: help is not on the way."[7]

A crowd gathers outside the gate of a mansion in Newport, Rhode Island. Framed by baroque fountains, the house projects the "density and permanence" desired by the nouveau American aristocracy the author knew well from Cape Cod. The grounds are neglected and overgrown, however, the master of the estate absent, ironically condemned to a body "no more substantial than a moonbeam." Winston Niles Rumfoord materializes like clockwork every fifty-nine days, and people fidget with anticipation even though his appearances are always a closely guarded affair. To his wife, Beatrice, the visits are a recurring humiliation, unfit for public consumption.

This time, a guest has been invited inside the high walls to observe the ritual. From a limousine emerges Malachi Constant, the playboy and "notorious rakehell," disguised behind dark glasses and beard. With his inherited millions he has devoted himself to a life of carousing and excess, in a vain effort to ward off feelings of emptiness. His name means "Faithful Messenger," and deep inside he harbors a noble aspiration. "He pined for just one thing—a single message that was sufficiently dignified and important to merit his carrying it humbly between two points." Mr. Rumfoord requests Constant's presence, insisting that they have business to discuss.

With his dog, Kazak, Winston Rumfoord was thrust into this cycle of birth and death years earlier when his chartered ship to Mars passed through a zone of "chrono-synclastic infundibulum," a region of the cosmos where space and time curve, where matter is various rather than fixed, where "there are many different ways of being right."

This, not coincidentally, was the principle Vonnegut learned in his anthropology studies at the University of Chicago as he compared traditions and practices from around the world. It was a simple idea, like so many profound concepts, and one he found congenial. As he explained in an interview, he only wished it was taught sooner in school.

> A first-grader should understand that his culture isn't a rational invention; that there are thousands of other cultures and they all work pretty well; that all cultures function on faith rather than truth; that there are lots of alternatives to our own society.

The relativism Vonnegut absorbed in the 1940s would become a tenet of his young audience twenty years later. In Chicago, he remembered, "we weren't allowed to find one culture superior to any other."[8]

Rumfoord appears on schedule and strides into the foyer, regal and erect. Based on Franklin Delano Roosevelt, his larger-than-life persona looms over the story as the mythmaking American president's did for the author's generation growing up. Even Rumfoord's frailty and physical limitations, carefully hidden from view, but more evident as the story advances, evoke FDR. "Rumfoord extended his soft hand, greeted Constant familiarly, almost singing his greeting in a glottal Groton tenor," and asked the young man about the secret to his legendary good fortune. "Who knows?" Constant shrugs, uncharacteristically off-balance. "I guess somebody up there likes me." His host found the conceit charming.

The two men pause in the hallway to admire a portrait of a young girl dressed in white, her face frozen as she grasps the reigns of a pony. This was Beatrice as a child, inhabitant of a sealed world of privilege who seems based in part on Vonnegut's own mother. Despite her advantages and creative gifts—she once published a volume of poems, as Edith Lieber Vonnegut tried to be a writer—Mrs. Rumfoord is paralyzed by bitterness, living like a prisoner on the now-decrepit estate. She sequesters herself upstairs as the meeting commences.

Rumfoord boasts to Constant of his fortune-telling abilities, a gift his wife found deeply upsetting. "It's a thankless job," he observes, "telling people it's a hard, hard universe they're in." Since his transformation Rumfoord has known that the Earthling view of life as a linear, sequential experience whose course could be discerned and controlled was mistaken. "Everything that has ever been always will be," he insists, "and everything that ever will be always has been." Vonnegut is broaching here a theme that will take another decade to develop, with the "unstuck in time" Billy Pilgrim of *Slaughterhouse-Five*.

Now comes Rumfoord's bombshell prediction that Malachi Constant and Beatrice Rumfoord, two radically different people united in their loneliness, will one day find themselves together, and will produce a child. The scenario for Constant includes stops on Mars, Mercury, and Titan, the largest moon of Saturn—a journey epic in scope, but not the mission for which the visitor has been looking. A consummate salesman, Rumfoord sweetens the pitch with assurances of Titan's pleasant climate and alluring women, slipping into his guest's hand a photograph of three females, mesmerizing in their beauty. He knows that Constant has a weakness for the sexual power of women. Then the old man fades into insubstantiality, his voice full of static as though "coming from a cheap radio"—another Rooseveltian touch—urging Constant to keep an eye out for his future son's good luck piece. "The grin remained some time after the rest of him was gone."

In the weeks that follow, Malachi Constant labors to preempt any chance of the fate Rumfoord described coming true. He jettisons investments in Galactic Spacecraft, the company in his portfolio that owns a ship capable of interplanetary flight. He uses the proceeds to acquire MoonMist Tobacco and deploys the white, gold, and brown Sirens of Titan in its new campaign of cigarette ads. Like Odysseus having himself tied to the mast of his ship, Constant hopes this will protect him from their hypnotic song. Meanwhile he dispatches letters to Mrs. Rumfoord exaggerating his leering side for maximum offense. And he turns to old habits, throwing himself into a bacchanalia of drugs, booze, and sex at his Hollywood bachelor pad.

We learn the curious story behind Constant's inheritance. His father, Noel, a traveling salesman, was languishing one night in a fleabag motel when he got a notion to speculate in stocks, guided by acronyms lifted at random from the Bible in his room. The method proved uncannily successful—he became wealthy beyond his dreams. "It looked as though somebody or something wanted me to own the whole planet," Noel observed with incredulity. He had a child, Malachi, by a maid compensated for her periodic company, but due to "complex inabilities to love"—one of those strikingly economical phrases Vonnegut generated with such abundance in his writing—he met his son only once, on the occasion of Malachi's twenty-first birthday. Fathers and sons are often estranged from each other in Vonnegut's novels, and reconciliation, if it comes at all, is provisional, incomplete, and perhaps too late to make a difference. Hearing the story of Malachi's father reveals the hole in the boy's heart, the seeds of his desire to create and nurture a family of his own.

The run of gambling luck had continued for years following Noel's death, but now it ends as suddenly as it began: Malachi Constant finds himself broke. Beatrice Rumfoord, meanwhile, is busy with her own problems. She has also been wiped out by the latest stock slide and vents anger at her husband for not alerting her in advance to the dip in the roller coaster ride. "If I seem indifferent to your misfortunes," he explains to her paternally, "it's only because I know how well things are going to turn out in the end."

Events converge to fulfill Winston Niles Rumfoord's predictions. Undercover agents recruit Constant for the Army of Mars, offering him an irresistible enticement: a chance "to think about your native planet from a fresh and beautifully detached viewpoint." They visit the Rumfoord estate in Newport, posing as bank representatives there to discuss the defaulted mortgage. As Beatrice tours the grounds with them a saucer is waiting out back, hidden in the dark. The scene anticipates Billy Pilgrim's kidnapping in *Slaughterhouse*.

The scene shifts to Mars, eight years later, in a vignette drawn from the author's experiences in uniform. Ten thousand soldiers stand at rigid attention on a surface of metallic orange, the atmosphere above them airless, cold, and silent. The beat of a snare drum is piped electronically into each man's skull. We fix upon one figure in the endless columns, a demoted officer who is now, in the words of his sergeant, "the platoon f-kup," just back from his latest reprogramming treatments. Maybe this time Unk—a nickname signifying his low rank and advanced age, a preliminary version of old soldier Edgar Derby —will be able to control his thoughts. At the front of the assembly, hands bound, stripped of his medals, is a convicted saboteur awaiting punishment.

It is a set piece of horror, recalling for readers the paces "brainwashed" American POWs were led through by their captors in the Korean War. Unk is chosen to consummate the ritual. A sharp pain rises in his head as he hesitates, then he proceeds with the job, strangling the prisoner with his bare hands. The dying man manages a last whispered message to him, something about a letter under a rock near barracks Twelve. Unk returns to his place, then marches off blankly with the formation to the radio-controlled cadence.

Outside the prefab structures wave banners of various Earthling nations, indicating the target for each unit in the invasion about to commence. As Unk cleans his rifle we wonder about its prospects. His weapon, like those of all his comrades, is an antique musket. Loose residual memories float in his mind—images of three women, one white, one brown, one gold. "Sell MoonMist," he mumbles to himself.

This draws the attention of Unk's squad mate, Boaz—the name a reference from Vonnegut's anthropology studies. The young black soldier has been Unk's buddy since basic training, his Bernard V. O'Hare. Though only a private, Boaz wears a tailored uniform and exudes a confidence unusual for his status. "Unk had the eerie feeling that he and Boaz were the only real people in the stone building," Vonnegut writes. "The rest were glass-eyed robots, and not very well-made robots at that."

Unk faints as he tries to explain his words. It was just this kind of mental activity that made him so stubbornly maladjusted. Boaz activates a device in his pocket and everyone freezes. He is one of the many double agents in Vonnegut's early novels, a commander for the upcoming campaign against Earth. The man just executed was also a member of the covert elite, until he befriended Unk and took too much interest in his efforts to think and remember.

Boaz's swagger hides an insecurity about how long he will keep his privileged position. He joined the Martian cause as a teenager with few life opportunities and now dreams that his pal will share with him the good luck for which he had once been so renowned. Unk will take him to night clubs when they return home as part of a victorious army of occupation. "Back there on earth, man," Boaz often reminds him, "you were King!"

During a recreation period—everyone in the Army of Mars is required to learn German batball, the esoteric pastime which, strangely enough, was a passion of Winston Niles Rumfoord—Unk searches for the letter under the rock. It is a kind of diary, its author unknown. *I am a thing called alive,* it begins, part of an army that *plans to kill other things called alive in a place called Earth.*

Even this rudimentary information was hard won, Unk realizes, and setting it to paper amounted to high treason. It symbolizes the price to be paid for exercising free will, pursuing individuality, being human. The diary continues: *You are afraid of the pain now, Unk, but you won't learn anything if you don't invite the pain. And the more you learn, the gladder you will be to stand the pain.*

Unk learns from the book that everyone on Mars, himself included, had emigrated not long ago from Earth, and he reads about his friendship with Stony Stevenson, whose identity as the man he strangled just hours earlier remains mercifully repressed. They had made a pact to share any insight about their circumstances that might come their way. The person in charge of everything, they figured out, was "a big, genial, smiling, yodeling man who always had a big dog with him," *a big charm boy*, who *fills everybody up with new ideas.*

The last entries in the letter speak of Stony's intuition that the coming military adventure would be a debacle, and inform Unk about his family on Mars. His mission is to gather his family to safety and escape *to somewhere peaceful and beautiful.*

Unk admires the person who wrote these words, so willing to "expose himself to any amount of pain in order to add to his store of truth." He imagines an Olympian figure, but as he turns to the final page the signature—in large letters, executed "with a smeary black kindergarten exuberance"—is his own name. *He* was the hero. It was the beginning of wisdom, the understanding that any answers to be had resided within.

The invasion begins as planned. The entire populace of Phoebe, the lone Martian city, mobilizes for the glorious effort. Early reports are promising; surrender terms are already being prepared. Unk, however, has other priorities. Marching in formation toward his ship, the ever-watchful Boaz at his back, he joins in the war whoops, like Paul Proteus cheerleading at the Meadows—but takes the first opportunity to steal away.

Stony's instincts were right. Like the Ghost Dance rebels in *Player Piano* waiting for Pittsburgh to fall, the Martian leaders wildly miscalculated their strength. Earth's nuclear response is devastating, and the sky turns burnt orange in the slaughter. Cohesion among the shocked troops disappears once their superiors are neutralized—preset controls in their saucers could not be adjusted to changing conditions. The few beachheads established collapse quickly. It was a suicide mission from the start.

Vonnegut was skilled in drawing images of battlefield chaos. He had been a small player in the disaster at the Bulge, one of the greatest reversals in U.S. military history. He knew what defeat looked and smelled and felt like, and would reprise it again and again in his stories.

Winston Niles Rumfoord, the operation's financier and mastermind, had engineered it for failure, as an object lesson in the futility of war and the need for universal brotherhood. He explained it all later in his *Pocket History of Mars*, a primer in the art of mythmaking.

Any man who would change the world in a significant way must have showmanship, a genial willingness to shed other people's blood, and a plausible new religion to introduce during the brief period of repentance and horror that usually follows bloodshed.

There was a role for Unk in Rumfoord's grand scheme. Not unlike Paul Proteus, he would serve as a symbol for the new religion. But, as we have already seen, Unk is no passive object—despite crippling limitations, his humanity is developing before our eyes, he is *becoming a character.*

Unk makes his way to a schoolyard where a group of youngsters is playing batball. The one with jet-black hair "growing in a violently counter-clockwise swirl" has to be his son Chrono. The boy dominates the game with a mixture of barely controlled rage and faith in his good luck charm, a piece of scrap metal from a flame-thrower factory that is invested with magic powers. Unk weeps when the boy spurns his fatherly overtures. Like everything else in the adult world, the plan of escape is a lot of "baloney," Chrono remarks, and he starts back to the field, eager to annihilate his next victim.

Meanwhile, Chrono's mother, Bee, is at her job instructing army recruits in how to breathe in oxygen-deprived atmospheres. Bee is dutiful in her work, but she is another hard case for the medical professionals. She has been hospitalized for the crime of writing poetry, and dark circles now frame her eyes. Bee shows no emotion when Unk appears to reveal his identity, however, and daydreams as he is taken into custody.

Unk is on a ship amid rows of other saucers ready to take off for battle. The garishly uniformed Winston Rumfoord materializes, Kazak in tow, to check on Unk's condition and offer some words of encouragement. Rumfoord flashes "a very small, v-shaped smile," but Unk cries out in bewilderment over what he sees as injustice. "I-I tried to bring my family together. That's all."

Rumfoord shares a parable about an Earthling volunteer who, to prove his manhood, forced himself upon the lone female on board his flight to Mars. "She was a woman that a fortune-teller had promised him would one day bear his child," he explains solemnly. The violation left the perpetrator with self-loathing and an intense desire for repentance. He had seen the depth of his capacity for brutish behavior and was "spoiled forever as a soldier."

> He became hopelessly engrossed in the intricate tactics of causing less rather than more pain. Proof of his success would be his winning of the woman's forgiveness and understanding.

Unk does not grasp it at the time, but *he* is the protagonist in Rumfoord's tale.

Male guilt, the theme of having caused grievous harm requiring forgiveness, runs throughout Kurt Vonnegut's work, and seems always to connect in some way to his feelings about his mother, whose suffering he could not alleviate. In *Palm Sunday* he describes a recurring dream in which the police arrive at his door to arrest him for having "murdered an old woman a long time ago." Was it, he wondered, his mother?[9]

Edith Vonnegut's struggles, leading up to her suicide, weighed heavily on Vonnegut's sense of self and his relationships. John Rauch, the family historian Vonnegut quotes at length in *Palm Sunday*, gives an account of Edith's last days, the despair she experienced as her son prepared to go off to war. "Bernard at twenty-four escaped the draft, but Kurt, Jr. at 19 was caught." Kurt Jr. had done nothing wrong, his fate was out of his control—but survivor guilt does not operate by the logic of reason. Unk's effort in this allegory to repair the damage caused by his clumsy assertions of manhood may well be the author's expression of his own helpless desire to heal his mother, to reconnect and make her whole again.[10]

Boaz arrives at the ship, eager to catch up with the rest of the invasion armada. But when he presses the "on" button, he and Unk are whisked off in another direction entirely. Rumfoord wants to keep his charge safe and out of sight for awhile.

"The planet Mercury sings like a crystal goblet," the interlude begins—a poetic rendering of the tension between the hemispheres of the sun's innermost planet. Boaz and Unk plunge down its twisting recesses, where they will be marooned for a long time.

The contrast in adjustment between the two castaways could not be greater. Simple, kindly Boaz finds peace among the *harmoniums,* small creatures that glow with nourishment from the vibrations of his beating heart. Unk's loved ones are elsewhere, however, and he is consumed by the need to reunite with them and insure their rescue. After two years, with the help of clues Rumfoord leaves for him during his periodic phantom visits, Unk at last figures out how to get the saucer airborne again and departs alone for the next stage of his odyssey.

The craft lands in a wooded area not far from Vonnegut's Cape Cod village of West Barnstable. A nearby cemetery is filled with Earthlings and Martians buried side-by-side, honored dead from the war. Everyone fancies themselves brothers and sisters now, just as Winston Niles Rumfoord had hoped. National borders have disappeared, wars have ceased, and people embrace the gospel of a god remote and apathetic about their affairs. No one will ever again claim divine sanction for their actions, no person or country can pretend to be favored by a deity. No more crusades, no more inquisitions. Rumfoord's humanistic anti-faith, the Church of God the Utterly Indifferent, is widespread by the time the prophesied Space Wanderer makes his return.

Church bells sound, announcing the star in the passion play. After some coaxing—the moment of re-entry for a soldier is daunting, what is expected of him?—Unk dons the costume prepared for the pageant, bright yellow with question marks. Flowers rain down and crowds cheer as he sits atop the engine of the local fire department. Did the author experience this kind of disorientation on his return from Europe in the summer of 1945?

The world has changed a lot since the Space Wanderer's departure, and Vonnegut the anthropologist has fun with the elaborations. Human beings, as they are apt to do, have remade in unexpected ways what was drawn up on paper, taking things in the egalitarian new order to extremes. The strong carry weights on their shoulders and attractive women disguise themselves with "frumpish clothes, bad posture, chewing gum, and a ghoulish use of cosmetics." "There were," Vonnegut tells us wryly, "literally billions of happily self-handicapped people on Earth."

When asked about the nature of his journey, the Space Wanderer responds with words inscribed above a church door, the mantra for Rumfoord's new millennium:

I WAS A VICTIM OF ACCIDENTS, AS ARE WE ALL.

Outside the Newport estate, vendors hawk cheap souvenirs. Among them are none other than Bee and Chrono. The child is now a delinquent registered with the local police; his mother, once the blue-blooded Beatrice, is now a weathered gypsy queen, her front teeth capped in gold.

Bee has little regard for the man about to materialize. "He cleaned out our minds the way you clean the seeds out of a jack-o-lantern," she protests to the veteran at the next booth, Unk's old sergeant on Mars. "He wired us like robots, trained us, aimed us—burned us out in a good cause."

The main event gets underway. On a scaffolding complete with loudspeakers and television cameras, the master of ceremonies appears. Pale and less steady than usual, he is determined to soldier on with the script. "It's the *contrast* they like," Winston Rumfoord, ever alert to the nuances of stagecraft, confides to the befuddled Space Wanderer. "The order of events doesn't make any difference to them. It's the thrill of the *fast reverse*—"

Rumfoord delivers his sermon with the cadence of a carnival barker, knowing that the audience needed a villain as much as it needed heroes— a principle Bokonon in *Cat's Cradle* would identify as "dynamic tension." "We are *disgusted* by Malachi Constant," Rumfoord bellows, recalling the name of the man who famously presumed favor from the hand of God ("I guess somebody up there likes me.")—the worst sin imaginable for members of the Church of God the Utterly Indifferent.

Rumford reveals that the man in the spotlight with him is Constant, and offers him now a chance for redemption. All he has to do is climb a ladder, as Christ once ascended to the cross, and leave in the saucer at the top of the high platform. He will disappear into exile on Titan, the seventh moon of Saturn, "taking all mistaken ideas about the meaning of luck, all misused wealth and power" with him.

In the audience Bee and Chrono dare Constant to comport himself with courage. He starts his lonely ascent, pausing to look over the home planet he will never see again. "Tell me one good thing you ever did in your life— what you can remember of it," Rumfoord demands from below. Constant thinks of the secret journal he kept on Mars. "I had a friend," he replies tentatively. Rumfoord seals the tragedy with another fast-reverse, identifying Constant as Stony's killer.

There is one more symbol of human folly left to be expunged. "The excesses of Beatrice were excesses of reluctance," Rumfoord declares, turning to his wife. "As a younger woman, she felt so exquisitely bred as to do nothing and to allow nothing to be done to her, for fear of contamination." Again we wonder how much of the author's mother lies in this indictment. "The proposition that God Almighty admired Beatrice for her touch-me-not breeding is at least as questionable as the proposition that God Almighty wanted Malachi Constant to be rich."

"The human race is a scummy thing, and so is Earth, and so are you," Bee responds as she and Chrono scale the ladder. "Good-by, all you clean and wise and lovely people," she adds bitterly as they enter the craft.

Saturn's largest moon is indeed a kind of paradise, with an oxygen-rich atmosphere through which large bluebirds fly majestically. Its maps betray Rumfoord's ego—Titan's seas are called Winston, Niles, and Rumfoord. In the middle of one of them stands his palace, another counterfeit in the grand American style, this time a replica of the Taj Mahal. Rumfoord's lone companion, aside from Kazak, is Salo, a squat, tangerine-colored emissary from the remote planet Tralfamadore, condemned to languish in this unlikely precinct due to a mechanical failure in his spaceship.

Salo's mission—to deliver a message to the far reaches of the cosmos—has been on hold for thousands of years as he awaits assistance in response to his distress signal. He receives communications from home by way of long-distance manipulations of human history. From above, the outline of Stonehenge translates into "Replacement part being sent with all possible speed." The same idea has been behind China's Great Wall, the Kremlin, the Palace of the League of Nations, we learn—all the highest works of man were really just alien telegrams, uniformly bland and unimaginative.

Salo pays a call to the Earthling for whom he has developed unexpected affection. Things are amiss on this day, however. Winston Niles Rumfoord displays electrical streaks in his figure and seems generally out of sorts. His cold manner reflects the deep sense of betrayal he is feeling.

Yes, he admits, Salo helped him plan his invasion project, but like all beings from Tralformadore he is in the end only a *machine* following instructions. Sweat gathers at his temples as Rumfoord struggles to maintain composure, inserting a cigarette into its holder and thrusting out his jaw. Even the limited free will he always thought his birthright turns out to have been a lie; he was as much a pawn in the game as anyone. The new residents of Titan are on their way now, with the boy's all-important good luck charm—the replacement part—so there is no longer any reason to continue the charade.

Salo, un-machine-like, is deeply wounded. With a voice like a bicycle horn he asks what he can do to make things right. Rumfoord has a very human request: he wants to know the reason he has been so systematically used. What *was* the message Salo had been sent to deliver?

The Earthling family lands on the shore of the Winston Sea. "I resign," Malachi Constant declares emphatically, lounging in the shade of a Titanic daisy. It was "a routine philosophy for all Martian veterans," and indeed for veterans of all wars—we can hear the author speaking loud and clear here. "We have taken part for the last time in experiments and fights and festivals we don't like or understand!" Bee endures patiently a harangue she has heard countless times on the long interplanetary flight.

Salo escorts the trio to a final audience with Mr. Rumfoord. They find him by the pool of his Taj, in extremis, stretched out on a lounge chair. "I am not dying," the old man weakly assures his guests.

> I am merely taking my leave of the Solar System. And I am not even doing that. In the grand, in the timeless, in the chrono-syn-clastic infundibulated way of looking at things, I shall always be here. I shall always be wherever I've been.

Again we have a preview of the philosophy that would help Billy Pilgrim get through his days after the war. Rumfoord points a charged finger at Chrono. "You, young man. You have in your pocket the culmination of all Earthling history."

"All I can say," he adds as light envelopes him, "is that I have tried my best to do good for my native Earth while serving the irresistible wishes of Tralfamadore."

Rumfoord was gone, but, like FDR, his impact was lasting and indelible. "They both have enormous hope for changing things," Vonnegut observed once of the two secular high priests. "Childish hopes, too. I don't think Roosevelt was an enormous success except as a personality. And maybe that's the only kind of success a president needs to have anyway." What Americans need in the White House, as the author would say elsewhere, was a humane "dreamer-in-chief" to bring out our best qualities, and leaders like that don't come along every day.[11]

Salo rushes too late to the courtyard, holding out the square of aluminum containing his message, a salutation of the most banal kind. His mission is an empty practical joke, the embodiment of absurdity. In despair over his friend's departure Salo scrambles to the beach and disassembles himself. Chrono drops his good luck piece among the parts in the sand. Wise beyond his years, he has no doubt that "sooner or later the magical forces of the Universe would put everything back together again. They always did."

The epilogue is as bittersweet—some might say sentimental—as anything Vonnegut ever wrote, a testament to the dignity of human beings in an existence they cannot understand, let alone control. Malachi Constant grows to contented old age, a long way from the insensitive "rakehell" we first encountered. He lives by himself in Salo's ship, tinkering with the robot's remains. If reassembled, perhaps his son could go back to Earth to build a life.

This proves unnecessary. In an example of the versatility of his species, Chrono "had made such a thorough and specialized adjustment" to his new environment "that it would have been cruel in the extreme to send him anywhere else." He has joined the Titanic bluebirds, wearing feathers and soaring with them as they travel to and from their nests. Sometimes when Constant is out gathering food he comes across a collection of sticks and stones left by Chrono, the expression of some kind of touchingly human religious impulse. The father tends to those that have fallen into disarray. "Tidying up the shrines was as close, spiritually, as Constant could get to his son."

Elderly Bee lives in the Taj at the center of the Winston Sea, devoting herself to a book challenging her husband's fatalism. People *are* largely determined, Vonnegut says through her. Tralfamadorian interests *have* undoubtedly been served over the millennia—but "in such highly personalized ways" that it didn't matter.

Bee makes a last entry in her journal as she spies the painting of herself as a child, the sad girl on the pony—the single artifact Rumfoord brought with him to Titan. "The worst thing that could possibly happen," she writes, "would be to not be used for anything by anybody." She has been on a hero's journey of her own, and, like Malachi Constant, has come a long way.

Bee takes her last breath and Constant lays her to rest under a sky darkened by thousands of bluebirds. Resplendent in his feather cape, Chrono cries out thanks to his parents for the gift of life and takes off with his flock. We have here, in its most lyrical form, the Vonnegut optimism about the young.

As Constant rows back to shore, Salo comes out toward him, buoyant on inflated spherical feet. He is whole again and eager to resume his cosmic errand, however foolish. "You finally fell in love, I see," Salo says to his grief-stricken companion. *This* was the purpose of life, the faithful messenger understands: "to love whoever is around to be loved."

Offered a lift to Earth, Constant curiously requests Indianapolis as his destination. In the wintry predawn darkness Salo's craft sets down in a vacant lot. "There's your stop over there, old soldier," the robot whispers, pointing to a bench. In a baggy suit once owned by Winston Niles Rumfoord, Malachi Constant waits in the snow for a bus that comes hours too late. As he drifts off he imagines a sunbeam breaking through the clouds, bearing a diamond-encrusted flying saucer. It is a happy death, courtesy of a posthypnotic suggestion.

Out of the saucer comes Stony, clad in the uniform of their old Martian Assault unit. "Hello, Unk," he says with joshing familiarity. Stony is taking his friend to Paradise, to join Beatrice. "Don't ask me why, old sport," Vonnegut perversely has his character say as the airlock seals, "but somebody up there likes you."

"Every mother's favorite child is the one that's delivered by natural childbirth," the author once told an interviewer, and so it was with *Sirens of Titan*, produced in the space of two months. A paperback original for Dell, it solidified, for better or worse, Kurt Vonnegut's reputation as a science-fiction writer, selling for 35 cents a copy at PXs and drugstores around the country, packaged behind a cover featuring mechanical monsters and a voluptuous woman cavorting in an asteroid belt. The sirens of its title, the publishers calculated, was its strongest selling point. There were no reviews for such an "unserious" piece of work—many of its ideas would be lost until later—but it provided a stream of income for a man supporting a suddenly expanded household, the family that *he* had assembled.[12]

And Vonnegut took advantage of the genre's freedoms to address large issues: the subjectivity of time, the pettiness of human concerns in the cosmic scale, the need to celebrate the smallest acts of friendship and community. It satisfies as the story of a man buffeted by life, finding strength and meaning within, learning how to make a home, how to *love*. It is a hero's journey, one Vonnegut and the men of his generation struggled to make as they dealt with the realities of their lives.

THREE

Mother Night

Nobody saw the honest me I hid so deeply inside.
—Howard W. Campbell Jr.

Mother Night (1961), another paperback original, is a taut study of identity in the modern world—the fragmentation of the self unhinged from community, the masks we wear to conceal the absence of a stable, rational center. Vonnegut teases out here the mystery of human motives, the ways in which good and evil, innocence and vanity, are always intertwined. The title is from a passage in Goethe's *Faust,* in which Mephistopheles anticipates the inevitable triumph of darkness over "supercilious" light.

To negotiate this terrain Vonnegut shifts from the otherworldly flights of *Sirens of Titan* to something decidedly more earthbound, set firmly in history. That is not to deny the story's surreality, however. Hitler's Reich, where *Mother Night* takes place, is as much a distant planet for us as Tralfamadore. But the issues raised under these conditions are embedded, if in less extreme form, in all of our lives.

As a book about a man walking the frontier between his American and German selves, *Mother Night* hits close to home for the author. The material is more disturbing and harder to engage with detachment than in his first two books. "My personal experience with Nazi monkey business was limited," Vonnegut felt the need to disclose in his introduction to a 1966 reissue. There were fascist sympathizers around during his youth, to be sure, and he vaguely recalled once seeing a copy of the *Protocols of the Elders of Zion,* the confection alleged to be the Jews' secret plan for world domination. But as was true for many at the time, Hitler was too remote and comical a threat to be taken seriously by the Vonnegut household. It was a family joke when an aunt married a "*German* German" and was required to show proof she had no "Jewish blood" in her background. Indianapolis officials "had fun putting ribbons and official seals all over the documents, which made them look like eighteenth-century peace treaties."[1]

Writing for the first time with such directness of his months inside Germany as a POW, Vonnegut describes in that introduction how with his companions he worked for his keep, mixing with civilians in the bejeweled "open" city of Dresden. Then came the night of the fire-bombing. "Everything was gone but the cellars where 135,000 Hansels and Gretels had been baked like gingerbread men," he reports. At gunpoint the prisoners became "corpse miners," harvesting valuables before bodies were burned. Grieving relatives hurled curses and rocks at the Americans as they went about their labors.[2]

Who bore responsibility for this landscape of death? Acknowledging the vagaries of fate, the author declines the posture of clean hands: this was the creation of human beings like himself. "If I'd been born in Germany, I suppose I would have *been* a Nazi," Vonnegut muses, "bopping Jews and gypsies and Poles around, leaving boots sticking out of snow banks, warming myself with my secretly virtuous insides. So it goes."[3]

Who can say they would not have been a "good citizen" in that situation, keeping doubts hidden from view? *Mother Night* expresses a warning about hubris; its moral, made explicit from the start, is a signature Vonnegut aphorism: "We are what we pretend to be, so we must be careful what we pretend to be."[4]

Vonnegut's third novel marks a shift in style for the author, toward the economy of his mature works. Its 45 chapters are compressed into 174 pages, and the humor is darker, more aggressively ironic as the reader is led through a maze of carefully laid "mousetraps" of oscillating tension and release. Jerome Klinkowitz has described its "absurdity to the third power," with each person and each event having at least three layers as the onion is unpeeled. In storytelling terms, "it's the thrill of the *fast reverse*" that keeps the audience involved, as Winston Niles Rumfoord might say.[5]

Here, too, we have for the first time the prototype Vonnegut narrator, an "epilogue man" shattered by circumstances and bad choices, recounting in noir flashback the road to the present dead end. Full of self-loathing, he is waiting to die.

This is literally true in *Mother Night*. Inspired by the capture and prosecution of international fugitive Adolf Eichmann, Vonnegut creates the figure of Howard W. Campbell Jr., an American held by Israeli authorities at a new prison in Jerusalem—in the same building as Eichmann—on the eve of his own trial for war crimes.

Campbell is a trophy, thanks to his activities as a high-profile voice for Hitler's propaganda ministry. Recalling real-life propaganda broadcasters "Tokyo Rose," Britain's Lord Haw-Haw, and Ezra Pound, Campbell's radio broadcasts from Berlin offered viciously anti-Semitic messages down to the dying days of the regime. All the while, however, he was a double agent, relaying information that undermined the Axis cause. The question that haunts even the accused himself is whether he did his job as a mouthpiece for evil *too* well. Is he a hero or a villain?[6]

As he did previously with science-fiction in *Player Piano* and *The Sirens of Titan*, Vonnegut here uses a commercial genre—in this case a spy story—to talk about the big things on his mind. "Simply on a circumstantial level," Klinkowitz observes, "think of Vonnegut's life, sitting in West Barnstable being a writer. That's like being a counterspy while everybody else is a storm-window salesman or a crab fisherman."[7]

The idea for the Campbell saga began in a cocktail party conversation Vonnegut had with a former U.S. Navy Intelligence officer. A comment about people in his line of work being "schizophrenic" struck Vonnegut as a metaphor for the modern condition. Spies have to believe, at some level, in the lies they tell, the parts they play. They have to exaggerate aspects of themselves, manage rogue thoughts, repress contradictions—on penalty of death. "They have to be insane," Vonnegut recalled the naval officer saying, "because otherwise they would either blow their covers or simply die of fright." But the question Vonnegut makes his own here is, at what point do they lose control, with no chance of turning back?[8]

The Haifa Institute for the Documentation of War Criminals has provided Howard Campbell with the means to record his "Confessions." The machine upon which he pecks away is identical to one he used when he worked for Hitler, including a key with parallel lightning strokes—the notation for the S.S. As a trafficker in symbols and myths—in a way, he is a cousin to Reverend Lasher in *Player Piano*—Campbell always appreciated the typewriter's "frightening and magical" effects. It was good stagecraft.

Campbell is under twenty-four-hour surveillance, and his guards represent different perspectives on the war. A bright schoolboy holds forth at length about "Tiglath-pileser the Third," marauder of the Canaanite city of Hazor in 732 BC, but draws a blank when the prisoner mentions his old boss, Goebbels. It wasn't in the textbooks. He is relieved by an Auschwitz survivor who confesses to having volunteered for the "Special Detail," shepherding inmates into gas chambers to delay his own rendezvous with death. Why did he do it? Complicity is an elusive thing. After two years of loudspeakers blaring "corpse-carriers to the guardhouse," the job suddenly sounded appealing. If one could answer the *why*, the former Sonderkommando told Campbell, "you would have a very great book."

The third guard sympathizes with the prisoner's alleged "crimes," urging him to speak without shame about "the things a man does to stay alive!" A Hungarian Jew, he too had been a deep-cover agent, using false papers to become the fiercest of S.S. men. "What an Aryan I made!" he boasts, so "pure and terrifying" he was assigned to investigate who was passing information to the resistance. "There was a leak somewhere, and we were out to stop it," he recalls, still in character, still righteous, "bitter and affronted"— even though *he* was the leak. "I am happy to say that fourteen S.S. men were shot on our recommendation."

Observing the prisoner's tortured efforts to sleep, the guard on the overnight shift finds in Campbell the only man he knows with a bad conscience. "Everybody else, no matter what side he was on, no matter what he did, is sure a good man could not have acted in any other way." Even Auschwitz commandant Rudolf Hoess slept soundly in his cell, he remembers. He feels no particular satisfaction in helping to hang him. "I was like most everybody who came through that war. Every job was a job to do, and no job was any better or any worse than any other."

Campbell had been casually intimate with Hoess and others at the highest levels of the Nazi hierarchy; he knew them as individuals. Political theorist Hannah Arendt's phrase of the time, "the banality of evil," perfectly applies to Vonnegut's discussion of the Nazi hierarchy's clumsy "Mickey Mouse" dancing, their intramural ping-pong matches, their hollow sentimentality while in the midst of perpetrating mass murder.

Campbell finds it curious that he never dreams about "the nightmare people" he knew during those days. All of his nocturnal talk, the guard tells him, was about a woman, and about his years after the war in New York City, living a kind of purgatory in a grim attic apartment in Greenwich Village. From its back window he could hear children calling out "olly-olly-ox-in-free," the "sweetly mournful cry that meant a game of hide-and-seek was over." He longed to hear those words of absolution for himself.

Acknowledging from the start his fragmented selves, Howard W. Campbell Jr. introduces himself as "an American by birth, a Nazi by reputation, and a nationless person by inclination." Born in 1912, he grew up in Schenectady, the only child of a globe-trotting General Electric engineer and his wife, from Indianapolis. His father was harsh and largely absent, his mother a "beautiful, talented, morbid person," probably drunk most of the time. Like the author's mother, she must have been the source of her son's dreamy side, his weakness for tragic romance and hunger for the uncritical love of a woman.

A work assignment took the family to Berlin in 1923, and Howard Jr. assimilated easily into his new culture. It is the inverse of Vonnegut's own experience. When Campbell's parents returned to America sixteen years later, he stayed. Political intrigue was no reason to abandon the perquisites he had earned as a playwright in his adopted language. Then, too, there was his marriage to the actress Helga Noth, elder daughter of Berlin's chief of police. Theirs was a love envied for its passion and glamour.

We fast-forward to April 1945 when, in flight as Nazi Germany collapsed, Howard W. Campbell Jr. was recognized and captured by

Bernard B. O'Hare, a U.S. army lieutenant. He was paraded around a death camp, to see up close the effects of his words. His image at the gallows became a cover for *Life,* nearly winning a Pulitzer Prize for its iconic power.

But Campbell did not hang—Allied authorities intervened to arrange his disappearance. All through the war he had been conveying coded intelligence in the form of "mannerisms, pauses, emphases, coughs, seeming stumbles in certain key sentences." Before the Normandy invasion his phrasing "sounded like the last stages of double pneumonia," he recalled, not hiding his satisfaction. He never knew the content of the messages, but delivered them with the skill of a master thespian.

Campbell's career in espionage began with an apparently chance encounter in Berlin's Tiergarten. He was the picture of contentment that sunny morning before the war, his plays—"medieval romances, about as political as chocolate *éclairs*"—making him the toast of Germany's theatergoing elite. Campbell sat by himself on a park bench, lost in thought about a new work he planned to write, a celebration of his marriage to be called *Das Reich der Zwei* ("The Nation of Two"). It would demonstrate "how a pair of lovers in a world gone mad could survive by being loyal only to a nation composed of themselves."

A "gasbag" tourist took a seat next to him, inquiring in "twanging Chicago English" what he thought about life in Hitler's New Order. Campbell demurred, with some annoyance, but the man persisted, sharing the outline of a "spy story" he claimed to have concocted. "There's this young American, see, who's been in Germany so long he's practically a German himself. He knows a lot of big-shot Nazis who like to hang around theater people." When war comes he pretends to be loyal to his adopted country, while serving as an Allied operative—right in the belly of the beast.

Campbell nervously laughed off the scenario, protesting his aloofness from the convulsions of history. He was an *artist,* after all, a man of peace. "This war isn't going to let anybody stay in a peaceful trade," the stranger replied, flashing a card identifying himself as Major Frank Wirtanen of the U.S. War Department. He did not soft-pedal the hazards of the assignment he was proposing. If Campbell agreed to do it he would be on his own, and

should he somehow miraculously survive, it would be impossible to reha-
bilitate his name, even if the right side won.

What made Wirtanen think this man might accept? From Campbell's
plays he had detected a weakness for melodrama that would make the
assignment too good for Campbell to pass up. "You'd be an authentic hero,
about a hundred times braver than any ordinary man," the major promised
seductively, his voice lowered as two uniformed Nazis brushed by.

From his cell Campbell notes that the U.S. government denies any
record of the only person on earth who could save him from the execu-
tioner's noose. The meeting in the park, the bargain that had its beginnings
so many centuries ago, is otherwise the figment of a fertile and desperate
imagination. Wirtanen's existence is so much a matter of private belief that
Campbell refers to him as his "Blue Fairy Godmother."

And his Mephistopheles had been right about him. Like a lot of people,
Campbell longed to be a character in an exciting story.

> I was a ham. As a spy of the sort he described, I would have an
> opportunity for some pretty grand acting. I would fool everyone
> with my brilliant interpretation of a Nazi, inside and out. . . . And
> I *did* fool everybody. I began to strut like Hitler's right-hand man,
> and nobody saw the honest me I hid so deeply inside.

He kept the secret even from his mate. "My Helga believed that I meant
the nutty things I said on the radio, said at parties," he remembers. It would
not have registered in any case. The realm to which they retreated together
allowed for no outside information, no troubling moral questions. They
simply amputated inconvenient portions of their humanity as the storm
swirled about them. "If we had listened for more, had thought about what
we heard," Campbell now anguishes, "what a nauseated couple we would
have been!"

A "Nation of Two" is by its nature a fragile arrangement, and from the time
Helga went missing while entertaining troops on the Russian front
Howard W. Campbell Jr. was rendered "stateless," an exile without allegiances of any kind. In his new life in New York he sleepwalked for more
than a decade. The few possessions he accumulated were, like himself, "war

surplus," his lone passion was the memory of his wife. Day after dreary day he conversed with Helga's ghost, and at night he drank candlelight toasts to their lost love.

In 1958 Campbell took a step out of his dream world. Driven by boredom and a half-conscious hunger for contact with a live human being, he knocked at the door of a neighbor in his building to solicit a game of chess. George Kraft, another grieving widower, welcomed him inside and a friendship, a marriage of sorts, was born. Sharing meals, debating politics and art (Kraft was a painter), "we built up between ourselves a pathetic sort of domesticity." Campbell spilled the details of his past to his sympathetic companion. The cocoon "was frayed a little, was weakened enough to let some pale light in." But with the light would come complications.

Not that his cover was ever that deep. In the metropolis he had settled into a life of open obscurity, following with amusement rumors about his whereabouts in Iran, Argentina, or Ireland. Nobody seemed curious whether the name on his mailbox belonged to *the* Howard W. Campbell Jr.

His single brush with exposure occurred when he paid a visit to another neighbor in the building to get treatment for a minor wound. The Epsteins were survivors of Auschwitz, and, like the guards in the Israeli prison, represented different attitudes toward the pain of recent history. The young physician wanted to move on; his childhood was a nightmare to be quarantined and forgotten. For his mother, though—"heavy, slow, deeply lined, sadly, bitterly watchful"—the war was ever present. She made a point to inquire about the visitor's suspiciously famous name. Campbell feigned ignorance, eluding her effort to get him to speak a little German.

But evasion would soon become impossible. In the mail one day with the usual handbills he found a letter from Bernard B. O'Hare, his wartime captor. "I was very surprised and disappointed to hear you weren't dead yet," O'Hare had written, cold hatred coming through on the American Legion stationery. "Now that I know where you are, I will be paying you a call real soon. I should have pushed you into a lime pit when I had the chance." O'Hare copied his correspondence to law enforcement agencies and outlets in the mainstream and fringe media.

Among the latter was something called the *White Christian Minuteman*, a free copy of which was also in Campbell's mail that morning. Upon inspection it proved to be what its masthead advertised, "a scabrous, illiterate, anti-Semitic, anti-Negro, anti-Catholic hate sheet" with headlines like "Supreme Court Demands U.S. Be Mongrel!" and "International Jewry Only Winners of World War II." Such sentiments were not in themselves startling to Campbell. It was, he thought to himself, "the sort of thing I said for a living in Germany." But one item raised alarm bells. "American Tragedy!" lamented his present circumstances, as the victim of "the conspiracy of international Jewish bankers and international Jewish Communists who will not rest until the bloodstream of every American is hopelessly polluted with Negro and/or Oriental blood." Campbell's address was listed for anyone who wanted to help.

Vonnegut now takes us into the lunatic underworld of home-grown fascism, where Campbell's wartime rhetoric lived on with a small but devoted audience. The Reverend Doctor Lionel Jason David Jones, "D.D.S., D.D.," the person behind the *White Christian Minuteman,* had been expelled from dental school for pushing his views on race, including "degeneracy in the teeth of Catholics and Unitarians." He ended up president of an embalming school in Arkansas, which for tax reasons transformed itself in the 1930s into the Western Hemisphere University of the Bible.

The *Minuteman* underwent striking changes as the decade wore on. The layout grew slicker, dentistry diagrams were replaced by emphatic pro-German commentary on current events. In 1942 Jones was convicted as a foreign agent, with evidence that the content of his newspaper had been supplied by a secret financier, the Nazi propaganda ministry. "It is quite possible," Campbell reflects with horror, "that much of his more scurrilous material was written by me." As Vonnegut would insist in *Breakfast of Champions,* once ideas entered into circulation they took on a life of their own.

Why has Campbell given us (with the research assistance of the Haifa Institute) this profile of Lionel Jason David Jones?

> In order to contrast with myself a race-baiter who is ignorant and insane.
>
> I am neither ignorant nor insane. Those whose orders I carried out in Germany were as ignorant and insane as Dr. Jones. I knew it. God help me, I carried out their instructions anyway.

The next week Jones paid a call to the martyred hero, accompanied by a menagerie of trusted associates. The meeting is one of Vonnegut's most effective burlesques, captured with all its absurdist color in Keith Gordon's 1996 film version of the novel. Each man has credentials in the field of paranoid hate mongering. The bodyguard, a former officer in the German American Bund, once arranged a summit with the New Jersey Ku Klux Klan, highlighted by his speech declaring the Vatican a front for the worldwide Jewish conspiracy. The idea was a staple of Campbell's broadcasts from Berlin. "A change of Popes and eleven years in a prison laundry had not changed his mind."

Jones's secretary was a defrocked, alcoholic priest, chaplain of a Detroit gun club—there are echoes of anti-Semitic radio priest Father Charles Coughlin here. The chauffeur, meanwhile, was another "erstwhile jailbird," the ridiculously costumed "Black Fuehrer of Harlem." He proclaimed to anyone who would listen his allegiance to "the colored folks' side" in the late war, evidenced by his service as a spy for Japan.

As Jones approached the top of the stairs, wheezing colleagues in tow, Campbell braced for attack, ready "to square him away so savagely that he would never think of me as one of his own kind again." He wanted to reclaim his good name with his fists, but was stopped cold by the announcement that the pale, anomalously youthful figure lagging below is his long-lost Helga.

The shock was profound. Could the ivory-haired woman possibly have survived the Red Army and years of slave labor? It could not *be*—and yet he accepted the story she told, woven on the same "crazy loom" of history that had produced his own remarkable journey.

There was no need for thanks, Jones assured Campbell as he took his leave. It was *he* who was due gratitude—"for having the courage to tell the truth during the war, when everybody else was telling lies."

Campbell welcomed the woman into his "war surplus" existence. As they awkwardly resumed the intimacies of their "Nation of Two" that night, she asked what he knew about the fate of her family. He recalled the last time he saw her parents and her "pretty, imaginative little sister, Resi," during the chaotic final weeks of the war that Vonnegut revisited so often in his writings.

Campbell stopped by the Noth estate as he fled Berlin on a commandeered motorcycle, just ahead of the Russian advance. To ease passage through a welter of checkpoints he had donned the blue-and-gold officer's uniform of the "Free American Corps," a "Nazi daydream" he had cooked up about a unit of American POWs who would join the fight against communism on the Eastern front. He recalled the bizarre normalcy of the mansion—like the Dresden Vonnegut would see when he arrived for his work detail, it "had not suffered so much as a cracked window-pane."

His father-in-law was supervising laborers as they loaded household possessions onto wagons. The scene crystallized for Campbell the dehumanizing morality he had helped to encourage. A Polish woman emerged from the house, nearly losing control of the heavy object she carried in her emaciated arms. Werner Noth charged toward her in a rage. Aggrieved, "close to unashamed tears, he asked us all to adore the blue vase that laziness and stupidity had almost let slip from the world."

"That's quite a uniform," Noth remarked to his son-in-law as they began their farewell conversation. It was the same costume Billy Pilgrim and Edgar Derby would see when Campbell visited their quarters in *Slaughterhouse*. On his dagger was "an American eagle that clasped a swastika in its right claw and devoured a snake in its left claw," representing "international Jewish communism." Noth made a joke, suggesting that the thirteen stars haloing the bird's head—copied from Campbell's original design, mistakenly drawn as six-sided Stars of David—stood for "the thirteen Jews in Franklin Roosevelt's cabinet."

This was a time for honesty, and Noth admitted that Campbell's marriage to his daughter had broken his heart. For years he waited for a misstep, a sign that the interloper was a spy. "I studied you. I listened to everything you said. I never missed a broadcast." Now it didn't matter whether he was a double agent or not. "You could never have served the enemy as well as you served us," Noth said, shaking his hand. "I realized that almost all the ideas that I hold now, that make me unashamed of anything I may have felt or done as a Nazi, came not from Hitler, not from Goebbels, not from Himmler—but from you."

Campbell was dispatched to shoot Resi's dog, who could not go along in the evacuation. He found Resi, the "ten-year-old nihilist," in the music room, and was startled to see how much she was coming to resemble her older sister. Now it was time for *her* confession, about the love she harbored for her dashing brother–in-law. "I used to envy Helga," Resi told him, voice flat, eyes vacant. "When [she] was dead, I started dreaming about how I would grow up and marry you and be a famous actress, and you would write plays for me." This was Resi's exciting story, her *Cinderella*, and Campbell was the perfect blank screen upon which to project it. What was behind the screen even he could not pin down for sure.

Sitting at a barber shop years later Campbell saw a photograph of his father-in-law's summary execution. "Hangwomen for the Hangman of Berlin" screamed the title of the article, filler for a spread of standard-issue 1950s pornography. (There could have been a Kilgore Trout story elsewhere in the magazine's pages.) In contrast to the well-fed maidens displayed on the cover, like those adorning Vonnegut's science fiction paperbacks, the females surrounding Noth's body as it dangled from a tree were "nameless, shapeless ragbags." Perhaps one was the woman who had been so careless with the vase.

Now Campbell beheld his "Helga," allowing himself thoughts of picking up where they left off. "Tomorrow, we'll find a bed like our old bed—two miles long and three miles wide with a headboard like an Italian sunset," he told her, his romantic imagination re-engaged. She had something else he had thought lost forever, a suitcase full of his collected works and other possessions. Included was a paean to the "Nation of Two."

> *I saw a huge steam roller,*
> *It blotted out the sun.*
> *The people all lay down, lay down;*
> *They did not try to run. . . .*
> *My love and I, we ran away,*
> *The engine did not find us.*
> *We ran up to a mountain top,*
> *Left history far behind us.*

As Campbell scanned the artifacts of his younger days, Helga asked why he had fallen silent, why he no longer wrote poems or plays. In the response we can imagine Vonnegut at this stage of his career, haunted by the long struggle for a form and language to tell *his* remarkable war story. "It's all I've seen, all I've been through that makes it damn near impossible for me to say anything," Campbell explained. "I've lost the knack of making sense. I speak gibberish to the civilized world, and it replies in kind."

On the street the next morning, attired in a suit he had not worn since his capture, complete with walking cane, Campbell has regained his swagger, dispensing opinions on all manner of passing scenes. He is taking in America for the first time in decades, and does not like much of what he sees. The stores were closed for "Veterans Day," a change from the "Armistice Day" of his youth. "It's just so damn cheap, so damn typical," he protests with disgust. "This used to be a day in honor of the dead of World War One, but the living couldn't keep their grubby hands off of it, wanted the glory for themselves. Any time anything of real dignity appears in this country, it's torn to shreds and thrown to the mob."

Did he hate his native country? "That would be as silly as loving it," Campbell replied.

> It's impossible for me to get emotional about it, because real estate doesn't interest me. It's no doubt a great flaw in my personality, but I can't think in terms of boundaries. Those imaginary lines are as unreal to me as elves and pixies.

We can admire Campbell's aversion to nationalism, an expression of the author's leanings, but also detect in his words a streak of arrogance, the habit of exemption from common concerns that allowed him to withdraw so thoroughly during the war years, to play the part of a Nazi so convincingly. "You've changed so," Helga commented with surprise. "People should be changed by world wars," he answered, "else what are world wars for?"

Campbell's moment back in the "supercilious" light was fleeting. The woman at his side was not who she pretended to be. Instead she is Resi, auditioning for the role of her older sister. "What is this strange crime I've committed," Campbell asked himself, appalled. "I'm Helga, Helga, Helga. You believed it." Understanding the weight of the lie, he made another bargain. "God forgive me. I accepted Resi as my Helga again."

His companion grew steadily more confident, more demanding now with each step. Could she be his muse? Campbell saw their reflection in a shop window: "The male ghost looked God-awful old and starved and moth-eaten," while "the female ghost looked young enough to be his daughter, sleek, bouncy, and full of hell." The Helga/Resi confusion here fits a pattern running through Vonnegut novels, the man befuddled and victimized by Janus-faced women—healers and idealized love objects one minute, betrayers the next.

The shocks continued, as we know they must. There was a swastika scrawled next to Campbell's mailbox. "Now the carnivores, scenting a freshly opened den, are closing in," he realized with dread. A man was waiting in the foyer, armed with a newspaper reporting Israel's campaign to bring the war criminal to justice. "Before the Jews put you in a cage or in a zoo or whatever they're gonna do to you," he said, knocking his prey to the floor, "I'd just like to play with you a little myself." He was there to avenge his fallen buddies from the war.

Campbell awoke in a cellar festooned with Nazi banners and a picture of Hitler over a cardboard fireplace. It was the headquarters of the "White Sons of the American Constitution," a refuge courtesy of Dr. Lionel Jason David Jones. "What is life without friends," Campbell mumbled darkly to Resi as he struggled to take in his surroundings. Kraft shot a pistol in an adjacent room. The target was a familiar one, "a caricature of a cigar-smoking Jew" Campbell dashed off early in the war, "standing on broken crosses and little naked women." Goebbels was so impressed he ordered copies by the million printed, and Himmler sent a letter of thanks for its role in improving the marksmanship of S.S. recruits.

This bit of lethal propaganda may have been "an excess of zeal," Campbell concedes—his first admission that he had lost some control of his shadow side, indulged it beyond what was necessary. He insists it was only to add credibility to his performance, but we wonder about the lines that have been crossed. He intentionally "overdrew" the sketch, with clichés that "would have been ludicrous anywhere but in Germany or Jones' basement," but now he realizes that crudeness was the secret to its appeal. "This is a hard world to be ludicrous in, with so many human beings so reluctant to laugh, so incapable of thought, so eager to believe and snarl and hate. So many people *wanted* to believe me!"

Using materials at hand, Campbell cobbled together an ensemble as outrageous as his Free American Corps uniform. It included a silver shirt, symbolic of the American Fascist movement, and "a tiny orange sports coat that made me look like an organ-grinder's monkey." Billy Pilgrim would wear the same jacket in *Slaughterhouse.* The news from outside, meanwhile, was all bad. Officials at the highest levels announced their readiness to extradite Campbell once he was captured. Street vigilantes poised to take more immediate measures, and Bernard B. O'Hare remained in hot pursuit. "I want this guy all for myself," he vowed to the newspapers.

In the public mind Campbell was a monster on the level of Eichmann, the fugitive he would meet in person for the first time in their Tel Aviv prison. The architect of the Final Solution, he was by then a pitiful harmless-looking figure, a "chinless old plucked buzzard" looking up from his typing chores, "beaming, beaming, beaming" a "saintly smile." Chilling in his ordinariness, Eichmann tried to mentor the new arrival, sharing his philosophy about the need to adapt to ever-changing environments. "Each one is very different from the others, and you have to be able to recognize what is expected of you in each phase. That's the secret of successful living." It was also the first principle of espionage.

"The more I think about Eichmann and me," Campbell concludes, "the more I think that he should be sent to the hospital, and that I am the sort of person for whom punishments by fair, just men were devised."

> As a friend of the court . . . I offer my opinion that Eichmann cannot distinguish between right and wrong—that not only right and wrong, but truth and falsehood, hope and despair, beauty and ugliness, kindness and cruelty, comedy and tragedy, are all processed by [his] mind indiscriminately, like birdshot through a bugle.
>
> My case is different. I always know when I tell a lie, am capable of imagining the cruel consequences of anybody's believing my lies, know cruelty is wrong. I could no more lie without noticing it than I could unknowingly pass a kidney stone.

A plan is revealed to get Campbell to Mexico. Anticipating their new life together, Resi cries for joy. Was she sincere? Just as Paul wondered about Anita's emotions in *Player Piano,* this was a perpetual question for Vonnegut men, and we are never sure of the answer. "Who knows. I can only guarantee that the tears were wet and salty." Campbell was asked to address the

Iron Guard of the White Sons of the American Constitution, gathered on folding chairs in the furnace room. A recording of a wartime broadcast was played to introduce the honored guest. "This is Howard W. Campbell, Jr., one of the few remaining free Americans," the voice crackled with smug menace.

Listening to himself in the darkness, Campbell was for a moment paralyzed with déjà vu, "unstuck in time." How could he live with what he had done? Through an ability to compartmentalize, a knack for cultivating "that simple and widespread boon to modern mankind—schizophrenia."

Just before stepping to the podium a note was thrust into Campbell's pocket warning of imminent danger. Signed by Colonel Frank Wirtanen, it directed him to exit through the coal bin to the vacant store across the street.

Campbell had met his "Blue Fairy Godmother" only once since the encounter in the park. "Well, what did you think of *that* war?" Wirtanen asked at Allied headquarters in Wiesbaden in 1945. "I would just as soon have stayed out of it," Campbell replied, bitterly. "You were a good soldier," the colonel assured him. "Of all the agents who were my dream children, so to speak, you were the only one who got clear through the war both reliable and alive."

It was cold comfort, since Helga had been one of the casualties—a fact Campbell discovered he unknowingly conveyed in code over the radio. *This* was a violation too far. "It represented, I suppose, a wider separation of my several selves than even I can bear to think about." Like Malachi Constant and Winston Niles Rumfoord in *Sirens of Titan*, Campbell raged now about all the ways he had been used.

Among the three people on earth who knew that he was a double-agent, Wirtanen revealed with a smile, was "the man you called Franklin Delano Rosenfeld, who used to listen to you gleefully every night." The rest "knew you for what you were too," he added, leaking for the first time mixed feelings about his prize operative. "Whoever it was, he was one of the most vicious sons of bitches who ever lived." Maintaining a Nazi persona was a difficult problem, he reminded Campbell, and "very few men could have solved it as thoroughly as you did." All he had to offer now in exchange, though, was passage out of Germany and a little cash.

Men like Campbell didn't do what they did for medals or money anyway, in Wirtanen's experience. The precise motivation varied from case to case, he observed, but at bottom, "espionage offers each spy an opportunity to go crazy in a way he finds irresistible," to unleash without restraint hidden impulses in his soul. The same could be said for the writers of novels.[9]

Now the two men met again. Wirtanen was older, but still full of surprises. He had come out of retirement because his "dream child" was an object of interest in the Cold War. Both Resi and Kraft were Soviet agents. Campbell's walk through the funhouse hall of mirrors seemed without end. There was one more thing to disclose. Campbell's diary of the most private recesses of his "Nation of Two" was published under another name by the Russian soldier who found it, and it had become an underground classic east of the iron curtain. Like a pig in the Chicago stockyards, every aspect of Campbell's identity had now been appropriated, sectioned, packaged, and digested:

> By God—I think they even found a use for my squeal! The part of me that wanted to tell the truth got turned into an expert liar! The lover in me got turned into a pornographer! The artist in me got turned into ugliness such as the world has rarely seen before.

Campbell's brief absence from Jones's basement had gone unnoticed. Hungry to reclaim some shred of his dignity, he confronted his companions at gunpoint about their intentions. The house was about to be raided, and Resi pleaded her fidelity a last time, asking him to join her in the ultimate sacrifice—like a hero in a Howard W. Campbell Jr. play. She swallowed cyanide, showing him "a woman who dies for love."

Campbell was soon on the streets again, more directionless than ever. Even the flickering life-force of curiosity, which allowed him to "move through so many dead and pointless years after the war," was now gone. Inertia took him back to his building, and after feeling his way up the blackness of the stairs he found his apartment looted, the windows broken out.

The sensation of moving into cold fresh air reminded him of the times he and his wife had been bombed out during the war. "Both moments at those splintered stairheads under the open sky were exquisite.... For a minute or two, Helga and I felt like Noah and his wife on Mount Ararat." But then it was time to return to the shelters, to wait with neighbors as the explosions above resumed their capricious path. "And they walked and they walked and they walked, and it seemed that they would never go away." This is another gesture toward Vonnegut's Dresden, where he, a German American prisoner, had been attacked from the air by his own side. It is a story as remarkable in its own way as Howard Campbell's.

Bernard B. O'Hare was lying-in-wait. In his mind, the figure before him represented "pure evil"—not a man but a dragon he intended to slay. Perhaps this mission was an antidote to the gray realities of O'Hare's life after the war, which as he rambled on, clearly "had not been years of merry blooming." Campbell surprised him with a blow that broke his arm. Exuding a passion he did not know still existed, he condemned the fantasy that had delivered the avenger to his room. "I'm not your destiny, or the Devil either!" he shouted.

> Look at you! Came to kill evil with your bare hands, and now away you go with no more glory than a man sideswiped by a Greyhound bus! And that's all the glory you deserve! ...That's all that any man at war with pure evil deserves.
>
> There are plenty of good reasons for fighting ... but no good reason ever to hate without reservation, to imagine that God Almighty Himself hates with you, too. Where's evil? It's that large part of every man that wants to hate without limit, that wants to hate with God on its side.

Campbell had learned some things on his journey. Experience had made him a realist, a believer in restraint, an evangelist for Rumfoord's "Church of God the Utterly Indifferent."

Now he delivered himself again to the door of the Epsteins, eager to be judged for his crimes against humanity. The mother insisted, over her son's objections, that the neighbor's wish be accommodated. They recognized his name from the internment days—between themselves they call him "Kahmboo," the persona Campbell now describes as "the undiluted evil in me."

Mrs. Epstein sat at the kitchen table, studying him intently. "They took all the light bulbs," she told Campbell in German, referring to the darkened stairwell he had just negotiated. In Europe it happened too. After the Gestapo had taken someone away, "other people would come into the building, wanting to do something patriotic. Such a strange thing for somebody always to do."

As volunteers arrived to turn Campbell over to the authorities, he felt a weight off of his shoulders. By way of a goodbye, the old woman leaned toward him, singing in the tone of a nursery rhyme: "*Leichentrager zu Wache.*" "Corpse-carriers to the guardhouse."

Campbell considers the circus around his upcoming day in court. He is a talisman, and the public is eager to see "Pure Evil" expunged. But an interesting piece of correspondence has today made its way into his stack of mail, a letter from his "Blue Fairy Godmother" offering to testify that the accused, "at personal sacrifices that proved total," was an asset for the Allies during the war. "If there must be a trial of Howard W. Campbell, Jr., by the forces of self-righteous nationalism," Colonel Frank Wirtanen has written, "let it be one hell of a contest!" Like the robot Salo in *Sirens of Titan* he is ready to violate his programming in the name of human feeling.

Campbell finds the chance for redemption "nauseating," and resorts to the last avenue of free will available to him, taking justice into his own hands. His "Confessions" are left as a cautionary tale, of "a man who served evil too openly and good too secretly, the crime of his times."

Like any human being, Vonnegut's protagonist in *Mother Night* was neither entirely good nor "Pure Evil." He took on risks few men would accept, and his work as a spy advanced a just and necessary cause. Campbell's mistake arose from the very qualities that allowed him to succeed in the assignment: egotism, an ability to separate from anything beyond himself, reflected in his earlier inner migration to the realms of art and erotic love.

He was blind to the costs of the bargain he made, thought, like many before him, that he could manage it all. But no one is exempt from the principle of "we are who we pretend to be." The words and actions we commit in public, regardless of our "secretly virtuous insides," have consequences. In "going crazy in a way he found irresistible," Howard W. Campbell Jr. lost himself, and there was no way back.

Kurt Vonnegut learned in war about the dangers of the Christian good-versus-evil narrative—what he saw was plenty of gray, in himself and in others as they negotiated their extreme circumstances in the struggle for survival. *Mother Night* is a meditation on the realities he witnessed, the tenuousness of our hold on even the most apparently stable signposts of our identities. In playing with the thought that "if I'd been born in Germany, I suppose I would have *been* a Nazi," he opens us to the disturbing malleability of the human soul, insisting that there is no place of purity and "clean hands" to which we can safely and finally retreat. We put down the book uncomfortable with our capacity for moral "schizophrenia," on notice to be vigilant against complacency.

FOUR

Cat's Cradle

What is sin?
—Felix Hoenikker

And I made up lies
So that they all fit nice,
And I made this sad world
A par-a-dise.
—Calypso from *The Books of Bokonon*

Half a century later it is easy to understand the word-of-mouth, "underground" appeal of *Cat's Cradle* (1963), its gently subversive effect on the counterculture then beginning to emerge on college campuses around the country. A rollicking burlesque of the Cold War, told in 127 bite-sized chapters, it was precisely in tune with the experimental freedom opening up in the wake of the Cuban Missile Crisis—as indispensable an artifact of that moment as Stanley Kubrick's cinematic black comedy, *Dr. Strangelove*. In both cases attitude and pace are as important to the impact as any of the plot devices.

Cat's Cradle is an insider's view of the military-industrial complex Vonnegut had seen after the war, and, with *Player Piano*, the second book to come directly out of his years in Schenectady. His job as a GE publicist from 1947 to 1951 required him to interview scientists given license to play on the frontiers of research, and the indifference he observed to the uses made of their discoveries, especially among those who came of age before World War II, gave him pause.

At his Cape redoubt Vonnegut immersed himself in family life (six growing children and a sheepdog) as he wrote *Cat's Cradle,* enjoying the pleasures of nature and his varied creative pastimes, including painting, wood carving, sculpture, and the clarinet—even as he kept a watchful eye on the chess moves of Kennedy and Krushchev. He held his breath with everyone else as crises over Berlin, Cuba, and other hot spots played out in rapid succession. Vonnegut knew about life in a bomb shelter, and he did not want to repeat the experience.

A project tying what he had witnessed at GE to the existential threat of thermonuclear war seemed obvious and timely. And after a decade of limited success Vonnegut had new reason for optimism on the career front, even as the demand for short stories continued their irreversible decline: in 1962 Samuel Stuart, an editor involved in issuing the *Sirens of Titan* project, moved to Holt, Rinehart & Winston, and was able to arrange a two-book deal in hardcover that promised at last to attract attention beyond the sci-fi "file drawer."

Cat's Cradle is a perennial favorite in the Vonnegut catalog, by the consensus of readers and critics alike. The author himself considered it possibly his most accomplished book. Again, part of the reason is style—the razor-sharp concision perfected in *Mother Night* continues here, in a lighter, seemingly more effortless key. Never has blackout comedy been fused more perfectly with horror and dread. The tension between these polarities vibrates in every enigmatic chapter title ("Vice-President in Charge of Volcanoes"), every twist in the road, every word, and keeps the adventure fresh even today.

A diligent student of good writing practice, Vonnegut was interested above all in connecting with his audience, and he stayed sensitive and alert to its needs. In a revealing 1974 interview, cited by Peter Freese in his comprehensive book *The Clown of Armageddon,* the author explained the approach he used in gluing together his trademark "mosaics" of jokes and set-pieces:

> The limiting factor is the reader. No other art requires the audience to be a performer, and you may write music which he absolutely can't perform—in which case it's a bust. Writers have had to change because the audience changes. We have a much shorter attention span perhaps, because of television and the film. We've been educated to quick cuts and very little exposition.[1]

But the fact that *Cat's Cradle* is fast and fun and user-friendly in no way implies a pandering to the audience in terms of content. This work remains the best example of Vonnegut's genius for addressing profound philosophical questions in simple language. It is the culmination of the primary concern of his first three novels: the *paradox* of the human need for myths, religions, stories—narrative structures by which to give order and meaning to our lives—in a universe where knowledge of the ultimate is beyond our reach.

We recall insights the author remembered from his anthropology studies: "that culture is not a rational invention, that all cultures function on faith rather than truth; that there are lots of alternatives to our own society." In *Player Piano* we observed the competition between a blind faith in technological progress and the romantic nostalgia of the Ghost Dance movement. In *Sirens of Titan* Winston Niles Rumfoord tried to counter bloodthirsty tribalism with a "plausible new religion" celebrating universal brotherhood. The results were mixed at best. And in *Mother Night* Howard W. Campbell Jr. volunteered to become an actor in the Nazi pageant of hate, losing his bearings along the way.

Now Vonnegut goes all the way, inventing a complete and self-contained theology out of whole cloth, *foregrounding* rather than concealing its artifice. It is indeed like the game to which the title refers, a network of intersecting lines and curves out of which we can imagine all kinds of patterns—forgetting after a while that what we are looking at is just a tangled length of string. "Nothing in this book is true," we are told from the start as we are delivered into the presence of a shaman unembarrassed to admit that his edicts are "shameless lies" cobbled together to "fit together nice." To enter the world of *Cat's Cradle* is to proceed down a slippery slope, to a recognition that *all* beliefs are up for grabs, *all* religions, ideologies, and received truths are subject to radical questioning. Amid the excitement of the civil rights movement and its challenge to racial hierarchies, the stress of nuclear brinkmanship during the age of "Mutual Assured Destruction," and the trauma of a charismatic president being murdered on a bright autumn afternoon, this was a journey many young people of the sixties were ready to undertake.

If religions were made-up Rube Goldberg contraptions anyway, why not assemble one that encouraged compassion rather than brutality? Vonnegut runs this experiment on the Republic of San Lorenzo, a fictional Caribbean island resembling Haiti under "Papa Doc" Duvalier, where inhabitants cope with wrenching poverty by practicing a mostly benign faith of recent origin. It comes with all the accessories needed to make it work—a foundation myth and an elaborate vocabulary, a mysterious, persecuted leader, and a scripture of commonsense axioms set to a smiling calypso beat, spiced with traditional native *vodou*. The author seems to have kept notes from his graduate classes in Chicago close at hand as he wove together the strands of the story. Bokononism amounts to a collection of *foma*—"harmless untruths"—aimed at exposing the futility of our delusions of power, reminding us of webs of connection in the most unlikely places. At its core it is a distillation of Vonnegutian humanism: "Live by the *foma* that make you brave and kind and healthy and happy."

For all the irreverence of *Cat's Cradle*, the ways in which it is an elaborate practical joke, it is important always to remember that this is a *doomsday* book. As in Kubrick's *Dr. Strangelove*, its laugh-provoking mixture of human vanity, recklessness, and lust for power ends badly. The man-made tornadoes, "deathly still" ruins, and valleys strewn with corpses of the last pages are a warning from the past to the present, evoking scenes the author lived through at Dresden.

"Call me Jonah," the narrator introduces himself. It is a deft blending of Melville's *Moby-Dick* and the Old Testament prophet, alerting us from the top that this will be a story in which the pursuer is swallowed up by the object of his search. Looking back, everything now makes sense to him as the unfolding of a mysterious larger plan. Jonah is a cousin to the characters in *Sirens of Titan* in acknowledging that he has been used for purposes he will never understand. "Somebody or something has compelled me to be certain places at certain times, without fail," he explains. At each cross-road on his circuitous path to Bokononism, "conveyances and motives, both conventional and bizarre, have been provided."

Jonah is a dissolute version of Vonnegut, a freelance writer who—"two wives ago, 250,000 cigarettes ago, 3,000 quarts of booze ago"—conceived a book project with a grandiosity we can grasp from its working title, *The Day the World Ended.* It would be a snapshot of what key players were doing on August 6, 1945, the date of the Hiroshima bombing.

Armed with the insights of his new faith, the "bittersweet lies" he encountered on the exotic Republic of San Lorenzo, Jonah has decided (with characteristic narcissism, rationalizing away his slothful work habits) that the manuscript he started was never meant to be finished. It was instead only a means to intersect with members of his *karass*—defined by Bokonon as a team organized to "do God's Will without ever discovering what they are doing."

Soon incorporated into the lexicon of the 1960s counterculture as insider shorthand for its communitarian ethos, the concept, like so many Vonnegut creations, came from a randomly observed found object—the Greek sur-name "Karass" was on the mailbox of a Cape Cod neighbor. "I didn't think too hard about them," he said in a 1991 interview, demystifying the origins of *Cat's Cradle*'s theological terms. "I don't suppose I spent more than ten minutes coining any one of those words." It was intuitive.[2]

As with all such constellations, Jonah's *karass* was "as free-form as an amoeba," defying the "national, institutional, occupational, familial, and class boundaries" imagined by men. Bokonon's Fifty-third Calypso puts it this way:

> *So many different people*
> *In the same device.*

Among the *karass*'s members were Angela, Franklin, and Newton, the three adult children of the late Nobel Prize physicist renowned for his work on the Manhattan Project, Felix Hoenikker. Newt, a premed student at Jonah's alma mater, Cornell, responds to a letter of inquiry with a portrait of his father as a distant eccentric sheltered from adult responsibilities by his employers, the General Forge and Foundry Company of Ilium, New York, and its chief client, the Pentagon.

The author based his mad scientist here on Irving Langmuir, the star of the GE Research Laboratory legendary for his dissociation from reality. "Langmuir was wonderfully absent-minded," Vonnegut explained in an interview. He loved puzzles and games and asked questions about things like whether turtle spines buckled or contracted. In Schenectady the story circulated that Langmuir once left a tip under his plate after his wife served him breakfast at home. It all *seemed* harmless enough.[3]

When the news about Hiroshima came over the radio, Newt recalled, Dr. Hoenikker was at home in pajamas, eager to demonstrate to little Newt his mastery of the age-old children's pastime cat's cradle. "Nobody could predict what he was going to be interested in next," Newt observes. "On the day of the bomb it was string."

Angela chastised her little brother when he ran out of the house, frightened by his father's strange behavior. "He's one of the greatest men who ever lived!" she cried. "He won the war today!" Frank, the third sibling, soon joined the ruckus, but Dr. Hoenikker remained inside, paying no notice. "People weren't his specialty," Newt explains, with typical earnest understatement.

Peter Reed speculates that the Hoenikker children represent in oblique form the youngsters growing up in the Vonnegut household in the 1920s and 1930s. By this account, the tall and gawky caretaker Angela is sister Alice, Frank is the budding scientist Bernard, and dwarfish, naïve Newt is the author himself, the baby of the family. The father here may be a version of the detached and dreamy Kurt Sr.[4]

A lot of human concerns evaded Felix Hoenikker. Newt closes his letter with an anecdote he heard about the first nuclear test earlier that summer of 1945. "Science has now known sin," a colleague intoned gravely, à la Oppenheimer, as his team of physicists observed with awe the tower of smoke they had erected in the desert. "What is sin?" Felix replied, blankly.

Questions surrounding the Hoenikker children linger in Jonah's mind over the coming months. Curious things have happened to each of them since their father's death two years earlier, at the family cottage on Cape Cod. After flunking out of Cornell, Newt was involved briefly in an affair with

Zinka, a beautiful Ukrainian dancer from a traveling Soviet ballet company. Spinster-in-training Angela managed to find a husband with a good job, something in U.S. government intelligence, and they have set up house together at his new posting in Indianapolis. The intensely private Frank, meanwhile—his nickname at Ilium High was "Secret Agent X-9"— dropped completely out of sight. He is now wanted by the FBI for involvement with smuggling operations to Cuba.

A year passes—"I loafed on my book"—before Jonah visited Ilium to delve deeper into these mysteries. He calls General Forge to arrange an interview with Asa Breed, longtime head of its research laboratory. Breed bristles at the idea that he had ever been Hoenikker's boss, no matter what the organizational chart said. "The man was a force of nature no mortal could possibly control," he insists over the phone.

"Ah, God, what an ugly city Ilium is! What an ugly city every city is!" So *The Books of Bokonon* tell us. Impaired after a night of drinking and debauchery, Jonah finds himself staring at morning gridlock in old Dr. Breed's sedan. Felix Hoenikker once abandoned his car in such a traffic jam, Breed remarks, a typical act of irresponsibility that set the stage for the accident that killed his wife. Breed clenches his teeth as he speaks of the late Mrs. Hoenikker. It is rumored around town that *he* is the father of her children.

Once past layers of security, the two men are met by Francine Pefko, a perky secretary we will encounter again in *Breakfast of Champions*. The Christmas bunting on display, the holiday carols performed so sincerely by the "Girl Pool" typists from the basement, strike the visitor as ironic in a place that birthed weapons of mass destruction.

In his office Dr. Breed launches into a defense of pure scientists, men encouraged to follow their imaginations without restraint in the interest of developing new knowledge—surely "the most valuable commodity on earth." Vonnegut must have heard sermons like this many times at GE. A Bokononist would have reacted to the conceit with cynical laughter.

To the military brass, Hoenikker and his kind were alchemists whose obsessions, however esoteric, could sometimes be put to practical use. They imagined him to be a miracle worker, "a sort of magician who could make America invincible with a wave of his wand." Full of can-do confidence that science solved all problems, a few dropped by the lab from time to time, sharing their wish lists and proposing crackpot schemes.

A Marine general who wanted relief from battlefield quagmires was a good example. He pestered Hoenikker in the building cafeteria about how to neutralize the mud that slowed down his charges. "In his playful way, and *all* his ways were playful," Breed remembers, sitting back in his chair, "Felix suggested that there might be a single grain of something—even a microscopic grain—that could make infinite expanses of muck, marsh, swamp, creeks, pools, quicksand, and mire as solid as this desk." If what we "skate upon and put in our highballs" could be imagined as ice-one, why not . . . ice-nine? We can imagine an American soldier in the jungle monsoons of Vietnam later in the decade, reading his battered copy of *Cat's Cradle* and entertaining the same fantasies.

Vonnegut admitted borrowing the notion of room-temperature ice from Irving Langmuir himself. He had suggested the concept to no less a figure than H.G. Wells during the legendary author's tour of Schenectady in the 1930s. "And then Wells died, and then, finally, Langmuir died," Vonnegut told an interviewer. "I thought to myself, 'Finders, keepers—the idea is mine.'"[5]

Ever the impertinent layman, Jonah presses Dr. Breed about unintended consequences. Once the chain-reaction to turn a surface into ice-nine started, when and how, exactly, would it stop? It was just a theory, Breed insists as he brusquely terminates the interview. Nothing to worry about.

The assurance proves wrong. Just before he died, Felix Hoenikker worked up a chunk of ice-nine in his kitchen, a "last batch of brownies" for the human race. Angela, Frank, and Newt secretly divided it among themselves, for purposes unknown at the time. The fate of those three blue-white "seeds of doom," Jonah will come to realize, was the *wampeter* of his *karass*, the pivot around which it revolved, "in the majestic chaos of a spiral nebula."

Ice-nine represents all the innovations science had contributed to the art of war in the modern era, including the dynamite that funded Nobel Prizes to men like Felix Hoenikker. In considering *Cat's Cradle* it bears repeating that Kurt Vonnegut was far from a knee-jerk Luddite. He admired scientific thinking, having studied chemistry and biology (albeit fitfully) at Cornell and mechanical engineering during his training days in the army. He was proud of his brother Bernard, an authority on the atmosphere who, among other achievements, figured out in 1946 how to seed clouds with silver iodide to produce rain.

But the Buck Rogers optimism of the author's youth, the quasi-religious faith of his generation in the "progressive," beneficent qualities of science, was severely undermined by World War II. Vonnegut described his disillusionment in the language of a lapsed believer:

> For me it was terrible, after having believed so much in technology and having drawn so many pictures of dream automobiles and dream airplanes and dream human dwellings, to see the actual use of this technology in destroying a city.... It's like being a devout Christian and then seeing some horrible massacres conducted by Christians after a victory.

It was much the same for Bernard, who was appalled to see his discoveries about clouds used as part of the air war in Vietnam.[6]

Felix Hoenikker's capacity for wonder, his ability to "see old puzzles as brand new," could certainly produce life-saving miracles. In many respects it was benign, even charming, and explained his absorption into the toys that littered his office at General Forge, now a cordoned-off shrine. But Hoenikker's truncated field of vision now endangers the entire planet. Like a lot of scientists of his age, "any truth he found was beautiful in its own right, and he didn't give a damn who got it next." If the moral of *Mother Night* is to "be careful about who we pretend to be," the message of *Cat's Cradle* is to "be careful about whose dreams we chose to make come true."[7]

This is true for everyone, but in Vonnegut's estimation some people bore special responsibilities. On a trip to the Soviet Union in the 1980s he was pleased to discover that scientists there were revered as artists because of their fertile, playful imaginations, like musicians and poets and novelists, and they were all held to a similar code of ethics. This confirmed his belief that storytellers, no less than their brethren in lab coats, needed to be mindful about their creations. Once into circulation they could be as dangerous as the most deadly poisons—and there was no retrieving them.[8]

Jonah has more stops to make before departing Ilium. First is the cemetery where Felix Hoenikker and his wife had been interred. The driver asks if he minds visiting the tombstone showroom nearby, and it proves a momentous detour. "Peculiar travel suggestions," Jonah quotes Bokonon, "are dancing lessons from God."

The proprietor, Asa Breed's brother Marvin, has nothing but contempt for the legend of the celebrity buried across the road as some kind of saint. "How the hell innocent is a man who helps make a thing like an atomic bomb?" Even more damning was his neglect of his wife, for whom Marvin, like his brother, carries a torch. "Sometimes I wonder if he wasn't born dead. I never met a man who was less interested in the living."

Browsing the inventory, Jonah chances upon a garlanded stone angel with his last name on its pedestal, shared with the German immigrant who long ago commissioned the statue. This spooky coincidence triggers visions of "the unity in every second"—a concept not far from the Tralfamadorian notion of simultaneity we know from *Sirens of Titan*. Jonah is suddenly unstuck in time. In Bokononist parlance, the experience is a *vin-dit*, a sudden shove in the direction of one's invisibly charted destiny. "Busy, busy, busy," the Bokononist believer says when confronted with evidence of how inscrutable and complicated is the machinery of life.

It is interesting to note that the author originally wanted to engrave "Vonnegut" onto the stone pedestal, a nod to his ethnic heritage and a gesture of identification with the protagonist—as he explained it, a kind of "Ingmar Bergman touch." He was restrained from doing this by his editor, who argued that the intrusion unnecessarily distracted the reader. It was a rule of the storytelling game he was testing but not quite ready to break.[9]

The last destination on Jonah's Ilium itinerary is the hobby shop where Frank Hoenikker had worked as a teenager. The owner remembers the boy's passion for engineering, the long hours he spent assembling scale-model miniatures. Frank was more comfortable living in his own world as a master builder than playing sports or chasing girls. Like his father, "people weren't his specialty." He was last seen hitching a ride out of town in a car with Florida plates. It is believed that he had been picked up by mobsters, and had almost certainly met with a bad end in their company.

Months later, while lounging with the Sunday newspaper, Jonah stumbles across another signpost: a glossy supplement for an obscure Caribbean island, hawking its desirability as an investment vehicle. What catches his eye is the young female on the cover, posed seductively on a beach as bulldozers clear palm trees. "The Republic of San Lorenzo on the move!" the caption announced. "A healthy, happy, progressive, freedom-loving, beautiful nation" opens its arms to the world, the future of its half-million inhabitants secure under the guidance of the elderly Miguel "Papa" Manzano. The model in the photograph is Manzano's adopted daughter, Mona. Inside the brochure is something almost as interesting to Jonah—a profile of Major General Franklin Hoenikker, the island's Minister of Science and Progress.

"As it was *supposed* to happen," Jonah receives an assignment to write about Julian Castle, the sugar trust heir who runs a free hospital in the jungles of San Lorenzo. Among the passengers sharing the flight from Miami is Horlick Minton, the veteran diplomat, along with his wife, Claire. Together they form a *duprass,* the Bokononist version of *Mother Night*'s "Nation of Two," erected in part as a defense during the ambassador's purge from the State Department a few years earlier. "I was fired for pessimism," Minton declares defiantly when the subject comes up.

Also on board is H. Lowe Crosby, a portly middle-aged businessman hell-bent on moving his bicycle factory from Chicago to the union-free environs in San Lorenzo that he has been reading about. "The people down there," he declares loudly over drinks in the back of the plane, "are poor enough and scared enough to have some common sense!" Crosby's wife Hazel, a well-meaning "barnyard fool," is thrilled to discover that Jonah was born in Indiana. "My God," she crows, "are you a *Hoosier?*" Wherever they travel, she beams with pride, Hoosiers are making their mark. Amid hugs she insists on being called "*Mom,*" her thinking, Jonah writes now as a confirmed Bokononist, based on the folly of the *granfalloon,* "a false *karass* of a seeming team that was meaningless in terms of the ways God gets things done." Other examples include the Communist Party, the General Electric Company, Cornell University alumni—and, Vonnegut the anarchist tells us, "any nation, anytime, anywhere."

Jonah immerses himself in a manuscript on the history of San Lorenzo included in Ambassador Minton's briefing materials. It details the life of Bokonon, the holy man who landed on its forbidding shores back in 1922. Born Lionel Boyd Johnson on Tobago, he won a scholarship to the London School of Economics, beginning an epic journey that included capture by a German U-boat, a shipwreck in Bombay harbor, and finally, a stop in Haiti, where he met a U.S. Marine deserter named Earl McCabe, anxious for a ride to Florida. High winds blew their craft onto San Lorenzo, where they emerged, naked and born again. As the scripture says,

> *A fish pitched up*
> *By the angry sea,*
> *I gasped on land,*
> *And I became me.*

We think of the multiple identities of Malachi Constant in *Sirens of Titan*, the masks of Howard W. Campbell Jr. in *Mother Night* as we consider this latest Vonnegut reinvention. In the native patois, Johnson became "Bokonon." The lifeboat of his vessel would eventually be painted gold and made into a bed for the presidential palace. According to a legend he would make up, it would sail again on the eve of the end of the world.

Castle Sugar relinquished its hold on the demoralized, disease-ridden population easily, and the new custodians divided the labor of their revitalization project. McCabe drew up a blueprint for the island's economy, while Johnson focused on spiritual matters, designing a theology to replace the Catholic Church.

Predictably, the utopia failed. Only the religion survived, as a guerrilla faith officially outlawed by McCabe and his successor, Papa, on penalty of the hook—a gruesome device awaiting anyone on San Lorenzo convicted of a crime. Why was Bokonon banished to the wilderness? It was stagecraft, a narrative trick Winston Niles Rumfoord would have appreciated. Johnson knew that good and evil had to be opposed in "dynamic tension," a phrase from a Charles Atlas bodybuilding ad he remembered from his youth. This would divert attention from miseries he and McCabe could not remedy. (We can't help noticing that the same principle lay at the heart of the Cold War.)

Jonah is so fascinated by his reading that he does not notice the two passengers who board the plane in San Juan. It is Angela and Newt Hoenikker, on their way to their brother's wedding. Jonah is crushed to learn that Frank's bride will be Mona, the object of his erotic fantasies.

On the ground in Bolivar, San Lorenzo's lone city, the guests are taken to a reviewing stand for welcoming ceremonies. Thousands wait before them in the midday heat until sirens herald the arrival of a motorcade. Soon the frail Papa Manzano emerges from his limousine. Behind him is Frank, who, in spite of his medal-heavy uniform, fails miserably to convey any kind of gravitas. He is another in Vonnegut's series of ludicrous boys straining too hard to pose as a man—as we've seen in Paul Proteus, the young Malachi Constant, and later, Billy Pilgrim. Mona, meanwhile, is even more ravishing in the flesh.

As Papa's greeting echos off the new glass buildings that frame the central plaza, he collapses suddenly, in obvious pain. His last utterance to Frank before the ambulance takes him away is one enigmatic, ominous word: *ice.*

Angela and Newt are taken to their brother's residence on a mountaintop cliff overlooking Bolivar, while Jonah is dispatched to a hotel, riding there in San Lorenzo's single antique taxicab. The Casa Mona is not quite ready to receive its first-ever registered guests, and on an upper floor looking for room supplies Jonah surprises a pair of hotel employees engaged in *boko-maru,* the ritual of sitting barefoot, sole-to-sole. (Note the pun.) It is the beginning of his realization that Bokononism is widely practiced on San Lorenzo.

Beyond the obvious sexual connotations, the "mingling of awarenesses" of *boko-maru* can be seen as a comment on the resilience of freedom and community even in a police state. This helps explain the enthusiasm with which *Cat's Cradle* and other Vonnegut novels were received when they appeared in translation on the other side of the iron curtain. Ham-handed censors missed the political implications.

"We passed through scenes of hideous want," Jonah recalls of the trip to Franklin Hoenikker's Scandinavian moderne house. Once there, he finds Newt out on the terrace napping next to an easel with his latest painting, a mass of spider webs scrawled on a black canvas. This is his representation of the game his father tried to show him on the day of the bomb. "For maybe a hundred thousand years or more," he complains as he wakes up, "grownups have been waving tangles of string in their children's faces."

No wonder kids grow up crazy. A cat's cradle is nothing but a bunch of X's between somebody's hands, and little kids look and look and look at all those X's. . . . *No damn cat, and no damn cradle.*

Perhaps without meaning to, Kurt Vonnegut had invented a rallying cry for the 1960s counterculture—"No damn cat, and no damn cradle"—in the voice of the earnest and aggrieved Newt.

Soon Angela walks in with Julian Castle, back from touring the House of Hope and Mercy in the Jungle. Gruff-voiced and brandishing a cigar, Castle is more movie gangster than Albert Schweitzer saint, and he serves here as a mouthpiece for the no-nonsense side of Vonnegut, the adult bringing the proceedings down to earth. After quizzing Newt about his canvas, he tosses it casually into the waterfall below.

Castle displays a similar brashness in admitting his conversion to the forbidden faith of the island, whose benefits he has come to appreciate in the depressing circumstances of his hospital. And, he tells Jonah, believers enjoy "more zest, more tang" in their lives with the prospect of the hook on their minds—an idea Johnson had borrowed from Madame Tussaud's in London.

Off-putting to "highbrow" critics, it is a Vonnegut specialty to build his stories on the junk ephemera of everyday life. In *Sirens of Titan* Chrono's good luck charm, so consequential in the affairs of Earth's mighty civilizations, is a piece of discarded metal. Here an entire faith is conjured out of ideas from the back of a comic-book and props from a tourist trap wax museum.

Every so often, Castle continues, McCabe and his successor, Papa, had to reinvigorate the drama by ordering their militias to arrest Bokonon, only to have him elude capture every time. "As the living legend of the cruel tyrant in the city and the gentle holy man in the jungle grew," Castle declares, "so, too, did the happiness of the people grow." San Lorenzans stayed hungry, but at least some of their needs were being met. "They were all employed full time as actors in a play they understood, that any human being anywhere could understand and applaud."

There was a price to pay for maintaining the performance, however. The lead characters risked surrendering parts of their humanity, a danger Howard W. Campbell Jr. could have warned them about. Over time the world demanded that "the pirate half of Bokonon and the angel half of

McCabe wither away." *We are who we pretend to be,* and one day the blood became real and people really did start dying on the hook.

Frank telephones the house from his vigil at the dying Papa's bedside, insisting that he and Jonah have urgent matters to discuss. A convoy of American-made military vehicles descend on the grounds and shock troops begin digging trenches to protect the next president of San Lorenzo.

In their meeting Frank deploys a series of macho clichés with Jonah ("I like the cut of your jib!") on the way to proposing a ruling partnership. Anxious to shed responsibilities he knows his narrow shoulders cannot bear, Frank appeals to the other man's vanity, almost always a successful strategy in Vonnegut novels. Jonah considers it the shove of another *vin-dit*—God must have work for him to do. And, if the salary of his new position isn't enough to seal the deal, the prospect of betrothal to Mona—a requirement for the next president, as prophesied in *The Books of Bokonon*—surely is.

The initial thrill of power wears off quickly, however. After their initiation into *boko-maru*, Jonah discovers that, like the good Bokononist she was raised to be, exclusivity is not in Mona's nature. It is clear, too, that the weight of decision making for the troubled republic is now entirely his. He tries valiantly to rise to the occasion. As he and Frank near the presidential castle the next day, a labyrinth out of a children's fairy tale, Jonah is appalled to see the hook poised menacingly over the entry gate. Full of good intentions, he vows to dismantle it at the first opportunity.

Papa lies on his deathbed, the gilded boat that delivered Johnson and McCabe to San Lorenzo so many years earlier. "Ice!" he calls out in his delirium, groping for the pendant around his neck. He orders that the search for Bokonon continue after he is gone, and that the people of the island be taught the gospel of science—"magic that *works!*" His doctor then joins him in *boko-maru*—the ceremonial last rite prescribed by scripture. Even Papa is a believer.

Attention shifts to the installation of the new president. Jonah composes an address in his head, hoping to set a tone of reconciliation. At heart he is a romantic American idealist, for whom new beginnings and utopian dreams come naturally. The most pressing question is what to do about

Bokonon. "I pondered asking him to join my government," he recalls, "thus beginning a sort of millennium for my people." But then come second thoughts. Papa's dying request makes sense after all.

> There would have to be plenty of good things for all to eat, too, and nice places to live—things Bokonon and I were in no position to provide. So good and evil had to remain separate; good in the jungle, and evil in the palace. Whatever entertainment there was in that was about all we had to give the people.

The stage is set, and Jonah's head swells like the nebbish in Woody Allen's *Bananas*. "I looked out at my guests, my servants, my cliff, and my lukewarm sea," he recalls of his ascent to the top battlement of his castle. Cardboard cutouts stand anchored offshore, more comic-book stagecraft designed to purge evil—caricatures of "enemies of freedom" like Marx, Stalin, and "old Kaiser Bill." They would serve as targets for the six vintage airplanes of the San Lorenzan Air Force in its annual display of righteous firepower. Mingling with his guests, Jonah keeps a watchful eye on Mona. He experiences an archetypal dilemma for the Vonnegut protagonist: is she "the highest form of female spirituality," or "anesthetized, frigid—a cold fish?" In the style of his new faith, Jonah prefers the more comforting view, imagining her as angelic, "sublime."

Down the spiral staircase Jonah sees Papa's physician outside the presidential quarters, agitated and obviously alarmed. His patient has ingested the contents of the cylinder around his neck and instantly was covered with a blue-white frost. The doctor is the next to go, carelessly touching the lips of the deceased. His crystallized body crashes into fragments on the floor.

Jonah rounds up the Hoenikker children for a family meeting that is much too late in coming. He makes them look at the wreckage caused by their selfishness: All three turned out to be as short-sighted as their father, trading on his creation to get the love he had denied them when he was alive. Vonnegut gives us more cloak-and-dagger moments, reminiscent of *Mother Night*, with the result that ice-nine has now entered into the Cold War arms race. Angela married a U.S. intelligence operative; Newt enjoyed a fling with a KGB agent posing as a dancer; and Frank used his chip of the deadly material to ingratiate himself with a brutal dictator. With brooms and a blowtorch they clean up the worst of the mess, then go back up to rejoin the festivities.

"It was a strikingly Bokononist speech," Jonah recalls of Horlick Minton's address to the crowd atop the castle tower. Minton speaks in the island dialect to honor the "Hundred Martyrs to Democracy" (*lo Hoon-yera Moratoorz tut Zamoocratz-ya*), the young men conscripted to join the fight against the Axis powers, whose mission was ended by a German torpedo even before they left Bolivar harbor. Minton insists on remembering them as they really were, young innocents sacrificed to the furies of bloodlust. His own son perished, too, in the Second World War. "My soul insists that I mourn not a man but a child," he says with sad dignity. It is a moment of reflection before all hell breaks loose, and a preview of the main theme of *Slaughterhouse-Five*. On the horizon Jonah notices his fighters "skimming my lukewarm sea" as they approached their targets.

Kurt Vonnegut boasted of his ability to stage Armageddon on a few pieces of blank paper, lauding the efficiency and power of the word to engage the reader's imagination. "The end of the world is not an idea to Vonnegut, it is a reality he experienced," his friend John Updike once observed, noting that his "come-as-you-are prose always dons a terrible beauty when he pictures vast destruction."[10] A plane in the formation catches fire and explodes into the castle cliff, triggering a rockslide. Masonry splits and cracks. The Mintons drop smoothly to the sea below, holding hands as they give a resigned wave. "Their good manners killed them."

The president's quarters rip open, discharging Papa's remains, still in the golden boat. The chain reaction Jonah had wondered about in Dr. Breed's office is now underway and beyond anyone's control. "I opened my eyes—and all the sea was *ice-nine*. The moist green earth was a blue-white pearl."

Everyone improvises their own means of escape. Jonah takes Mona into a bomb shelter Papa had built for himself, with all the amenities readers of the time would have expected for such a chamber—canned goods, ventilation powered by a stationary bike, even reading material: a full set of *The Books of Bokonon*. The image resonated for the children of duck-and-cover drills, as a satiric rendering of their darkest fears. "During our first day and night underground," Jonah recalls, echoing Vonnegut's time in the subterranean meat locker, "tornadoes rattled our manhole cover many times an hour. Each time the pressure in our hole would drop suddenly, and our ears would pop and our ears would ring."

Jonah and his Eve find themselves a clumsy, uncommunicative pair—certainly not a *duprass*—as they wait for the storms above to subside. They are no exception to the rule that romantic love ends disappointingly in Vonnegut novels. Respect, mutual care, a world-weary modus vivendi is usually the best resolution we can expect. But Mona is too remote even for that.

When they finally venture outside "the air was dry and hot and deathly still," the earth beneath their feet encased in frost as far as the eye could see. "There were no smells. There was no movement." As it was for Vonnegut and the other American prisoners on corpse-disposal detail after the bombing of Dresden, extreme caution is the watchword. "Death has never been quite so easy to come by," Jonah warns his companion. "All you have to do is touch the ground and then your lips and you're done for." This anticipates Edgar Derby's absurd death in *Slaughterhouse-Five*, the result of picking up a teapot in the Dresden rubble.

If only there was a father to offer answers and reassurance, Jonah thinks to himself. "Daddy, why are all the trees broken?" he would ask. "Daddy, why are all the birds dead?"

Near Mount McCabe they come upon the remains of thousands of San Lorenzans who had been asking the same questions. Bodies lie like statues, arranged in positions of *boko-maru*. Reading *Cat's Cradle* today, the scene is reminiscent of the Kool-Aid drinkers of Jonestown. The San Lorenzans had complied with Bokonon's casual remark that the creator "was done with them, and that they should have the good manners to die."

Walking among the dead, Mona laughs. "It's all so simple, that's all," she says—Vonnegut pondering through her the attractions of suicide. "It solves so much for so many, so simply." Mona reaches to the ground, touches her fingers to her lips, and dies as precipitously as Resi Noth in *Mother Night*.

Jonah is found later by the Crosbys, Newt Hoenikker, and Frank. Over the following months the group—"Mom" dubs them "Swiss Family Robinson"—achieves a kind of community in the ruins, "not without a certain Walt Disney charm." Jonah writes, Newt paints, and Frank resumes his old hobby of harmlessly tending to an ant farm. There is even a noble, unifying purpose in this unlikely folk society. Hazel sews strips of cloth into a primitive American flag, which they determine should be planted at the top of Mount McCabe.

Driving in the cab that had somehow come through the big freeze unscathed, Jonah understands now the mission of his *karass*. "It's been working night and day for maybe half a million years to get me up that mountain," he realizes. But what, besides delivering the flag, is he supposed to do once he gets there? He finds the old holy man, Bokonon, sitting on a rock beside the road, etching the last entry of his scriptures. If he were younger, Bokonon writes, he would create "a history of human stupidity" to use as a pillow while he ingested a particle of ice-nine and thumbed his nose at "You Know Who." Jonah's memoir turns out to be that history.

Vonnegut blamed politicians and military strategists for Dresden and Hiroshima, and for the balance of nuclear terror that held the world hostage at the time he was writing his doomsday fable. But plenty of other people were complicit. Felix Hoenikker "was allowed to concentrate on one part of life more than any human being should be allowed to do," the author observed of his childishly reckless mad scientist.

> He was overspecialized and became amoral on that account. It would seem perfectly all right to see a musician vanish into his own world entirely. But if a scientist does this, he can inadvertently become a very destructive person.

Again we have a case study in the "schizophrenia" of the modern condition, a warning against tunnel vision and ceding too easily parts of our humanity. As Vonnegut illustrated in *Mother Night*, it can be a bargain with catastrophic consequences.[11]

Cat's Cradle reaffirms the theme of Vonnegut's earlier books, that we create our own meaning and it is important to take care what beliefs we choose to embrace. It is hard to find characters here who really get the message, however. The narrator remains hapless and shallow throughout, and his mission at the end is as empty as Salo's errand in *Sirens of Titan*. Bokonon's accommodation with evil was always unstable—he accepted the hook and ended up in a dead end of impotent bitterness. The Mintons have their noble qualities but are too involved in *duprass* to serve as role models. Maybe the closest thing to a hero in this tale is Hazel Crosby, "barnyard fool" though she may be. At least kindly Mom was trying to build a family—even if it was based on a *granfalloon*.

Vonnegut's fourth novel raised hopes that he would be granted respect by critics and discovered by a mainstream audience. There were some enthusiastic notices—Terry Southern praised the work in the *New York Times Book Review*, and the British literary icon Graham Greene dubbed Vonnegut "one of the best living American writers" on the strength of this latest work. But aside from college bookstores—*Cat's Cradle* joined Joseph Heller's *Catch-22* and Ken Kesey's *One Flew Over the Cuckoo's Nest* as standard backpack equipment—initial sales were anemic. It was still early on the wave of changing values; the author would have to spend more time as an esoteric, "cult" taste.[12]

Later, Vonnegut would be able to point to one bit of life business the book helped him to complete. In 1971 it was accepted by the University of Chicago anthropology department in belated fulfillment of his Master's degree. The recognition brought to mind things he had in common with another veteran and alumnus of the program, Saul Bellow. As men with families they could not go on research expeditions like the other graduate students. "You must be young in order to take the summer off or to take a year or two off," Vonnegut explained in an interview.

> And neither one of us could afford it or spare the time. So he made up the field trip in his most amusing book, *Henderson the Rain King*. He totally invents Africa. He's never been there. I made up a Haiti. . . . These two frustrated anthropologists, who were never able to go out into the field. Each one of us invented a field trip anyway.[13]

FIVE

God Bless You, Mr. Rosewater,

or, *Pearls Before Swine*

Jesus Christ—these aren't soldiers. They're firemen!
—U.S. Infantry sergeant, World War II

For more than a decade Kurt Vonnegut had supported his family largely on his writing income, which ebbed and flowed with his production. When words flowed and several pieces sold in succession, an air of prosperity filled the house and it was time to invite the neighbors for a party to celebrate. During fallow periods—he had a bout of writer's block for a year after his father's death in 1957—things were tight. "We were back to eating cereal again until the next story," neighbors remember Jane saying about the roller coaster ride. Overall, Vonnegut described his earnings during this period as about what he would make being "in charge of the cafeteria at a pretty good junior-high school." But the market for short stories was dying with the competition of television and the demise of regular customers like *Collier's* and the *Saturday Evening Post.*[1]

His novels did not help much, winding up each time on remainder shelves, on the way to going out of print. The same fate might befall this project, the second and last installment on his two-book hardcover deal with Holt.

"I grew up thinking everything would be perfect if we just had a little more money," Mark Vonnegut recalls of his childhood years. His father periodically considered abandoning the typewriter in favor of another stab at a day job, and every book looked like it could be the last. Writing was always on some level a *job*, the means of fulfilling a duty to provide for his family, and for men of his generation, if things weren't working out it was time to get another one.[2]

These concerns about identity and occupation manifest themselves in a variety of ways in *God Bless You, Mr. Rosewater* (1965). There are no super-computers or Tralfamadorians or metastasizing ice crystals here, but we meet for the first time Kilgore Trout, scorned prophet, *moraliste* for an age of doomsday weapons and trash pop culture. Vonnegut conceived Trout as an homage to Theodore Sturgeon, the prolific, internationally acclaimed science fiction master he befriended in the mid-1950s and acknowledged as an important influence. "When I met him on Cape Cod," Vonnegut remembered, "he was down on his luck, making a penny a word." Trout was also a projection of fear—"the lonesome and unappreciated writer I thought I might become," Vonnegut admitted.[3]

The title character, meanwhile, is a man devoted with childish zeal to the practice of altruism. With his gentle New Testament humanism, Eliot Rosewater was also drawn from life, inspired by an accountant who shared with Vonnegut an office over a liquor store. Vonnegut explained it in an interview:

> I could hear him comforting people who had very little income, calling everybody "dear" and giving love and understanding instead of money. And I heard him doing marriage counseling, and I asked him about that, and he said that once people told you how little money they'd made they felt they had to tell you everything. I took this very sweet man and in a book gave him millions and millions to play with.

A strength here, evident in his work generally, is Vonnegut's ability to empathize with people on both sides of the wealth divide. Even those *with* money were people, subject like anyone else to feelings of insecurity, self-loathing, loneliness. Affluence, by itself, was no answer to the most profound human needs.[4]

Even more important, we have in *God Bless You, Mr. Rosewater* the further unburdening of Vonnegut's war story. It is the journey of a combat veteran haunted by the fragility of human materials, so ready at any moment to combine with oxygen and burn. We can see the author nearing his destination on the long road back to Dresden.

What makes this work a breakthrough and gives it staying power—it was always a favorite in the eyes of the author, and remains so among his most devoted readers—is its unabashed heart. As he moves along in his writing, with nothing to lose, we see Kurt Vonnegut getting more personal, allowing himself to become more and more the main character, dropping protective layers and letting us in on his gentlest, most naïve self. The irony that pervades his earlier novels is largely absent here; the wounded idealist, warts and all, is presented for all to observe.

Is Eliot Rosewater psychotic, or is he the sanest man in America? This is the question at the heart of Vonnegut's novel, and its answer will have far-reaching consequences. It is the financial ones that preoccupy Norman Mushari, an unscrupulous young lawyer for the firm that represents Eliot's family, lusting for a payday. He is the rare unredeemed villain in Vonnegut's novels—Mushari's role models in childhood were the bare-knuckled opportunist Joe McCarthy and his rabidly dogged associate, attorney Roy Cohn. Mushari schemes to prove Eliot's mental unfitness in court as a way to remove him as custodian of the Rosewater Foundation, a tax shelter originally designed to preserve the family's enormous wealth. Eliot has complicated matters by taking its humanitarian mission literally, and has engaged in a pattern of behavior that, to some, looks like madness.

Poring over the files after hours, Mushari unearths the smoking gun he thinks will make his case. It is a letter Eliot meant to keep sealed until after his death, expressing a less-than-admiring attitude about how his ancestors had amassed their riches. We can read these passages as a darker version of Uncle John Rauch's family history of the Vonneguts published in *Palm Sunday*—the Vonnegut dry-goods business and the Lieber brewery were founded on skill, hard work, and fair dealing, but the Rosewater family business does not have such noble origins. For the author, it is an opportunity for a history lesson in robber-baron avarice.

"Like so many great American fortunes, the Rosewater pile was accumulated in the beginning by a humorless, constipated farm boy turned speculator and briber," Eliot wrote. Great-grandfather Noah inherited a saw factory and six hundred acres of southern Indiana land, "dark and rich as chocolate cake." When the Civil War erupted he hired a substitute to fight in his place and converted operations to meet the demand for food and munitions. "Noah priced his merchandise in scale with the national tragedy."

From the fruits of this profiteering he built a financial empire. Noah married the ugliest woman in Indiana to get access to her family's capital, then, driven by a reluctance to be a victim in the Darwinian struggle, acquired controlling interests in an Indianapolis slaughterhouse, a Pittsburgh steel mill, and several mining concerns. Eventually the gritty world of swords and pork was transcended altogether, as Noah moved into abstractions—banking, securities, stocks, and bonds, often designed to bilk investors in an age when the rules of the game were fast and loose.

The excesses of Noah Rosewater and his kind were tolerated, Eliot continued, because of the widespread notion that "the continent was so vast and valuable, and the population so thin and enterprising, that no thief, no matter how fast he stole, could more than mildly inconvenience anyone." It is the American myth of the endless frontier, of resources without limit.

> Thus did a handful of rapacious citizens come to control all that was worth controlling in America. Thus was the savage and stupid and entirely inappropriate American class system created.
>
> Thus the American dream turned belly up, turned green, bobbed to the scummy surface of cupidity unlimited, filled with gas, went *bang* in the noonday sun.

Eliot's letter concluded with an account of those who came after Noah, ignorant and unconcerned about the origins of privileges they took for granted. Over time members of the Rosewater clan styled themselves aristocrats, gravitating to the genteel arena of politics, journalism, and culture, seasoned with the occasional philanthropic gesture. Norman Mushari can barely contain his glee as he finishes reading.

Eliot was born in Washington, DC, in 1918, cloistered in a world of private schools, Grand Tours, vacations, skiing, and sailing. His mother, Eunice, died on the water in 1937, in an accident for which he always blamed himself. The first rule of storytelling Vonnegut imparted to his writing students was to make their characters *want* something, even if it was only a glass of water. In his own work, though, the imperative seems to be to give protagonists the sense of having committed a crime. The thing they want is peace of mind, release from their self-imposed burden of guilt.

All we learn about Eunice is that she was different from her husband in her concern for the poor. Eliot grew up to be his mother's son—he would find a way, somehow, to help them, to realize her impossible dream of a more just world.

In common with a lot of Americans, members of Eliot's family maintained only the most tenuous connections to their roots, making an excursion once a year to Rosewater County, as much a backwater in its way as the island of San Lorenzo in *Cat's Cradle*. After Pearl Harbor Eliot did his duty, leaving Harvard the day after the Japanese attack to join the army, where he would rise to the rank of infantry captain—a source of particular pride to his father, a U.S. senator. Near the end of the war Eliot was hospitalized for combat fatigue, and in the hospital he met his future wife, Sylvia, daughter of a classical musician on a tour entertaining wounded American troops.

> *The Second World War was over—and there I was at high noon, crossing Times Square with a Purple Heart on.*

Eliot's famous phrase, a soldier's bawdy double entendre—"Heart on"/"hard-on"—deployed as the novel's epigraph, is the kind of wordplay the author seemed to create with ease throughout his career. Aside from its comic import, it conveys with economy the sense of displacement, fear, vulnerability, and possibility millions of men like Eliot Rosewater, and also Kurt Vonnegut, experienced on their return home. After such close exposure to death, how does one now go about building a life? Would the wounds heal?[5]

After the war Eliot assumed the presidency of the family foundation, with responsibilities "exactly as flimsy or as formidable as he himself declared them to be." He opted for the latter reading. From his office on Fifth Avenue in Manhattan he distributed largess to all manner of charitable endeavors. "Rosewater dollars fought cancer and mental illness and race prejudice and police brutality and countless other miseries, encouraged college professors to look for truth, bought beauty at any price." But the results were too abstract and scattershot, the method too bloodless and top-down, to bring him real satisfaction.

In 1953 Eliot vanished for a week, in an alcohol-fueled search for a better means to express his crusading spirit. Vonnegut has his protagonist crash a convention of science-fiction writers at a motel in the crossroad of Milford, Pennsylvania—a real gathering the author once attended with his son Mark, then age twelve. Norman Mushari has a transcript of the impromptu remarks Eliot delivered that day—further evidence, surely, of mental instability.

"I love you sons of bitches," Rosewater declared to his audience, in one of the iconic passages in the Vonnegut lexicon. "You're all I read anymore. You're the only ones who'll talk about the *really* terrific changes going on." Although most of those in the room "couldn't write for sour apples," it was true—a nod to the author's ambivalence about life in the science-fiction drawer—style was beside the point. Vonnegut here defends his own life project:

> You're the only ones with guts enough to *really* care about the future, who *really* notice what machines do to us, what wars do to us, what cities do to us, what big, simple ideas do to us, what tremendous misunderstandings, mistakes, accidents and catastrophes do to us. You're the only ones zany enough to agonize over time and distances without limit, over mysteries that will never die, over the fact that we are right now determining whether the space voyage for the next billion years or so is going to be Heaven or Hell.

"I only wish Kilgore Trout were here," Eliot concluded unsteadily, invoking the man he considered the greatest among them all. Trout couldn't afford to come, languishing as he did in minimum-wage obscurity in a stamp redemption center on Cape Cod. As Mushari learns in the course of his research, Trout's dozens of cheaply packaged novels were scattered in the discount bins of adult book stores around the country. Vonnegut's books were almost as hard to find.

Eliot ended his performance by suggesting the need for a sci-fi examination of the phenomenon of wealth. "Just think of the wild ways money is passed around on Earth! You don't have to go to the Planet Tralfamadore in Anti-Matter Galaxy 508 G to find weird creatures with unbelievable powers."

The road trip continued. Alcohol and tears flowed freely as Eliot visited firehouses and declared his devotion to the heroes who manned them, another underappreciated group. "When you think about it, boys," he told them at each stop, "that's what holds us together more than anything else, except maybe gravity. We few, we happy few, we band of brothers—joined in the serious business of keeping our food, shelter, clothing and loved ones from combining with oxygen."

These passages bring to mind Vonnegut's days as a volunteer firefighter after the war, Badge 155 in Alplaus, New York, outside Schenectady, and then during his years on Cape Cod. The service was both a way to continue the male bonding he had experienced as a soldier and also a survivor's mission, an effort to memorialize Dresden. One of the most diabolical aspects of the Allied assault on that city was the use of bombs before incendiaries to drive emergency crews down into the shelters. When the firestorm got going, hardly anybody was above ground to try to contain it. Volunteer fire departments also embodied the communal spirit of a vanishing America, the small-town ethic of neighborliness and mutual help Vonnegut had learned about growing up in the Midwest. His character here longs to revive that spirit.[6]

After a night in the drunk tank Eliot was back home in Manhattan, sheepish and contrite, but a month later he was gone again, carousing with firefighters in Clover Lick, West Virginia, and New Egypt, New Jersey. He swapped his expensive clothes with the common men he encountered. "I don't want to look like me," he told more than one bewildered recipient. "I want to look like you." Sylvia watched in horror as her husband's closet became "a depressing museum of coveralls, overalls, Robert Hall Easter specials, field jackets, Eisenhower jackets, sweatshirts."

Eliot was sick, of course, but no one around him was equipped to deal with the problem. His father, Senator Lister Ames Rosewater, was too immersed in political combat in Washington to give the matter proper attention. "He's experimenting," he reassured advisors when they warned him of his son's antics. "He'll come back to his senses any time he's good and ready."

The senior Rosewater is a mouthpiece for blustering paleo-conservativism, a friend to Joe McCarthy famous for speeches decrying the country's moral decline, à la Rome during its late-period decadence. His name evokes the mouthwash Listerine, and he has campaigned obsessively against the loosening of free speech boundaries, condemning all references to bodily functions and sex as rank pornography, "filth." (The senator no doubt would have favored the hook used in *Cat's Cradle* as a way to enforce his standards of propriety.) He considered his son's vulgar soldier's language and disregard for personal hygiene an abomination, and, in contrast to Eliot's do-gooder sentimentality, preached an undiluted social Darwinism. "We must be hard," he thundered in the well of the Senate, "for we must become again a nation of swimmers, with the sinkers quietly disposing of themselves."[7]

Psychoanalysis had no effect on Eliot's behavior, and Sylvia's efforts to calm her husband and maintain appearances were futile. A night at the opera started out well enough—dressed in his last remaining suit, Eliot's blue eyes were "glittering with mental hygiene" for most of the performance of *Aida*. But during the finale, in which the lovers on stage were doomed to suffocate in an airtight burial chamber, he fell apart again. "You will last a lot longer, if you don't try to sing," he cried to the actors from his balcony seat. "Maybe you don't know anything about oxygen, but I do."

Ever a student of jokes, always a character in his stories, the author drew this surreal vignette from a childhood memory. In a 1991 interview he remembered the radio operas that used to fill the Vonnegut house in Indianapolis every Saturday afternoon when he was a boy. "My father said about the last scene in *Aida* 'You know, it would last a lot longer if they wouldn't try to sing it.' That's really a very funny thing to say."[8]

Ten days after the opera incident Sylvia received a letter from her husband—one of dozens she would turn over to Norman Mushari, her lawyer in the divorce action. This time Eliot was in Elsinore, California, reporting with enthusiasm about the equipment and methods used by the fire department there. "They are wonderful people," he gushed, "like the Americans I knew in the war." He identified with Shakespeare's Hamlet in his search for purpose. "Don't worry, I do not hear voices," Eliot insisted, "but there is this feeling that I have a destiny far away from the shallow and preposterous posing that is our life in New York. And I roam. And I roam." From Texas to Iowa he traveled, visiting firehouses and delivering barroom sermons on the gospel of good citizenship and economic justice.

Eliot has a wide-eyed quality that seems less like the author than his wife, a Quaker and would-be social worker. "Jane had an utter and complete lack of distance from people with problems," Mark Vonnegut remembers of his mother.

> As long as it was all in a book and hypothetical she was ok, but as soon as she met flesh-and-blood people with real problems, she thought long and hard about what could be done and could never escape the idea that she, Jane, should move in with the family and straighten things out.

Jane's religiosity and sense of mission would be a source of friction in the Vonnegut household over the years, and it is likely that elements of her personality appear here in both Eliot and Sylvia.[9]

If we look closely, we also find plenty of autobiography in Vonnegut's title character. Born into wealth and privilege, like Paul Proteus in *Player Piano*, Eliot becomes a "traitor to his class" and feels more comfortable mixing with people outside that world, the Reeks and Wrecks, even though he can never really be one of them, just as Vonnegut found himself scratching out short stories to make ends meet, a far cry from the lifestyle of his childhood, before the stock market crash. His sometimes harsh judgments on the quality of their lives betray remnants of his father's prejudices, a noblesse oblige arrogance unbecoming of a saint. Eliot's childlike demeanor and too-desperate hunger for companionship, meanwhile, reflects the feeling of arrested development many veterans experienced, a legacy of their emotional scars from the war. It is a recurrent Vonnegut motif. Only their brothers-in-arms *really* understood.

Eliot's quest ends finally in the Indiana county that bears his family's name. There he would minister to the "rickety sons and grandsons of the pioneers," he grandly told Sylvia from a phone booth, the call monitored and recorded by Mushari. It is a homecoming of the sort the author must have imagined often in his life.

Like so many places in the American landscape, there was nothing grand at all about Rosewater, an undistinguished stretch of real estate whose bustling days had long since passed. Vonnegut knew the terrain well, having seen it as a boy on car trips with his father outside Indianapolis to inspect the Bell Telephone installations he had designed. The layout accentuated its bleakness, roads without curves tracing a featureless prairie. Rail tracks rusted from disuse, and a "sizzling double-barreled highway," the symbol of rootless mobility we will encounter again in Vonnegut's Midland City novels, *Breakfast of Champions* and *Deadeye Dick,* missed the county seat by eleven miles. It might as well have been eleven light-years.[10]

A canal from great-grandfather Noah's stock-and-bond Ponzi schemes lay abandoned and overgrown, the heirs of its long-ago investors reduced to fishing its stagnant waters. Noah's company was still around, but production had been transferred outside town, overseen by a few technocrats like *Player Piano's* Ilium Works. They lived aloof from the natives in a subdivision given the faux-Shakespearean name Avondale.

Only hints of past glories remained. In a corner of the county stood what was left of New Ambrosia—Vonnegut's version of New Harmony, a utopian community on the Wabash River in Southwestern Indiana, founded in 1814 by Johann George Rapp and later sponsored by socialist reformer Robert Owen. New Ambrosia went under in the canal fiasco, leaving behind only its brewery.

Most of the structures in Rosewater proper were jerry-built and crudely functional, but a few exuded permanence, spoke of loftier ambitions. In the center square was a red-brick Parthenon, its columns gone to seed. Bella's Beauty Nook now occupied its basement. Next door was the ghost of the Rosewater Saw Company, its clock tower a nest for barn swallows and bats. On the next block was the opera house, "a terrifyingly combustible wedding cake" to Eliot's trained eye, now converted, ironically, into a firehouse. In the city park stood the empty family mansion, not far from Noah Rosewater Memorial High, home of the once-proud Fighting Sawmakers. All else to the horizon was "shithouses, shacks, alcoholism, ignorance, idiocy and perversion."

What, exactly, did Eliot intend to do there, asked Sylvia, with whom we increasingly sympathize. Her youth was spent in the cosmopolitan sophistication of Paris, and she could not imagine that land anywhere could be so flat, its people so dull. "I'm going to *care* about these people," came the earnest reply. Eliot had found at last his canvas. "I'm going to love these discarded Americans, even though they're useless and unattractive. *That* is going to be my work of art." Maybe young Kurt had such dreams as he looked out the car window on excursions to the hinterlands with his father.

Sylvia dutifully agreed to join her husband at his outpost. They took up residence in the big mansion, opening its doors to the have-nots of the county. Lavish banquets were occasions for townspeople to sound off about their "misshapen fears and dreams," to which the hosts listened attentively. Eliot became an officer in the fire department; Sylvia was elected president of the Ladies' Auxiliary. But after five years she reached the limit of endurance, suffering a nervous collapse and torching the firehouse.

"In his heart, Eliot doesn't love those awful people out there any more than I do," Lister Ames Rosewater insisted to his long-time lawyer, Thurmond McAllister. His son's efforts to improve the rabble were doomed to futility, a case of pearls before swine. If he would only stop drinking, surely his misplaced compassion would play itself out. The senator turned to Sylvia, bemoaning the couple's childlessness as another part of the puzzle. McAllister reminded his client that in any event the Rosewater line was not ending, another branch of the family existed—one we will meet later in the story—a thought banished with contempt.

Looking at a photograph of Eliot as he appeared in uniform, Lister began to cry. "So clean, so tall, so purposeful," he exclaimed. "How puffy and pasty he looks these days ... eats a balanced diet of potato chips, Southern Comfort, and Rosewater Golden Lager Ambrosia Beer." Although the father-son disconnect typical of Vonnegut stories prevails here, the senator is not a cold-blooded villain. His aggression hides his sadness and is a clumsy expression of concern. In his bull-in-a-china-shop way, he has a point about how his son's indiscriminate embrace of the world at large, his attempt to "play God to people," shortchanged those closest to him. Eliot "did to the word *love* what Russians did to the word *democracy*," Lister complained. "If Eliot is going to love everybody, no matter what they are, no matter what they do, then those of us who love particular people for particular reasons had better find ourselves a new word." Sylvia loved Eliot, too, and defended his quixotic ways. "It's beautiful what he's doing. I'm simply not strong enough or good enough to be by his side any more." McAllister urged his client against self-recrimination for his son's troubles, but it was no use. "I have spent my life demanding that people blame themselves for their misfortunes," the senator declared. "Good for you," his friend replied. "And while you're at it, be sure to hold yourself responsible for everything that happened to Eliot during World War Two."

Now we arrive closer to understanding why Eliot could not take ownership of his princely birthright. We flash back to a factory in Bavaria, thought by his platoon to be infested with enemy troops. Leading the charge toward the burning structure, Captain Rosewater pitched a grenade and went in, blinded by smoke, confused and alarmed by the shouts in German. After stumbling over several bodies he was confronted by a fearsome, helmeted figure in a gas mask and instinctively thrust forward his bayonet.

A voice from his left yelled for the assault to stop. "Jesus Christ—these aren't soldiers ...!" Before he knew what was happening Eliot had killed two older men and a teenager, "ordinary villagers, engaged in the brave and uncontroversial business of trying to keep a building from combining with oxygen."

Minutes later he lay on his back in the middle of a road, trucks just missing him as they rumbled past. Rigid and uncommunicative, Eliot was shipped to the rear, then to a hospital in Paris. Already burdened with survivor guilt over his mother, he now had to deal with what he had encountered in the fiery chaos of war. Like the author, he is driven by a hunger to do penance, to make things whole again.

Back in Rosewater, Eliot continued his lay ministry, moving into a tiny second-floor room in the center of town. The furniture was war surplus, but unlike Howard W. Campbell Jr.'s Greenwich Village apartment, this was for Eliot no deathly purgatory. He slept like a baby, oblivious to the blinking neon advertising the liquor store conveniently below him. Etched on his office door was a logo:

ROSEWATER FOUNDATION
HOW CAN WE HELP YOU?

From his window Eliot admired the new fire station he had subsidized, with six gleaming engines. The red phone by his cot was for fire calls, a prompt to activate the bullhorn installed under the courthouse cupola. Once the main air-raid siren of Berlin, it was the loudest alarm in the Western Hemisphere. In its overkill it refers to the alarm Vonnegut remembered from the Alplaus, New York, fire station, and reflects the exaggerated vigilance of a trauma victim.

The black phone, meanwhile, connected callers with problems to discuss, and in extreme cases it served as the county's suicide hotline. Like the mom-and-pop accountant upon whom he is based, Eliot dispensed tax information, gave out parole forms, offered medical diagnoses at any hour of the day or night, and kept a careful record of every transaction.

Throughout his life Kurt Vonnegut thought long and hard about the Rosewater Problem, how to help people who could not help themselves in a culture lacking the security of large extended families. Eliot was trying to address it one person at a time. In *Slapstick* the author proposes a government scheme to assign everyone artificial relatives. And, ever the tinkerer, he once floated the idea of a nonprofit organization called Life Engineering. "If you didn't know what to do next and you came to us, we'd *tell* you," he explained to *Playboy*. "You'd have to absolutely promise to do whatever we'd say, and then we'd give you the best possible answer we could." As with the other approaches he toyed with, the problem was enforcing compliance. "We couldn't bring in a couple of hit men from Detroit."[11]

Eliot idealized the people he served as children of a yeomanry that had cleared forests, drained swamps, and like him, come to the defense of country in wartime. In truth they were a demoralized lot, manifestly lacking the ability or the will to transcend their desperate circumstances. Diana Moon Glampers phoned late one night just to hear the reassurance of Eliot's voice. He listened, bottle at his side, as she complained childishly about her ankles and her loneliness. "You gave up everything a man is supposed to want, just to help the little people, and the little people know it," she thanked her only friend as they said goodbye. "God bless you, Mr. Rosewater."

One evening Eliot's father called, barking commands and demanding answers. "Are you," he asked out of habit, "or have you ever been a communist?" Sylvia took the phone, and she and Eliot arranged to see each other one last time—"a dangerous thing for two such sick and loving people to do"—in Indianapolis. In the meantime he was on his way to baptize a set of twins just born outside of town. "Hello, babies," he would tell them. "Welcome to earth. It's hot in the summer and cold in the winter." He planned to share with them the one rule he knew they had to hold on to during their short stay on the planet, delivered with a soldier's no-nonsense vulgarity: "God damn it, you've got to be kind."

Norman Mushari had been eavesdropping, as usual. The summit between Eliot and Sylvia jeopardized all the groundwork he had been laying, and it was time to execute the next stage of his plan.

In a digression amounting to the kind of short story that had been Vonnegut's stock-in-trade, we learn about the Rhode Island Rosewaters, descended from Noah's brother George, who led a rifle company during the Civil War. George returned to Indiana a blinded hero, only to discover that he had been swindled out of his half of the saw works and farm. George resettled out East to work in a factory employing disabled veterans. By the boom years of the 1920s his grandson Merrihue was prospering, making a paper fortune in real estate and marrying into the prominent Rumfoord family of Newport. Merrihue committed suicide after it all collapsed with the crash on Wall Street.

We now meet George's son Fred, struggling to make ends meet peddling life insurance on Cape Cod. How he got there, his connections to the famous Rosewaters of the Midwest, is a story lost to him. "Like most Americans of modest means, Fred knew nothing about his ancestors." In common with the fishing villages Vonnegut got to know on Cape Cod, Pisquontuit had developed by Fred's time into a microcosm of the country's class system. It was the summer home for two hundred wealthy clans, with a thousand ordinary families, the Reeks and Wrecks of the resort community, dependent on them for their modest livelihoods. The portrait of the town is a damning one. "The lives led there were nearly all paltry, lacking in subtlety, wisdom, wit or invention—were precisely as pointless and unhappy as lives led in Rosewater County, Indiana." Money, or the lack of it, was not the main issue. The problem was a spiritual one.

Fred, like the author, straddled the social divide in his village. He had attended Princeton briefly, knew how to sail, and could hobnob with the elite—but in fact he was "gruesomely poor" by their standards. Fred made his rounds on another desultory morning, chatting up regulars at a newsstand diner. No one was in a position to buy, but "they knew in their hearts that he was offering the only get-rich-quick scheme that was open to them: to insure themselves and die soon." A staple of his pitch was the satisfaction he always felt when the widow of a client told him, on behalf of her children: "God bless you, Mr. Rosewater."

Fred came home one evening to find his wife sleeping off the drinks consumed during the weekly luncheon engagement with her obnoxious best friend. Caroline let Fred know all the time how disappointed she was with the life he had given her, and in his despair he decided now he couldn't take it anymore. But while looking for a rope to hang himself he came upon *A History of the Rosewaters of Rhode Island*, a volume put together by his late father, covered in dust on a basement shelf. Fred discovered in its opening pages an epic story, filled with characters of nobility and courage. It was lifesaving gold.

"We *are* somebody," he told Caroline excitedly. "Those phony bastards you think are so wonderful, compared to us—compared to *me*—I'd like to see how many ancestors they could turn up that could compare with mine." For the first time in his life he was comfortable in his own skin. In his defiance we can hear the voice of Vonnegut, the downwardly mobile prince, the undiscovered, struggling writer trying to support a family:

No more apologies! So we're poor! All right, we're poor! This is America! And America is one place in this sorry world where people shouldn't *have* to apologize for being poor. The question in America should be, "Is this guy a good citizen? Is he honest? Does he pull his own weight?"

But in the kind of O. Henry twist he favored in his magazine stories, the author withdraws Fred's new identity before he has a chance to enjoy it. The rest of the Rosewater manuscript was hollowed out, its pages consumed by termites. As he resumed his suicide attempt, there was another interruption. Norman Mushari stood at the front door, announcing his intention to represent him in a suit against his rich Hoosier relatives. It is a different kind of gold being offered, a lottery ticket, and it is hard to blame Fred when he grabs it without hesitation.

In Indiana, Eliot was making preparations for his meeting with Sylvia. He was groggy after a night of calls from clients afraid, in spite of assurances, that their patron saint would not be coming back. The streets were quiet as Eliot made his way to the Greyhound stop at the Saw City Kandy Kitchen. "There had been a lot of frantic, lame-brained planning of an appropriate farewell" in town, including a triumphal arch of water from fire hoses, but no one had stepped forward to lead. The grief felt was too sharp, the dread about the future too overwhelming.

The few people Eliot passed along the way recognized that he was not himself, his mind was as empty as the town's sidewalks. He could not remember their names, and he had visions as he put one foot in front of the other. In the glare of the afternoon sun two figures idling in front of the courthouse appeared as "charred stickmen surrounded by steam."

An ex-con, Noyes Finnerty, perhaps a cousin of the rebel leader in *Player Piano*, stopped his sweeping in the firehouse to watch. He understood what the look in Eliot's eyes meant. An internal "click" had gone off, signaling a subtle but unmistakable change he had seen before in fellow inmates. "That thing that bothered him so will never click on again. It's dead, its *dead*. And that part of that man's life where he had to be a certain crazy way, that's *done!*"

Eliot certainly felt that way. He had done his best in Rosewater, and as the town receded in the rear window of the bus he lost himself in a Kilgore

Trout paperback he had purchased at the Kandy Kitchen. When he looked up an hour later, the city ahead was engulfed in flames. Eliot rose from his seat, to behold the firestorm of Indianapolis.

> He was awed by the majesty of the column of fire, which was at least eight miles in diameter and fifty miles high. The boundaries of the column seemed absolutely sharp and unwavering, as though made of glass. Within the boundaries, helixes of dull red embers turned in stately harmony about an inner core of white. The white seemed holy.

"Poo-tee-weet?" Eliot awakens to find himself in the garden of a sanitarium, the same one where Sylvia recovered after her breakdown. Tennis racket in hand, he has no memory of the past twelve months—the fight with the bus driver, the straitjacket and shock treatments, the suicide attempts.

The firestorm, he understands, never happened—at least not in Indiana. The blank year anticipates the amnesia at the core of the Dresden experience that Vonnegut describes in the early pages of *Slaughterhouse-Five*. In his blackouts, his otherworldliness and time-travel, his flat affect and attention to the soothing distractions of birdsong, Eliot is a rough draft of Billy Pilgrim.

He is in a strategy session for a hearing on his mental fitness, surrounded by a brain trust that includes his father, the lawyer McAllister, and another person he does not at first recognize—a man with features "like those of a kindly country undertaker." Eliot is unable to complete a thought he started to express before blacking out. "I can't find the words," he whispers, confused, to the doctor.

I can't find the words.

The mystery man is none other than a clean-shaven Kilgore Trout, summoned, at Eliot's request, to explain—as he cannot—the meaning of his recent activities. Lister Rosewater chortles as he begins to speak, thinking it all brilliantly manufactured hokum that just might sell in court. But Trout is not kidding. "What you did in Rosewater County was far from insane," he tells the patient.

It was quite possibly the most important social experiment of our time, for it dealt on a very small scale with a problem whose queasy horrors will eventually be made world-wide by the sophistication of machines. The problem is this: How to love people who have no use?

Again we have the question we encountered in *Player Piano.* "Americans have long been taught to hate all people who will not or cannot work, to hate even themselves for that," Kilgore Trout continues. "We can thank the vanished frontier for that piece of common-sense cruelty." Nor did the problem afflict only the poor. The sermon rises to its central message: "Uselessness will kill strong and weak souls alike, and kill every time."

Trout has nothing but admiration for the man before him, seated precariously on the edge of a bird bath. Eliot's regard for fire departments made perfect sense. "They rush to the rescue of any human being, and count not the cost. The most contemptible man in town, should his contemptible house catch fire, will see his enemies put the fire out." Trout falls silent, arms raised like a Jesus figure.

"If there had only been a child," the senator interrupts, still looking for a legal defense. Old McAllister laughs. There were plenty of offspring around if they were really needed. As part of the conspiracy to discredit Eliot, Mushari has bribed dozens of women in Rosewater County to file paternity claims against him, on behalf of their sons and daughters.

Emboldened by Trout's speech, Eliot comes back to life, reassuming leadership of his foundation. After writing a settlement check to his cousin Fred, he orders papers drawn up acknowledging all of the claimants entitled to affection and support as his children. In one stroke, he has become the patriarch of a large and beautiful brood.

In *God Bless You, Mr. Rosewater,* trauma is transmuted into hope and renewal—a feat captured inventively in a musical production of the novel the author helped to mount in the late 1970s. In it, Eliot welcomes his children on stage in song and is joined by the rest of the cast. "Each is carrying a baby, and in the end you have this lovely, triumphant finale," Vonnegut explained in an interview. He loved the statement for its open-heartedness, conveying in a way he did not anticipate the spirit of the last scene, as the hero's odyssey ends in healing, home, and familial love—just as Malachi Constant's does in *Sirens of Titan*.[12]

We read *God Bless You, Mr. Rosewater* today in the context of what followed in Vonnegut's writings, and it is impossible not to see it as the last leg in the author's Dresden journey. But what if Kurt Vonnegut had been forced by financial pressures to give up on his writing career at this point, what if this had been his last novel? Even if he was able somehow to continue, could he find the words—could he, like Eliot, find resolution for his painful memories of war? After several gestures toward the blinding light of the firestorm, the author was at a crossroads.

SIX

Slaughterhouse-Five,

or, *The Children's Crusade: A Duty-Dance with Death*

*On about February 14th the Americans came over, followed
by the R.A.F., their combined labors ... destroyed all of Dresden—
possibly the world's most beautiful city. But not me.*
—Private Kurt Vonnegut Jr., May 29, 1945

Centered on his capture and imprisonment by the Germans during the
waning months of World War II, *Slaughterhouse-Five* (1969) is Vonnegut's
signature achievement. After several approaches, he confronts finally his
experience of apocalypse, the Allied firebombing of Dresden, in his sixth
novel. Everything was destroyed that February night, tens of thousands
killed, he wrote his family from a Red Cross station after his release a few
months later. *"But not me."* The words bear a heavy weight.[1]

This was a book that resisted being written, with a subject defying language and the conventions of narrative. "There is nothing intelligent to say
about a massacre," Vonnegut cautions in its first pages. He often downplayed
the importance of the event in his life, in part out of concern that his reflections might be seen as special pleading by a German American. One thing he
had in common with Mark Twain, Vonnegut said once in an interview, is that
they were both associated with the enemy in a war (referring to Samuel

Clemens' brief stint on the side of the Confederacy). "And so you have to be funnier than most people," he added, as well as circumspect in describing the privations of the other side. The war was something he experienced from the outside, as though a visitor on another planet. "Being present at the destruction of Dresden," Vonnegut insisted, "has affected my character far less than the death of my mother, the adopting of my sister's children, the sudden realization that those children were no longer dependent on me, the break-up of my marriage, and on and on." The attitude seems to some degree a defense, an attempt to quarantine the episode and minimize the part of himself he lost in the inferno. In later years Vonnegut declared Dresden off-limits in interviews—only to bring it up himself, again and again, like a compulsion. The struggle to commit his story to print, and the power of the finished product, leave no doubt that *Slaughterhouse-Five* was the fulfillment of a survivor's mission, the expression of a deeply held need to bear witness.[2]

A number of things came together to allow Vonnegut to complete his mission. In 1965 he left the isolation of Cape Cod for a residency at the Iowa Writers' Workshop, making the long drive west alone in a dilapidated Volkswagen. There he was able for the first time to rub shoulders with a community of writers, including Nelson Algren, Vance Bourjaily, Richard Yates, and José Donoso, as they worked with students on the mechanics of storytelling. John Irving, later the author of *The World According to Garp*, was Vonnegut's most promising protégé. It was in Iowa, Jerome Klinkowitz has observed, that Vonnegut came to understand the real subject of a book about Dresden would be himself—his reactions—rather than the event. The framework was beginning to take shape.[3]

Meanwhile, Vonnegut's career was gaining new traction. An audience beyond the science-fiction "file drawer" and the campus underground was taking notice of his earlier novels, reissued in paperback by Dell and Avon. Pieces for the *New York Times, Life,* and *Esquire*, reviews and commentary in the manner of the first-person "new journalism" then emerging, raised his profile among the literati. The legendary editor Seymour Lawrence was impressed enough to offer Vonnegut a contract for three novels and became, like Knox Burger and Kenneth Littauer before him, a friend and mentor of enormous influence. "How much money do you need to live on for the time it will take you to write your book?" Lawrence is said to have asked about the Dresden project when they first met. With that vote of confidence, and a Guggenheim fellowship supporting a trip to East Germany to revisit the scene, the table was set.[4]

Slaughterhouse-Five is a tale of defeat rather than victory, in itself a departure in our relentlessly affirmative national story. "It goes against the American storytelling grain to have someone in a situation he can't get out of," Vonnegut told *Playboy*, "but I think this is very usual in life." It is his intimate "duty-dance" with the reality of meaningless death, the most taboo of subjects in any culture.[5]

Suffused with irony (encapsulated in the famous tag line, "so it goes"), *Slaughterhouse-Five* is rich in interludes of comic relief. But it is the author's unfunniest novel, an American version of *Trümmerliteratur*, the spare and haunted "rubble literature" pioneered in the late 1940s by his friend and fellow infantry soldier, Heinrich Böll. Vonnegut compared it to Böll's stories of men who leave and come home, "with the war part missing." "That is like my memory of Dresden," he told a student audience in 1969. "Actually there's nothing there."[6]

In its reduction of things to their constituent elements—individuals turned to inert objects or steam, prisoners oozing like liquid out of boxcars, a city transformed into minerals—it also bears comparison to fellow chemist Primo Levi's accounts of his experiences at Auschwitz. Each man adopts the scientific detachment that was part of their training, as both a means of survival and, later, a mode of communication. Each records his extreme circumstances as though observing an experiment in human behavior. In their economy of expression and eye for detail emerges a kind of poetry different than one might expect from storytellers with more orthodox pedigrees.[7]

Vonnegut had no illusions about the commercial prospects of what he had to say, and he dismissed any ambition that his small testimony might affect the workings of history. Was it an antiwar statement he was trying to deliver? "Why don't you write an anti-*glacier* book instead?" a skeptic at a cocktail party told him. But his experience had to be recorded, and it turns out that a public in the throes of seismic change was ready to embrace it.

Slaughterhouse-Five's protagonist, Billy Pilgrim, caricatures the decidedly unheroic child the author imagined himself to be during the war. "We were baby-faced," Vonnegut told an interviewer in 1977. "I don't think I had to shave very often. I don't recall that that was a problem." Like Eliot Rose-water, Billy suffers from what would today be called post-traumatic stress disorder. His story is rendered through understatement, unfolding on three alternating trajectories. First is the realism of the POW experience, Billy's trials as a droplet in the "Mississippi of humiliated Americans" that moved eastward after the Battle of the Bulge disaster. Second is his postwar success story, as a benumbed ghost for whom "pretty much everything is alright." Like other returning veterans he sleepwalks through the expected rites of passage—marriage, family, career, and a house in the suburbs. Free will is not an issue in this determined life.[8]

A third level takes place in the realm of Billy's imagination, on a remote world of healing and wisdom into which he escapes during moments of stress. He lurches without warning between times and locales—it is like watching television with another person impulsively changing channels.

The author acknowledged that he was always a character in his books. While both Billy Pilgrim and Edgar Derby, the Indianapolis schoolteacher who is the other key figure in this novel, were modeled on real people, we can also see Vonnegut using them to express facets of his own complex identity, to convey the experience of his random flights to different locations in his own life trajectory. The essence of being *unstuck in time*, after all, is the idea of fragmentation, doubleness, multiplicity—the sense of floating from one moment to another, and back again, regardless of circumstances and without much control. Billy is the child-soldier, a frightened neophyte, as young Vonnegut was in 1944 and 1945. Derby is the author looking back at that boy from his present middle-age, trying to understand what happened to him during the war.[9]

The opening chapter of *Slaughterhouse-Five* annihilates the boundary between fiction and autobiography, inviting us into Vonnegut's uncertainty about just what he has written. It is a dance, rather than an exercise in cold objectivity. "All this happened, more or less," he writes. "The war parts, anyway, are pretty much true." The facts sometimes make no more sense than the dirty limericks and scraps of soldiers' doggerel that also stick to his memory. Years of aborted outlines, wastebaskets overflowing with discarded pages had brought him no closer to conveying his experience. "I would hate to tell you what this lousy little book cost me in money and anxiety and time." Dresden is a black hole, and pinning it down is made more difficult by the lack of corroborating information. Details about the Allied raid were still classified. People inquiring about the project reacted with platitudes or got defensive when Vonnegut told them what it was about. In the grand scheme, measured against the Holocaust and other atrocities, the suffering of one more Nazi city did not amount to much.

The crystallizing moment for Vonnegut in his preparation for writing his "famous Dresden book" occurred on a trip he made to Pennsylvania to visit his army buddy and fellow POW Bernard V. O'Hare. He tells us that O'Hare's wife, Mary, eavesdropping on two old soldiers trying to dredge up anecdotes at the kitchen table, interrupted their conversation with tears and anger. Another swashbuckler was in the works, a shapely story with heroes and villains and neatly trimmed edges—and she found it disgusting. "You'll pretend you were men instead of babies, and you'll be played in the movies by Frank Sinatra and John Wayne or some of those other glamorous, war-loving, dirty old men." It would be one more bit of fuel to fire the cycle of madness for future generations.

Chastened, Vonnegut assured Mary he was not interested in cashing in, and promised that his book, if it ever saw the light of day, would not traffic in the Hollywood clichés that had brainwashed even the war's participants. The subtitle—"The Children's Crusade," a reference to a particularly bloody episode in the religious wars of the Middle Ages—would make sure of that.

The road to expression was long and torturous. "I must have written five thousand pages by now, and thrown them all away," Vonnegut told Mary O'Hare. In an interview he reflected on the consuming, frustrating nature of the task:

> Anyway, I came home in 1945, started writing about it, and wrote about it, and *wrote about it*, and WROTE ABOUT IT. This thin book is about what it's like to write a book about a thing like that. I couldn't get much closer. I would head myself into my memory of it, the circuit breakers would kick out; I'd head in again, I'd back

off. The book is a process of twenty years of this sort of living with Dresden and the aftermath.[10]

Finally, when the job was done, the book was written, Vonnegut apologized for the results. It was a failure, he explained to Sam Lawrence, "so short and jumbled and jangled." How could it be otherwise? "Everybody is supposed to be dead, to never say anything or want anything ever again." Why bother, then, with the dance? Vonnegut found inspiration in the Old Testament story of Lot's wife, who looked back at the destruction of Sodom and Gomorrah as she fled with the other refugees. She could not help herself, despite the certainty of becoming a pillar of salt.

Billy Pilgrim migrates "spastically" from youth to old age, from birth to death and back again. He is a wanderer manipulated by mysterious, larger forces, not unlike the chrono-synclastic infundibulated Winston Niles Rumfoord in *Sirens of Titan*. "The trips aren't necessarily fun."

Born, like Vonnegut, in 1922, Billy grew up in Ilium, New York. He was an awkward youth—"tall and weak, and shaped like a bottle of Coca-Cola." When war came he was drafted, sent to Europe, and taken prisoner by the Germans. He returned home and married the earnest but dramatically unattractive Valencia, daughter of the head of the optometry school where he completed his degree. It was a successful readjustment, interrupted only briefly by a "mild nervous collapse." He and Valencia have two children.

Billy often drifts back to the war. A chaplain's assistant in the army, he was attached to a combat regiment in Luxembourg just as it was disintegrating in the face of a ferocious German counterattack. "He had no helmet, no overcoat, no weapon, and no boots. On his feet were cheap, low-cut civilian shoes which he had bought for his father's funeral." Lost behind enemy lines, Billy was adopted by a pair of army scouts and a bullying, over-equipped little tank gunner named Roland Weary. For days in a December blizzard they operated without maps or food. "They ate snow."

Bringing up the rear across ditches and roads, Billy was numb. Sometimes he wanted nothing more than to lie down, to die quietly. "You guys go on without me," he said softly. But Weary took a sadistic interest in Billy's survival, as part of the "true war story" he was concocting in his head. The "Three Musketeers" would rescue this weakling on their way to Bronze

Stars. "Get out of the road, you dumb motherfucker," Weary screamed when the bullets flew. "Saved your life again, you dumb bastard," he shouted, slapping and kicking his hostage to keep him moving.

In the quiet of a forest, eyes closed, Billy had his first experience of being unstuck in time. He ranged across the arc of his life, "passing into death, which was violet light." He watched himself as a child, getting sink-or-swim lessons from his father at the Ilium YMCA. In middle age he visited his mother at a nursing home, then shifted to his son's Little League banquet, then forward to a drunken infidelity at a New Year's Eve party.

Suddenly he was back in 1944, shaken to his senses by Roland Weary. They could hear voices and dogs barking nearby. Crouched in a creek bed, Billy didn't care what happened next. "If everybody would leave him alone for just a little while, he wouldn't cause anybody any more trouble. He would turn to steam and float up among the treetops." Weary was enraged that *his* fantasy has been derailed, and started to beat his companion with renewed ferocity. Looking down at them in puzzlement were five German soldiers.

In a 1977 "Self-Interview" for *Paris Review,* Vonnegut described his actual memories of the Bulge. He was as frightened, ill-prepared, and lost in the confusion as anyone else, he insisted. Most of his training had been in the operation of the cumbersome 240-millimeter Howitzer rather than the infantry. And now he was a battalion scout, gangly and easy to spot in his olive drab clothing. Winter camouflage was a luxury enjoyed only by the enemy. "I imitated various war movies I'd seen," Vonnegut remembered of his survival scheme.[11]

Eventually he found himself with perhaps fifty other GIs in a gully not unlike the one that held Billy Pilgrim. Over a loudspeaker the Germans demanded surrender, but Vonnegut and his comrades instinctively fixed bayonets instead. "It was nice there for a few minutes. . . . Being a porcupine with all those steel quills," he recalled with some satisfaction of his wartime experience, so closely mimicked by Billy's experience in the novel. "I pitied anybody who had to come in after us." Then came a deadly turn of "artificial weather," a barrage of eighty-eight-millimeter fire.

> The shells burst in the treetops right over us. Those were very loud bangs right over our heads. We were showered with splintered

steel. Some people got hit. Then the Germans told us again to come out. We didn't yell "nuts" or anything like that. We said, "Okay," and "Take it easy," and so on.[12]

The protagonist in *Slaughterhouse-Five* did not put up a fight, as Vonnegut and his brothers-in-arms tried to do in real life. Billy looked up from the ditch expecting the fearsome Wehrmacht warriors of his imagination, and instead saw rag-tag old men and angelic boys, barely weaned from their mothers' breasts. They herded the prisoners toward a stone cottage being used as a collection point. Exhausted, bobbing clumsily up and down along the road on the missing heel of his shoe, Billy kept crashing into Roland Weary and his damaged feet. ("We were supposed to get combat boots, but they never arrived," Vonnegut recalls of his own experience.) Warmed by furniture alight in the fireplace inside, Billy and his vanquished brothers stared blankly into the flames. "Nobody talked. Nobody had any good war stories to tell."

Billy falls asleep a prisoner in occupied Belgium and travels to his optometrist's office in a shopping center on the outskirts of Ilium, imagining a city remarkably like Vonnegut's Schenectady. A noise outside jolts him as he finishes with a patient. "He was expecting World War Three at any time." It was a firehouse alarm, like the one that sounded every day in Rosewater County, harmlessly announcing the arrival of noon. Billy finds himself split in two, "simultaneously on foot in Germany in 1944 and riding in his Cadillac in 1967," headed to a businessmen's gathering across town. In a burned-out, still-smoldering section of the black ghetto, where his childhood home once stood, he drives past sidewalks crushed by National Guard tanks and half-tracks. The war at home, the anarchic racial violence in cities and towns across the nation, was in the headlines and on Vonnegut's mind as he wrote. Billy's old neighborhood is like the surface of the moon, like Dresden after the big air raid.

The speaker at the businessmen's lunch that day was a Marine officer just back from Vietnam. He urges fortitude in the struggle against the Communists and suggests "bombing North Vietnam back into the Stone Age" if necessary. Billy, the only one in the room in a position to know what that would be like for the people below as the bombs fell on them, is not moved either way, even as he accepts congratulations for the service of his Green Beret son. What would happen is out of his control in any case. He lives by the serenity prayer of Alcoholics Anonymous—like the Sermon on the Mount, a favorite Vonnegut reference point—asking for the wisdom to accept what he cannot change.

After lunch Billy drives to his house and tries to take a nap. A doctor had prescribed the regimen for a problem he had lately been experiencing:

> Every so often, for no apparent reason, Billy Pilgrim would find himself weeping. Nobody had ever caught Billy doing it. Only the doctor knew. It was an extremely quiet thing Billy did, and not very moist.

Billy finds himself a prisoner again, his tears caused by the biting wind. He marched past trucks carrying enemy ordinance and reserves in the other direction, to the front. The cold and rough treatment left him dizzy and seeing colors. A kind of Saint Elmo's fire glowed around objects in his field of view. Vonnegut evokes here in the novel the terrible beauty he himself had witnessed under similar circumstances:

> At each road intersection Billy's group was joined by more Americans with their hands on top of their haloed heads. Billy had smiles for them all. They were moving like water downhill all the time, and they flowed at last to a main highway on a valley's floor. Through the valley flowed a Mississippi of humiliated Americans. Tens of thousands of Americans shuffled eastward, their hands clasped on top of their heads. They sighed and groaned.

This was the timeless fate of defeated armies. It was no doubt the scene the author had in mind when I saw him speak in 1991, and he declared solidarity with the columns of frightened young Iraqis we saw paraded on television at the end of the first Gulf War. Prisoners of war, for him, were a sacred brotherhood, beyond the boundaries of nation or epoch.

As darkness fell Billy's group reached a rail yard filled with boxcars, poised to ship more human cargo to the already overflowing camps deep within Germany. "Flashlight beams danced crazily" as the men were sorted according to rank. "You one of my boys?" a colonel to the side asked Billy, coughing and delirious from double pneumonia. "You from the Four-fifty-first?" The man was searching for his destroyed regiment, promising with tragic frontier bravado a barbecue reunion when they all made it back home. "If you're ever in Cody, Wyoming," he croaked in his death rattle, "just ask for Wild Bob!"

Billy was loaded with the other privates into an unheated cattle car. He could see some light outside through a ventilator. Locomotives sounded their departure whistles one by one, but his train sat motionless for two days. Billy imagined that the guards outside thought of each sealed container as a unit, "a single organism which ate and drank and excreted through its small openings." Again, there is lyricism in Vonnegut's description of the prisoners as they improvised ways to live together. In the most desperate of circumstances there are moments of grace, examples of spontaneous, divine community.

> Human beings in there were excreting into steel helmets which were passed to the people at the ventilators, who dumped them. Billy was a dumper. The human beings also passed canteens, which guards would fill with water. When food came in, the human beings were quiet and trusting and beautiful. They shared.

The men took turns standing up and lying down as finally the train began inching its way across the icy landscape. "Somewhere in there was Christmas," Vonnegut writes, reflecting the collapsed sense of time of the world inside the boxcars.

Billy Pilgrim travels forward, to the evening after his daughter's wedding. Valencia snores as he creeps downstairs for the rendezvous with aliens that he knows—had always known—are about to come. A movie about American fliers in World War II is on TV and it rewinds in his head as he waits.

> The formation flew backwards over a German city that was in flames. The bombers opened their bomb bay doors, exerted a miraculous magnetism which shrunk the fires, gathered them into cylindrical steel containers, and lifted the containers into the bellies of the planes. The containers were stored neatly in racks. The

Germans below had miraculous devices of their own, which were long steel tubes. They used them to suck more fragments from the crewmen and planes. But there were still a few wounded Americans, though, and some of the bombers were in bad repair. Over France, though, German fighters came up again, made everything and everybody as good as new.

The bombs were returned to the United States, transformed into minerals and buried, "so they would never hurt anybody ever again." The pilots handed in their uniforms and went back to high school. Soon everyone in this veteran's impossible dream of wholeness—even Hitler—was a baby again.

It is time now for Billy to make his way to the backyard. With its zap gun and little green men, the craft that materializes there is a B movie cliché. Billy is drawn through its airlock and strapped to a recliner for the duration of the trip. It is all a parody of his capture during the war.

Vonnegut's technique here was not a new one. "The science-fiction passages in *Slaughterhouse-Five* are just like the clowns in Shakespeare," he explained to *Playboy*. "When . . . the audience had had enough of the heavy stuff, he'd let up a little, bring on a clown or a foolish innkeeper or something like that, before he'd become serious again."[13]

"Why me?" Billy asks his kidnappers, who are from the distant planet Tralfamadore that we recognize from *Sirens of Titans*. They have encountered the question before and they find it as puzzling as the human conceit of free will. We are all simply "trapped in the amber of this moment," they respond telepathically. "There is no *why*." It is a good philosophy for a child of the Depression, with its worries and its setbacks and dislocations. It is good, too, for a soldier tossed about by the random fortunes of war.

The saucer's acceleration sends Billy back to the boxcar in Germany. Vonnegut recalled that his train was attacked at night by British mosquito bombers—"I guess they thought we were strategic materials of some kind." Roland Weary has died in the car ahead—but not before spinning fevered tales of his adventures as one of the Three Musketeers, singling Billy out as his Judas. After another stretch the doors open, and those who survived the trip spill out onto a platform. Overcoats, worn by Russians who are now dead, lie waiting for them in frozen piles. Billy dons a flimsy civilian's garment, crimson with a fur collar, ventilated with bullet holes.

Past barbed-wire fences they move, past row upon row of grey sheds. At the delousing station Billy gets his first look at the occupants of Weary's car. One is Edgar Derby, a schoolteacher from Indianapolis, at forty-four the oldest man in the group. He had to pull strings to get into the army at his advanced age—there are echoes of the old soldier Unk from the Army of Mars in *Sirens of Titan* here. Derby worries all the time about his son serving in the Pacific and regards Billy and the rest of the youngsters around him with paternal concern. Another prisoner is Paul Lazzaro, a thief from Chicago who traveled in the same boxcar as Roland Weary and has vowed to avenge his ghastly death at the first opportunity. Like Weary, Lazzaro has a taste for self-aggrandizing melodrama and he enjoys assembling lists of enemies with whom he would one day get even.

Scalded by the shower, a shock that killed some of his companions, Billy escapes in his mind to the more pleasant baths he received as an infant. Then he is a middle-aged optometrist again, sinking a Sunday morning putt on a golf green. Then he is back on the space ship.

Billy learns on the voyage that the "rarefied, luminous spaghetti" he sees outside the craft are actually stars, incorporating where they have been and where they are going rather than distinct points of light. Similarly, Earthlings resemble millipedes, with "babies' legs at one end and old people's legs at the other." Storytelling on their planet is not a matter of sequential narrative. "There is no beginning, no middle, no end, no suspense, no moral, no causes, no effects." The idea is to convey "the depths of many marvelous moments seen all at one time." Here Vonnegut is expressing his renunciation of the simplistic notion of time on Earth that defines and imprisons us. This novel marks his boldest effort to be free of those strictures.

Lights flash and Billy steps out of the delousing chamber. His thawed-out coat, made "for an impresario about as big as an organ-grinder's monkey," confirms his status as an emasculated object of derision. The Americans were brought to a building where a contingent of British officers suddenly emerged, as in a music hall farce, belting out a welcome. Captured early in the war, the British POWs were thoroughly accommodated to their surroundings, models of hygiene and discipline who "made war look stylish and reasonable and fun."

The surreality continued inside. A barracks feast had been prepared, toiletry kits laid out, an all-male amateur production of that ultimate happy-ending story, *Cinderella*, rehearsed to make for a proper celebration. It was all illuminated by the "ghostly, opalescent" light of candles made in camps further to the East. Only after the excitement fades did the Brits begin to notice the condition of their guests. It was not what they had expected. "My God—what have they done to you, lad?" exclaimed one officer to Billy after rescuing him from the flame of the stove. "This isn't a man. It's a broken kite."

Watching the play was too much stimulation for Billy. Edgar Derby volunteered to watch over him as he was taken to a hospital quarters. An Englishman shared with Derby his surprise at the youth and inexperience of the Americans. "You know—we've had to imagine the war here," he confided, "and we imagined that it was being fought by aging men like ourselves. When I saw those freshly-shaved faces, it was a shock."

Morphine dreams take hold, and Billy is in the mental ward of a veterans' hospital back in the States three years later. Sharing his room is none other than Eliot Rosewater, an infantry captain struggling to cope with his own traumatic memories. A trunkful of musty paperbacks sits under Eliot's bed, including some by his favorite author, Kilgore Trout, which he shares with the enthusiasm of a religious convert. Having "found life meaningless, partly because of what they had seen in war," Vonnegut writes, the two patients become brothers in "trying to re-invent themselves and their universe."

Billy returns to the zoo on Tralfamadore, his home now for the past six Earth months. His climate-controlled dome is outfitted with all the comforts of postwar suburban living—end tables, wall-to-wall carpeting, even a color TV. Thousands of spectators observe as he goes about his daily routine.

Billy asks how they had learned to live together so harmoniously. "Earthlings must be the terror of the Universe!" he exclaims. It is all charmingly naïve to his listeners. Some days are indeed peaceful, a guide tells him, others are bloody and cruel in the extreme. The universe *would* end violently, no doubt about it—but not due to anything that happened on Billy's planet. It would be a simple matter of mechanical failure, as with Salo in *Sirens of Titan*. A Tralfamadorian test pilot would set in motion a final cataclysmic chain reaction as he engaged the starter button on his craft. It was not mysterious, and yet nothing could be done to prevent it. "He has *always* pressed it, and he always *will*. ... The moment is *structured* that way," the guide explains patiently. The key to living, he continues, is not to attach to big stories with conclusions at the end, not to dwell on bad times or the inevitability of death, but to "spend eternity looking at pleasant moments— like today at the zoo. Isn't this a nice moment?"

We can hear in these words the voice of Vonnegut's Uncle Alex, acknowledging whatever small joys came his way as precious gifts. "If this isn't nice, I don't know what is," he was prone to observe. But the author was not prescribing here feel-good passivity or "dropping out," as some of his young fans must have imagined when they read the novel for the first time. "I've never been sympathetic to the Leary movement," he told an interviewer in 1980. "I think all I was describing in *Slaughterhouse-Five* was a very real *memory* process," one based on the fact that nobody he talked to could remember anything about the Dresden bombing. The dialogue here is a meditation on the power of the human mind to distort and repress, an effort at making peace with the sensation of multiplicity—the subjective experience, common to soldiers and non-soldiers alike, of being *unstuck in time*.[14]

Billy tries to follow the Tralfamadorian creed. He drifts to his honeymoon bed, where all seems right with the world. Valencia's father is setting him up in business and surprises the newlyweds with a brand new house and car. The marriage, Billy knows, "was going to be at least bearable all the way." Between bites of her ever-present Three Musketeers bars, Valencia promises to lose weight, and she asks if the war still troubles him. Fumbling with the light switch, Billy is back in the prison camp.

It was still his morphine night. As he stepped outside Billy was serenaded by the moans of prisoners sick from their welcoming feast. Their hosts recoiled in disgust. The Americans were a disappointing lot—"weak, smelly, self-pitying," one Brit complained, "worse than the bleeding Russians." A German assured the British officer that the imposition was only temporary. The new arrivals were shipping out, to work as contract labor. Under his arm he carried a tract by the notorious American Nazi Howard W. Campbell Jr.

Billy drifted in and out of consciousness, emerging as a widower facing the wrath of his daughter for neglecting the furnace of his empty house.

Under an electric blanket his thoughts run to a more congenial model of femininity. Montana Wildhack, the movie sex symbol, a GI's pin-up ideal of voluptuous submission, was delivered one day to his habitat in the extra-terrestrial zoo. The Tralfamadorians wanted to watch the mating rituals of Earthlings. To calm his terrified new companion, Billy gallantly demanded the privacy of the night canopy. Light from a lamp set off the "baroque detailing" of Montana's nude body—like the "fantastic architecture in Dresden, before it was bombed."

By midday the prison camp was alive with the sounds of a new latrine being constructed. Lazzaro frothed about the justice he means to exact against the man who broke his arm the night before as he was caught in the act of larceny, and he glared menacingly at Billy, the villain he believed had killed his boxcar pal.

Decades later Lazzaro would make good on his vendetta. Billy witnesses the scene in his mind frequently. "It is high time I was dead," he calmly announces to a large crowd gathered at a Chicago ballpark, just before the fatal gunshots ring out. The audience was there to hear his insights about Tralfamadorian culture. Here Vonnegut incorporates into his story the assassinations of Robert Kennedy and Martin Luther King Jr. that wrenched the country as he was writing his book. The greeting Billy had learned from his intergalactic hosts—"farewell, hello, farewell, hello"—would be his final words.

Along with Lazzaro and Derby, two extremes of humanity, Billy walked from the infirmary to the shed where they had first been welcomed, his coat wadded around his hands like a lady's muff. Inside, the floor was packed with men trying to sleep. Near the makeshift stage, Billy donned its blue curtain and tried on the slippers from the play, a pair of airman's boots painted silver. Now "Billy Pilgrim was Cinderella, and Cinderella was Billy Pilgrim."

An Englishman took the stage for a pep talk to the dissipated assembly. He confessed envy about the adventure on which the Americans were about to embark, assuring them they would be out of danger, in an open city. The final act of the protocol was choosing a leader, something the Brits considered a matter of survival. When there were no volunteers, Edgar

Derby was nominated by default and elected by a few half-hearted "ayes." Humbled by the gravity of his new responsibilities, Derby promised to do all he could to get his charges home in one piece. "Go take a fuck at a rolling doughnut," razzed Lazzaro from the back row.

Unlike their journey from the front, the soldiers' ride to Dresden was brief and pleasant, "a lark." There was soup and bread and real cigarettes, and the caress of suddenly milder weather. After a couple of hours the boxcar doors opened to late afternoon sunshine, framing the loveliest man-made sight most of the men had ever seen. One soldier—the author himself—declared it "Oz."

Even that late in the war, Dresden "had not suffered so much as a cracked windowpane." Air-raid sirens sounded daily, but the bombers were always headed elsewhere. Vonnegut remembered the muffled sounds of the attacks on other places—*whump a whump a whump a whump*. Here, in contrast, the defenses were down and shelters were scarce, here prevailed an amazing normalcy. "Steam radiators still whistled cheerily," electricity flowed, streetcars rumbled across intersections. There was even a functioning zoo—the inspiration, certainly, for Billy's Tralfamadorian flights.

Eight haphazardly uniformed figures crossed the yard to take the prisoners into custody. Again it was old men and youngsters, pressed into service just the day before. They approached warily, expecting "cocky, murderous American infantrymen" fresh from the killing fields. Instead there was Billy with his toga and silver shoes, Lazzaro with his bandaged arm, and, at the head of the receiving line, Edgar Derby, "mournfully pregnant with patriotism and middle age and imaginary wisdom." Fear dissolved into laughter. "Here were more crippled human beings, more fools like themselves," the guards realized. "Here was light opera."

Dresdeners gathered to watch the parade as it "pranced, staggered and reeled" through the city streets. Billy, in his otherworldly costume, was enchanted by the fanciful buildings, which would all be gone in a month. In a while the column reached the threshold of a sprawling slaughterhouse complex. The guard who spoke English ordered the men to memorize their new address, cement building number 5, *"Schlachthof-funf."*

Billy is transported to 1968, to relive the crash of a chartered plane headed for an optometrists' convention. On board, as a barbershop quartet breaks into song just before impact, he understands there is nothing he can do to prevent the rendezvous with that Vermont mountainside. Lying dazed in the snow, Billy, the only survivor, is rescued by a team of Austrian ski instructors who speak German as they sift through the wreckage. In their masks, they looked to him like "golliwogs," blackface performers from a minstrel show. Is this some "amazing new phase of World War Two?" A golliwog leans down to make out the words Billy whispers: *"Schlachthof-funf."*

In the hospital Billy travels back to the first days in Dresden. He and Edgar Derby were pushing a cart, accompanied by a German armed with an antique musket who could have been his kid brother. A group of teen-aged girls, newly-arrived refugees, screamed as the trio stumbled onto them in a dressing room. In the kitchen a war widow ladled soup into bowls. "All the real soldiers are dead," she mumbled with contempt, surveying the line of misfits.

Billy watched as he and his companions labored in the weeks that followed, sweeping floors and washing windows. By some strange good luck they had been assigned to a factory that made vitamin-enriched syrup for pregnant women. His starved body "shook him with ravenous gratitude and applause" when he got clandestine spoonfuls. Derby burst into tears when it was his turn for a taste.

This nice moment was interrupted by the appearance of an official visitor—Howard W. Campbell Jr., in the flesh. As though out of a comic book, Campbell was resplendent in his red, white, and blue costume, accessorized with a ten-gallon hat, cowboy boots, and a swastika armband. He was there to recruit volunteers for his Free American Corps, a unit that would fight the communist hordes in the East in exchange for freedom, glory, and, more immediately, all the steak and mashed potatoes they could eat. As emaciated as his audience was, there were no takers.

The lone response came from Edgar Derby, who "lumbered to his feet, for what was probably the finest moment in his life." Vonnegut sets the scene:

> There are almost no characters in this story, and almost no dramatic confrontations, because most of the people in it are so sick and so much the listless playthings of enormous forces. One of the

main effects of war, after all, is that people are discouraged from being characters. But old Derby was a character now.

"His stance was that of a punch-drunk fighter. His head was down. His fists were out front, waiting for information and battle plan." Derby glared at his adversary and called him a snake, then "spoke movingly of the American form of government." He lauded its ideals of "freedom and justice and opportunities and fair play for all." His men were ready to *die* for these things, he said, united in brotherhood with the Russian people to make them come to pass. The whine of an air-raid siren cut short the showdown. Everyone scrambled downstairs to the whitewashed coolness of the meat locker. It was a false alarm—the bombs would not drop until the next night.

Vonnegut was diffident about his wartime exploits, as he was about so many things in his life—a combination of background, temperament, and undoubtedly a large degree of survivor guilt. But we know that he, too, became a character during his months as a POW. Like Edgar Derby he resisted his circumstances and stood up to his captors, at great personal risk. In his letter from the Red Cross station, published after his death in the collection *Armageddon in Retrospect,* young Vonnegut refers to being the spokesman for his companions thanks to the fragments of German he understood and could speak. "After desperately trying to improve our situation for two months and having been met with bland smiles," he wrote his family, "I told the guards just what I was going to do to them when the Russians came. They beat me up a little. I was fired as group leader."[15]

Vonnegut's use of Derby to voice the American civic faith, unfashionable in the late 1960s and often overlooked or misunderstood by the readers who first championed the book, is not meant as a joke. It is the author's unashamed tribute to both the futility and the tremendous appeal of the values for which he was proud to have fought, ideals he came to appreciate in new ways in the cold and hunger of incarceration, far from home.

In the shelter the next night, "there were sounds like giant footsteps above. The giants walked and walked." These are words Vonnegut has used before to convey the sound and feel of those fateful hours. When the prisoners came up the next day they encountered a swath of ruin overwhelming in scale. The tableau is reminiscent of the doomsday ending in *Cat's Cradle*, with British incendiaries replacing ice-nine as the agent of destruction here:

> The sky was black with smoke. The sun was an angry little pin-head. Dresden was like the moon now, nothing but minerals. The stones were hot. Everybody else in the neighborhood was dead. So it goes.

Billy looked at the guards as they "drew together, rolled their eyes." Mouths open, "they looked like a silent film of a barbershop quartet."

On Tralfamadore, Montana, six months pregnant, asks for a bedtime story. Billy remembers the aftermath of the firestorm—the "little logs lying around," charred remains of people, the collapsed buildings with melted glass undulating to the horizon. After a while the prisoners were led across the jagged surface in search of food and water. American Mustangs swooped low to finish the job, strafing anything that still moved.

In an introduction to the twenty-fifth anniversary edition of *Slaughter-house-Five* Vonnegut styled his effort "a nonjudgmental expression of astonishment" about what he saw after he emerged from "the best bomb shelter in town." He was reluctant to direct blame at individuals, from commanders down to the pilots and crews who executed what was in effect a bureaucratic exercise, the logical playing out of a machine gone beyond control. "One reason they burned down Dresden," he said in 1977, acknowledging the role of inertia, "is that they'd already burned down everything else. You know: 'What're we going to do tonight?'"[16]

In essays and speeches over the years he expressed understanding for those who considered the operation justified retribution for Nazi crimes. What bothered him was the imposition of collective guilt, the death penalty applied to babies, old people—even himself and his buddy O'Hare, who should have been dead in the whirlwind. The city was filled with Polish slave laborers and refugees of various backgrounds, making an accurate final accounting of the casualties impossible. He thought 135,000 dead was the best estimate, more than the number who would perish in either Hiroshima or Nagasaki six months later. (The zoo animals were not exempt. "You should have seen the giraffe after the firestorm," he commented in 1991's

Fates Worse Than Death.) The raid came as the enemy was collapsing on all fronts, and it "didn't shorten the war by half a second, didn't weaken a German defense or attack anywhere, didn't free a single person from a death camp." In *Fates Worse Than Death* Vonnegut concluded that Dresden was about symbols rather than military science. "It was religious. It was Wagnerian. It was theatrical. It should be judged as such."[17]

As disturbing as the attack itself—primarily a British operation, revenge for the carnage of the Blitz—was the fact that the American role was kept from the public back home. "It was a secret, burning down cities—boiling pisspots and flaming prams," Vonnegut wrote three decades after the war. It reassured people, as it does still today, to think of aerial warfare as a surgical procedure with minimum collateral damage. But it always looks different from the ground.

> There was all this hokum about the Norden bombsight. You'd see a newsreel showing a bombardier with an MP on either side of him holding a drawn .45. That sort of nonsense, and hell, all they were doing was just flying over cities, hundreds of airplanes, and dropping everything.

When Vonnegut came home he could find almost nothing about the Dresden attack in the official record or in the newspapers. Did it even happen?[18]

As the weak light of day faded, Billy and his fellow "moon men" came at last upon signs of life. At an inn nestled in a suburb, "on the edge of a desert," there was a desperate attempt to maintain the appearance of business as usual. Its staff "polished the glasses and wound the clocks and stirred the fires" in the fireplaces, "and waited and waited to see who would come." But the only patrons that evening were the American prisoners and their guards, who bedded down together in the straw of the stable. Thus the nativity verse that frames the book:

> *The cattle are lowing,*
> *The Baby awakes.*
> *But the little Lord Jesus*
> *No crying He makes.*

Not long after the crash of the chartered plane, middle-aged Billy snuck off to New York City, hoping to spread the Tralfamadorian gospel there on television. In the window of a Times Square adult bookstore he saw a stack of Kilgore Trout paperbacks, complete with the usual lurid cover art. One told of an Earthling man and woman kidnapped for an extraterrestrial zoo. As he stood at the register a magazine in the discount bin caught his eye, trumpeting the question *What really became of Montana Wildhack?* Billy smiled, knowing that she had not been killed by mobsters as the story alleged. Soon he was safely home on Tralfamadore. "Time-traveling again?" Montana asked sweetly as she nursed their child. Billy noticed the locket between her breasts, etched with the words of the serenity prayer.

There is no resolution to the story. Vonnegut begins the last chapter with a postcard from later in 1968. The country reels from the murders of Martin Luther King Jr. and Robert Kennedy, and "every day my Government gives me a count of corpses created by military science in Vietnam," all the more dubious a cause in the wake of the Tet Offensive. "So it goes." He describes his recent return to Germany, where, from the plane at night he imagined "dropping bombs on those lights, those villages and cities and towns." How did he and his traveling companion O'Hare make it from the war to their present comfortable circumstances? We can imagine the mordant smile in response. The journey was simply "*structured* that way." Like everyone else they were condemned to spend eternity unstuck in time, transported from youth to old age and back again, and they were still learning to make the best of it.

We journey one last time to the war, when Billy Pilgrim and his fellow POWs were deployed as "corpse miners" in the Dresden ruins. There was no telling what the next shovelful would turn up—"it was a terribly elaborate Easter egg hunt," Vonnegut once said elsewhere. They found people asphyxiated in subways and basements, like figures in a wax museum. Initially the bodies were carried to city parks, to be cremated in large communal pyres. As days passed the process had to be streamlined. The prisoners were made to harvest valuables before flamethrowers consumed the dead where they had been entombed.

"Somewhere in there the poor old high school teacher, Edgar Derby, was caught with a teapot he had taken from the catacombs. He was arrested for plundering. He was tried and shot. So it goes." Delivered with the flat concision of a dispatch for the Chicago City News Bureau, the episode encompasses the loss of bearings, the absurd disproportion and injustice, that always comes with war.

"And somewhere in there was springtime." One day Billy Pilgrim walked through an unlocked gate and into freedom. It was a moment to savor. Birdsong queried: "*Poo-tee-weet?*"

Vonnegut wrote his "famous Dresden book" as an exercise in catharsis, and also as an act of political engagement. In bringing to light the things he had seen and experienced, his endeavor was patriotic in the highest sense of that word. It is fair to say that *Slaughterhouse-Five* was more than an "anti-glacier" book. It had a real effect on the consciousness of people questioning our involvement in Vietnam and other foreign crusades. With Billy's adventures in mind, war could never look so glamorous again to its readers. Mary O'Hare must have been proud.

And in Edgar Derby we see the virtues of the ordinary Americans the author admired and celebrated his entire life, unbroken by the futility that engulfs him. With a few brush strokes, Derby is the heroic focus of the book—in his stewardship of his boys, his willingness to stand up to evil, his ability to find meaning in dehumanizing circumstances. In *becoming a character* he strikes a blow for dignity, autonomy, free will. Derby is the part of Kurt Vonnegut who never unlearned his junior civics lessons from PS 43 in Indianapolis, the expansive democratic dream he absorbed so innocently as a child during the Great Depression.

And yet it is all undercut by the tone of the narrative. Are good intentions and humane values *enough* in an absurd world? Vonnegut is doubtful. *Characters* get steamrollered all the time—Derby was shot, Dresden was destroyed. The author's ambivalence is captured perfectly in the phrase for which he today remains most identified. "So it goes" conveys a bone-deep sense of irony and resignation in the face of defeat—and a will, nonetheless, to carry on.

SEVEN

Breakfast of Champions,

or, *Goodbye Blue Monday!*

I have no culture, no humane harmony in my brains.
I can't live without a culture any more.
—from the Preface

Still wavin', man.
—Eddie Key

Everything changed for Kurt Vonnegut after *Slaughterhouse-Five*. A critical and commercial success, it lifted him almost overnight to iconic status. He was a celebrity profiled by *Life* and *60 Minutes* as America's most successful writer, a hip and rumpled guru who could explain members of the Woodstock generation to their parents. At forty-seven this child of the Great Depression was in the money—"fabulously well-to-do," he overheard a youngster say as he passed him on the street. It was a turn of fortune he welcomed but also had trouble trusting. And after years of struggling to be breadwinner for his children, the timing of the sudden prosperity had a "slightly mocking quality," as they were all in various stages of starting their own lives.[1]

In his recent memoir Mark Vonnegut gives us a sense of the new reality after the *Slaughterhouse-Five* breakthrough. His "impeccably dressed in

147

Brooks Brothers clothing father, increasingly recognized and recognizable," belonged to the world now, he realized as he entered his twenties, and "there was never enough Kurt to go around." Mark was surprised by his dad's admission toward the end of his life that he was "glad he had been able to restore the family fortune." It adds up, though, when we consider the side of the author who remembered the propriety and social standing of his forebears, and longed to heal the wounds fate had inflicted on his family. Not immune to the pull of Horatio Alger stories, he was a boy who grew up wanting to make his mother's impossible dreams come true, and when it finally happened it must have been deeply satisfying.[2]

The moment of redemption was accompanied by new turbulence in Vonnegut's private life, however. In 1970 Kurt and Jane separated after twenty-five years together, as he took up full-time residence in Manhattan. "Six children were children no more," he said of the loneliness he had been feeling in West Barnstable.

> It was a time of change, of good-bye and good-bye and good-bye.
> My big house was becoming a museum of vanished childhoods—
> of my vanished young manhood as well.... I was drinking more
> and arguing a lot, and I had to get out of that house.

Another family had disintegrated for him, and though it was his choice to leave, the loss was profound. Like a lot of couples, he and his wife "woke up in different ambulances, so to speak," he remembered in *Palm Sunday*.

> The shock of having our children no longer need us happened
> somewhere in there. We were both going to have to find other sorts
> of seemingly important work to do, other compelling reasons for
> working and worrying so.[3]

With a mixture of relief and guilt—and embarrassment about the reaction of some of his Indianapolis relatives to the split and eventual divorce, a rarity in the history of his clan—Vonnegut labored at the task of reinvention, pushing himself to exhaustion at times. Besides the demand for his services as a campus speaker and his involvement in the antiwar movement for which he was now a leading figure, he undertook a dangerous aid mission to Biafra and was elected vice-president of the international writers' human rights group, PEN. Vonnegut also returned to the academy, teaching creative writing at Harvard and later at City College of New York. Being *inside* had its appeal. He liked his time at Harvard, he wrote Mark, "because it gave him a chance to know people who were *at home in the world*." Vonnegut shelved a novel-in-progress, declaring that there would be no more books, and threw himself into the new family assembled to bring his play *Happy Birthday, Wanda June* to the stage at the Theatre de Lys off-Broadway in the fall of 1970. It was there that he became close to the accomplished photojournalist Jill Krementz, with whom he would soon be living. She was documenting the play's rehearsals, and the author was taken by her courage and adventurous spirit. Jill had spent time in Vietnam and other war zones, and had flown in a cockpit with the Israeli icon Ariel Sharon, a fact Vonnegut reported with awe to his friend and confidant from the Iowa City days, Loree Rackstraw.[4]

Through this period of change Vonnegut confessed to Rackstraw of suffering a kind of "postpartum depression." It was a natural letdown upon completing his war story, the task that had driven him for so many years. Now that the Dresden book was done, what, if anything, was next? "After I finished *Slaughterhouse-Five*," he told *Playboy* in 1973, "I didn't have to write at all anymore if I didn't want to."

> I suppose that flowers, when they're through blooming, have some sort of awareness of some purpose having been served. Flowers didn't ask to be flowers and I didn't ask to be me. . . . I had the feeling that I had produced this blossom. So I had a shutting-off feeling, you know, that I had done what I was supposed to do and everything was OK. And that was the end of it. I could figure out my missions for myself after that.[5]

The chaos in Vonnegut's personal life and the struggle to find a new direction is reflected in *Breakfast of Champions*, which appeared in bookstores after much delay in 1973. It is a commentary on the American Dream as the insurgent hopes of the sixties collapsed, a harrowing tour through the anomie the author saw in a country alienated from its own history, without a center of gravity, without a sense of its culture. People in the novel careen around deserts of parking lots, moving fast so they can avoid thinking about the blight that engulfs them. Isolated and driven by chemical reactions, they "swing off" interstate highway exits to destinations no more exalted or welcoming than hamburger chains and cinderblock motels. Private longings, joys, and disappointments lie deeply buried, making individuals appear to each other as robots, benumbed automatons. A sense of place, nourishing rituals, opportunities for human-scaled enterprise— these are all defunct, or headed rapidly in that direction. Corrupted speech clouds thinking at every turn, and conversation degenerates into monologue, clichés from the latest television commercials, empty sounds. Even the title and subtitle of the book are advertising slogans.

To more casual members of Vonnegut's burgeoning audience this darkly outrageous experiment came as a shock, both for its content and its intentionally vulgar style. Many found its directness on the issues of racism and sexuality particularly unpalatable. *Breakfast of Champions* documents a society (and perhaps a writer) in the process of a nervous breakdown. Its moments of brutality are meant to jolt the reader into seeing familiar things in new ways, questioning the most mundane words and gestures for the (often toxic) baggage they carry. Sad and angry as it is, however, Vonnegut's seventh novel is also invigorating, funny, and full of deftly choreographed burlesque. We cheer with recognition as he uses his machete to cut through the thicket of lies that strangle his characters. In the clearing we are relieved to breathe the fresh air, to find evidence of the dignity of the human spirit and the possibility of free will—even in a wasteland.

The preface to the book gives fair warning about what is to follow. Vonnegut dedicates the book to Phoebe Hurty, a fortyish widow he and his teenaged friends visited after school in the late 1930s. She wrote cleverly risqué ads for a downtown Indianapolis department store, and was a revelation in her brashness, quite unlike the other adults they knew. "She would talk bawdily to me and her sons, and to our girlfriends when we brought them around," Vonnegut remembers warmly. "She was funny. She was liberating. She taught us to be impolite in conversation not only about sexual matters, but about American history and famous heroes, about the distribution of wealth, about school, about everything."

"I now make my living by being impolite," Vonnegut observes. The attitude is in fashion after the assault on authority of the last decade, but it lacks the grace of before, the sense she exemplified, that defying convention might lend "shape" to an American paradise in the future. Today's bad manners are pure cynicism, an end in themselves. "I sure miss Phoebe Hurty."

The author explains the origins of his suspicion that human beings might be nothing more than machines, amalgamations of wires and gears controlled by chemicals. During his youth it was common to see syphilitic men crossing the street, backs rigid, kicking their legs out like chorus girls. Tiny corkscrews had insinuated themselves into their neurological equipment. Then there were the unfortunates with goiters, grotesquely inflamed thyroid glands, a condition later found to be remedied by small doses of iodine. Vonnegut reminds us that his mother "wrecked her brains with chemicals, which were supposed to make her sleep." And he alludes to the prescription drugs he used to address his bouts with depression, "postpartum" and otherwise. The implications of the power of the little pills to affect his mood were both liberating and disturbing. "I used to think I was responding to Attica or to the mining of the harbor of Haiphong," he told *Playboy*, only half tongue-in-cheek. "But I wasn't. I was obviously responding to internal chemistry."[6]

Vonnegut offers *Breakfast of Champions* as a fiftieth birthday present to himself, a project he is seemingly "programmed" to undertake to clear his head of "all the junk in there." He gives himself permission to write in childlike prose, explaining the most basic things from scratch. It is a distancing technique that makes America circa 1972 as exotic as the most far-flung galaxy. He punctuates the story with digressions and graffiti, primitive line drawings from a felt-tipped pen, and pledges to jettison anything superfluous—including the characters from his previous books. "No more puppet shows," he insists, a promise he will not be able to keep. "I think I am trying to make my head as empty as it was when I was born onto this damaged planet."

> The things other people have put into *my* head, at any rate, do not
> fit together nicely, are often useless and ugly, are out of proportion
> with one another, are out of proportion with life as it really is out-

side my head. I have no culture, no humane harmony in my brains. I can't live without a culture anymore.

Looking at his biography, we can say that Kurt Vonnegut actually lost *two* cultures in his lifetime—the European *Kultur* of his parents and grandparents, suppressed in the nativist fevers of World War I, and the world of buoyant civic optimism he learned in grade school during the Great Depression, the ideals embodied in *Slaughterhouse-Five*'s Edgar Derby—a dead letter, he feared, in the age of Watergate and the Vietnam War.

Breakfast of Champions builds over its pages to an intersection between "two lonesome, skinny, fairly old white men." As usual they represent different aspects of the author himself. Kilgore Trout, the angry, unreconciled *outsider*, is again the failed writer Vonnegut was on his way to becoming only a few years earlier. Dwayne Hoover, in contrast, appears to be the most conventional of men, a Pontiac dealer from Midland City, Ohio, a thinly disguised version of Vonnegut's hometown. Dwayne is an *insider*, admired and envied by his neighbors for living the American Dream in high style, but material abundance leaves him cold. He is losing a solitary battle with despair, descending inexorably into a madness no one else sees.

It is interesting in terms of the author's method to note that *Slaughterhouse-Five* and *Breakfast of Champions*, so different in tone and subject matter, were originally conceived by the author as a single book. The Billy Pilgrim and Dwayne Hoover alter egos are both middle-class "success stories," and Vonnegut, the onetime Saab salesman, thought about making Billy a car dealer. He explained his second thoughts in a 1980 interview:

> I realized the automobile business was so damned interesting, especially in a car-crazy country like America, that it would take over *Slaughterhouse-Five* sooner or later. It occurred to me that, no matter what I did, the very nature of the business would make the reader forget all about the World War II "portion" of the novel. So I deferred the automobile business to *Breakfast of Champions* and got Billy Pilgrim into optometry after the war. If you involve a character in optometry, you're giving him and the reader a good

deal of time for introspection—and both Billy and the reader needed that time in *Slaughterhouse-Five.*⁷

Vonnegut establishes the context for the Trout/Hoover showdown with a decidedly impolite history of the United States. Like a grade-school primer with doodles scrawled in the margins, it deconstructs much of the iconography put into his head when he was a boy. Edgar Derby would, no doubt, be offended. In this account the words of the national anthem amounted to "pure balderdash," a snatch of "gibberish sprinkled with question marks." The flag was attractive enough as an object, but laws exempting it from being lowered in parades betrayed an unseemly arrogance born of insecurity. And the motto on the currency, *E pluribus unum,* declared a unity of purpose that never existed, in a language no longer spoken. Its masonic imagery was an indulgence in the "baroque trash" that preoccupied the founders, aristocrats anxious to "show off their useless educations."

The symbols were empty for most people, but they were not the harmless *foma* of *Cat's Cradle*—they concealed great crimes. The number 1492, for example, marked not the discovery of the continent but "the year in which sea pirates began to cheat and rob and kill" the millions of inhabitants already here. They used human beings for machinery. "Color was everything," with consequences that reverberated still. How did the invaders become so dominant? Superior technology had something to do with it, but even more important was their "capacity to astonish." "Nobody else could believe, until it was much too late, how heartless and greedy they were."

The tradition continued. In this country, as Eliot Rosewater's ancestors knew, everyone "was supposed to grab whatever he could and hold onto it." Dwayne Hoover was good at the game. Kilgore Trout, like so many others, was terrible at it. The share of the planet he owned added up to "doodley-squat."

Trout rents a basement apartment in Cohoes, New York, eking out a living installing aluminum storm doors and windows. His lone companion is a parakeet named Bill, to whom he harangues daily about mankind's willful stupidity and imminent, well-deserved demise. Trout lacks *charm,* that essential ingredient for success in America that involved "making strangers like and trust a person immediately, no matter what the charmer had in mind."

As we know, Trout is a prolific storyteller, but he has never found a reputable publisher for his science-fiction fables. Instead they provide bulk for increasingly graphic pornography—"beaver books," in the vernacular of the street. Since Kilgore Trout and Dwayne Hoover and Kurt Vonnegut had been little boys, knowledge of the parts of the female anatomy to which the vulgarity referred, "ten thousand times as common as real beavers," had been designated "the most massively defended secret under law." When he accepted the 1979 Nobel Prize for Medicine, Trout would observe that the madness for images of that forbidden sight, like the mania of the old sea pirates for gold, revealed the susceptibility of his species to bad ideas. "I thank those lusts for being so ridiculous," he would tell his Stockholm audience, "for they taught us that it was possible for a human being to believe anything, and to behave passionately in keeping with that belief—*any* belief."

In *Palm Sunday* Vonnegut lamented the fact that many of his relatives back in Indiana stopped reading him once he began to traffic in what they considered to be obscenity. But the sketches of vaginas and underpants and even his own asshole in *Breakfast of Champions* did not, he insisted, represent the rebellion of "a small boy sticking out his tongue at the teacher," as a critic for *Indianapolis Magazine* complained. The author's bad manners were an effort "to make the Americans in my books talk as Americans really do talk," as well as to shine a light on things concealed and repressed in our taboo-ridden culture, he insisted. "Even when I was in grammar school," Vonnegut wrote, "I suspected that warnings about words that nice people never used were in fact lessons in how to keep our mouths shut not just about our bodies, but about many, many things—perhaps too many things." In Queen Victoria's time, rules of taste forbade mention of the exploitation of the Irish or the coming of the world war; today it was Indochina and racism and prisons and the inequality of wealth.[8]

Trout prizes his invisibility, and is not happy when it is disrupted one day by a piece of fan mail filled with childish praise of his work. The letter is from Eliot Rosewater, the philanthropist dedicated to getting his hero recognized as the greatest living American novelist. "Keep the hell out of my body bag," Trout snaps at this invasion of his privacy, referring to the plastic envelope for corpse disposal newly invented during the Vietnam War. Soon another letter arrives, this one inviting him to an arts festival in Midland City, Ohio. Examining the enclosed honorarium check, he wonders if it is a joke.

After a few days Trout decides to teach the philistines in the provinces a lesson. "They don't want anybody but smilers out there," he tells Bill. "But maybe an unhappy failure is exactly what they *need* to see." He would show up all right, wearing the moth-eaten tuxedo he keeps in a steamer trunk, as "a representative of all the thousands of artists who devoted their entire lives to a search for truth and beauty—and didn't find doodley-squat!" Vonnegut relishes his character's subversive mission. It expresses his own ambivalence about success and the need to be charming, his unease about the expectations of his new, mainstream audience.

In Midland City, meanwhile, imbalances in Dwayne Hoover's neurochemistry affect his thoughts and actions in progressively bizarre ways. In this book, as Vonnegut told *Playboy*, "we don't give a shit about the characters' childhoods or about what happened yesterday—we just want to know what the state of their bloodstreams is." Dwayne sees eleven moons over the illuminated sphere of the new Mildred Barry Arts Center one night. His behavior in public remains within acceptable bounds, however, and hardly anyone sees his breakdown coming. This was not unusual in America, where speech and gesture were mostly rote, the chaos of private lives carefully hidden from view. Midland City is a sprawling, updated Winesburg, Ohio, in this respect. Vonnegut captures the thinness of community in such a world:

> It didn't matter much what Dwayne said. It hadn't mattered much for years. It didn't matter much what most people in Midland City said out loud, except when they were talking about money or structures or travel or machinery—or other measurable things. Every person had a clearly defined part to play. . . . If [they] stopped living up to expectations, because of bad chemicals or one thing or another, everybody went on imagining that the person was living up to expectations anyway.[9]

At Dwayne Hoover's Exit Eleven Pontiac Village—a Potemkin Village if there ever was one—business carries on as usual even as Dwayne's connections to reality deteriorate. He whistles and sings to himself, cheerful, reassuring sounds, as he passes through the new car showroom and across the parking lot to the lobby of his new Holiday Inn. "If I owned what he owns, I'd sing, too," an employee at the motel restaurant comments one day. Francine Pefko, Dwayne's secretary, considers him happier than he has been in a long time. "I kept thinking," she tells a reporter from her hospital bed after his rampage, "he is finally getting over his wife's suicide."

Harry LaSabre, the square, insecure sales manager, is the only person at work troubled by changes in his boss. He has worked for Dwayne since before the operation moved from the advancing edge of "the Nigger part of town" decades earlier. (In the parlance of many white Midland City residents, "a Nigger was a human being who was black," the narrator explains, as though viewing the scene from outer space.) But lately Harry has been singled out for abuse. Dwayne lights into him for his monochromatic suits and mortician's demeanor, hardly conducive to selling products promising customers a glamorous, youthful adventure. He orders Harry to come in after the holiday weekend with an ensemble in keeping with the Hawaiian Week promotion about to begin. Harry wonders if Dwayne suspects that he is a closeted transvestite. Harry does not want to end up in the sexual offenders' wing at Shepherdstown correctional facility as a result of his hobby.

Dwayne goes through a rough patch at home that night. Sleepless and agitated, he takes out the revolver he keeps under his pillow and sticks it in his mouth. He changes his mind just before squeezing the trigger, shooting up tiles in the bathroom instead. Nobody in the hermetically sealed neighborhood hears the noise. He gets the Plymouth Fury he had taken in trade that day out of the garage and goes for a drive, bouncing on and off the interstate until sliding to a stop in a vacant lot.

"Suicide is at the heart of the book," Kurt Vonnegut told *Playboy* of *Breakfast of Champions*. "It's also the punctuation mark at the end of many artistic careers. I pick up that punctuation mark and play with it in the book, come to understand it better, put it back on the shelf again but leave it in view." We can see in Dwayne Hoover's crisis the author's deepest fears as he negotiated his post-*Slaughterhouse* life.[10]

Dwayne ends up on the roof of his Holiday Inn, looking out over the pre-dawn city. He was born there, and now owns an extraordinary share of its properties—three Burger Chefs, five car washes, pieces of a drive-in theatre, and a par-three golf course. But he feels only the displacement that afflicts so many of Vonnegut's characters. As an adult, a question always dogged Vonnegut as he checked into whatever anonymous accommodation had been arranged on his visits to Indianapolis: "Where is my bed?" Here, now, is Dwayne Hoover, asking: "Where am I?"[11]

Hundreds of miles away, Kilgore Trout is readying himself to be the beggar at the banquet at the arts festival. His first task is a reconnaissance trip to Manhattan to unearth samples of his work in the derelict establishments of Times Square. Sandwiched between covers promising "Wide-Open Beavers" he finds a number of his stories, including *Now It Can Be Told,* the one with the ideas that would be so toxic to Dwayne's diseased mind.

In the evening Trout dozes in a theater showing blue movies. He has gone there mainly for effect—it was the kind of thing dirty old men did, and "he wished to arrive in Midland City as the dirtiest of all old men." Bored in the darkness he conjures a story about what pornography might look like on a planet where the food supply has been exhausted. Crowds flock to watch images of humanoids eating meat, fresh fruit, cake, and pie—all fake, of course. The audience goes wild at the climax, when in tight focus the overstuffed diners dump their leftovers into a garbage can. It is the kind of dream hungry Billy Pilgrim might have had in the prison camp.

Trout emerges onto Forty-Second Street suddenly aware of how risky it is to be there at that hour. "The whole city was dangerous, because of chemicals and the uneven distribution of wealth and so on." Oppressed by squalor, people who live in the area ingest drugs in a doomed but very human effort "to make their insides beautiful." Trout has a sense he is being followed, and the next thing he remembers is sitting under the Queensboro Bridge, battered and slightly bleeding. Who were the assailants? "For all I know," he tells the police, "that car may have been occupied by intelligent gas from Pluto."

This throwaway line demonstrates the power of ideas to spread like a virus. Once they are out there, as *Mother Night* teaches us, there is no controlling them. Tabloids pick up the story about the depredations of the Pluto Gang, and New Yorkers have a focus for their perpetual fears. A band of Puerto Rican youths adopt the name, hoping to convey ferocity to the predators besieging their neighborhood.

Trout is ready now to begin his pilgrimage west. He hitches a ride at the mouth of the Lincoln Tunnel, in a truck pulling a load of Spanish olives. The scenery is not inspiring, to say the least. First are the poisoned marshes of New Jersey, then a bridge shrouded in smoke, named for Walt Whitman. Soon Trout finds himself rolling through West Virginia, its landscape denuded by strip mining. It is startling to think how fast the destruction has taken place during the rush to transform coal into energy. "Now the heat was all gone, too—into outer space," Trout supposes. "It had boiled water, made steel windmills whiz around and around. America was jazzed with electricity for awhile."

Trout is forced into banter with the driver, an amateur philosopher hungry for companionship. As they talk about storm windows and aluminum siding, the driver seems disappointed that his passenger does not try to make his life sound more interesting than it is. "All the same," he says, pressing for a better story, "you've got buddies you see after work. You have a few beers. You play some cards. You have some laughs." These are things the driver, whose name Trout cannot remember, misses in his wanderings on the interstate.

The awkwardness of the interaction is an example of the difficulty of communicating in a world of random, superficial encounters. The signs lining the road do not help, all of them manipulations to charm strangers, to get them to "buy or sell some damn thing." Vonnegut delivers his semiotics lesson in the plainest language possible. Trout is struck by the paradox of "Pyramid Trucking Company," the logo on the side of the vehicle. Why *Pyramid*, he asks, for a business specializing in high-speed transportation? Because, the driver explains with rising impatience, his brother-in-law "liked the *sound* of it."

As they continue through the hills and hollows, the mailboxes in one area all seem to bear the name "Hoobler." This was once the home of the family that adopted Dwayne. They changed their name to "Hoover" after arriving in Midland City. "It was embarrassing," Dwayne's stepfather once explained to him. "Everybody up here naturally assumed Hoobler was a *Nigger* name."

After a few hours sleep Dwayne emerges from his motel room relaxed and refreshed. He orders the Number Five Breakfast at the lounge, the Tally-Ho Room, and everything outside the large windows looks reassuringly familiar in the light of day—the six-lane interstate, the concrete channel built to contain polluted Sugar Creek, the white sphere of the new Mildred Barry Arts Center. A flat expanse of farmland, perhaps the future site for a strip mall or tract housing, stretches off into infinity. It feels like we are back in Rosewater County, Indiana.

As Dwayne walks across the parking lot, however, it dips elastically with each step. He manages his way to the used car lot, where a young black man burnishes a Buick Skylark with a rag. Freshly paroled from Shepherdstown, Wayne Hoobler is there to apply for a job with the father figure he knew from the radio ads that circulated all the time in the prison. ASK ANYBODY, they proclaimed in confident tones, YOU CAN TRUST DWAYNE. Innocent of life outside institutional walls, Wayne took the statement at its word. The prospect of joining Dwayne's family has become the one purpose in his life, a way out of the cycle of being "put in cages all the time." "Our names are so close," he pleads as Dwayne brushes past him.

In the showroom the ground solidifies again, but the surreality continues. Dwayne has forgotten all about Hawaiian Week and does not know what to make of the palm trees set up for the occasion, let alone the sight of Harry LaSabre greeting him in a grass skirt. Dwayne keeps walking, leaving another disappointed soul in his wake.

Later he drives to one of his Burger Chef franchises for lunch, across from the John F. Kennedy High School. "Presidents of the country were often shot to death," the narrator adds darkly. "The assassins were confused by some of the same bad chemicals which troubled Dwayne." Listening to the car radio, he begins mechanically repeating the last words of each sentence—a pure, soothing *sound*.

Patty Keene, the teenager who took Dwayne's order, is in awe of the power she knows Dwayne possesses to lift her out of her hard life, as the "Blue Fairy Godmother" did for Cinderella. She feels sorry for him, too. It is common knowledge that his wife Celia had killed herself in the most ghastly manner, ingesting Drano, the everyday remedy for clogged plumbing. Patty thinks her "brand-newness" could heal Dwayne's middle-aged angst, and tries to engage him in conversation. But she is too nervous and self-conscious to get through, too embarrassed about her language skills to be assertive. "Patty Keene was stupid on purpose," like a lot of women in town, aware that any unusual ideas their big brains produced might attract enemies. "So, in the interests of survival, they trained themselves to be agreeing machines instead of thinking machines."

As Dwayne absent-mindedly makes his way back to work, Vonnegut parodies the American obsession with measurement, quantification, comparison. Characters are reduced to numbers, and things are described with bloodless precision, from the size of male sex organs to the value of life insurance policies. Statistics diminish everyone, as advertisers know so well.

Dwayne passes by the most imposing structure in the relentless horizontality of Midland City: an obelisk in Calvary Cemetery topped by a marble football, erected to honor a high school athlete who died in a game back in 1924. No one remembers him now—his relatives moved away years ago and the movie theatre that once bore the family name has become a cut-rate furniture store. "It was a very restless country, with people tearing around all the time. Every so often, somebody would stop to put up a monument."

Back at the dealership Dwayne looks for something to divert his racing mind. In an office drawer he comes across a pornographic brochure, which sets in motion another round of chemical chain-reactions. He phones Francine at her desk, and they arrange to meet at their usual motel outside Shepherdstown.

Francine is a generous, voluptuous woman, one of Vonnegut's mother figures. Her husband's remains were recently returned from Vietnam in a body bag. She tries to relax Dwayne with idle conversation—looking out from their room across Route 103, she wonders if the empty land near the adult correctional center might not be a good location for a fast-food outlet. Dwayne winces at the suggestion, then lets loose a torrent of paranoia, delivered, for all of its heat, in the practical language of the Midwest.

> He told her that every woman was a whore, and every whore had her price, and Francine's price was what a Colonel Sanders Kentucky Fried Chicken franchise would cost, which would be well over one hundred thousand dollars by the time adequate parking and exterior lighting and all that was taken into consideration, and so on.

An agreeing machine, Francine tearfully protests her good intentions. Most of the inmates at the prison are black, and, she figures, the relatives who come to visit them would be natural customers for such a restaurant. "So you want me to open a Nigger joint?" Dwayne snarls, channeling his racist stepfather. Harry LaSabre was right, Francine cries—Dwayne *has* changed. "Maybe it was time!" he replies with defiance. "I never felt better in my life!"

He downshifts fast, from aggression to childlike dependency. "I'm so confused," he sobs in Francine's arms. "Tell me what life is all about." Maybe God is using him like the prototypes in "destructive testing" he had observed at Pontiac headquarters.

> I've lost my way. I need somebody to take me by the hand and lead me out of the woods. I want to hear new things from new people. I've heard everything anybody in Midland City ever said, ever *will* say. It's got to be somebody new.

Francine risks another suggestion. Maybe someone at the arts festival has the ideas he is seeking.

Night falls in Midland City as "Bunny" Hoover, Dwayne's estranged son, prepares to go to his job at the keyboard of the Holiday Inn's cocktail lounge, the Tally-Ho Room. He rents a room at the once-grand Fairchild Hotel, a long-neglected structure in the poorest section of downtown. Bunny has not spoken to Dwayne for years, ever since being shipped off to a military academy. An exemplary cadet, he was still gay, and could never become a man in his father's eyes. Bunny was loyal to his mother, despite the fact that she became "crazy as a bedbug" on her journey into self-destruction. Bad chemicals were to blame. Vonnegut gets personal here.

> Listen: Bunny's mother and my mother were different sorts of human beings, but they were both beautiful in exotic ways, and they both boiled over with chaotic talk about love and peace and wars and evil and desperation, of better days coming by and by, of worse days coming by and by. And both our mothers committed suicide. Bunny's mother ate Drano. My mother ate sleeping pills, which wasn't nearly as horrible.

Leaving his room Bunny pauses in front of the mirror, as he always does, uttering the mantra he learned at boarding school: "Can do." It has a comforting ring to it.

In the Tally-Ho Room Dwayne Hoover sits before his martini, presented with a flourish by the waitress as the "Breakfast of Champions." He is lost in thought, waiting for the out-of-town festival guests to arrive. Francine Pefko is back at the dealership, catching up on the lost afternoon's paperwork. Bunny goes about his craft at the piano, filling the room with a tinkling, soothing quality evocative of the music boxes his mother used to collect. The sounds have attracted troubled souls from all over. It is an outlet for Bunny to communicate his joy and pain, and people appreciate the human feeling behind it. This is *not* a player piano.

Wayne Hoobler, meanwhile, remains on the used car lot, sounding out letters on the signs and talking to the rush hour traffic "sizzling" by on the interstate. He is lonely and misses the security of prison, brutal as it was, and wonders, without really minding, if he might die of exposure that night. Eldon Robbins, a dishwasher and fellow Shepherdstown alum, brings Wayne into the kitchen of the cocktail lounge for a meal. Motioning to a peephole into the Tally-Ho Room, he invites his guest to "watch the animals in the zoo."

Like a stage set, almost everything is in place for the meeting of the protagonists. But Kilgore Trout is still on the interstate, in a Ford Galaxie just short of Dwayne's Exit Eleven Pontiac Village, waiting for an accident to clear. Vonnegut takes the opportunity of the delay to insert himself as a character, seated in a darkened corner of the lounge, incognito behind sunglasses. It is the kind of authorial intrusion he has been heading toward for a long time.

As he washes down one of his mood-management pills with a second drink, the waitress inquires if the author can see anything through those mirrored lenses. "The big show is inside my head," he responds, wondering if perhaps *he* is the one going crazy. The frontier separating his midlife crisis from Dwayne's is blurring. This far into the narrative he is full of ambivalence about its quality, unclear how things are going to turn out. Even *he* is open to surprise.

One thing Vonnegut knows is that he does not want to add to the already overflowing pool of bad ideas warping people's sense of reality. Other books, movies, and TV shows have already done that, and he is not interested in contributing to the problem. They imposed a false order on things, fostering the illusion that "life has leading characters, minor characters, significant details, that it had lessons to be learned, tests to be passed, and a beginning, a middle, and an end."

As I approached my fiftieth birthday, I had become more and more enraged and mystified by the idiot decisions made by my country-men. And then I had come suddenly to pity them, for I understood how innocent and natural it was for them to behave so abominably, and with such abominable results: They were doing their best to live like people invented in story books.

Vonnegut resolves to avoid using the tricks of his trade to mold this work into coherence. He would insist on the truth that "there is no order in the world around us, that we must adapt ourselves to the requirements of chaos instead." Perhaps he should just quit now: the best ending for a tale about a person on Earth might simply be "... and so on," or "etc.," the abbreviation for "sameness without end." It was better, certainly—if less efficient—than the gunshots lazy writers so often used to punctuate their creations.

Two of the festival's featured guests now enter the lounge. The writer Beatrice Keedsler grew up in Midland City, and with her is Rabo Karabekian, the celebrated abstract painter from New York. "This *has* to be the asshole of the Universe," Rabo remarks loudly as they make their way to Bunny's piano. Clad in an appropriately bohemian sweatshirt, Rabo has even more reason than usual for self-regard that night, after closing on the sale of his latest piece to the Mildred Barry Center for the Arts. An oversized canvas of green wall paint adorned with a strip of Day-Glo orange tape, mystifyingly titled *The Temptation of Saint Anthony*, the artwork commanded a sum of money that raised eyebrows all around town.

Rabo drips with sarcasm as he engages the waitress in conversation. "This distinguished lady," he informs Bonnie MacMahon, pointing to his drinking companion, "is a famous storyteller, and also a native of this railroad junction. Perhaps you could tell her some recent true stories about her birthplace." A smiling machine at work, Bonnie does not catch the condescension and begins sharing details about the local scene. Her uniform—a get-up that could have been designed by Howard W. Campbell Jr., with its cowboy boots and sequined leotard, pink cotton attached to its rear—glows as she speaks. Ultraviolet lights in the ceiling activate the leotard's fluorescent chemicals, a bit of otherworldly ambience alternating at the bartender's flick of a switch.

Vonnegut's parody is so acute here because he had observed with the sharp eye of an anthropologist the decorum and protocols of arts festivals in the hinterlands many times himself during the lean years. This same world appears in his earlier writing, when Eliot Rosewater visits a science-fiction convention in Milford, Pennsylvania, for example, and in the author's description for the *New York Times Book Review* of a writers' conference he attended in the 1960s in Macomb, Illinois, sponsored by the local state university (reprinted in *Wampeters, Foma & Granfalloons*). To avoid a campus prohibition against alcohol, a party to get acquainted was held at the Travelodge Motel, "between the Coin-A-Wash and the A & W Rootbeer Stand." Vonnegut empathized with the earnest junior instructor in charge of the event who, "above the Muzak and the sounds of drag races out on Route 136," apologized for the sparse turnout. In some ways the author was more comfortable at these functions than he was at Harvard or the hallowed halls of the American Academy of the Arts and Letters, where he was inducted in 1972.[12]

Rabo begs for more from the waitress. Who is the girl on the cover of the festival program? Bonnie beams with the pride everyone feels about Mary Alice Miller, recounting the regimen she had maintained for years, under her father's guidance, to become women's two-hundred-meter breaststroke champion of the world. "What kind of a man," Rabo replies with mock credulity, "would turn his daughter into an outboard motor?"

He has a point—people treat their loved ones like machines all the time. But this is meant as a provocation, and it triggers "the spiritual climax" of the book, Vonnegut tells us, a tectonic shift in the way he sees the world. "I did not expect Rabo Karabekian to rescue me. I had created him, and he was in my opinion a vain and weak and trashy man, no artist at all. But it is Rabo Karabekian who made me the serene Earthling which I am this day." Bonnie MacMahon explodes in unfiltered rage, telling Rabo that he ought to be ashamed of stealing money for his ludicrous painting. Her judgment receives hearty support from the other patrons in the lounge. Rabo has crossed a line, tapping into a fear that, beneath all the boosterism, their lives might be ridiculous.

Instead of slinking off in defeat, however, Rabo stands and faces the mob, delivering the speech of his life, a defense of his *Temptation of Saint Anthony* in all its minimalist glory. "I now give you my word of honor," he declares with a thespian's solemnity, "that the picture your city owns shows everything about life which truly matters, with nothing left out."

> It is the immaterial core of every animal—the "I am" to which all messages are sent. It is all that is alive in any of us—in a mouse, in a deer, in a cocktail waitress. It is unwavering and pure, no matter what preposterous adventure may befall us. A sacred picture of Saint Anthony alone is one vertical, unwavering band of light. If a cockroach were near him, or a cocktail waitress, the picture would show two such bands of light. Our awareness is all that is alive and maybe sacred in any of us. Everything else about us is dead machinery.

Rabo's band of light manifesto draws enthusiastic applause. Maybe it was heartfelt, maybe just self-serving *foma*, but in either case his Creator was sold. Unfortunately, Dwayne Hoover, seated nearby, is too immersed in his own ruminations to hear a message that might have saved him.

Kilgore Trout abandons the Galaxie and starts toward Exit Eleven Pontiac Village on foot. As he trudges across the concrete ditch of Sugar Creek, a mysterious plastic substance hardens around his feet. It is waste from the local defense contractor, Barrytron, a byproduct of the antipersonnel bomb it was making for the Air Force.

At the registration desk Trout presents himself as a wretched abominable snowman, but is deflated to learn that the clerk is one of his few fans. Soon he enters the Tally-Ho Room in his baggy tux, feet still encased in plastic, making his way to the table between his Creator and Dwayne Hoover. Dwayne mumbles to himself an advertising slogan for a washing machine he remembers from the Midland City of his youth: "Goodbye, Blue Monday." On the table in front of Trout sits the dog-eared copy of *Now It Can Be Told*.

"As three unwavering bands of light, we were simple and separate and beautiful," Vonnegut observes, reveling in the triangulation he has set up, the effects of the alcohol and the prescription drugs taking effect. "As machines, we were flabby bags of ancient plumbing and wiring, of rusty hinges and feeble springs." Noticing the neon glow, Trout wonders what is going on. "Like most science-fiction writers, he knew almost nothing about science."

The light reflecting from his ruffled blouse lands in Dwayne Hoover's eyes, rousing him from his catatonia. "Give me the message," Dwayne demands as he crashes down next to Trout, chin thrust into his shoulder. Is it in the book? To relieve his discomfort, Trout nods blankly that it is. The story is in the form of a letter from the Creator of the Universe, and Dwayne takes it in as though intended solely for him. "Dear Sir, poor sir, brave sir," it begins, "You are the only creature in the entire Universe who has free will." Everyone else he has encountered in his life, indeed every other person who ever lived, was an unfeeling machine designed to elicit his reactions. It is a narcissist's dream, the key unlocking so many of the mysteries that haunt Dwayne. His parents had been *built* to be fighting machines and self-pitying machines, he now realizes, to gauge the effects on his development growing up. His mother would berate her husband for being a defective money-making machine, and his father was programmed, in turn, to yell at her for being an inadequate housekeeping machine. For purposes of destructive testing, they were paired to behave as defective loving machines.

Now It Can Be Told is vindication for Dwayne Hoover. His path of destruction—there would be eleven victims in all, detailed in the newspaper the next day with dotted lines on a map—begins with his son Bunny. Dwayne laughs as he approaches the piano, calling Bunny "a God damn cock-sucking machine." Next he breaks Beatrice Keedsler's jaw and punches Bonnie MacMahon in the stomach, believing their reactions to be fake. "All you robots want to know why my wife ate Drano?" he asks the stunned onlookers. "I'll tell you why: She was that kind of machine!"

Dwayne exits the lounge looking for more targets. Wayne Hoobler leaps to the safety of a truck bed as his assailant rants on about his efforts to help black robots, many of whom were designed in advance to be ungrateful. Then the madman drags Francine out of the dealership office to avenge what he imagines to be her fully programmed faithlessness. "Best fucking machine in the State," he tells the gathering crowd. "Wind her up, and she'll fuck you and say she loves you, and she won't shut up till you give her a Colonel Sanders Kentucky Fried Chicken franchise."

Dwayne now marches into the oceanic roar of the interstate, to a median between the cars and trucks whizzing past, where he finally is brought down and put into a straitjacket. "Goodbye, Blue Monday!" he shouts to his puzzled victims as they ride together to the emergency room. He likes the sound of it. Kilgore Trout is among the wounded, the tip of his finger having been bitten off during the melee. (Even Vonnegut sustained some minor damage.) Dr. Cyprian Ukwende is on duty in the back of the ambulance bus, while in the driver's seat is Eddie Key, a young black man descended from the composer of the national anthem.

Like Ukwende and his relatives back in Nigeria, Eddie has extensive knowledge of his family tree. In the manner of a griot, he could name hundreds of ancestors of various races, with an anecdote about each. Eddie believes he is the eyes and ears of his forebears, which include some of Wayne Hoobler's kin. He quietly acknowledges his most famous relative whenever he sees the American flag: "Still wavin', man."

For Eddie, the Edgar Derby of *Breakfast of Champions*, the iconography of the country is still an inspiration, not a collection of meaningless words, dead slogans, empty sounds. His connection to a living past makes him healthier and more human than Dwayne Hoover or Kilgore Trout, or the author.

> We had no sense of anybody else using our eyes—or our hands. We didn't even know who our great-grandfathers and great-grandmothers were. Eddie Key was afloat in a river of people, who were flowing from here to there in time. Dwayne and Trout and I were pebbles at rest.

After his crack-up Dwayne finds himself more disconnected than ever, "one more withered balloon of an old man" on downtown's Skid Row. "See him?" people say, pointing as they drive by. "Can you believe it? He doesn't have doodley-squat now, but he used to be fabulously well-to-do." With his memories of the Great Depression, Vonnegut knew it was not out of the question for him to meet the same fate.

The epilogue finds Kilgore Trout emerging from the basement of the Midland City hospital, beginning the long hike toward the Mildred Barry

Center for the Arts. He does not know that the festival has been cancelled.

Trout's Creator sits waiting for him in a rented Plymouth Duster, on a stretch of shuttered factories and warehouses along Fairchild Avenue. The life has been drained out of the area by the highways, including the new Robert F. Kennedy Inner Belt Expressway, constructed over the right-of-way of a long-defunct railroad line. Vonnegut gets out of the car and, puffing on his Pall Malls, pauses to consider the old Keedsler mansion, where the World War I flying ace Will Fairchild had gone on a killing spree back in 1926. It reminds him of the dream homes his grandfather had designed for Hoosier millionaires in Indianapolis, now all "mortuaries and guitar schools and cellar holes and parking lots."

Kazak, the Doberman from *Sirens of Titan,* now programmed to be an attacking machine, hurls himself violently against a chain-link fence. From a distance Trout sees yet another astonishing sight in what has already been a long, bewildering day. His bloodstream flooded with adrenaline, Vonnegut leaps over an automobile to evade the animal's lunge. "Are you from the Arts Festival?" Trout asks, terrified, as his Creator catches up with him in his car. "I am from the *Everything* Festival," the stranger replies, assuring him of better days ahead. Like Tolstoy and Jefferson he is freeing his serfs, the characters from his books, to pursue their own destinies. It is an act of cleansing, and another rebellion against the expectations of the audience. Vonnegut holds out an apple, like the one Adam had eaten back in Eden, "a richly-colored and three-dimensional and juicy" symbol of the kind for which Americans hungered. Trout's Creator offers it as a prayer that together they might all create "wholeness and inner harmony" out of their broken lives.

Breakfast of Champions signals Vonnegut's turn to the aggressively autobiographical approach of his later works, a decision to foreground from now on the contours of his turbulent interior life. "I want to get into more intimate matters," he told an interviewer in the wake of the success of *Slaughterhouse-Five.* "I want to go on more of an ego trip now that I'm free to do it." Despite strong sales—it became an immediate number-one bestseller and was a selection for the Literary Guild and other major book clubs—not everyone was prepared for the ride, and the novel took a bashing among critics. One famously described it as the work of a "writer in trouble," another wondered if it was "in some buried way, a calculated insult" to his readers. Vonnegut himself was not that pleased with the results, despite his usual painstaking care in putting it all together. The idea of a film version to be directed by Robert Altman, on the heels of George Roy Hill's acclaimed adaptation of *Slaughterhouse-Five*, never materialized, and the uneven quality of the later project by Alan Rudolph (1999) is a testimony to the challenges of bringing this material to the screen.[13]

But *Breakfast of Champions*, at once one of Vonnegut's most beloved and most controversial enterprises, remains fresh today thanks to its outrageousness and relentless honesty about an author and a culture in crisis, the dangers of closed eyes and the debased language of advertising. It is a bravely public effort, as he said at the time, to "[make] peace with certain things that happened to me during the breakfast of my life," and in its way the book winds up on an affirmative, if highly unresolved, note. The abbreviation *ETC.*, accompanied by a self-portrait with a tear in the eye, as he imagined encountering his dead parents in the void, ends the book and indicates the depth of the issues involved. An earlier version of the book had Vonnegut winding up in an asylum with Dwayne Hoover. According to Jerome Klinkowitz, Vonnegut changed it when the courier taking his manuscript pages to Delacorte Press complained that he did not think it fit. Suicide, another convenient and time-tested device to end stories, is off the table for Vonnegut, no longer an option, he assured his *Playboy* interviewer.[14]

"One thing writing *Breakfast* did for me," Vonnegut concluded in retrospect, "was to bring right to the surface my anger with my parents for not being happier than they were. . . . I'm damned if I'll pass their useless sadness on to my children if I can possibly help it." Rabo's epiphany in the Tally-Ho Room about the awareness that makes human life worth living is often lost amid the book's downbeat, riotous satire. In those *unwavering bands of light* hope survives, and the author's unburdening process opens a whole repertoire of unexpected new possibilities. "I think my wind is still good enough for me to go chasing after happiness," Vonnegut told *Playboy* as he looked forward—"something I've never really tried."[15]

EIGHT

Slapstick,

or, *Lonesome No More!*

We need all the relatives we can get in a country
as big and clumsy as ours.
—Dr. Wilbur Daffodil-11 Swain

Kurt Vonnegut's sister, Alice, died from cancer in 1958, at the age of forty-one. The blow was so grievous that it would take him nearly eighteen years to channel his grief over her unfinished life into novelistic form, in *Slapstick* (1976).

Allie was Vonnegut's closest companion growing up, and he often acknowledged the inspiration of her mordant humor and artistic bent on his own sensibility. It was a source of frustration to him that she was careless in the stewardship of her own creativity. "I bawled her out one time for not doing more with the talents she had," Vonnegut recalled in an interview. "She replied that having talent doesn't carry with it the obligation that something has to be done with it. This was startling news to me. I thought people were supposed to grab their talents and run as far and fast as they could."[1]

Slapstick, the word Allie whispered to her brothers, Bernie and Kurt, as she lay dying in a hospital bed, was her protest against melodrama, her stoic refusal to think of life's tribulations as anything other than "accidents in a very busy place." It resonates with the affection she shared with them for the newspaper aphorisms of Kin Hubbard, a "Hoosier Oscar Wilde," and the movie and radio comedians of the 1930s who modeled such humanity in the face of recurring defeats—Jack Benny, Fred Allen, and Fibber McGee and Molly. "You got your little dose of humor every day," Vonnegut remembered, and the medicine was delivered with a charming innocence. "Man is not evil, they seem to say," he wrote in a 1975 foreword to *Write If You Get Work: The Best of Bob & Ray*. "He is simply too hilariously stupid to survive."[2]

"Exhaustion, yes, and deep money worries, too, made her say toward the end that she guessed that she wasn't really very good at life," Vonnegut tells us of his beloved sister. "Then again: Neither were Laurel and Hardy." In the "grotesque situational comedy" we all face every day, Stan and Ollie— to whom *Slapstick* is dedicated—taught the dignity of persistence, the importance of always "bargaining in good faith with destiny."

With this novel Vonnegut for the first time dropped the "Jr." from his name, an act of "Freudian cannibalism" he did not take lightly. Almost twenty years after his father's death it was time to move on, to act out another signifier of manhood. He was established now in Manhattan, sharing with his partner, Jill Krementz, a four-story brownstone on the city's East Side, not far from the United Nations complex. There was an abundance of creative energy around him in New York, and plenty of opportunities for companionship. Still, he mourned the recent disintegration of his Indianapolis and Cape Cod families.

While attending the July 1975 funeral of Uncle Alex, his most reliable adult friend when he was younger, Vonnegut thought about how people coped with the loss of their loved ones. He came to believe that "the orphans," the boys he and Jane had adopted after Allie and her husband, Jim, died in quick succession, could scarcely remember their parents. Vonnegut saw this forgetting as a defense mechanism designed to ward off unbearable grief, a particular blessing for children. But he wondered how the same process of amnesia had worked in his own life.

Slapstick presents a darkly tragic vision of the sibling relationship, told from a child's limited perspective, soaked in an adult's survivor guilt. That is why, Vonnegut tells us in the first pages, it is an allegory about "desolated cities and spiritual cannibalism and incest and loneliness and death." Allie was his muse, "the secret of whatever artistic unity I had ever achieved," he declared. But now she had faded from his imagination. Was forgetting a form of murder?

The story unfolds as the autobiography of Wilbur Daffodil-11 Swain, a tall, "blue-eyed, lantern-jawed" man now one hundred years old. Wilbur surveys the ruins of New York City from his makeshift home on the first floor of the Empire State Building. Smoke from a cooking fire rises over the jungle enveloping Thirty-Fourth Street, the pavement is uneven, bridges and tunnels are down. Visitors from the mainland are rare—Manhattan is known far and wide as the "Island of Death." Vonnegut must have imagined this scene many times walking the malaise-ridden streets of his city in the 1970s.

Clad in a toga fashioned from draperies—a costume that reminds us of Billy Pilgrim—Wilbur composes his memoir by the light of a burning rag. He is a medical doctor and a former president of the United States—the last one, in fact—and now lives with his adopted teenaged granddaughter, Melody Oriole-2 von Peterswald and her boyfriend, Isadore Raspberry-19 Cohen. Their nearest neighbor, Vera Chipmunk-5 Zappa, runs a benevolent plantation along the East River.

The gravity is light today, Wilbur observes, a weather pattern in which all males have erections—purely "hydraulic experiences," we are assured. You could fling a manhole cover into New Jersey, things are so weightless at the moment. "In this superbly simple fancy . . ." John Updike wrote in his *New Yorker* review of *Slapstick*, "Vonnegut gives enormous body to his own moodiness, and springs a giddy menace upon the city he inhabits."[3]

Wilbur is not sure anyone will be reading his story. Melody and Isadore are proudly illiterate and impatient with any discussion of the past. "As far as they are concerned, the most glorious accomplishment of the people who inhabited this island so teemingly was to die, so we could have it all to ourselves."

Wilbur was born into wealth in old Manhattan—his original middle name was Rockefeller. But he and his twin sister, Eliza Mellon Swain, were christened in a hospital rather than a church. No cooing relatives welcomed them into the world. "The thing was," Wilbur explains, "Eliza and I were so ugly that our parents were ashamed."

The pages that follow present—in surreal, stylized form—the emotional landscape the Vonnegut children faced growing up in their troubled household—the distance they felt from their parents, the thwarted efforts to connect with them and to ease their suffering. Wilbur and Eliza had the misfortune to be born as "hideous *neanderthaloids*" with extra toes and fingers, course black hair, massive brow ridges and "steamshovel jaws." Allie and Kurt, both tall and awkward themselves, may have felt this grotesque at times. The infants were presumed to be imbeciles, and expected to have mercifully short lives.

Their parents, Caleb Mellon Swain and Letitia Vanderbilt Swain, "two silly and pretty and very young people," had good intentions, and Wilbur never blamed them for their shortcomings. "Anyone would have been shattered by giving birth to Eliza and me," he offers in their defense. Counseled not to raise the twins in their Turtle Bay townhouse, Caleb and Letitia decided to "entomb" them in the ancestral mansion up in rural Vermont. No expense was spared readying the house for their special needs. Thick padding was laid down under the carpets and the dining room was lined in tile so that mealtime debris could be hosed off into floor drains. Fences ringed the apple orchards of the estate to prevent the intrusion of prying eyes.

The household staff was drawn from local country folk, glad to suppress their horror to keep their jobs. As the twins grew larger and ever-more appalling in appearance, safety concerns took priority. Alarms were installed in every room to be sounded should Eliza and Wilbur become violent in their play. Caleb and Letitia stayed away, visiting the children only once a year, on their birthday.

The twins made the best of circumstances they accepted as natural, forming an emotionally self-sufficient "nation of two." They kept things to themselves, including a long-forgotten network of trap doors and sliding panels they discovered that permitted stealth movements around the mansion. The staff interpreted noises from this hidden world—sneezes, laughter, creaking stairways—as proof that the place was haunted.

"I was born into a house which was designed and built by my father in 1922, the year of my birth," the author wrote in *Palm Sunday* of his earliest memories. "It was so full of treasures that it was like a museum." The Swain estate in Vermont mimics the hermetic isolation of the Vonnegut children. "Edwardian lives of a sort were conducted there for seven years," he wrote of that period in Indianapolis, until the stock market crash changed every-thing. For young Kurt what followed was an adventure, with a different school and new friends to learn about. "To my parents, who were great lovers of music, it must have been as though a full orchestra had played the first seven bars of a symphony, and then gone home."[4]

In *Slapstick* the twins' biggest secret was their intelligence. "Cultivating idiocy" seemed to be what the adults wanted, so they obliged, speaking gib-berish and eating library paste. Mental fluency was no advantage, "simply one more example of our freakishness, like our extra nipples and fingers and toes." Adapting to expectations, disguising their talents, it was all a game, and surely the best course for everyone involved. The caretakers, Wilbur explains, "could be heroically Christian in their own eyes only if Eliza and I remained helpless and vile."

The pair lived happily within this cocoon for years, doing "all we could to make each day exactly like the one before" in front of their nurses. Mean-while, in the snug recesses of the house they developed their minds, functioning as "a single genius." Wilbur learned to read and write, working methodically through the volumes in their grandfather's library. Since noth-ing had been added since 1912, the information available there—like the worldview of the Vonnegut parents in real life—stopped abruptly on the eve of the First World War. Eliza specialized in imaginative flights, the "great intuitive leaping" that would guide all their decisions and behavior. Together the children spent hours debating Darwin's theory of evolution and wondering whether variable gravity in the distant past explained how the pyramids were built. It was a perfect division of labor: Eliza spoke of her visions and dreams, and her dutiful brother wrote it all down.

We can read in these passages Vonnegut's longing for his own sister Allie, and the pain he still felt nearly two decades later around her loss. Allie, who was the talented partner in their relationship, with a native, unforced orig-inality that put to shame his own plodding and imitative efforts. It is a primordial feeling he was never able to shake. In terms of worldly success, why me, and not her? It is a common burden for survivors, bringing to mind the judgment by the Dresden widow ladling soup to Billy Pilgrim and Edgar Derby in *Slaughterhouse-Five,* near the end of the war: "All the real soldiers are dead."

The twins speculated, too, about how to make people happier. Intuitively they knew that something was missing from their lives, and they conceived what Wilbur later considered their masterpiece: an amendment to the Constitution guaranteeing that "every citizen, no matter how humble or crazy or incompetent or deformed, somehow be given membership in some family." It spoke to their own hidden longings.

The children did not blossom as in a fairy tale. Instead they just got taller and "more preposterous with each passing day," counting it as good luck that they were so unattractive. "We knew from all the romantic novels I'd read out loud in my squeaky voice that beautiful people had their privacy destroyed by passionate strangers," Wilbur recalls. "We didn't want that to happen to us, since the two of us alone composed not only a single mind but a thoroughly populated universe." Even as they wondered about the world beyond the fences of the estate, they wanted to keep it out.

But the carefree years ended abruptly on the occasion of Wilbur and Eliza's fifteenth birthday. During their "annual space voyage to our asteroid" Caleb and Letitia maintained the usual smiles and small talk, trying to mask their revulsion. The twins played their part in the ritual, staging food fights and feigning ecstatic surprise about the presents they would open the next morning on their "Fuff-bay."

After being put to bed in their oversized cribs, they snuck through a trap door to eavesdrop on their parents. "They appeared, as they had always appeared to Eliza and me, to be under some curse which required them to speak only of matters which did not interest them at all," Wilbur tells us. "And indeed they *were* under a malediction. But Eliza and I had not guessed its nature: That they were all but strangled and paralyzed by the wish that their own children would die."

Unaware that she was being observed, Letitia let out a shriek of anguish. "Her hands closed convulsively. Her spine buckled and her face shriveled to turn her into an old, old witch. 'I hate them, I hate them, I hate them,'" she cried to her husband. "'I would give anything for the faintest sign of intelligence, the merest flicker of humanness in the eyes of either twin."' Was this the volatile Edith Vonnegut, in one of her late-night meltdowns?

Eliza and Wilbur were not dismayed. If they were responsible for their parents' discomfort, it would be easy enough to make things right. "We enjoyed solving problems." Maybe now they could all be a real family.

"Thus did Eliza and I destroy our Paradise—our nation of two." Rising early, they dressed themselves for the first time, in clothes elegant enough to fit their reborn identities. "Good morning, Oveta," Eliza greeted the nurse with shocking decorum. "A new life begins for all of us today. As you can see and hear, Wilbur and I are no longer idiots. A miracle has taken place overnight. Our parents' dreams have come true. We are healed."

Their efforts had the opposite of the intended effect. Letitia stayed in bed, too upset to face the strangers. Caleb, "palsied and drawn," made it down to the breakfast table, but could barely respond to the children's salutations, addressed to him in the various foreign languages in which they were fluent. "He was sick with guilt, of course, over having allowed intelligent human beings, his own flesh and blood, to be treated like idiots for so long." In growing up, in being themselves—and in trying to please—the twins only made themselves more repulsive, and there was no going back.

Now the attendants who once treated them with such indulgence delighted in opportunities for revenge. "They were suddenly entitled to bawl us out." Wilbur recalls. "What hell we caught from time to time!" Once again the experts were consulted, and the twins were subjected to a battery of aptitude tests, administered separately, to determine the nature of their metamorphosis. "I felt as though my head were turning to wood," Wilbur remembers of the solo examinations. "I became stupid and insecure." They invented names for their diminished selves in a new twist on the Vonnegut theme of fractured identity. Eliza and Wilbur became, in their private language, "Betty and Bobby Brown."

Cordelia Swain Cordiner, a renowned child psychologist, was brought in to evaluate the situation. It was she who insisted that the twins be separated permanently. Dr. Cordiner affected a professional demeanor in the presence of adults, but alone with the children she was another Vonnegut Jekyll-and-Hyde female, reminding her patients that she was no "sweet Aunt Cordelia." Taking the tests together was out of the question. "In case nobody has told you," she scolded sharply, "this is the United States of

America, where nobody has a right to rely on anybody else—where everybody learns to make his or her own way." It was time they learned the hard rule: "Paddle your own canoe."

Dr. Cordiner reported the children "dull normals." Eliza was especially impaired and needed to be institutionalized for the rest of her life. Wilbur, on the other hand, if properly trained, was salvageable. In a last-ditch maternal effort on their behalf, Letitia demanded that they be allowed to answer questions jointly, and their "single genius" reasserted itself—the score was perfect. But the intensity of their involvement, portrayed in graphic, physical imagery, was too frightening. Wilbur was sent away the next day to an academy for disturbed children on Cape Cod—a reference to the author's time as a teacher at Hopefield School for disturbed children in the 1950s.

"Even as we rolled through the lovely countryside, my forgettery set to work," Wilbur admits. The amputation left no trace of even phantom pain as he attended posh summer camps, traveled to Europe, and performed unexpectedly well at school. His skills were mundane compared to his sister's—he was "patient, orderly, and could sort out good ideas from heaps of balderdash"—but they were enough to win the approval of the world, and in time even to gain admission to Harvard. Only occasionally was he reminded "that somewhere I had a twin sister who was little more than a human vegetable." Eliza faded from his thoughts, she was "only a name." In medical school Wilbur lived like a squire, hosting parties at his Beacon Hill townhouse and enjoying chauffeured rides to classes. It pains him now to look back on the depth of his betrayal. "I was then not only a stupid Bobby Brown, but a conceited one." Here we have an expression of Vonnegut's ambivalence about money and success, his guilt about the one he left behind.

After Caleb's death Wilbur received a visit from Norman Mushari Jr., son of the conniving lawyer from *God Bless You, Mr. Rosewater*. Mushari was carrying on the family tradition, representing Eliza in a lawsuit to get her share of the Swain inheritance. She now reemerged with a vengeance, her tone appropriately outraged, her voice a "rowdy contralto" riddled with smoker's cough. The scandal made Eliza a tabloid celebrity, and she was asked for her opinion on all sorts of issues. How did she feel, for instance, about the People's Republic of China abandoning its new embassy in Washington? "What civilized country could be interested in a hell-hole like America," she answered, not missing a beat, "where everybody takes such lousy care of their own relatives?"

Eliza showed up finally at Wilbur's door, a parade of photographers in tow. "I was just some kind of tumor that had to be removed from your side," she told her brother. But soon her pent-up fury subsided, and to reaffirm their bond she invited him to embrace her. "We became a single genius again," Wilbur recalls with awe. But once again the union had a visceral, convulsive quality that disturbed those looking on. "We went berserk. It was gorgeous and it was horrible." The next thing he knew Eliza had been taken away, and this time the separation was for good.

Letitia Vanderbilt Swain staged a gala celebration for her son when he graduated from Harvard Medical School (albeit at the bottom of his class). In his moment of triumph Wilbur was summoned to the gardens across the street from the hotel, where Eliza said a last goodbye and gave her blessings on his passage to manhood. She appeared to him as an angel in a dream.

Dr. Swain outgrew his selfishness and devoted himself to a life of service, converting the old Vermont mansion into a children's hospital. "The years flew by"—and suddenly he was fifty. "Yes, and I found the hospitality of my mind to fantasy pleasantly increased as machinery died, and communications from the outside world became more and more vague."

One night he was visited by an emissary from China, interested in the papers he and Eliza had composed together on variable gravity during their days as a "single genius." Wilbur obliged, leading him through a secret passageway to the urn where they had been stowed away. It had to have been another dream.

Three weeks later a letter arrived at the post office, announcing Eliza's death. "An extraordinary feeling came over me," Wilbur recalls. At first he took it to be grief. "I seemed to have taken root on the porch. I could not pick up my feet. My features, moreover, were being dragged downward like melting wax." In fact, it was a sudden spike in gravity. In other parts of the world "elevator cables were snapping, airplanes were crashing, ships were sinking, motor vehicles were breaking their axles, bridges were collapsing." Another apocalyptic—and impossibly beautiful—Vonnegut moment.

Time flew, "a blurry bird now—made indistinct by ever-increasing dosages of tri-benzo-Deportamil," a mood-stabilizing drug for which Wilbur had developed an addiction. (Brain chemistry was never far from Vonnegut's mind during this period.) Now Dr. Swain was a senator from Vermont, running for president and championing the ideas about extended families he and Eliza had once concocted together. If elected he would see to it that every citizen was assigned a new middle name, unconnected to the categories of men—flowers or fruit or nuts, animals or minerals or chemical elements—paired with a number. These would designate the clans to which they would now belong.

Vonnegut told *Playboy* that the scheme elaborated in *Slapstick* started as the premise of a Kilgore Trout story. "The trouble with the country," the chief executive announces, "is that nobody has enough relatives within shouting distance. Everybody has to fill out forms." He was here trying to adapt the model of the "folk-society" he remembered from anthropologist Robert Redfield's lectures at Chicago to the anomic mass of modern America.[5]

Vonnegut suggested the slogan that is the novel's subtitle to friends he knew in the George McGovern presidential campaign in 1972. "I wanted Sarge Shriver [McGovern's running-mate] to say, 'You're not happy, are you?'" he explained in an interview. "Nobody in this country is happy but the rich people. Something is wrong. I'll tell you what's wrong: We're lonesome!" The stump speech would build from there, a piece of populist oratory that would have made Eugene Debs proud:

> They *want* us lonesome; they want us huddled in our houses with just our wives and kids, watching television, because they can manipulate us then. They can make us buy anything, they can make us vote any way they want. How did Americans beat the Great Depression? We banded together. In those days, members of unions called each other "brother" and "sister," and they meant it. We're going to bring that spirit back, Brother and Sister! We're going to vote in George McGovern, and then we're going to get

this country on the road again. We are going to band together with our neighbors to clean up our neighborhoods, to get the crooks out of the unions, to get the prices down in the meat markets. Here's a war cry for the American people: "Lonesome no more!"

"That's the kind of demagoguery I approve of," Vonnegut told *Playboy*. Since the politicians rejected his proposal (and McGovern lost in a landslide to incumbent Richard Nixon), Vonnegut decided to introduce it into his fiction, creating a futuristic country in which artificial extended families are mandated by executive fiat. To foreground the experiment, he considered calling his eighth novel *The Relatives*.[6]

These ideas also bear the influence of a 1970 trip Vonnegut made to Biafra during its civil war with Nigeria. He heard the sounds of live artillery for the first time in twenty-five years, and was on the last plane out before the final collapse. Vonnegut was moved by the dignity of the people he met there, maintained even under the most extreme conditions. The key to their resilience and spirit was the dense web of support and mutuality in traditional Ibo society. "They all had the emotional and spiritual strength that an enormous family can give," he wrote for *McCall's*.

> And there were no orphanages, no old people's homes, no public charities—and, early in the war, there weren't even schemes for taking care of refugees. The families took care of their own—perfectly naturally.[7]

Wilbur Rockefeller Swain, MD, easily won the election, with a mandate to implement his and Eliza's communitarian vision. Soon everyone, himself included, received a registered letter confirming their new name. Wilbur painted the Oval Office yellow to celebrate his membership in the Daffodil family, and he and the White House dishwasher hugged when they discovered they were now brothers.

Not everyone was pleased with the new order. The president's wife, the former Sophie Rothschild (reminding us of the snobbish Beatrice Rumfoord in *Sirens of Titan*), could not abide her assignment to the Peanut clan, a notoriously "ground-hugging bunch." She loathed the spectacle outside the White House grounds, where thousands assembled to proclaim their new allegiances.

Wilbur was undeterred. "I am glad we have those people outside the fence to think about," he told the First Lady. "They are frightened hermits who have been tempted out from under their damp rocks by humane new laws. They are dazedly seeking brothers and sisters and cousins which their President has suddenly given to them from their nation's social treasure."

Families compiled directories to facilitate contact. Wilbur read about the remarkably diverse constellation of cousins in his—a small-town chief of police, a prima ballerina from Chicago, even Muhammad Daffodil-11 X, the heavyweight boxing champion. Regional clubhouses were established and newsletters circulated everywhere. Quaintly chaotic, pre-digital vehicles for social networking, they offered classified ads, profiles of family triumphs and tragedies, opinion pieces on all manner of issues. The Peanut-family journal, the *Goober Gossip*, for example, declared government-run law enforcement a thing of the past. "If you know of a relative who is engaged in criminal acts," its editors urged, "don't call the police. Call ten more relatives."

For all of the randomness of their creation, the artificial clans did show some patterns and statistical oddities. Pachysandras were musical, Watermelons heavier than average, and Wilbur's family was unusually concentrated in Indianapolis, Indiana, known as Daffodil City. Human nature being what it was, signs of hierarchy and varying degrees of xenophobia crept in from the start, and religious cults flourished. "Eventually, of course, the Chromiums would start thinking that they were just a little bit better than the Daffodils," Vonnegut conceded to *Playboy*. But overall Wilbur had reason to be pleased with the early stages of his experiment.[8]

"Just when ... Americans were happier than they had ever been, even though the country was bankrupt and falling apart," a series of mysterious plagues broke out. In Manhattan it was the "Green Death." Was this, like variable gravity, the handiwork of the scheming Red Chinese? Soon America descended into regional warfare. When the Oval Office phone rang the president would find himself talking to "some sort of mythological creature—'The King of Michigan,' perhaps, or 'The Emergency Governor of Florida.'" Things fell apart fast.

"It was a day of such salubrious gravity that our helicopter expended no more energy than would have an airborne milkweed seed," Wilbur remembers of his journey to the Midwest. An air force pilot flew him over the Battle of Lake Maxinkuckee in northern Indiana, site of the Vonnegut family's village of summer cottages when the author was a boy. In Indianapolis Wilbur was treated to parades and a lavish banquet, in honor more of his status as a Daffodil than his high office. Vonnegut must have daydreamed about such a homecoming from time to time.

Wilbur was invited to a family meeting. Selected by lot, the chairperson that week was an eleven-year-old black girl named Dorothy Daffodil-7 Garland. The guest watched with satisfaction as she presided over the raucous assembly with firmness and efficiency. Dorothy "might have been some sort of goddess up there, equipped with an armload of thunderbolts" as she enforced that blueprint for democratic deliberation, *Robert's Rules of Order*. It is Vonnegut's American Dream brought to life.

The most pressing business that evening was choosing replacements for Daffodils who had fallen in the army of the King of Michigan, in his war with the Great Lakes pirates and the Duke of Oklahoma. Here the body accorded itself most proudly, allowing freedom of expression but imposing wise, humane limits on individual emotions and impulses. A teenager rose to proclaim his eagerness to fight. "There's nothing I'd rather do than kill me some 'Sooners,'" he announced hotly. Wilbur describes what happened next:

> To my surprise, he was scolded by several speakers for his military ardor. He was told that war wasn't supposed to be fun, and in fact wasn't fun—that tragedy was being discussed, and that he had better put on a tragic face, or he would be ejected from the meeting.

"Young man," an elder charged with authority, "you're no better than the Albanian influenza or the Green Death, if you can kill for joy." The youngster was disqualified in any case because he had fathered a number of illegitimate children. "He wasn't going to be allowed to run away from caring for all those babies."

Next on the agenda was a discussion of how to care for refugees arriving from the various theatres of combat. Again, fairness and common sense prevailed. A woman, "beautiful but disorderly, and clearly crazed by altruism"—a version of Eliot Rosewater perhaps, or Vonnegut's first wife, Jane—offered to take in at least twenty of the displaced Daffodils. The idea was shot down quickly. She was so careless, someone reminded her, that her own children had to leave the house to be raised by other relatives. No cruelty was intended—the over-enthusiastic volunteer meant well, and was, after all, everyone's sister or cousin. She stayed, "looking sympathetic and alert," for the rest of the meeting. "Once a Daffodil, always a Daffodil" was the family credo.

Finally it was the president's turn to address the gathering. "You have nobody but your doddering Cousin Wilbur here," he admonished as the applause died down. Like many before him he had failed in the search for peace and stability, the country he had tried to fix proved ungovernable. But there was progress to report. "Because we're just families, and not a nation any more, it's much easier for us to give and receive mercy in war."

> I have just come from observing a battle far to the north of here, in the region of Lake Maxinkuckee. It was horses and spears and rifles and knives and pistols, and a cannon or two. I saw several people killed. I also saw many people embracing, and there seemed to be a great deal of deserting and surrendering going on.
>
> This much news I can bring you from the Battle of Lake Maxinkuckee:
>
> It is no massacre.

For a person like Kurt Vonnegut, who had witnessed a massacre and its aftermath up close, this was no small achievement. War might sometimes be necessary, but it was understood as a horrific last option when he was a boy, when Americans inclined to pacifism in world affairs and his birthday was still called "Armistice Day." Like all schoolchildren of his generation, he was required to memorize the words of U.S. Navy Captain J. W. Philip as he watched the *Vizcaya* go down in flames in Santiago Bay, during the 1898 war with Spain: "Don't cheer, boys, those poor devils are dying." Romantic myths and the hunger for rites of passage to manhood made war seem an exciting adventure to the uninitiated. Maybe Wilbur's policies would reverse the trend.[9]

From Indianapolis the president flew to a summit with the King of Michigan, where he signed a document ceding the area of the old Louisiana

Purchase. It was a dead letter anyway—most of that real estate, he noted, was already in the possession of the Duke of Oklahoma or claimed "by other potentates and panjamdrums unknown to me."

In the last entry of Wilbur Daffodil-11 Swain's diary we circle back to where we started, to the overgrown ruins of midtown New York City. He aches from a party the night before that was arranged by his granddaughter and her friend, Isadore, in celebration of his 101st birthday. Years earlier Melody had come to Manhattan as a war refugee, and, Vonnegut tells us in the prologue, she symbolized the vestiges of the author's "optimistic imagination." There are always seeds of hope in destruction, victories amid the larger defeat, birth on the frontiers of death.

Isadore is a member of the food-gathering Raspberries, who live in the shell of the New York Stock Exchange. They had been responsible for the delicacies everyone enjoyed at the birthday picnic. Vera Chipmunk-5 Zappa presented Wilbur with beer and wine and wax candles, to go into the dozens of ornate holders he had accumulated during his years as the lone doctor on the Island of Death, where he was known to all as the good "King of Candlesticks." Wilbur recalled the peace he felt as the candles were lit, one-by-one. "Standing among all those tiny, wavering lights, I felt as though I were God, up to my knees in the Milky Way." It was a moment of grace, in the company of a loving family. He wished that his sister could have been there to share it with him.

A posthumous epilogue describes Wilbur's last communication with Eliza, another of Vonnegut's dialogues across the void. She finds the afterlife disappointing and dull, and pleads with her brother to join her as soon as possible to alleviate the boredom. As he ponders their imminent reunion, Wilbur thinks of a poem, a fragment of a sonnet by Shakespeare, to commemorate their gift to the world:

> *And how did we then face the odds,*
> *Of man's rude slapstick, yes, and God's?*
> *Quite at home and unafraid,*
> *Thank you,*
> *In a game our dreams remade.*

Slapstick was mostly savaged by the critics, who complained that its digressions and sci-fi devices did not hold together with the cohesion of Vonnegut's earlier works. Perhaps it had been a mistake to dismiss his alter ego Kilgore Trout as the vehicle for such fantasies. The author himself complained to his friend Loree Rackstraw of the unfinished quality of the manuscript, rushed into print to meet the demands of the market. "One thing that troubles me," he told her, "is that anything I write now sells like crazy and my publishers won't tell me honestly what they think of my work, since their opinion doesn't mean a damn thing commercially. We just publish, and off we go."[10]

An exception to the overall negative response was a review by John Updike for the *New Yorker*. Establishment commentators missed the point, Updike insisted, they did not have an ear for what the author was trying, in his idiosyncratic way, to accomplish. "There need be no scandal in Vonnegut's wide appeal, based, as I believe it is, on the generosity of his imagination and the honesty of his pain." He considered the novel within the larger arc of his friend's work.

> The pain in Vonnegut was always real. Through the transpositions of science fiction, he found a way, instead of turning pain aside, to vaporize it, to scatter it on the planes of the cosmic and the comic. His terse flat sentences, jumpy characters, interleaved placards, collages of stray texts and messages, and nervous grim refrains like "So it goes" and (in *Slapstick*) "Hi ho" are a new way of stacking pain, as his fictional ice-nine is a new way of stacking the molecules of water. Such an invention looks easy only in retrospect.[11]

We know from *Mother Night* that a nation of two is a tenuous, doomed thing, and so it was with the siblings in this tale. But the survivor here manages to transmute the pain of his loss into helping others. Vonnegut imagines creating families in a nation of strangers, and, like all grand schemes, the results fall short of expectations. But we can smile at the spirit of the effort, admire the commitment to keep on "bargaining in good faith with destiny," even in the face of endless pratfalls and mistakes.

"It's a sunny little dream I have of a happier mankind," the author protested to *Playboy* when challenged about the workability of his ideas. "I couldn't survive my own pessimism if I didn't have some kind of sunny little dream."

> That's mine, and don't tell me I'm wrong: Human beings *will* be happier—not when they cure cancer or get to Mars or eliminate racial prejudice or flush Lake Erie but when they find ways to inhabit primitive communities. That's my utopia. That's what I want for me.

It was a dream born in the affection between a lonely young boy and his older sister a long time ago. No passage of time, no amount of "forgettery," could extinguish it.[12]

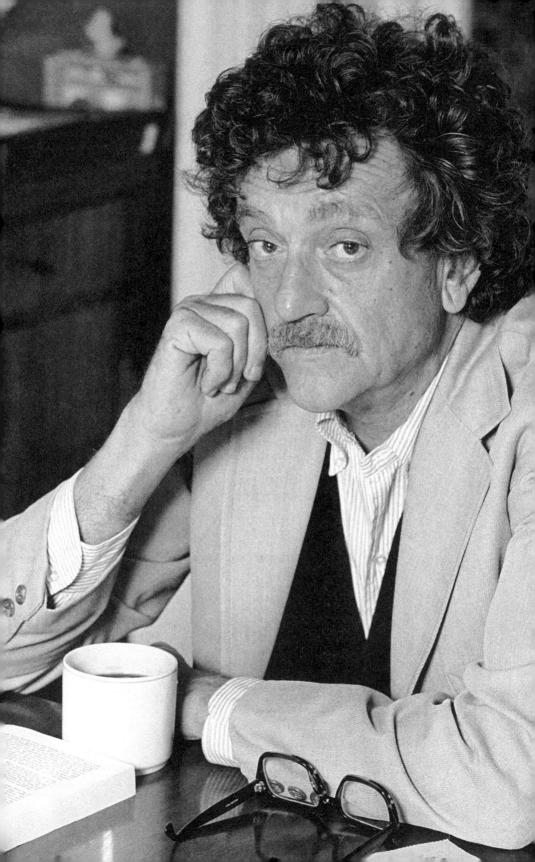

NINE

Jailbird

The economy is a thoughtless weather system—and nothing more.
—Walter Starbuck

At least you tried to believe what the people with hearts believed,
so you were a good man just the same.
—Mary Kathleen O'Looney

Beginning in the 1970s Vonnegut's novels are a cycle of first-person reflections, weighing the merits of a messy life lived in a troubled, perhaps doomed, world. There is regret about dashed dreams and missed opportunities, even as the protagonist moves, haltingly and without ever fully arriving, toward acceptance and forgiveness, self-love and a world-weary gratitude.

Writing was a vehicle in this search for reconciliation as the author advanced in middle age and dealt with encroaching thoughts of mortality. "I keep losing and regaining my equilibrium," he wrote in the introduction to his mid-1970s collection *Wampeters, Foma & Granfalloons,* "which is the basic plot of all popular fiction. And I myself am a work of fiction." A ten-year period of turmoil—sudden celebrity, the breakup of his first marriage, the move to Manhattan—was ending with relative stability, at least on the

189

surface. The books continued to sell and Vonnegut remained in demand even as the young who first embraced him moved on in their lives. The Cinderella story was not about to end abruptly. In 1979 Vonnegut and Jill Krementz married, formalizing their long-term relationship.[1]

He was dogged as always by self-doubt, had reason to look back and wonder about the journey. His preoccupations were not so different from those endured by others at his age of maturity—the scattering of children, the deaths of friends, the passing of familiar landmarks, physical and spiritual.

Creatively, Vonnegut felt newly alone and rudderless, a victim, ironically, of his own success. In his 1977 "Self-Interview" he admitted the absence of a mentor to whom he could be accountable:

> I guess I'm too old to find one. Whatever I write now is set in type without comment by my publisher, who is younger than I am, by editors, by anyone. I don't have my sister to write for anymore. Suddenly there are all these unfilled jobs in my life.[2]

Vonnegut's work since *Slaughterhouse-Five* had received a lot of criticism, and notices for his latest expressionist experiment, *Slapstick,* were especially brutal. "I felt as though I were sleeping standing up on a boxcar in Germany again," he confessed of his sensitivity to the backlash. He was willing to concede shortcomings—"everybody else writes lousy books," he protested, "why shouldn't I?" What stung was the breadth of the attacks, the demand that readers "admit now that I had never been any good." A literary establishment that never liked him in the first place was exacting its revenge.[3]

Vonnegut returned to a more accessible form, and initiated a "comeback" of sorts, with *Jailbird* (1979), a comic romp inspired by the Keystone Kops machinations of the Watergate affair. The embattled romantic dreams of his youth are on full display here. With its New Testament compassion for the "losers" in our tempestuous weather system, I read this a sequel to *God Bless You, Mr. Rosewater.*

At the center of *Jailbird* is Walter Starbuck, one of Vonnegut's most loveably hapless protagonists, the most obscure and the least guilty of the president's men to serve time. Walter's American Dream has had its ups and downs, its share of self-inflicted wounds and bad luck, including, as the title infers, the humbling shame of incarceration. But he retains his innocence, never succumbing entirely to cynicism. For all of his self-recriminations Walter is an example of grace in defeat, and with him we discover that the meek, the "saints" among us who act with decency and kindness, do, sometimes, inherit the earth.

In contrast is the figure, real and mythological, of Richard Nixon, with whom Walter's life has been oddly entwined. Nicholas Shrimpton and Peter Freese speculate that Vonnegut chose the name "Starbuck" to identify his character here with the "accidental man" of *Moby-Dick,* the "good-hearted but ineffectual first mate" of another Ahab, the darkly obsessive Nixon. "Well, I don't think that he's evil," the author said when asked for an opinion about his fellow child of the Great Depression. But Nixon, an embittered survivor who managed to claw his way to the top, represented to him the most pinched, "envying, life-hating" tendencies of their generation, and lacked the imagination to use his pulpit creatively. It was a catastrophe for the country, Vonnegut told *Playboy,* that "the lessons Nixon has taught us have been so mean." The president "must dream the biggest dreams of all for us," and his were too often petty and vengeful.[4]

Vonnegut sets up the story by recalling the day when, just back from the war, he met Powers Hapgood, a man of larger dreams, a real-life hero of the American labor movement. The archly conservative Uncle Alex, Hapgood's Harvard classmate, arranged the luncheon to indulge his nephew's idea about working for the CIO after his discharge from the army. "Unions were admirable instruments for extorting something like economic justice from employers then," Vonnegut reminds us. Waiting for their guest to arrive, Alex expounded on the cautionary tale of the Hapgood family's cannery business in Indianapolis, an early twentieth-century experiment in enlightened workplace democracy. Employees were brought into management decisions and granted generous benefits and incentives. "It went bust," said Alex, his smile betraying a "grim, Darwinian satisfaction."

Also present at the table that afternoon was Kurt Vonnegut Sr. His architecture practice long defunct, his wife, Edith, having "surrendered and vanished from our table of organization" the previous year, he was "a good man in full retreat from life," regressing to a state of childlike detachment. The author understood the impact of the blows, and empathized with the response. It all made sense intellectually, but remained nonetheless a source of frustration and anger. "Once he made that decision to disengage," Vonnegut lamented, "he wound up leaving behind very little for a son to relate to."[5]

Powers Hapgood was unremarkable in appearance when he entered the restaurant, save for the small union badge attached to his lapel. It spoke of a life in social justice battles—coal mines, walking picket lines to protest the executions of Sacco and Vanzetti, barricades in the organizing drives of the 1920s and '30s. Instead of joining a Wall Street law firm he had chosen to endure death threats, beatings, and stints as a Debsian jailbird. The judge that morning, he told his lunch companions, asked why a man of his pedigree would associate himself with striking workers. "Because of the Sermon on the Mount, sir," was his reply.

Here we are presented with a continuum, four different approaches to the challenges of the world, each containing elements of the author. Vonnegut's creation Walter Starbuck is an object, slow to react, overmatched by events, doing well to preserve any dignity as he plays out the string. He is a familiar alter ego. In contrast to Walter are figures from real life. Nixon is the misanthrope, Vonnegut's shadow side, so poisoned by hard times he can never be comfortable in his skin. The author's father, Kurt Sr., has none of Nixon's brutality but is just as damaged. He represents the temptations of escape, of internal migration from a destiny too heartbreaking to "bargain with in good faith," to borrow the phrase from *Slapstick*. And then there is the resolute Powers Hapgood, advocate for the dispossessed. In common with *Slaughterhouse-Five*'s Edgar Derby, he is intent on asserting himself as a character, able to find meaning in the most difficult circumstances, "still full of ideas about how victory might yet be snatched from the jaws of defeat." Hapgood is a quiet hero, undeterred by long odds—a man to follow.

Vonnegut shifts now to a passion play, a fictionalized amalgam of late nineteenth-century labor battles convincing in its detail and theatrical effects. With the Hapgood anecdote it serves to establish historical sweep for the story, the context for Walter Starbuck's dreams as a young man. As with the strikes at the Pullman Palace Car Company in Chicago, led by Eugene Debs, and Andrew Carnegie's Homestead steel mill in Pennsylvania, so we find the Cuyahoga Bridge and Iron Company of Cleveland in the fall of

1894, roiled by a standoff between ownership and workers protesting a wage cut. Self-made Daniel McCone aims to use the occasion to teach his heirs about the enterprise they would inherit one day, especially his stammering younger son, Alexander. Freshly graduated from Harvard, it was time he got his hands dirty.

As weeks passed the governor dispatched guardsmen to protect the plant, ill-trained farm boys without local ties. The echoes are here of another Ohio militia, brought in to contain student demonstrators at Kent State in the spring of 1970.

On Christmas morning, as things came to a head, Alexander hoped for a peaceful "pageant" in which the workers would be brought to their senses and convinced to go home quietly. Standing in the clock tower, near where marksmen were poised, lying in wait to perform the service for which they had been hired, his heart sank. On command the uniformed men below commenced an advance. They averted their bayonets, but in the chaos some were pulled to the ground by their heavy packs. "They refused to shoot," Vonnegut notes admiringly. "They formed a defensive heap instead, a paralyzed porcupine" of the sort he remembered from the snow and cold of the Bulge. Another order was given, and this time the sharpshooters raked the crowd with fire. "Like it or not, boys," thundered Dan McCone to his sons as they surveyed the carnage, "that's the sort of business you're in." It was a particularly gruesome rout in a long line of defeats suffered by the poor at the hands of the powerful.

For Alexander McCone the traumatic effects would be permanent. He never again visited the factory complex, and from the seclusion of his mansion across town formed only one relationship in all the years after the massacre. This relationship was with Walter, the only child of his immigrant cook and chauffeur. In exchange for long hours as his chess companion, McCone, another "Blue Fairy Godmother," would make the young man's American Dream come true—he would send him to his alma mater, that magic gateway to insider status.

Walter's parents agreed to anglicize their name, from "Stankiewicz," thinking it a small price to pay in the bargain. But it would foster confusion in the boy about his identity, the deep sense of duality and fraudulence so common among Vonnegut characters. It reminds us in a way of the author's parents, cutting the children off from their German heritage to prove their patriotism after the First World War.

Now in his sixties, Walter Starbuck faces release from the minimum-security correctional facility that has been his home for the last two years. It is a perennial Vonnegut theme, the oscillation between captivity and release, blind determinism and the challenges of free will. The year is "Nineteen-hundred and Seventy-seven," a device to remind the reader how we demarcate our lives with disruptions, natural and manmade, usually beyond our control. As a boy the author heard lots of talk among his older relatives about the legendary "Blizzard of '88." And there were, of course, the storms in the uneven weather of the economy. "A terrible flaw in Capitalism is that every so often a depression comes along," Vonnegut explained in an interview.

> My father would refer frequently, and with good reason, to the setback of '22, for instance. Then there was the Great Crash of '29, then the one in '32, then the one in '39. I have similar recollections of booms.

In the collective memory of each generation, years assumed human characteristics.[6]

Walter sits on the edge of his cot, staring blankly at the wall as he awaits final processing. On good days he allowed himself to look forward to a welcoming face when he got out, but today he has to face the truth. "There would be no one to greet me at the gate," he knows, not even his son, Walter Jr. "Nowhere in the world was there anyone who had a forgiving hug for me."

The white-collar criminals in the prison go about their work details as usual. Celebrities and "shoals of disbarred lawyers" are so common inside the fences they draw no particular notice. The facility teems with Watergate alumni, many of them Ivy Leaguers. Vonnegut indulges himself here in tweaking the establishment that has been so hard on him. (We note also that his character's estranged son is a book reviewer for the *New York Times*.)

Walter's Harvard degree was in the liberal arts. Mr. McCone insisted that he develop his mind as broadly as possible in preparation for a career in public service—clearly the highest calling in a democracy. When he went to work in Franklin D. Roosevelt's Department of Agriculture during the

New Deal, "more and more posts were being filled by Harvard men," whose moral and intellectual superiority was taken for granted. "It seems mildly comical to me now," he admits.

Walter thinks of the heroes of his younger days, figures of substance like the martyred anarchists Sacco and Vanzetti and those who had fallen earlier at the Cuyahoga Massacre. Though it had taken place long before he was born, even before his parents had immigrated from Poland, images of that bloody Christmas morning are vivid in his mind, passed on to him by his mentor during their chess matches.

Walter notes in passing that Cuyahoga Bridge and Iron, the fearsome colossus of industrial-age Cleveland, has been absorbed as a "mere division" of RAMJAC, the faceless conglomerate that seems to have its fingerprints on every enterprise in the American economy.

These ruminations, like all of Walter's thoughts, are interrupted at regular intervals by a bawdy drinking song he recalls from his fraternity days at Harvard. Its refrain, so shocking when he first heard it, was part of a ritual meant to "coarsen" the feelings of youngsters like himself on the brink of adulthood.

> *Sally in the garden,*
> *Sifting cinders,*
> *Lifted up her leg*
> *And farted like a man.*
> *The bursting of her bloomers*
> *Broke sixteen winders.*
> *The cheeks of her ass went—*

"Here the singers, in order to complete the stanza, were required to clap three times." These vulgarities were recited, Walter remembers, "not by middle-aged roughnecks, but by college boys, children really, who, with a Great Depression going on and with a Second World War coming, and with most of them mocked by their own virginity, had reason to be petrified." Here Vonnegut remembers again the trials the child-warriors of his generation faced.

Women would expect them to earn good money after they graduated, and they did not see how they could do that, with all the
businesses shutting down. Women would expect them to be brave
soldiers, and there seemed every chance that they would go to
pieces when the shrapnel and bullets flew.

For the survivors, the Eliot Rosewaters and Billy Pilgrims, the burdens
would continue even after they returned home. They would have to put
aside the things they had lost, cover up their injuries and keep moving.
There would be demands for intimacy, expectations they become husbands
and fathers and breadwinners they felt grievously ill-equipped to satisfy.
Looking back, the saloon song was poignant false bravado, a protest against
fear and powerlessness. No wonder Walter can't get it out of his head.

The death in 1977 of Kurt Vonnegut's friend James Jones—a midwesterner,
the author of *From Here to Eternity*, and a fellow member of "the last recognizable generation of full-time, life-time American novelists"—prompted an
effort at stock-taking as they began their exit from the center of American
life. "We appear to be standing more or less in a row," Vonnegut observed at
the start of *Palm Sunday*. "It was the Great Depression which made us similarly edgy and watchful. It was World War II which lined us up so nicely,
whether we were men or women, whether we were ever in uniform or not."[7]
Vonnegut used a review of Joseph Heller's second novel, *Something Happened*, in the mid-1970s to explore the same issues. He applauded Heller's
attempt to put forward a more realistic narrative to replace the bromides
about the veterans who came back to marry and have children after World
War II. "The proposed myth has it that those families were pathetically
vulnerable and suffocating," Vonnegut writes, thinking, too, of his own
experience. "It says that the heads of them commonly took jobs which were
vaguely dishonorable or at least stultifying, in order to make as much
money as they could for their little families, and they used that money in
futile attempts to buy safety and happiness." The compromises required
were deeply damaging, the results often less than encouraging.[8]

Walter Starbuck's unlikely journey to prison started with his appointment
as President Nixon's "Special Advisor on Youth Affairs." It was a kind of

reunion—Walter had encountered Nixon years earlier, during the rising politician's period on the House Un-American Activities Committee, and their lives were never the same. Was this the return of a favor, an act of generosity? Was Nixon in his *karass?*

As an indication of the importance attached to the post, Walter was assigned to a windowless subbasement in the Executive Office Building. His desk was directly below a room where a cabal of Ivy Leaguers hatched plans for the burglaries and other dirty tricks that would go so famously awry. Walter spent his days underground in chain-smoking isolation, cataloging student newspapers to monitor the political temperature of young people for the famously tone-deaf Nixon inner circle. His carefully annotated memoranda went unread, ending up "shredded and baled with all the rest of the White House wastepaper."

Walter assumed he had been tapped as interpreter of the campus Left due to his own history of activism back in the 1930s. At Harvard he became a proud communist, until the Hitler-Stalin pact made him a "cautious believer in capitalistic democracy again." His views were acceptable at the time, no obstacle to a government job or, later, to military service. And Walter's idealism, hedged and underdeveloped as it has always been, persists. "I still believe that peace and plenty and happiness can be worked out in some way," he admits. "I am a fool."

This bit of self-deprecation reflects the author's sense of his own politics, as "unsystematic" and heartfelt, in his estimation, as his ideas about literature. Vonnegut was embarrassed sometimes to try to articulate them. "The beliefs I have to defend," he admitted in *Palm Sunday,* "are so soft and complicated, actually, and, when vivisected, turn into bowls of undifferentiated mush. I am a pacifist, I am an anarchist, I am a planetary citizen, and so on."[9]

No one would have noticed if Walter had stayed home more during the Nixon years, and he now regrets not helping his wife with her interior decorating business, the enterprise that kept them afloat during the lean years, when he could not find a job. He was always the child in the relationship, the bumbling romantic. Ruth was the hard-boiled cynic, a survivor of the concentration camps.

Walter was in uniform when he first laid eyes on Ruth, in Nuremberg, Germany, in the late summer of 1945. Again we are transported to that *Ur*-moment in the Vonnegut universe, the chaos of the end of World War II. Walter had been put in charge of accommodations for the war crimes trials about to begin. Looking for translators as he rode through rubble-strewn streets, in a Mercedes once belonging to Himmler, he noticed a gaunt figure in fatigues and shorn hair, conversing expertly with refugees from various countries. Only reluctantly did Ruth agree to get into the car. "She was uninterested in ever trusting anybody with her destiny anymore." Like *Hamlet*'s Ophelia, and like so many other displaced persons at the time, she had wrapped herself in a dream world, determined to "roam alone and out-of-doors forever, from nowhere to nowhere, in a demented sort of religious ecstasy."

Walter delivered his fragile recruit to the medical care of a Harvard classmate, and within a few weeks Ruth was once again the "sane and witty Viennese intellectual" she had been before the war. Things went smoothly on his big assignment, mostly thanks to her competence. "I was Ruth's inferior, you might say," he readily concedes.

Walter's optimism was a source of amusement and horror to Ruth when they began courting. A particularly American kind of naïvety allowed him to think that a new millennium was dawning. "The closing chapter to ten thousand years of madness and greed is being written right here and now—in Nuremberg," Walter announced to her with excitement as they strolled through the ruins of a cathedral. Remaking things, perfecting the world was a natural part of his outlook. The young warriors Vonnegut knew harbored some of the same millennial hopes.

Ruth agreed to marry Walter anyway. They arrived in Washington with their infant son in 1949, his faith now transformed into "bricks and mortar and wood and nails," the modest bungalow that would be the only home they ever owned.

As Walter sits in his cell "waiting for freedom to begin again," he is far from sure he is up to the challenge. His involvement in the Watergate fiasco had been absurdly incidental—he allowed a trunk filled with illicit cash to be smuggled into his office—and no one cared about his story. It was certainly not worthy of the television appearances or book deals scored by some of his fellow inmates. Walter lacks star power, too, because he had fallen once before, and his descent this time was nothing compared to the "belly-whoppers from the tops of church steeples" others were now taking. In any case, after Ruth's death he has had little will to try to clear his name, no interest in cashing in.

"At least I don't smoke anymore," Walter muses, looking for something to feel good about. His Brooks Brothers suit is waiting for him in the prison supply room, pocked with holes from the nicotine habit he shares with the author. Strangely enough, this was what attracted the president's attention the one time he paid him any notice. In May 1970 Walter was summoned to the White House for an emergency meeting, to deal with fallout from the Kent State shootings. All the heavyweights were there, including Henry Kissinger, Spiro Agnew, and future jailbirds H. R. Haldeman and John Ehrlichman.

Thinking no doubt of the Cuyahoga Massacre, Walter stayed up the night before drafting recommendations on how the moment might be seized for reconciliation. "The President should call the tragedy a tragedy," he wrote in his report, "should reveal himself as having had his heart broken. He should declare a day or perhaps a week of national mourning, with flags flown at half-mast everywhere."

Vonnegut reacted to Kent State and other violent clashes of the Vietnam era with horror, of course, refracted through the eyes of a man with experience in the infantry. He warned young people anxious to get to the barricades what it was like on the business end of tanks and high-powered automatic weapons. Meanwhile, he considered the government's heavy-handed response to their protests—reminiscent of its role in the labor battles of the 1890s and 1930s—indefensible in a democracy. The militias deployed were woefully undertrained, "draft dodgers" in many cases, and it was a certain recipe for bloodshed. "What's disconcerting about Kent State," Vonnegut said in a discussion of *Jailbird*, "is the fact that it shows we still cling to this dream that every American man is a potential Minuteman the minute he's handed a rifle."[10]

Here Vonnegut asks us to ponder how things might have gone differently if Walter's approach had been considered. But at the meeting he was not invited to speak, and no one expressed the slightest interest in the folder he held in his shaking hands. When he lit his fourth simultaneous cigarette, Nixon cracked a joke from the head of the table that drew laughter all around. "We will pause in our business," he said with his unhappy little smile, "while our special advisor on youth affairs gives us a demonstration of how to put out a campfire." It was not in the president's nature to grasp the possibilities of a compassionate response. He was a defective dreamer-in-chief, interested only in damage control.

In his cell Walter's time-travels are interrupted by the appearance of the gospel-singing Emil Larkin, a Charles Colson figure transformed from a hatchet man to a devout and evangelizing Christian. Brother Starbuck tries to tune out his harangues about the wrath of a vengeful Jesus.

With a twist of sadism, Larkin revisits the day in 1949 when Walter Starbuck inadvertently committed career suicide. Called to testify before a House subcommittee on domestic subversion, he responded to questioning from an aggressive congressman from California with examples of men like himself who had served their country well in spite of past affiliation with radical causes. Among the names he mentioned was Leland Clewes, a Yale man who closely resembles the real-life Alger Hiss.

By outing Clewes, Walter handed young Richard Nixon a publicity windfall, one on which he would build his meteoric career. At the same time, it became convenient shorthand to link "Starbuck and Clewes" as poster boys for disloyalty. They were finished as public servants. The pain of the mistake lingered still in Walter's heart, this was a crime, committed so innocently, for which there seemed to be no absolution.

Emil Larkin is an easy target for parody, his jailhouse conversion a particularly grotesque example of religious faith as expediency. But the author's "Christ-worshipping agnostic" side comes through in *Jailbird* as his protagonist begins to take his first steps back into the world. Penniless and disowned by even his son, Walter Starbuck walks the stations of the cross, experiencing solace and love rather than abuse. In conveying the sheer ordinariness of the offerings, in his eye for the power of the smallest gesture, Vonnegut succeeds in redeeming this otherwise tragic story. We awaken, with Walter, to the grace and poetry of everyday life.

Guard Clyde Carter, cousin to the current occupant of the White House from Georgia, arrives to rescue the parolee from his long-winded tormentor. He had taken a correspondence course in bartending with Walter, and now Clyde is sure that in no time his friend will be running his own watering hole in Manhattan. "This was kindness on his part, and not genuine optimism," Walter concludes. "Clyde was trying to help me be brave."

As they walk across the prison yard Walter encounters an inmate spearing litter with a spiked stick, "small and old" like himself, and the man scolds Walter one last time for his youthful dalliances. The man's utter lack of remorse for the trail of damage his manipulations of public funds left in their wake prompts Walter to consider that "every successful government is of necessity a Ponzi scheme." "How else to account for the gyrations in economic weather that plagued so many people?"

> How else am I to explain to my polyglot grandchildren what the United States was like in the nineteen-thirties, when its owners and politicians could not find ways for so many of its people to earn even the most basic necessities?
>
> And then suddenly, there were formerly poor people in officers' clubs, beautifully costumed and ordering filets mignon and champagne. There were formerly poor people in enlisted men's clubs, serviceably costumed and clad and ordering hamburgers and beer. A man who two years before had patched the holes in his shoes with cardboard suddenly had a Jeep or a truck or an airplane or a boat, and unlimited supplies of fuel and ammunition.

The attendant at the supply room is Dr. Bob Fender, a lifer known for writing science-fiction tales that sometimes made their way into disreputable magazines. (Vonnegut alerted us in the prologue that Kilgore Trout would be back, the promises of *Breakfast of Champions* notwithstanding, and indeed this was one of Fender's noms de plume. Trout "could not make it on the outside," the author explains. "A lot of good people can't make it on the outside.") Fender is another accidental criminal, convicted of treason during the Korean War thanks to an affair with a nightclub singer who turned out to be a spy. On Walter Starbuck's liberation day he plays at top volume a recording of the Edith Piaf song his girlfriend used to sing in Tokyo, "*Non, je ne regrette rien.*"

As a going-away present Fender took the trouble to have the suit with the cigarette burns repaired. Walter becomes a civilian again, "as dazed and shy and tremble-legged as any other newborn creature." The full-length mirror in the dressing room is turned against the wall—"another example of Fender's delicacy," Walter explains, to delay the moment when departing jailbirds have to see what a stretch in prison has done to them. His companions stay upbeat as the time to leave now arrives. "Good morning, Mr. Ambassador," Fender bows deferentially as his friend takes his leave. "Another crisp and bright day. The queen is expecting you for lunch at one."

Freedom, exhilarating and terrifying. Waiting for the bus in the Georgia sun, Walter is as unstuck in time as Billy Pilgrim. He drifts back to when he was last cut adrift from the government in 1953. He had not been prosecuted like Leland Clewes, but his purge was no less certain in coming, starting with demotion to a lower classification at the Defense Department. Once he was fired there was no place else to go. "Alas, whereas life for me had been so long a sort of Virginia reel, as friends handed me on from job to job, no one could now think of a vacant post anywhere." He was blacklisted, excommunicated from the Harvard family. The worst thing about it all was the impact on Ruth, who lost her friends in the Pentagon social circle. Crushing guilt toward a woman seems to be a requirement for Vonnegut's male characters.

A limousine screeches to the front gate of the prison, disgorging Virgil Greathouse, über-mastermind of the burglaries, wiretaps, and IRS harassment schemes uncovered in the Watergate investigations. Pipe clenched in his teeth, Greathouse resembles Nixon's attorney general, John Mitchell. Surrendering himself with the arrogance of a potentate, he does not notice his co-conspirator sitting on the bench, never anything to him but "a little mouse from the White House pantry."

The driver, Cleveland Lawes, offers Walter a ride to the airport, and en route tells him *his* Korean War story. A Harvard-trained operative in his POW camp convinced him to defect, and it took delicate high-level negotiations to secure his return. "They couldn't stand it," Lawes explains, "that even one American, even a black one, would think for even a minute that maybe America wasn't the best country in the world." He bears the RAM-JAC logo on the breast pocket of his blazer.

From Atlanta Walter flies to New York, where he had reserved a room at the Hotel Arapahoe, now a flophouse in the squalor of Times Square. He remembers his first visit there, as a college freshman in the antediluvian year 1931, under orders from Mr. McCone to take a date to the fanciest restaurant in town after the Harvard-Columbia football game. He had $40 in his wallet. "I could have bought the whole state of Arkansas for forty dollars cash," he recalls in amazement of those days.

His companion for the evening was Sarah Wyatt, a Yankee heiress whose father, a Harvard man, had jumped off a Wall Street ledge two years earlier. In her family's diminished circumstances are echoes of the atmosphere in the Vonnegut household when the author was a child. At the restaurant Walter inadvertently tipped the violinist with one of his twenty dollar bills, an act Sarah took as a vulgar display of arrogance. Vonnegut developed an acute sensitivity for such slights as a child, when ostentation was in bad taste and discussions of money forbidden, a kind of pornography. It was all a mistake, Walter pleaded to Sarah—he was not the bon vivant he pretended to be, but instead just "a robot invented and controlled by Alexander Hamilton McCone."

Sarah and Walter became friends, and in time she even accepted his proposal for marriage. She dropped out of private school to become a nurse, and moved by the suffering she observed, joined the Communist Party. "She would make me join, too," the ever-compliant Walter remembers. There may be traces of Jane, Vonnegut's first wife, in Sarah's social activism. More generally we can see in *Jailbird* a pattern in the author's later novels of the female characters becoming more powerful and admirably assertive. As the alter ego here concludes, they are "more virtuous, braver about life, and closer to the secrets of the universe than I could ever be." Vonnegut scholars Kathryn Hume and Peter Freese find in this progression evidence that the author is moving beyond the confusion and anger toward his mother that had "so contaminated his inner picture of women" for so long.[11]

Half a century later Walter walks into the Arapahoe again, its once breathtaking lobby now subdivided and barricaded with masonry and iron bars. The clerk at the reception desk is Israel Edel, holder of a doctorate in history. This was the best job he could find. Edel looks up in shock when the man tells him about his letter requesting a room. It is unprecedented, he thinks to himself, "like making a reservation in a burn ward." When Edel sees the return address on the envelope, it is clear he is dealing with a newly released ex-con.

"The least we can do," Dr. Edel announces cheerfully as he reaches for the room key, "is to give you the Bridal Suite." When Walter inquires what is on the other side of the wall, where the restaurant had once been, Edel cringes with the thought of having to initiate a dignified older gentleman into a world in which images of sexual depravity could be marketed as entertainment. He apologizes, explaining it all as patiently and euphemistically as possible. "He might have been my father," Walter recalls, touched, "and I was his little child."

Walter's sleep that night is plagued by dreams of what might have been. He should have become the member-in-good-standing of the Harvard club that Mr. McCone wanted him to be, today the head of a foundation or perhaps a cabinet official. He rises from bed early, as per his prison routine, and steps outside to be baptized by the fresh air. The author takes us on a walk through midtown at dawn, at the moment of Walter's resurrection. Everything is miraculous to the senses.

> I walked out into a city stunned by its own innocence. Nobody was doing anything bad to anybody anywhere. It was even hard to *imagine* badness. Why would anybody be bad?

Like all Manhattanites, natives or recent arrivals, Kurt Vonnegut had mixed feelings about life in the metropolis. "The Capital of the World," it was *the* place for an artist to find stimulation and congenial company, of a kind that could not be had where he grew up or in the wilds of Cape Cod. But in its cacophony and squalor the city could be monstrous, too—recall his images of the Island of Death in *Slapstick*. And the anonymity one enjoyed, blending into street crowds, was double-edged—relief for a shy celebrity, but also sometimes a source of deep loneliness. In *Palm Sunday* he wrote of the thinness of many New York "friendships."[12]

In *Jailbird* we get the city as lyric dream, full of possibility and warm human contact amid the rat race. It is the view of a man from the provinces, looking for those things. "You know what the trouble is with New York?" Vonnegut recalled being asked at a party by the actress Marsha Mason, from St. Louis. "Nobody here," she said, answering her own question, "believes that there is such a thing as innocence."[13]

Walter revels in the newness that surrounds him, marveling at the sight of a "baby-faced policeman." He enters a coffee shop, and finds himself in another vision of heaven.

> To the waitress everybody was "honeybunch" and "darling" and "dear." It was like an emergency ward after a great catastrophe. It did not matter what race or class the victims belonged to. They were all given the same miracle drug, which was coffee.

The diner reminds us of Eliot's Rosewater Foundation office in its open-hearted embrace. "The profit motive was not in operation." Setting the tone is the owner, Frank Ubraico, endlessly scolded by his employees for abandoning the register to help with tables and in the kitchen. No job is beneath him. Ubraico's hand had been burned once when, without thinking, he reached into a vat of oil to retrieve a wristwatch. The scars were a kind of stigmata, making him all the more beatific.

After breakfast Walter finds a park bench to sit and read his newspaper, and is intoxicated by the sights and sounds—flowers in bloom, joggers going through their paces, workaday traffic noise. The peace does not last long. A young man sits down across from him, his oversized portable radio blaring oppressively. It was a common sight in the city, the machines a kind of "prosthetic device," Vonnegut writes, allowing young men to assert their power and exude "an artificial enthusiasm for the planet." As Walter, in flight, reaches a crosswalk, another miracle happens. The prison daydream of a familiar face does indeed come to pass, but not in the way he had expected. Amid a city of millions, Leland Clewes is headed right in his path, a "husk of the man" he once was in his battered suit, buoyantly lugging the sample case of an unsuccessful salesman.

Now Vonnegut gives us a moment of burlesque street theater, drawing upon a decade of close study living in Manhattan. It is also a convenient plot device to bring his characters together—he was always thinking about the mechanics of stories, and how to keep the reader engaged. "An author gets to a point where he needs a couple of coincidences to keep the story moving," he said of the Clewes/Starbuck encounter in *Jailbird.* "So, he takes a deep breath and treats himself to a coincidence." As the Bokononist might say, "busy, busy, busy."[14]

Walter is suddenly between a man with a sandwich board and a shopping-bag lady clad in oversized basketball shoes, shouting profanities at gawkers as they pass by. With Clewes closing in, he resists the urge to run, burning to prove that he is every bit as honorable as the person whose gold-plated cover he had once blown. "The little Slavic jailbird" holds his ground in the face of "the former Anglo-Saxon champion." We admire this rare moment of pride.

"Walter F. Starbuck, I presume," the man says, extending his hand. This is no showdown. (Perhaps Walter is the bitter one, since it was Clewes who had long ago stolen his fiancée, Sarah.) As he gathers himself to respond with the gravity the occasion demanded, a shriek of recognition erupts from the homeless lady at his side. "Oh, my God! Is that really you?" she cries, leaning her bags against his leg she grabs his wrist.

"Leland, all I want to say to you is that I know what jail is now," Walter blurts out preemptively, "and, God damn it, the thing I'm sorriest about in my whole life is that I had anything to do with sending you to jail." But there is nothing to forgive. Clewes had chosen to view his misfortunes as opportunities, and going to jail was a blessing, he observes with a welcoming smile. Together he and Sarah built a love that had "stood up to the hardest tests."

As Clewes departs, Walter has to deal still with the woman in his face. Remarkably, she is Mary Kathleen O'Looney, another ghost from his past. "Now that I've found you, I'll never let you go again!" Mary Kathleen vows as a crowd encircles them. Walter imagines how the exchange must look to their eyes. He and Mary Kathleen are actors in a play, enacting "a miracle that our audience must have prayed for again and again: the rescue of at least one shopping-bag lady by a man who knew her well." Succumbing to the exhortations of the onlookers, he hugs her, and feels in his arms "a bundle of dry twigs that was wrapped in rags." For the first time since Ruth's death, he is in tears.

Mary Kathleen sounds mentally ill—people are after her, she insists. But Walter's return to her life—a man she could trust, still faithful, she imagines, to their youthful ideals—is a sign of deliverance. She leads him down into the old locomotive repair shop under Grand Central Station that is her refuge for the moment, like the catacombs where the early Christians hid. From out of the labyrinth they emerge into the lobby of the Chrysler Building, that cathedral of American free enterprise completed just as the house of cards collapsed. An elevator whisks them up to the celestial space of its crown, home still to its original tenant, a harp company—just absorbed by RAMJAC.

We discover—well before it dawns on Walter—that Mary Kathleen is married to Jack Graham Jr., founder of RAMJAC, a "Cinderella in reverse," as Peter Freese puts it. She is the majority stockholder of her late husband's conglomerate. Maybe her fantasies of being pursued are more than paranoia. Mary Kathleen is not involved in day-to-day management decisions, and has no idea that the business has become synonymous with corporate piracy.[15]

Now perhaps Walter can tell her why the world had gone so cold. "Nobody will even speak to me," she sobs. He knows it is not that simple. "There was a limit to how much reproachful ugliness most people could bear to look at, and Mary Kathleen and all her shopping-bag sisters had exceeded that limit."

But all is not lost, people are not inherently bad, even in a system that encourages inhumanity. Walter assures Mary Kathleen that he has experienced "almost nothing but kindness" in his new life, brief as it has been, flashing back to the generosity of the prison guard and the supply room clerk and the limo driver. "So there are still saints around!" she exclaims. Walter recounts the hospitality of the Arapahoe night clerk, and the coffee shop waitresses who lifted his spirits just that morning. Not least, there was his street encounter with the man he long thought to be his worst enemy.

Mary Kathleen produces from her shoe a battered photograph of Walter with Kenneth Whistler, the Harvard-trained labor organizer (based on Vonnegut's hero, Powers Hapgood) from 1935. Whistler was on campus to raise money for striking miners in Kentucky. That day was memorable also for the surprise visit by Alexander McCone, who wanted to see for himself how his surrogate son was using his opportunities. "I had somehow neglected to tell him that I had become a communist," Walter remembers sheepishly. When McCone found him in bed with Mary Kathleen, a portrait of Karl Marx hanging on the dorm room wall, he slammed the door in a stuttering rage, never to return. "What a daring young man I was! What a treacherous young man I was!" The memories are fraught with guilt. Walter posed as a campus radical more for the attention of women than out any deep-seated political conviction. Even then he was planning to abandon Mary Kathleen at the end of the school year. "She was too low class," he remembers thinking, with renewed self-loathing.

Kenneth Whistler cut a dashing figure at the lectern, bandages and arm cast complimenting his suit and carefully shined shoes. Mary Kathleen and Walter held hands in the front row as he began speaking, imagining his appearance to be the result of another scuffle with "the forces of evil." Whistler thrilled his audience with an indictment of the American class system and its hereditary plutocrats—many of them Harvard men.

He ended with a solemn retelling of the saga of Sacco and Vanzetti, at the time still "planetary celebrities" canonized for their sacrifices to the new millennium Whistler promised was just over the horizon. Vonnegut knew their legend as a boy, and he did his homework to include their "crucifixion" here in the right way. "Because, damn-it, the story is so shaking and moving—one of the most impressive I know," he said in an interview. "The Christ story is marvelous, but it's not really about people like us."[16]

Vonnegut often bemoaned the disappearance of shared reference points in our culture, books and works of art, stories and myths that people could use as a foundation to engage with each other about values and morality. "So I've been trying to crystallize a few things," he told Peter Reed in a discussion of the thinking behind *Jailbird*.

> Like, let's all be able to talk about the Sermon on the Mount (I mean if I were cultural dictator), let's have that part of the package because it's so influential as a typical outrage in America, the sort of miscarriage of justice that's possible, because of ruling class conspiracy and xenophobia and so forth, let's keep the Sacco and Vanzetti thing alive. I thought it was reason enough to write the book, just to talk about Sacco and Vanzetti again.[17]

Decades later the martyrs have been forgotten, and Walter has failed miserably to live up to their example. "I have been in a lot of trouble over the years, but that was all accidental. Never have I risked my life, or even my comfort, in the service of mankind. Shame on me."

Jailbird concludes in typically rollicking, bittersweet Vonnegut style. Walter is arrested in the showroom of the harp company Mary Kathleen had taken him to, on suspicion of involvement with a fencing operation. He is taken to the police station and locked in a basement cell for hours. It reminds him of his exile as Special Advisor on Youth Affairs to the Nixon administration. Lacking the fortitude of a Kenneth Whistler, he cracks, sobbing and bouncing off the walls before blacking out.

Walter awakens to what seems a particularly surreal dream. Exercising her "cosmic powers" as Mrs. Jack Graham—we think of the magical qualities of money at the center of *God Bless You, Mr. Rosewater*—Mary Kathleen, a version of Eliot Rosewater, has retained the toughest attorney in New York to get Walter out of jail. This is Roy Cohn, middle-aged but still as lethal as he was during the McCarthy years. "He was on my side now," Walter observes, noting the irony. A stretch limousine arrives carrying two passengers—Leland Clewes and Israel Edel. Frank Ubriaco, Cleveland Lawes, and Bob Fender would be gathered up next. They were all RAMJAC vice presidents now.

Walter descends underground to look for his angel, embarking too late on another rescue mission. She is hiding in a bathroom stall after being sideswiped by a taxi. Blood is coming from her nose, but "there were worse things wrong with her," he knows. "I cannot name them. No inventory was ever taken of everything that was broken in Mary Kathleen." In her gym shoe is a will, bequeathing RAMJAC to its rightful owners, the American people. She thanks Walter for hugging her in front of the crowd that day, and for his youthful declarations of idealism and love, however insincere. "At least you tried to believe what the people with hearts believed," she reassures him as he starts to cry, "so you were a good man just the same."

Two years later Walter Starbuck is about to become a jailbird again. He concealed Mary Kathleen's will to insure that her eleventh-hour executive appointments went into effect. Walter has taken full advantage of his perquisites—he was living the gentleman's life for which he had been groomed by Alexander McCone. But now the parent company, which owns "19 percent of the country," is being dismantled, its parts auctioned off to Saudi princes and other cash-heavy foreign suitors. RAMJAC's myriad businesses had been engineered strictly for profit anyway, so by design they were as aloof from human needs "as, say, thunderstorms," Walter concludes philosophically. "Mary Kathleen might as well have left one-fifth of the weather to the people."

Leland and Sarah Clewes throw a going-away party for their old friend. The guests that night include even Walter Jr. and his grandchildren. The festivities end with everyone listening to a 78-rpm recording of the last minutes of Walter's infamous congressional testimony from 1949. Congressman Nixon is heard asking why a son of immigrants had proven so "ungrateful" to America and its economic system. "Why?" the witness responded, echoing the words of Powers Hapgood. "The Sermon on the Mount, sir." Walter can now bask in the applause.

Just as it would be wrong to characterize Kurt Vonnegut as an opponent of technology, despite misgivings about its dangers, so it is in error to see him as a knee-jerk enemy of American free enterprise. As a child of the Depression he admired entrepreneurship and could be a shrewd, if not always successful, businessman, whether the product was oil-burning Saabs or mass-marketed books. He lauded those who made things work every day in the great engine of our economy, from the managers on down to the "Reeks and Wrecks."

His critique was directed at the inequities built into the system, the stacked deck and perpetually "loaded dice" that condemned so many to needless suffering. And Vonnegut had a well-earned fatalism about whether this state of affairs would ever change. Concentrations of wealth would endure, Ponzi schemes would rise and fall, corporations would continue to treat their employees like disposable machinery—whether through the naked brutality of Cuyahoga Bridge and Iron or the more bloodless methods of multinationals like RAMJAC. The "winners" would mostly win, through booms and busts, calm seas and typhoons. Any ground gained against them would be isolated and provisional, and those who anguished about the injustice of it all would continue to be demonized. The dream of a humane "revolution," whether from above or below, might never come to pass.

But Walter Starbuck has learned, late in life to be sure, that community, kindness, small acts of generosity can get us through all kinds of rough weather. His triumph, and Vonnegut's too, is an openness to such moments of grace. Meanwhile, we keep alive the struggle, hold close the mythical inspiration of Debs, Sacco and Vanzetti, Powers Hapgood—long-distance warriors, men to follow.

TEN

Deadeye Dick

It may be a bad thing that so many people try to make good stories
out of their lives. A story, after all, is as artificial as a mechanical
bucking bronco in a drinking establishment.
—Rudy Waltz

This is as much Shangri-La as anywhere.
—Otto Waltz

Kurt Vonnegut admitted that his self-esteem was on the line with each book. Reviews for *Jailbird*, fortunately, were mostly enthusiastic. Even the author gave himself an A grade for the effort. Relieved and validated, at least for the moment, in the next novel he would return to a more intensely personal voice, exploring the contradictions of his life as a successful writer cut off, in many ways, from the sources that had shaped and nurtured him.[1]

With its more nuanced view of Midland City, Ohio—the thinly-veiled surrogate for Vonnegut's Indianapolis, whose flat contours he charted in *Breakfast of Champions*—*Deadeye Dick* (1982) represents a major step in the author's rapprochement with his past. It was a trajectory signaled by an essay on writing he crafted for an ad campaign by the International Paper Company two years earlier, appearing in magazines from *Time* to *Rolling*

Stone. The message he wanted to get across was to be yourself, to understand that the materials for a creative life were always close at hand if you were open to them. A grounded authenticity was the key to Vonnegut's connection with a broad audience, and, like his hero Mark Twain, he understood that being provincial allowed him to be universal.[2]

Vonnegut admitted he grew up in an environment that, for an artist, could feel uninspiring, where the common speech "sounds like a band saw cutting galvanized tin." And yet he had no choice but to be true to those influences, to try to divine their poetry. No matter how hard he might try he could never become an East Coast Brahmin or an English gentleman, or a continental aristocrat like his ancestors so energetically aspired to be. "I trust my own writing most, and others seem to trust it most, too," he insisted, "when I sound most like a person from Indianapolis, which is what I am."[3]

As he mounted art shows and enjoyed summers in the Hamptons, Kurt and Jill were busy with plans to adopt a baby—Vonnegut's seventh child, Lily. For him it was a vote of confidence in the future, the expression of a resilient family instinct even as he dealt with the reality of first wife Jane's grueling battle with ovarian cancer. He found himself a wanderer between worlds, still feeling the pull of nostalgia as the years moved inexorably forward.

The American Dream celebrates freedom, restlessness, mobility—the idea of "lighting out" to pursue a grand destiny elsewhere. Vonnegut lived this dream, and now challenges its wisdom. The rewards out there are not always what they are cracked up to be. Again it is the hero's journey, the conflict faced by all exiles in one way or another, between the security of a place they never really wanted to leave and the attractions of "Shangri-La," the world beyond. Vonnegut's most self-consciously theatrical novel, *Deadeye Dick* is a meditation on our stories and how they define, nourish, and imprison us. Whether we leave or stay home, is it possible to make peace with the narratives imposed upon us, to go beyond the pain of our parents and the mistakes we feel we have made, to take hold of our own destinies?

Rudy Waltz is a middle-aged pharmacist, an everyman the author uses to imagine what it might have been like to stay home in Indianapolis. The city he inhabits for most of the novel, the place of his birth, has a stifling quality, to be sure. Rudy is saddled with the nickname that is the book's title, a badge of disgrace he cannot remove. It is another Vonnegut tale of crime and punishment, guilt and penance, and we wonder if the protagonist this time can get out from under the weight.

The initial signs are not encouraging. Rudy begins his memoir with metaphors of disease.

> I have caught life. I have come down with life. I was a wisp of undifferentiated nothingness, and then a little peephole opened quite suddenly. Light and sound poured in. Voices began to describe me and my surroundings. Nothing they said could be appealed. They never shut up. Year after year they piled detail upon detail.

Rudy feels determined by his circumstances, condemned to believe, even before his life really begins, that autonomy and full participation are not options. The things to which others aspire so casually are, for him, off-limits.

The early chapters focus on Rudy's father, Otto, son of a German American commercial dynasty with obvious similarities to the Vonnegut and Lieber families of Indianapolis. In the late nineteenth century the Waltzes built a pharmaceutical empire on the success of "St. Elmo's Remedy," a mixture of grain alcohol, opium, and cocaine.

Otto's mother indulged his creative side by providing him a studio in the loft of their carriage house, its windows allowing in the north light so favored by painters. The tutor she retained for him, however, a "rapscallion German cabinetmaker," took advantage of the parents' naïvety and corrupted the boy. Excursions to out-of-town museums were really an apprenticeship in debauchery, saloons, and whorehouses, and the pupil gladly went along for the ride. "Was either one of them about to acknowledge," Rudy asks, "that Father couldn't paint or draw for sour apples?"

At the age of eighteen Otto was sent to live with relatives in Vienna, where he would enroll in the prestigious Academy of Fine Arts. It was the romantic adventure he would cling to for the rest of his life. The city teemed then with bohemian energy "and so much wine and music that it seemed to Father to be a fancy dress ball," Rudy tells us. Otto adapted himself to the occasion, deciding "to come the party as a starving artist."

He was less than diligent in his studies, however, and with his modest gifts, almost everything he painted, Rudy intimates, "wound up looking as though it were made of cement." When a professor dismissed his portfolio it was an assault on the ego Otto could not abide. He bought his way out of the humiliation, impulsively declaring the canvas of another student, also about to be terminated from the academy, a work of genius and offering cash for it on the spot. Its creator turned out to be young Adolf Hitler. It is a classic Vonnegut intersection, and a demonstration of how easy it is to make catastrophic mistakes in life. But for this intercession, the future Führer might have frozen to death in the streets that winter.

The two outcasts struck up a friendship, "jeering at the art establishment which had rejected them" on long walking trips together. The watercolor sealing their bond hung in the master bedroom of the Waltz home when Rudy was growing up.

In 1914 Otto assumed, like many others, that "the fancy dress ball was to become a fancy dress picnic," and as war broke out he finagled a commission in the Hungarian Life Guard, whose panther-skin uniforms he fancied. Told that this would endanger his U.S. citizenship (and, more important, his allowance), Otto abandoned his dreams of martial glory and returned home.

Except for the friendship with Hitler, Otto's journey mirrors those made by the Vonnegut and Lieber men who were sent on Grand Tours abroad, went East for a gentleman's education, then complied, more or less reluctantly, with the expectation they return to Indianapolis and set themselves up with professions and families. There is some of Kurt Sr., who traveled widely in his youth and embraced European high culture as ardently as any of his cousins, in this portrait of Otto. He came back, only to watch the German colony into which he was born fall apart in his adult years.

In *Palm Sunday* the author expressed a particular feeling of identification with his grandfather, Bernard, an artist who loved his brief time in New York and never adapted to the confines of his hometown. For all of Bernard's success as a local architect, his was, in the end, a tragic story. "He was to surrender to the gravitational pull of the tremendous mass of respectability which his father and mother had amassed in the American wilderness," Kurt Vonnegut observed, commenting on Uncle John Rauch's family history. "He should have disobeyed."[4]

There are also elements here of the men in young Edith Lieber's life. Uncle John tells us about her father, Albert, the brewery heir and "rascal" who spent his time in London "the very model of Victorian sartorial elegance" with his Savile Row suits, silk hats, and handmade boots. Albert was "extroverted, flamboyant, sociable, and a big spender," and he brought these habits with him when he returned to Indianapolis. He was a corrupt, absentee custodian of business matters and an inattentive father to his three children. After their mother's death he did not protect them from his second wife, in Kurt Vonnegut's telling a woman as harsh as the witch in *Cinderella*. Albert Lieber's "emotional faithlessness" was a major cause of Edith's problems later in life. As a beautiful American princess she had her pick of suitors during extended stays each year in Dusseldorf, and was briefly engaged to a "heel-clicking" Prussian army captain, "a dashing figure in his colorful dress uniform" who may have reminded her of her father. Otto Waltz seems to be a blend of these Edwardian dandies.[5]

Otto moved into the carriage house, "a little piece of Europe in southwestern Ohio" with cobblestone floors, oak beams, and a conical slate roof. Rudy's lifelong sense of difference owed in no small measure to having grown up in such an unusual abode, with its empty spaces and large sliding doors that never opened. Otto took pride in his part in its design, evidence that he was not completely without creative talent, but it was cold and lonesome for a child.

Neighbors considered the Waltz place spooky, and indeed there was a kind of black magic up in the attic. That was where Otto stored his collection of antique guns, "junk from Europe" he brought back from a trip after the war. The author may be alluding here to the burdens of his parents' Old World heritage. "Father thought them beautiful," Rudy tells us ominously of the artifacts, "but they might as well have been copperheads and rattlesnakes. They were murder."

In interviews Kurt Vonnegut expressed an aversion to the Hemingway ethos of ritual violence, admitting with embarrassment that he came from a long line of confirmed "gun nuts." It was, he suspected, a legacy of the frontier mythos, a matter of proving one's masculinity in a culture that relegated the arts to the female sphere. "My father was right on the edge of the woman's world as an architect," he explained. "His father had been in the same spot. So they'd collect guns and go hunting with the best of them." As a youngster Kurt Jr. was himself a skilled marksman—"maybe the best shot in my company when I was a PFC," he observed with pride. But he worried about the proliferation of firearms among civilians, whether they were criminals, suburbanites braced for the next race war, or ill-trained militias like the one at Kent State. It was a recipe for disaster in a culture of such free-floating, vigilante individualism.[6]

Otto was a principal stockholder in the Waltz Brothers Drug Company. With adolescent cheek, he enjoyed showing up to board meetings in beret, smock, and sandals, oozing contempt for relatives he considered "intolerably humorless and provincial and obsessed with profits." This burlesques the tension within the Vonnegut/Lieber clans between artists and free spirits like Bernard and Albert and the men of practical affairs, the managers of the hardware stores and the brewery.

A local farmer named John Fortune accidentally dropped a beam on Otto's foot while helping with the renovation of the carriage house, foreclosing any second chance he might have had to be a warrior. Until his death Otto bemoaned missing the opportunity to prove himself in battle, and envied Fortune and the other men in town who came back from the trenches with medals on their chests. His lone civic honor would be for organizing scrap drives during the Second World War, a recognition that only added salt to the wound.

Otto married the young and painfully shy Emma in 1922, and when they returned from a honeymoon in Europe they found themselves "the only Waltzes in town." The headquarters of the drug store chain had been quietly moved to Chicago. Emma seemed content to live in the shadow of her husband's outsized personality, even though she was the one with a college degree. "He could certainly lecture on history or race or biology or art or politics for hours," Rudy remembers of his father, "although he had read very little." Otto's ideas were "cannibalized from the educations and miseducations of his roistering companions in Vienna before the First World War." Among them, of course, was Hitler.

In 1933 Otto sent a message of congratulation to his old friend, along with the painting he had bought from him two decades earlier. The following year he traveled with Emma and their older son, Felix, to see in person the vibrant Germany being created out of the ashes. The infant Rudy was left in the care of servants, all black, whom he came to regard as his closest relatives. From them he learned how to do housekeeping chores and to cook, which explains the recipes for soul food and German delicacies, chemistry formulas delivered with brio, that punctuate the narrative. They are a signature Vonnegut gesture, giving the protagonist (and the reader) a break from the demanding material, a version of Billy Pilgrim's Tralfamadorian interludes in *Slaughterhouse-Five*. "I think it really worked," Vonnegut said of the device. "I think a swell way to celebrate life, really, no matter how bad it gets, is to think about food. I wanted [Rudy] to forget his troubles and start talking about how to make sauerkraut."[7]

The Midland City *Bugle-Reporter* covered the return of the Waltzes as local color and a celebration of ethnic pride, featuring a photograph of the father in lederhosen and Felix in the uniform of Hitler Youth. Vonnegut is playing here with the complexities of his German American identity, imagining in grotesque form how suspicious neighbors might have viewed his family in the 1930s. Nobody objected when Otto flew a swastika flag "as big as a bedsheet" from the cupola of the carriage house. With enthusiasm he embraced a new mission, traveling around the Midwest with a slide show to promote the Nazi experiment. "This was quite a mistake."

Rudy's fondest memories are of the cocoon of the kitchen, "so hot and fragrant." "It was the only room in the house where any meaningful work was going on, and yet it was as cramped as a ship's galley," he remembers. It was a window onto another, more congenial way of living. On cold days the staff gathered there as family, and he was their adopted son. "Everybody would talk and talk and talk so easily, just blather and blather and laugh and laugh. I was included in the conversation. I was a nice little boy. Everybody liked me." If only he could return to this state of innocence.

This digression pays homage to the vitality of an African American culture largely invisible to white society in those days, but attractive to an observant child hungry for companionship. In particular it evokes Ida Young, the Vonnegut family cook and Kurt Jr.'s surrogate mother, who modeled for him at a tender age a warm and dignified humanity. "I probably spent more time with her than I spent with anybody," he remembered.

She knew Bible stories by heart, told him anecdotes about her ancestors, and read sentimental poetry to him—"about love which would not die, about faithful dogs and humble cottages where happiness was, about people growing old, about visits to cemeteries, about babies who died." Vonnegut acknowledged the depth of her influence on his vision of the world, the landscape of his most vulnerable side. "I am aware of my origins—in a big, brick dreamhouse designed by my architect father, where nobody was home for long periods of time, except for me and Ida Young."[8]

"Somewhere in there the Nazi flag came down." Hate mail arrived at the house as the international climate changed, and even John Fortune stopped speaking to Otto, declaring him "a dangerous nincompoop" to everyone in town. Already a war hero, Fortune would soon be enshrined as an even greater local legend. In 1938, after his wife died and the bank foreclosed on his farm, he packed up and left for the Himalayas. Inspired by the story *Lost Horizon,* John Fortune was "in search of far higher happiness and wisdom than was available, evidently, in Midland City, Ohio."

Rudy interrupts his memoir with a bulletin from the present. A neutron bomb has "depopulated" his hometown. In targeting only people it was quite an advance from the ordinance Vonnegut saw destroy Dresden in World War II. The authorities have characterized it as an accident, a "friendly bomb." A tractor-trailer crashed and exploded on the interstate, it was reported—not far from Dwayne Hoover's Exit Eleven Pontiac Village, the spiritual epicenter of Midland City we remember from *Breakfast of Champions.*

In its looming mystery the episode reminds us of the "Airborne Toxic Event" of Don DeLillo's iconic novel of 1980s dread, *White Noise.* Beyond its real dangers, for Vonnegut the neutron bomb was a metaphor for a more personal sense of loss, representing "the disappearance of so many people I cared about in Indianapolis when I was starting out to be a writer." The city is there, he tells us in the preface, "but the people are gone." There is no going home.

Rudy has reason to be skeptical about the official story. A demonstration test and cover-up was plausible, and its success might well be celebrated in some quarters. After all, "every one of the television sets in the new Holiday Inn is still fully operable." (We assume that the Day-Glo lights in the Tally-Ho Room are working too.) Even the sphere of the Mildred Barry Center for the Arts (its emptiness, Vonnegut jokes, a symbol of his head on the eve of his sixtieth birthday) emerged from the blast unscathed, still perched precariously over Sugar Creek atop its stilts. Anonymous and remote from the centers of power, were the thousands who perished considered somehow expendable? "Has the world lost anything it loved?"

Vonnegut used the doomsday weapon of *Deadeye Dick* to comment on the effects of the economic recession of the early 1980s, the indifference in high places to its human toll in cities and towns across the nation. "Like Terre Haute," he told Peter Reed. "The last business just closed down there—Columbia Records just closed down its plant there permanently. You know this place has got twenty-seven churches, it's got a railroad yard, it's got all this, and it might as well have been neutron bombed." For those affected it was another Great Depression, but it didn't really register with the people who could do something about it.[9]

Vonnegut was reacting also to the renewed Cold War arms race under Ronald Reagan and to loose talk at the Pentagon of "manageable casualties" in such a conflagration. It was Dresden all over again, this time on a planetary scale, and the public response seemed to be a kind of bored acquiescence.

> I swear I'm right that if a neutron bomb did go off accidently in Terre Haute, it would be on the news for about three days because the feeling is that these people weren't really of any importance. [We now live in] a society of people who matter and who don't matter, and Americans have taken this to heart.[10]

By the late 1930s Otto Waltz was "wholly a creature of the past, forever twenty years old or so," enchanted by a promise that would never develop. "He would paint wonderful pictures by and by. He would be a devil-may-care soldier by and by. He was already a lover and a philosopher and a nobleman." These fantasies served to insulate him from his mundane surroundings. "I don't think he even noticed Midland City before I became a murderer," Rudy declares. "It was as though he were in a space suit, with the atmosphere of prewar Vienna inside."

Like Otto, Vonnegut's parents were "wholly creatures of the past" by the time he came along. Their best years were behind them; the world described in Uncle John's genealogy had already been damaged beyond repair. They, too, were unstuck in time, inhabiting a bubble their children could little understand, with the atmosphere of prewar Indianapolis inside.

Otto's theatrics were a source of embarrassment for his sons. Felix cringed when his father insisted on addressing his teenaged friends in the language of Greek mythology and Shakespeare—"no doubt lively subjects in Viennese cafes before the First World War." Rudy's young playmates, meanwhile, "children of uneducated parents in humble jobs," responded with baffled looks when Otto spoke to them. This reminds us of how the author's friends from public school reacted to his father when he brought them by the house. The opposite of a Nazi in his gentle otherworldliness, Kurt Sr. was different from their fathers, as rare and beguiling as a unicorn.

Otto's "most dumbfoundingly inappropriate greeting" happened during World War II. In need of a last-minute date for the prom, Felix invited Celia Hildreth, a pretty but unassuming nobody from his class. Celia's family was so poor they lived in the black part of town, but here now was an opportunity for her to move up in the world. "A new Cinderella is born every minute," Rudy observes. We remember her as car dealer Dwayne Hoover's deceased wife in *Breakfast of Champions*. Not exempt from his father's vanity, Felix bragged all week about Celia's diamond-in-the-rough beauty, and, in exchange for the use of the family car, Otto demanded that she be brought around for his inspection.

Otto was like a schoolboy himself as the big night approached. "Who is Celia?" he intoned as he wandered the upper floor of the loft in the carriage house, invoking Shakespeare. "What is she? That all her swains commend her?" Rudy now understands the pain behind his father's curious performance.

> Oh, he was leading scrap drives in those days, and he was an air-raid warden too. And he had helped the War Department draw up a personality profile of Hitler, who he now said was a brilliant homicidal maniac. But he still felt drab and superannuated and so on, with so

many battle reports in the paper and on the radio, and so many uniforms around. His spirits needed a boost in the very worst way.

It was the old disease of uselessness again.

Otto prepared a reception fit for a princess. Dressed in his old scarlet-and-silver Hungarian Life Guard uniform, he illuminated candles to create the properly ethereal mood. Eleven-year-old Rudy witnessed the spectacle from a balcony, his head swirling with the myths of his father's imagination. "I was inside a great beehive filled with fireflies. And below me was the beautiful King of the Early Evening." Rudy's words remind us of Wilbur Daffodil-11, *Slapstick*'s "King of Candlesticks." As the car pulled up to the house Otto unbolted sliding doors that had not been disturbed for thirty years. "A wall of my home vanished," Rudy recalls with wonder. "There were stars and a rising moon where it had been. Never before had there been such beauty in Midland City."

"Let Helen of Troy come forward, to claim this apple if she dare!" Otto announced regally—but Cinderella did not take her cue. Like a lot of Vonnegut women (Sarah Wyatt in *Jailbird*, for example, and Marilee Kemp in *Bluebeard*), Celia felt the attention her physical beauty attracted to be a curse. She took flight, casting off her dancing shoes as she receded into the darkness of the spring night. "And fear and anger and stocking feet, and that magnificent face, made her as astonishing as anyone I have ever encountered in a legend from any culture," Rudy recalls. "Midland City had a goddess of discord all its own."

Felix was drafted into the army the next year, and spent his last weekend at home. It was the weekend of Mother's Day 1944—a day freighted with trauma for the author, as it was the date of his mother's suicide. For young Rudy that Sunday morning started out well enough. Accompanying his father and brother to the Midland City Rod and Gun Club, he earned a marksmanship trophy on the shooting range. In recognition of the achievement Otto directed Felix to hand over to him the key to their house's gun room, a ceremonial rite of passage unusual for a boy so young. It was another mistake, so human and well intended, yet so grievous in its consequences. "I could feel the key," Rudy remembers, "burning a hole in my pocket."

A luncheon guest was expected that afternoon—none other than Eleanor Roosevelt, on a tour of war plants "in the boondocks." Like other prominent visitors to Midland City, the First Lady would be required to see its most renowned landmark, the Waltz's hexagonal carriage house with its cupola and fanciful Salzburg weather vane. Otto had taken the trouble to sprinkle turpentine and linseed oil on the air registers so that the place would smell like an active studio, but no one in the entourage asked to see his work.

The single painting on display, a small canvas clamped to an easel, its "brush strokes laid down exuberantly and confidently, and promisingly, too," captured the poignancy of Otto Waltz's unfulfilled story. It was evidence, the son imagines, that "when my father was a young, young man, he must have had a moment or two when he felt that he might have reason to take himself and his life seriously."

We think of Kurt Sr.'s thwarted dreams as we read these words. Indeed, as his architecture practice contracted in the 1930s he began spending hours painting in a studio on the top floor of the house. "He had reason to be optimistic about this new career," Vonnegut remembered in *Fates Worse Than Death*, "since the early stages of his pictures, whether still lives or portraits or landscapes, were full of *pow*. Mother, meaning to be helpful, would say of each one: 'That's really wonderful, Kurt. Now all you have to do is *finish* it.' He would then ruin it."[11]

To show off to the guests as they were leaving, Otto sent Rudy upstairs to finish his chores in the gun room. Cradling the Springfield rifle he had used so masterfully in the morning, Rudy climbed to the top of the house to savor the moment in all of its richness. "I wanted to sit up there for awhile, and look out over the roofs of the town, supposing that my brother might be going to his death, and hearing and feeling the tanks in the street below" rolling out of the Barrytron assembly plant. Rudy inserted a cartridge into the chamber, slid the bolt forward, and—in ecstatic consummation of his coming-of-age day—squeezed the trigger.

Rudy did not grasp at first that his life had irrevocably changed. "The bullet was a symbol," he reassured himself as he descended the stairs, "and nobody was ever hurt by a symbol." But soon the police chief was at the front door, investigating the death of a pregnant housewife killed some distance away by a rifle shot through the window. He described to Otto the calibre of the fatal bullet.

"You know, I did that," Vonnegut admitted in an interview in 1989. "I didn't kill anybody. But I fired a rifle, out over Indianapolis. I never told anybody about it until I was an adult. I cleaned the gun and put it away." Trusted with his father's guns, what was it about the episode that made it so frightening to him, something he felt he had to hide for so long? "That I was such a person," he explained. "That I could be that silly. Because it was silly. I had no intent. The gun was an abstract thing. It wasn't aimed. It was just very easy to fire."[12]

Given the timing of the protagonist's "crime" in *Deadeye Dick,* we can speculate about its symbolic meaning for the author. "So this was Mother's Day to most people," Rudy tells us, "but to me it was the day during which, ready or not, I had been initiated into manhood." Here was a boy carelessly flexing the muscles of maturity, experimenting with his newfound power—and a woman died. Could this reflect young Kurt's feelings as a soldier preparing to ship out to a war zone when his mother took her life?

"I died," Rudy tells us. "But I didn't die." Doubleness, fragmentation, estrangement—things have instantly become unstuck for Rudy Waltz. His transgression is a metaphor for Vonnegut's guilt, representing, as he told us in the novel's preface, "all the bad things I have done."

"Oh, Jesus," exclaimed Otto. "The boy did it, but it is I who am to blame. I am to blame!"

Years later Felix offered his brother an explanation for their father's uncharacteristic acceptance of responsibility that fateful afternoon. He was reluctant to consider it heroic. "It was the first truly consequential adventure life had ever offered him," Felix speculated. "He was going to make the most of it. At last something was happening to him! He would keep it going as long as he could!"

Indeed what followed was quite a display—Otto Waltz's greatest work of art. Full of adrenaline, he marched upstairs and smashed the lock to the gun room door. "Everybody was too awed to stop him," Rudy recalls. For the

Wagnerian finale, Otto climbed to the cupola and severed it from its foundations. Everyone watched as it crashed onto the police car parked below. "What a hair-raising melodrama Father had given to Midland City, Ohio. And it was over now. The leading character was above us, crimson-faced and panting, but somehow most satisfied, too, exposed to wind and sky."

Otto seemed surprised that his theatre of contrition did not settle accounts. The story had spun beyond his control. At the station he dictated an accounting of the day's events, and we are impressed by its sobriety. "I alone am responsible," Otto kept insisting, firmly and unequivocally. "Leave him out of this."

Father and son were led to different parts of the building as again we are led through the psychological horror of incarceration, a perennial Vonnegut subject. Over the next hours Rudy endured "a tentative, moody, slow-motion and incomplete lynching" that may be an expression of the author's experience after his mother's suicide, as the most private recesses of the Vonnegut household were exposed to public scrutiny. Tall for his age but weighing "about as much as a box of kitchen matches," Rudy was handled roughly and "faceprinted" with black ink, then put on display in a basement cell for a crowd growing in size and ferocity as word spread of the shooting. "Look at the monkey!" someone said as citizens arrived to participate in "The Rudy Waltz Show." Celia Hildreth was there, escorted by her future husband, Dwayne Hoover, a civilian inspector for the Army Air Corps.

"My audience behaved as though they were quite accustomed to taunting bad people," Rudy observes now with detachment. "They may have done a lot of it in their dreams." From the present, in his hotel in Haiti, he reflects on its cathartic meaning. It was an exorcism, a kind of voodoo. "A curiously carved bone or stick, or a dried mud doll with straw hair would have served as well as I did, there on the bench, as long as the community believed, as Midland City believed of me, that it was a package of evil magic inside." Here is Vonnegut the anthropologist speaking, presenting us with another ritual purging to consider. "Everybody could feel safe for awhile. Bad luck was caged." On the ride home the patrolman christened the boy-murderer with his new name, "Deadeye Dick."

At the trial Otto made no effort to defend himself. "My father, the master of so many grand gestures and attitudes," Rudy tells us, "turned out to be as collapsible as a paper cup." He served two years in Shepherdstown prison for manslaughter, and the Waltz family lost everything, save for the carriage house.

From then on Rudy resigned himself to a life as his parents' caretaker, replacing the servants that had to be let go. "What a good boy was I!" he insists. After school he cooked and cleaned. Gone was the youngster who aspired to full-blooded manhood. "During my time in the cage, all covered with ink, I concluded that the best thing for me and for those around me was to want nothing, to be enthusiastic about nothing, to be as unmotivated as possible, in fact, so that I would never again hurt anyone." It is the numbness of survivor guilt.

The lone exception to Rudy's pledge of renunciation began with a school assignment, encouraged by a teacher who, like so many others in Midland City, felt herself a "nobody" bound for nowhere. Touched by his essay on John Fortune, the dairy farmer who disappeared in Nepal, she insisted that Rudy pursue his talents and become a writer. "And you must get out of this deadly town too—as soon as you can," she told him. "You must find what I should have had the courage to look for. Your own Katmandu."

Rudy baked a Linzer torte ("a great favorite in Vienna, Austria before the First World War!") and presented the idea to his parents. "This is as much Shangri-La as anywhere," Otto scoffed. It was a truth Rudy would not come to understand until later. Otto continued, with more energy than he had shown in years:

> Be a pharmacist! Go with the grain of your heritage! There is no artistic talent in this family, nor will there ever be! . . . [We] are descended from solid, stolid, unimaginative, unmusical, ungraceful German stock, whose sole virtue is that it can never leave off working.

This is another glimpse into the war between the artists and the businessmen in the author's family, as well as the discharge of some unresolved disappointment about his father's decision to send him to Cornell to get a "useful" degree in the sciences.

Rudy graduated from Ohio State, then returned to a job on the graveyard shift at a twenty-four-hour chain drugstore. He enjoyed his lonely vocation, despite the dangers. His predecessor was murdered by a man who randomly "swung off the Shepherdstown Turnpike" to rob the place. Rudy also had to put up with nightly phone calls inquiring if he was "Deadeye Dick." During slow stretches he pecked away on a typewriter in the stock room, converting his high school essay into a stage drama. He mailed the finished manuscript to a contest advertised in the back of a magazine and won first prize—a professional production in Greenwich Village. The larger world beckoned.

The theater was a lifelong passion for Kurt Vonnegut, both as a means of expression and as an ideal form of community. In his memoir *New York in the Fifties,* Dan Wakefield recounts how as a public relations man for GE Vonnegut took advantage of cultural opportunities on trips into the city. He stayed at the Algonquin ("because it was the writers' hotel") and attended all manner of performances during that golden age just after the war. "I was thrilled by Tennessee Williams and William Inge the way a later generation was thrilled by the Beatles," Vonnegut told him. "Their plays were my Beatles albums."[13]

He resorted frequently to the techniques of the stage in his fiction—here Rudy's habit of recasting traumatic events into playlets recalls Billy Pilgrim's flights in time and space as a coping strategy, a way to detach from and manage his memories. After the Dresden book was finished, Vonnegut considered leaving novel writing altogether to focus on writing plays. He threw himself into *Happy Birthday, Wanda June,* a project that opened off-Broadway in the fall of 1970, to decidedly mixed reviews. Rudy's episode here as a playwright is a reference to this and Vonnegut's other humbling experiences as a dramaturge.

On the afternoon of Valentine's Day 1960, Rudy Waltz looked up through the snowflakes to see his name on the Greenwich Village marquee, feeling a mix of pride and indifference about what was to transpire that evening. He had lost interest in what he now admitted was a "ridiculous" script about the "quite pointless death of John Fortune, written by a person who longed to be as far from home as possible." Now that Rudy was away and relieved of his oppressive story, life seemed full of new and more interesting possibilities.

I was startled not to be Deadeye Dick anymore.

I felt like a gas which had been confined in a labeled bottle for years, and which had now been released into the atmosphere.

I no longer cooked. It was Deadeye Dick who was always trying to nourish back to health those he had injured so horribly.

Rudy had arrived at a place of gloriously liberating anonymity, where he was free to reinvent himself. "I wasn't going to be arrested. I wasn't going to be displayed in a cage, all covered with ink." Perhaps he would get a job in the city like his brother Felix, now a successful broadcast executive. "And then, step by step, I would experiment with having a home of my own and a life of my own, maybe try pairing off with this kind of person or that one, to see how that went." He was ready to move beyond his nickname, seize control of his narrative—risk becoming a character.

But the moment of broad horizons was fleeting. *Katmandu* closed after only one performance, and critics (the same ones so eager to knock down Kurt Vonnegut over the past decade) "found it hilarious" that the playwright had never been to India or Nepal and had a degree in pharmacy. Rudy was back to feeling "that almost anything desirable was likely to be booby-trapped"—a sense of resignation no doubt shared by many of the people he passed on the streets. "Father had his studio, with its dusty skylight and nude model in Vienna, where he had found out he couldn't paint. Now I had my name up on a theatre marquee in New York City, where I found out I couldn't write."

The morning after the dead-on-arrival opening Rudy and Felix made an emergency trip back to southwestern Ohio, which had been hit by a mammoth blizzard. Looking down from the cabin of the plane, owned by Midland City magnate and arts patron Fred T. Barry, the placid white landscape concealed thousands of bodies, a foretaste of the neutron bomb incident to come.

The pilot talked to Felix about a girl they had both dated briefly, Celia Hildreth. "She was lucky to have married an automobile dealer who didn't care what was under her hood," he observed. Celia was a "cream puff," like a car "which was flashy and loaded with accessories—and never mind whether it ran or not." Vonnegut deploys here the vernacular speech he knew so well from keeping company with Reeks and Wrecks and army privates and carpenters and plumbers, the language from his days as a Saab salesman. It is a long way from the operatic flights of Otto Waltz.

Celia had been taking night classes at the YMCA, the pilot continued, and her marriage to Pontiac dealer Dwayne Hoover was said to be in trouble. In its sexlessness it was like a lot of relationships down there, he concluded with a laugh. "Some towns better pay attention to business. It would be a terrible thing for the country if they were all like Hollywood and New York."

The county hospital overflowed with refugees. Rudy took his place in a line pressing toward the information desk and was thrust back uncomfortably into his identity as "Deadeye Dick." Like all prodigal sons making their return, Vonnegut must have experienced this sensation on visits back to the Midwest. "I had a feeling, while I inched forward in the crowd," Rudy remembers, "that invisible insects were buzzing around my head." The sensation, he now knows, was a result of his sudden awareness of "little bits of information I had about this person or that person, or which this or that person had about me."

In November 1982 Jill Krementz organized a black-tie dinner party for her husband's sixtieth birthday, a happy occasion attended by John Updike, Norman Mailer, and a host of Kurt Vonnegut's friends from other backgrounds and the various chapters of his life story. Loree Rackstraw was there, and she recalled his visit the next day with a cousin visiting from Indianapolis.

> I listened raptly as their conversation continued with humorous anecdotes about shared childhood experiences and Indianans with onerous conservative values. She had a warm sense of humor and their mutual affection was clear. After she left, Kurt sat quietly for a moment. "She's about the only friendly relative left in Indiana," he smiled.[14]

Vonnegut wished there had been more. For all of his admirers around the world, for all of his relief at escaping the limitations of his birthplace, he longed, too, for the approval of the community that knew him when he was young, people with whom he shared the "little bits of information" that constitute true intimacy, and it stung him when it was withheld. Even though he could liken them to insects buzzing in his ear, he still longed for their attention. Mark Twain in Connecticut and other sons and daughters of the provinces were often condemned to endure the same repudiation. Vonnegut spoke often of family members back home who did not like his books, who recoiled at his increasingly "impolite" style or his politics and admitted they "could not bear to read [him] anymore." In truth, he shared many of their deepest values, and was an advocate of restraint rather than the excesses they imagined. But the gulf seemed impossibly wide, and the pain of the estrangement ran deep. He, too, was the infamous "Deadeye Dick," and the judgment was not an easy one to appeal.

A hospital volunteer fielding questions seemed to Rudy "an idealized representative of compassionate, long-suffering women of all ages everywhere," an archetypal nurse. The angel of mercy was Celia Hildreth Hoover, the notorious cream puff, who patiently directed him to the intensive care ward where his father lay dying. Later he saw Saint Celia sleeping on a couch in a waiting room lounge, watched over by her eleven-year-old son, Bunny.

Otto Waltz was humble, even gallant in his deathbed scene, expressing the hope that "he had at least brought some appreciation of beauty to Midland City, even if he himself hadn't been an artist." He was buried in a painter's smock, according to his wishes, his thumb hooked through an artist's palette.

Rudy resumed his night job, and with his mother was forced to move into "a little two-bedroom shitbox" in Avondale, a tract development built on what was once John Fortune's dairy farm. Felix, meanwhile, was living a spectacular version of the American Dream in New York as a highly paid executive with a television network. Like Kurt Vonnegut, he had been "a citizen of the world" since his army days—Midland City was a quaintly remote abstraction, if he thought about it at all. "Any city in any country, including my own hometown, was to me just another place where I might live or might not live," he explained later to his brother. "Who gave a damn?"

> So I treated my own mother and father and brother as natives of some poor, war-ravaged town I was passing through. They told me

their troubles, as natives will, and I gave them my absentminded sympathy. I cared some. I really did.

We are reminded of Wilbur's "forgettery" of his sister Eliza in *Slapstick*. Felix was a celebrity, known for his lavish lifestyle and a series of spectacularly dysfunctional marriages. He is a version of the author, who found his fortune in the bright lights of the metropolis but is haunted by a sense of displacement and guilt.

Rudy remembers his last encounter with Celia. He was in good spirits that night at work, scat-singing out back to chase away the blues (as he had learned to do as a boy in the kitchen of the carriage house). He imagined the noise of the trucks on the interstate nearby as the roar of ocean surf. When the service bell rang he made his way to the front counter, unsure as usual if he would be met by a customer or another predator with a sawed-off shotgun.

Standing by the sunglasses rack was Celia, now "a demented speed freak, a hag." Rudy recalls it as a scene in a play, but not of the kind she pleaded now for him to write for her. She had been the female lead in the local high school revival of *Katmandu*, but that seemed a long time ago now. "You are the only person in this town who ever made me glad to be alive," she cried. "Give me more words!" She was really after pills. "What a team we'd make," she continued, agitated and hostile when he did not comply. "The crazy old lady and Deadeye Dick." Again we have the Jekyll-and-Hyde Vonnegut female, perhaps a reference to mother Edith in the throes of her barbiturate addition.

Celia escaped into the night across the broken glass of the parking lot, in a hellish reprise of the magical prom night. Rudy phoned her son at his flophouse hotel, but the voice at the other end of the line told him to mind his own business. The Waltzes had enough problems in their own family to worry about—a news report said that Felix had just been fired from his big job. "They finally caught up with him," Bunny observed with bitter satisfaction. "He's just another fake from Midland City."

Your father was a fake. He couldn't paint good pictures. I'm a fake. I can't really play the piano. You're a fake. You can't write decent plays.

It's perfectly all right, as long as we all stay home. That's where your brother made his mistake. He went away from home. They catch fakes out in the real world, you know. They catch 'em all the time.

To Vonnegut, one of the things lost in the transition from the intimate world of the folk society to mass culture was the pleasure of self-expression. In the idealized past, those with an aptitude for making music or drawing or telling stories were celebrated for the sheer joy they brought to themselves and their communities. In an age of electronic media, where everything is reduced to a commodity and the market is national, even global, these life-sustaining human activities are devalued, and people retreat into passivity and silence. "We used to have our own boxers, our own wrestlers, our own songwriters, singers and painters," Vonnegut reminisced of the Indianapolis of his youth. "Now it's all got to be from out of town. You think you're funny? You're not funny. We're going to get Bob Hope. Think you're going to sing? Sinatra's going to sing—you're not good enough."[15]

Felix phoned to announce that he was coming home, ready to "rediscover his roots." "He said that everybody in New York City was phony," Rudy remembers, "and that it was the people of Midland City who were real."

A cocktail of prescription drugs in his system, Felix careened west across the country in his Rolls convertible. "Kill the fatted calf!" he shouted with his father's theatricality after coming to an abrupt stop on the lawn of the Avondale house. Emma and Rudy were just leaving for Celia Hoover's funeral, and Felix insisted on driving them, convinced all of a sudden that they had been sweethearts. "She was what I was looking for all the time," he sobbed on the way to the church, "and I never even realized it."

Arriving late, the Waltzes watched the ceremony from the back row. Only the husband of the deceased, Dwayne, and the black maid, Lottie Davis, shed any real tears before the closed casket. (Celia, we know from *Breakfast of Champions*, killed herself by ingesting Drano.) "There was no reason to expect that anything truly exciting or consoling would be said," Rudy recalls thinking as he sat there. It would be an exercise as empty as the lives of the people who bothered to show up. The author exposes his most resigned side here:

Not even the minister thought that every life had a meaning, and that every death could startle us into learning something important, and so on. The corpse was a mediocrity who had broken down after a while. The mourners were mediocrities who would break down after a while.

The planet itself was breaking down. It was going to blow itself up sooner or later anyway, if it didn't poison itself first. In a manner of speaking, it was already eating Drano.

Then came a surprise, a luminous Vonnegut moment of redemption. In his homily, the minister, who played John Fortune in Rudy's play at the high school, paid tribute to the "blissful unselfishness" of the cast in bringing its message to the audience. "As only a gifted actor could, the Reverend made the Mask and Wig Club's production of *Katmandu*, especially Celia's performance, sound as though it had enriched lives all over town." She would not be around for the opening of the Mildred Barry Arts Center, but the spirit Celia Hildreth Hoover represented existed long before that project was ever conceived, and if nurtured would never die. Indeed, he declared, "the most important arts centers a city could have were human beings, not buildings. There in the back sits an arts center named 'Rudy Waltz.'"

The minister's eloquence was interrupted by Felix's inconsolable wailing. Rudy and Emma managed to get him to the parking lot, but as they fumbled for the car keys Dwayne Hoover came out of the church and strode menacingly toward them. "It was like a scene in a cowboy movie," Rudy recalls, "with the townspeople all huddled together, and with a half-broken, tragic, great big man going to meet destiny all alone." Who said Midland City had no drama?

Again we are surprised—in narrative terms, "it's the thrill of the *fast-reverse*," as Winston Niles Rumfoord might say. It is another showdown, like the encounter between Starbuck and Clewes in *Jailbird*, that melts quickly into forgiveness rather than revenge. There is no violence, no resort to gunfire—a convenient way to end stories, Vonnegut the writing teacher has more than once observed. "Where do you fit in?" Dwayne demanded of Felix, but all he wanted was consolation that their love affair might have given his poor wife some happiness. "She was like this Rolls-Royce here, you know?" Dwayne said with vulnerability. We learn more about the pain of the man who went amok in *Breakfast of Champions*:

> "I just ran away from her, she was so unhappy, and I didn't know what to do about it—and there wasn't anybody else to take her off my hands. I'm good for selling cars. I can really sell cars. I can really fix cars. But I sure couldn't fix that woman. Never even knew where to get the tools. I put her up on blocks and forgot her. I only wish you'd come along in time to rescue the both of us."

Even car salesman were capable of deep feelings, of poetry.

"We all see our lives as stories," Rudy Waltz steps back to observe, sounding like the stage manager in *Our Town*. "If a person survives an ordinary span of sixty years or more, there is every chance that his or her life as a shapely story has ended, and all that remains to be experienced is epilogue. Life is not over, but the story is." Vonnegut is pondering these things for himself at sixty, wondering about his future direction and maybe even the point of continuing at all. He commented on the perils of this kind of existential crisis in *Breakfast of Champions*—it is the "and so on" and "etc." that are so difficult for people—and he would explore the theme with renewed urgency in his next novel, *Galápagos*. For some, like Celia Hoover, like his own mother, the prospect of sameness without end is so intolerable they commit suicide. Otto Waltz did not make such an exit, but it might have been better for him if the curtain had come down and the words "THE END" had appeared on the day of his arrest.

"Maybe my own country's life as a story ended after the Second World War," Rudy muses, "when it was the richest and most powerful nation on earth, when it was going to ensure peace and justice everywhere, since it alone had the atom bomb. THE END."

For the Waltz brothers, though, and for their mother, Emma, epilogue proved to be the best part of their lives. Rudy's burden as "Deadeye Dick" had been lifted by the funeral oration, and Felix was able to beat his drug habit, embracing a simpler existence at a radio station in South Bend, Indiana. Happiness is living without a story, Rudy now understands—

something, after all, "as artificial as a mechanical bucking bronco in a drinking establishment."

Rudy and his mother lived quietly in their Avondale house until it was discovered that the cement in the fireplace mantle, from Oak Ridge, Tennessee, was radioactive. Emma developed brain tumors, an infirmity that turned her for the first time into a character, "combative and caustically witty, a sort of hick-town Voltaire." It was her rebellion against an upbringing that "virtually decreed that she live only a pipsqueak story," Rudy tells us. If only the author's mother, Edith, had been able to traverse her troubles. Could she have enjoyed such a second act?

"I have now seen with my own eyes what a neutron bomb can do to a small city," Rudy Waltz comments from the 1980s. He and Felix now operate a hotel in Haiti, bought with money from the lawsuits over their mother's death. Camera crews record the intactness of what remains, and the president emphasizes the bright side of the tragedy, declaring the depopulated zone perfect for the resettlement of waves of Haitian refugees recently landing on American shores.

Was the explosion an accident, like Rudy's rifle shot, or was it by design? In either case life goes on, new seeds have to be planted. Back in Midland City with his brother to reclaim the family effects, Rudy is not unhappy about the Haitian homesteading scheme. Calling them "the most prolific painters and sculptors in the history of the world"—another homage to a vibrant black culture—he hopes that someone among them would be given possession of the old carriage house, its studio bathed in golden north light. "It is time a real artist lived there."

Meanwhile, conspiracy theories abound. On the fringes of the blast area a group of angry picketers march, organized as "Farmers of Southwestern Ohio for Nuclear Sanity"—an unlikely heartland branch of the nuclear freeze movement with which the author sympathized. They are fighting to make people outside the region care. Who is to say, their leaflets warn, that Terre Haute or Schenectady will not be next on the hit list?

Before returning to Haiti, Rudy and Felix are permitted a visit to their parents' graves at Calvary Cemetery. With them is the headwaiter of their hotel, Hippolyte Paul De Mille, who offers to raise the spirit of a departed person. The chosen spirit is Will Fairchild, the long-lost flying ace. Thus does Rudy Waltz, "the William Shakespeare of Midland City," bequeath to his hometown something every human community needed—a legend of a god made earthbound, in this case, a ghost wandering in search of his parachute.

Joseph Heller and Kurt Vonnegut once speculated to each other about what they might have become if not for the Second World War. Heller would have stayed with his family's dry-cleaning business in Brooklyn; Vonnegut imagined himself garden editor for the *Indianapolis Star*. In his 1977 "Self-Interview" he speculated about being an Indianapolis architect, like his father and grandfather. "I still wish that had happened." When the going got rough, and the arrows of the critics flew, Vonnegut must have wondered sometimes if he, too, was "just another fake from Midland City" who should go back to where he came from. It was not such an abhorrent idea—there was fulfillment and adventure, beauty and myth to be experienced, even in precincts dismissed as "flyover country" by people in more glamorous locales.[16]

Each of the characters in *Deadeye Dick* transcended their stories, at least for a while, proving Otto Waltz's hard-won insight that "this is as much Shangri-La as anywhere." So it was for the author in the city of his childhood, lacking in cosmopolitan style and Old World charm perhaps, but with free libraries and a beloved symphony orchestra, "cheap movie houses and jazz joints everywhere." The people one met, even if their voices sounded like "a band saw cutting galvanized tin," were funny and tragic and lovable. Some were walking, breathing "arts centers," like Rudy Waltz. And then there were those mornings in the warm kitchen of Ida Young.[17]

"Castles?" Vonnegut reflected in *Palm Sunday*, with what we envision as a sweetly faraway smile. "Indianapolis was full of them."[18]

ELEVEN

Galápagos:

A Second Noah's Ark

This was a very innocent planet, except for
those great big brains.
—Leon Trotsky Trout

Long a student of the natural world, Kurt Vonnegut always wanted to visit the Galápagos Islands, and in 1982 he and his wife, Jill, had the opportunity to make the trip. It was a sacred place for scientists, and seeing it raised for him all kinds of big questions. "Darwin just really could not believe that God had done all this—you know, why would he make thirteen sorts of finch for one environment or three separate species of land tortoise just a few miles from each other?" he commented to Peter Reed. "I could have unscrewed their heads, if I had wanted to," he joked a couple of months after his return in a speech at St. John the Divine cathedral in New York, remembering how he had walked among the innocent blue-footed boobies and observed their strange mating rituals. When confronted with such creatures, he told the audience,

> you are bound to think what Charles Darwin thought when he went there: How much time Nature has in which to accomplish

239

simply anything. If we desolate this planet, Nature can get life going again. All it takes is a few million years or so.[1]

Human beings were distinguished by their nervous systems, easily the most elaborate in the animal kingdom. But what was once an advantage, the basis for survival and then dominance, had reached a point of diminishing returns. When considered from a distance, our equipment was as bizarre an adaptation as the webbed feet of Galápagos birds or the chandelier-sized antlers of the Irish elk—and considerably more dangerous. The "cumbersome computers" in our heads, upon which we based our understanding of reality and our choices, were, it turns out, highly unreliable.

A voice from the distant future assures us, though, that we will survive our current brush with extinction. A second Noah's Ark will save us from the flood we created, evolution will, in the fullness of time, sculpt a form simpler and more durable than the one that so spectacularly misfired in the "era of big brains and fancy thinking."

On one level, *Galápagos* (1985) is a commentary on the politics of the 1980s, which were hard on Kurt Vonnegut. He anguished as the electorate twice embraced Ronald Reagan, "an amiable, sleepy, absentminded old movie actor" (and fellow alum of the PR department at General Electric), repudiating what he saw as the best of his country's egalitarian dreams. The Reagan administration used its skill in stagecraft to create escapist imagery of "Morning in America," stoking an aggressive style of patriotism alien to Vonnegut's ideals of planetary citizenship. The result was a new arms race and a series of bloody "show-biz" military engagements—hard for the veteran of a Just War to endure. At home, too, things seemed to go backward on all fronts, from the environment to civil rights, and trickle-down economics now returned with a vengeance. The beaming "Dreamer in Chief" had long-ago abandoned his youthful hero, Franklin Roosevelt, and the gulf between rich and poor widened accordingly.

In *Breakfast of Champions* Vonnegut tried to explain what he called "the idiot decisions made by my countrymen" as an attempt to realize the fantasies drummed into them from infancy. "They were doing their best to live like people invented in story books," he wrote, declaring his intent to abandon traditional narrative conventions. Now, like a good scientist, he traces the process back to its source—the biological matrix that generated and attached to those stories.

Despair over the direction of the country undoubtedly fed into what was reported as a suicide attempt by the author in the spring of 1984, ending in the emergency room of St. Vincent's Hospital in Manhattan. In his introduction to *Armageddon in Retrospect*, Vonnegut's son, Mark, a pediatrician with his own experiences of unruly brain chemistry, downplayed the role depression may have played in the episode. He challenged the common view of his father as a man plagued by gloom, capturing well his contradictions:

> He was like an extrovert who wanted to be an introvert, a very social guy who wanted to be a loner, a lucky person who would have preferred to be unlucky. An optimist posing as a pessimist, hoping people will take heed.

The pills ingested weren't toxic, Dr. Vonnegut insisted, and the next day the patient could be observed "bouncing around the dayroom playing Ping-Pong and making friends. It seemed like he was doing a not very convincing imitation of someone with mental illness."[2]

In *Fates Worse than Death*, however, the author was unambiguous about his intentions, and we need to take him at his word about the seriousness of the crisis with which he was dealing. "It wasn't a cry for help," he wrote. "It wasn't a nervous breakdown."

> I wanted "The Big Sleep" (Raymond Chandler). I wanted to "Slam the Big Door" (John D. MacDonald). No more jokes and no more coffee and no more cigarettes:
> I wanted *out* of here.[3]

Vonnegut soon returned to public life and to his comfort zone in front of the typewriter. His work was not done; there was more he wanted to say to the world. So, beneath the detached, scientific tone and the moments of soapbox commentary, the playful and well-crafted tricks of irony to which he had become accustomed, there is more than usual at stake for the author with this outing as he wrestles with the most profound existential questions. "It is a very mixed blessing," he had written earlier, in *Palm Sunday*, "to be brought back from the dead." On a personal level, *Galápagos* reads as an allegory about his own journey to the brink, and back again.[4]

The story opens in late 1986 at the Hotel El Dorado, an oasis of first-world luxury in squalid, desperately poor Guayaquil, Ecuador. The resort reminds us of San Lorenzo's Casa Mona in *Cat's Cradle*. A guest named James Wait is the lone patron in the cocktail lounge. To Jesús Ortiz, the bartender, the price tag still attached to Wait's shirt identifies him as a comically ordinary American tourist, of the kind Vonnegut might have seemed on his trip there.

In truth this is a ruse. James Wait, we discover from our mystery narrator, is an accomplished con artist, a ruthless predator. His specialty—his "survival scheme," in Darwinian terms—is the serial defrauding of widows with money. He wound up in this stagnant backwater by pure chance, after choosing Guayaquil from the departures board at Kennedy Airport while escaping his latest entanglement.

Wait is registered as "Willard Flemming," the alias on his forged Canadian passport. It is an early signal from the author that, as usual, identity is an unstable affair, multilayered and elusive. Wait sits watchful and alert, "keen for the next test," having just signed on to an adventure that under normal circumstances would provide fertile fishing grounds for his talents: an excursion to the nearby Galápagos Islands, set to depart the next day. For months the trip has been advertised around the world as the "Nature Cruise of the Century."

Something is amiss, however. From the air-conditioned lounge one can see only two boats anchored in the usually bustling waters of the port as it stretches off to the horizon.

James Wait is from, of all places, Midland City, Ohio, his pathology an adaptation to the broken social order in which he grew up. After enduring a series of foster homes he escaped to Manhattan. ("I, too," the narrator confides, "was once a teenage runaway.") There he made a living on the streets as a prostitute, learning to size up and manipulate strangers. Wait committed a murder, without any feelings of remorse. He had gone through seventeen wives, making himself wealthy in the process. Now he scans his surroundings for clues about how to bait and hook another victim.

Wait is one of Vonnegut's most repellent characters, and it takes some doing to find in him elements of an alter ego—but they are there. Again we have the odyssey of escape from province to big city, with its corruptions and dog-eat-dog ethics as well as its liberation. The author reveals his shadow side here as he considers the different identities he has had to take on in the various chapters of his life. It begs the question of *Mother Night*— what, if anything, is beneath "what we pretend to be"?

"It is hard to believe nowadays that people could ever have been as brilliantly duplicitous as James Wait," the voice from the future observes, "until I remind myself that just about every adult human being back then had a brain weighing about three kilograms! There was no end to the evil schemes that a thought machine that oversized couldn't imagine and execute."

Guayaquil's claims as a tourist attraction begin and end with the white-bearded figure in the portrait above the bar, featured also in the hotel brochures and on T-shirts available, at grossly inflated prices, in the lobby gift shop. As a young man Charles Darwin visited the area for five weeks, aboard the HMS *Beagle*. His interpretations of what he saw on the volcanic rocks west of the mainland, with their menagerie of geckos and iguanas and flightless birds, caused a sensation when they were finally published in 1859. Indeed, the volume he produced would become the most influential scientific treatise in the age of big brains, doing more "to stabilize people's volatile opinions of how to identify success or failure," our guide tells us, "than any other tome."

"I'm not very grateful for Darwin, although I suspect he was right," Vonnegut told *Playboy* in 1973. "His ideas make people crueler."

> Darwinism says to them that people who get sick deserve to be sick, that people who are in trouble must deserve to be in trouble. . . . And any man who's on top is there because he's a superior animal. That's the social Darwinism of the last century, and it continues to boom.[5]

In the Age of Reagan these ideas about "winners" and "losers" gained renewed legitimacy. Darwinian notions underlay greed, racial hierarchies, and aggressive nationalism. It was a lifelong preoccupation for Vonnegut. *Armageddon in Retrospect* presents a drawing produced in his last years, a skull-and-crossbones with the caption: "Darwin gave the cachet of science to war and genocide." At the core of Vonnegut's humanism was an effort to challenge this perverse tenet of the American Dream. Darwin was surely "right" in material terms, but we as a society have the duty to strive for something more noble and generous, modeled on the example of the family rather than the law of the jungle.[6]

By his words, Darwin transformed Guayaquil from "just one more hot and filthy seaport" into a gateway to imaginative wonder. There was no change to the physical characteristics of the nearby archipelago, previously of such little interest to the rest of the world. When tiny Ecuador declared the islands to be under its sovereignty in 1832, a year after Darwin's visit, it was as though the country "had annexed a passing cloud of asteroids."

What Darwin set in motion was a shift in how people saw the islands. "That was how important mere opinions used to be," the narrator observes, with a mixture of pity and astonishment.

> Mere opinions, in fact, were as likely to govern people's actions as hard evidence, and were subject to sudden reversals as hard evidence could never be. So the Galápagos Islands could be hell in one moment and heaven in the next, and Julius Caesar could be a statesman in one moment and a butcher in the next, and Ecuadorian paper money could be traded for food, shelter, and clothing in one moment and line the bottom of a birdcage in the next, and the universe could be created by God Almighty in one moment and by a big explosion in the next—and on and on.

Owing to dramatically reduced brain size, human beings in distant millennia were no longer troubled by such whimsical turns of mind, no longer "diverted from the main business of life"—which is, and has always been, food.

By the time James Wait arrived in Guayaquil, a sudden revision of opinion about the value of currencies was eviscerating the tourist business everywhere. This is not science fiction: debt crises and their attendant dislocations, especially in Latin America, were a staple of the news in the 1980s. Another network of Ponzi schemes was crashing down, "simply the latest in a series of murderous twentieth century catastrophes which had originated entirely in human brains." The passenger list for the "Nature Cruise of the Century," once boasting celebrities like Jacqueline Onassis and Henry Kissinger, is now pocked with cancellations. Only five guests have registered in the two-hundred-room El Dorado, all expecting still to make the voyage.

They are a varied lot, each with an oversized brain spinning out baroque stories and dilemmas and plans. Besides Wait, there are Japanese computer genius Zenji Hiroguchi and his pregnant wife Hisako, American venture capitalist Andrew MacIntosh and his blind daughter Selena, and Mary Hepburn, a middle-aged schoolteacher from Ilium, New York—the Edgar Derby of *Galápagos*. To accentuate the determinism that pervades the novel, Vonnegut uses an asterisk before the name of any character whose demise is imminent, who will "shortly face the ultimate Darwinian test of strength and wiliness," and fail. It is the inverse of *Slaughterhouse-Five*'s posthumous "so it goes."

Even before seeing Mrs. Hepburn, Wait has targeted her as textbook prey. Mary has not left her room since arriving and is at the end of her endurance following a series of personal disasters. She is at war with an unwieldy brain, which has addled judgment enough to deliver her for a cruise that will surely be canceled. Now it demands that she end the misery by suffocating herself with a garment bag, the one encasing the "Jackie dress" she planned to wear to dinner parties on the *Bahía de Darwin*. Mary is walking a precipice well-known to the author, and the outcome is very much in doubt. We have no inkling yet that she will be the indispensable person of her epoch, indeed the savior of the human race.

The year 1986 started out hopefully for Mary Hepburn, but then things, as they will, fell apart quickly. Her husband, Roy, walked out on his job at the Ilium Works without warning one day, signing up for the "Nature Cruise of the Century" billed in the window of a travel agency he passed on the way home. It was no garden-variety midlife crisis that motivated this impulsiveness. Roy, it was discovered, had a brain tumor—the same affliction that transformed Rudy Waltz's mother in *Deadeye Dick*.

Roy died before the cruise, full of regret that he and Mary never had children. "We Hepburns are as extinct as the dodoes now," he lamented— as much an evolutionary dead end as the Irish elk, Tyrannosaurus rex, or George Washington. With his last breath Roy made his wife promise to go through with the cruise as planned.

Compounding the private trauma of Roy's illness during these months was the disaster that overtook the larger community. The conglomerate that acquired Ilium's principal industry contracted a Japanese firm to automate operations, rendering most of the employees at the works superfluous. From then on "it was," Mary Hepburn would recall, "as though the Pied Piper had passed through town." Families packed up and left, the high school closed its doors for good in June.

Vonnegut based his earnest heroine here on Hillis L. Howie, the Indiana naturalist to whom he dedicates *Galápagos*. Howie organized an expedition to the Four Corners of New Mexico in 1938, broadening the horizons of the boys he mentored and cementing their interests in science. It was an important rite of passage for the author. "That's part of the American experience," he told an interviewer of this surrogate father figure, "to suddenly come across a truly great person who never becomes rich or famous, but who is enormously beneficial just to those near him." Young Kurt enjoyed his brief career as a mammalogist that summer, trapping a subspecies of the tawny whitefoot mouse that may have ended up in Chicago's Field Museum. "When I was in the army telling someone about this," he remembered later with a laugh, "he immediately named it Meesis Vonnegeesis." Career-wise, it was another road not taken.[6]

Mary devoted her last school lecture to the Galápagos Islands and their amusingly freakish examples of the evolutionary process. In mid-sentence she was overcome with doubts about what she had been peddling with such enthusiasm all these years. Vonnegut must have had bouts of the same vertigo on his college lecture tours. "Maybe I'm just a crazy lady," Mary thought to herself, "who has wandered off the street and into this classroom and started explaining the mysteries of life to these young people." Who was she to be doing that, when, like her husband, like the greatest minds throughout history, she had been "utterly mistaken about simply everything."

As Mary Hepburn contemplates suicide in her room and James Wait ponders his next moves down in the bar, the situation outside the El Dorado is deteriorating fast. The Ecuadorian currency, the sucre, is worthless, food supplies are running out, and soldiers patrol the streets as Guayaquil descends into anarchy. All commercial flights at the airport are canceled.

Wrapped in their own melodramas, the other guests are also oblivious to these developments. Zenji Hiroguchi, the computer wunderkind, argues with his wife about how to extricate themselves from what their "supposedly wonderful brains had done to them." They are hostages of Andrew MacIntosh, the investment banker—like Wait, he was a skilled predator. MacIntosh had lured the couple to this remote place to exploit the young man's value in the economic collapse he knew was coming.

Zenji's latest invention is Mandarax, a pocket device capable of a variety of advanced functions, from language translation to retrieval-on-demand of information from world history and literature. Through it Vonnegut sprinkles quotations to comment on the action, the best wisdom of the big-brain era, most of it having to do with human arrogance and folly. He is also expressing ambivalence about new generations of cyber-hardware intruding into daily life in the 1980s, personal computers far surpassing in speed and potential for mischief the behemoths Paul Proteus worried about in *Player Piano*. Despite the claims of enthusiasts for this latest stage in the automation of society, it all came with costs—economic, social, and spiritual. The impact in evolutionary terms was uncertain.

Zenji and Hisako enter data into Mandarax to determine if they have indeed been kidnapped by a madman. After some processing, its screen displays the words "pathological personality" to describe MacIntosh. Epidemic in scale, a lack of empathy for others is at the heart of the syndrome. It provided certain immediate, individual advantages in the struggle for survival, and those afflicted were "among the happiest people on the planet." But the wider effects were disastrous.

The tensions between Zenji and Hisako illustrate the near-impossibility of communication in the age of elaborate neural circuitry—especially within the bonds of marriage. As they volley back and forth, Hisako only gradually reveals what is bothering her. Zenji has programmed tapes of her classes in ikebana, the traditional Japanese art of flower arranging, into Mandarax. "A little black box could not only teach what she taught," she protests, "but could do it in a thousand different tongues." We are back to the problem of *Player Piano*. Zenji insists on his good intentions, but Hisako is not listening. "That was how bad things had become back in 1986," the narrator observes. "Nobody believed anybody anymore, since there was so much lying going on."

Andrew MacIntosh is wheeling and dealing in his suite down the hall on the same floor, waiting for a call from panicked local investors ready to turn over properties in assets exchange for the abstraction of still-good American dollars. When consummated, "Ecuador could wire or radio pieces of the mirage to fertile countries and get real food in return"—averting mass starvation for a few days, at most.

Outside, hastily erected barbed wire protects the hotel from the citizens now crowding around it. None of this concerns MacIntosh, who casually places a room service order from the El Dorado's well-stocked larder. Jesús Ortiz, the bartender, is pressed into delivery duty as other employees begin to vanish.

Jesús believes in the entitlements due to the rich, like the celebrities he still expects to arrive for the Nature Cruise. "Señora Kennedy" in particular occupies the status of a saint in his imagination, and her visit would be a miracle from which widespread plenty would surely follow. Like millions of people at the lower reaches of the economic order, Ortiz hopes one day to join the elect, to be Cinderella. "His big brain liked to show movies in his head which starred him and his dependents as millionaires."

MacIntosh gazes out the window at the properties he plans to own before the end of the day. Not wanting to be interrupted, he waves off the meal when it arrives, commanding that the steaks be put on the floor for Selena's dog.

Ortiz takes the gesture as a sharp blow. The dream has become a nightmare; the portrait in his mind of the formerly beatific Jackie "grew fangs like a vampire, and the skin dropped off the face." After pacing the perimeter of the building several times, his mercurial brain causes him to rip out the telephone lines in a rage.

Our narrator is the ghost of the *Bahía de Darwin*. He is an American marine who knows all about pathological personalities like the one displayed by MacIntosh—they were in charge of the war in which he served, in Indochina. He deserted to Sweden after his unit committed a My Lai–style massacre. He was decapitated during construction of the *Bahía de Darwin,* in the port of Malmo, after which his spirit attached to the brain of Adolf von Kleist, the alcoholic bon vivant scheduled to be the ship's captain. Von Kleist looked like a man of the sea and was so charming he had become a regular on the television talk-show circuit. But he knows almost nothing about the Galápagos Islands or, for that matter, the basics of navigation. He is the comic bumbler of the novel, and with his German name serves as a Vonnegut alter ego conveying the author's perpetual sense of his own fraudulence.

Our first look into the mental world of Captain von Kleist, woozy from all the champagne he had imbibed on the flight down from New York, does not inspire confidence. In the cab ride from the locked-down Guayaquil airport, his attention is fixed not on the crowds filling the streets but on the dangers posed by meteorites, like those that doomed the dinosaurs. It is a subject von Kleist ponders compulsively, drawn from one of the rare lectures he could remember from his misspent days at the Naval Academy. "This was often my experience back then," the narrator interjects. "I would get into the head of somebody in what to me was a particularly interesting situation, and discover that the person's big brain was thinking about things which had nothing to do with the problem right at hand."

But the captain's ruminations also make a kind of sense. Like the author, Adolf von Kleist "had already been hit by a meteorite." In yet another instance of nature's determinism, the threat of imminent disaster loomed in his thoughts ever since he found out about his father's Huntington's Chorea, a hereditary neurological disorder whose symptoms do not manifest themselves until middle age. This parallels Vonnegut's dread about his mother's mental illness, the shadow cast by her suicide.

It is amazing how slow the captain's brain is to catch on to the urgency of the dangers around him. When Hernando Cruz, his first mate (the person really in charge of the *Darwin*) briefs him on the situation, von Kleist smiles blankly and heads up to his suite for a hot shower. "This is another human defect," the ship's ghost tells us, one that even a million years of natural selection has yet to remedy: Full bellies are a recipe for fatal complacency. What made the problem so critical back in 1986 was the fact that "the people who were best informed about the state of the planet were by definition well fed. So everything was always just fine as far as they were concerned."

Cruz has a family back on shore, and their empty bellies weigh more and more heavily on his mind as the afternoon progresses. At sunset he watches as large stores of food and fuel are loaded onto the only other vessel in the harbor, owned by Colombian drug dealers. As with Jesús Ortiz, something snaps in Hernandez's brain in the face of all this brazen corruption. Concern for his blood relatives trumps duty to post, and he walks off the gleaming white ship, abandoning it to the supervision of his woefully unprepared boss.

The logic of evolution proceeds in ways that resist our human narratives. Adolf von Kleist's incompetence turns out to be fortunate, just what natural selection needed to transform his craft into a second Noah's Ark. The bumbler is about to be an inadvertent hero.

Random things happen in quick succession, and all will have enormous consequences in evolutionary terms—which, in the long run, are the only ones that matter. Miffed at his wife's accusations, Zenji Hiroguchi storms out of their room at the El Dorado and pushes the button for the elevator. The doors open to Andrew MacIntosh, the person he least wants to encounter. Siegfried von Kleist, the captain's brother and manager of the hotel, shouts from behind the registration desk as Zenji bolts through the lobby and out into the tumult of the Calle Diez de Agosto, MacIntosh in hot pursuit. It is too late—the men are gunned down within seconds.

The assassin is Geraldo Delgado, an army private whose diseased brain makes him see enemies everywhere. Besides killing two men who otherwise might have made it onto the *Darwin*, Delgado does one other thing that will have incalculable impact: He leaves a door ajar through which a group of starving young street girls enter the cordoned-off zone, thus arriving in time for their places on the Ark. They are the last survivors of the Kanka-bonos, an aboriginal tribe from Ecuador's depleted rain forest. All people a million years in the future will be descended from their race, once so close to extinction. It is a clever and instructive reversal, delivered with relish by Vonnegut the anthropologist.

The worldwide financial panic has destabilized governments everywhere.

To "divert the big brains of their people from all their troubles," the leaders of Peru's military junta declare war on the neighbor to the north. A chain reaction is now in motion, as irreversible and as much a human creation as ice-nine in *Cat's Cradle*. For the reader it is by now a patented Vonnegut specialty.

After wrapping her head in the polyethylene bag of her "Jackie dress," just on the edge of letting go, Mary Hepburn changes her mind and heads downstairs to meet the other passengers on the Nature Cruise. For her, and for the author after his flirtation with suicide, it is not time yet for the Big Sleep.

Mary sees James Wait feeding cocktail peanuts and olives to the Kankabonos. This first impression is a powerful one: her brain conjures a wholly mistaken story of Wait as a selfless humanitarian. It makes her even more vulnerable to his disguise as a grieving widower. The role is so easy to play, and the girls such perfect bait for his purposes as a fisherman.

But Vonnegut endows even his most reprehensible characters with humanity, and James Wait, the abused and neglected "child of the devil," finds himself astonished at the joy he feels when acting for the first time as a healer. "The opportunity to be charitable had simply never presented itself before, but here it was now, and he was loving it." We think of Otto Waltz in *Deadeye Dick,* seizing his chance to be a responsible adult after a lifetime of narcissistic excess. These are men who, at least momentarily, transcend their stories, exercise free will—become characters.

Wait's time to experiment with his new identity is short, however. There is now an asterisk by his name.

"How people used to talk and talk back then!" our narrator exclaims in exasperation. "What could most of that blah-blah-blahing have been but the spilling of useless, uncalled-for signals from our preposterously huge and active brains? There was no shutting them down! Whether we had anything for them to do or not, they ran all the time!" In their blaring distraction they were like the ghetto blasters many young people carried on their shoulders in the 1980s.

The mistakes and deceptions continue. Siegfried von Kleist directs his guests to round up blind Selena and pregnant Hisako for what he downplays as a precautionary trip to the airport. The radio announces that the Nature Cruise has been canceled, news the crowd outside takes as a signal that the food in the hotel is up for grabs. "Take it from somebody who has been around for a million years," the ghost declares. "Food is practically the whole story every time." We hear Billy Pilgrim and Edgar Derby echoing hearty "amens."

Rioters rock the bus, activating in its occupants varied instincts for survival. James Wait's first impulse is self-preservation, but Mary pulls him down into the aisle to shield the girls from flying glass. In the exertion his heart seizes up, the result of an inherited defect. In the driver's seat, meanwhile, Siegfried has his own genetic booby traps to contend with. He convulses as he struggles to steer the vehicle through the mob, the Huntington's Chorea passed on from his father choosing the worst possible time to become active.

His brother, meanwhile, spared the family disease, is acting less than courageously at the waterfront. The captain hides in the crow's nest of his ship as looters strip it clean. The brand-new vessel now has fewer amenities and navigational aids than were on board the *Beagle* back in 1831. As the human wave recedes the captain scrambles down to his cabin and finds the last remaining consumable, a half-bottle of cognac. Adolf shouts and laughs to himself, unaware that the boat is starting to drift from its moorings, attached to the mainland only by a single rope. "Poetically speaking," Vonnegut the mythmaker observes through his narrator, mindful of how his own life had so recently been hanging by a thread, "that stern line is the white nylon umbilical cord of all modern humankind."

It is fortunate the bus does not make its destination. Outside the city hospital, to which Siegfried has diverted out of concern for his stricken passenger, the earth shakes with a deafening explosion as the airport is destroyed. The people huddled on the floor (and their descendants) would believe ever after the captain's explanation that it was the impact of a meteor shower.

But Adolf von Kleist, as usual, is wrong. It was high-tech, big-brained warfare. Vonnegut conveys the eroticism of the air-to-ground missile attack through the mind of the young Peruvian pilot who launched it, encased in the cockpit of his jet, high in the upper atmosphere. Although computers did the work, he felt a postcoital satisfaction once the deed was done. All he needed was a cigarette.

Yes—and that rod which became a dot and then a speck and then nothingness so quickly was somebody else's responsibility now. All the action from now on would be on the receiving end.

He had done his part. He was sweetly sleepy now—and amused and proud.

Like the bombardiers who released their payloads over Dresden in 1945, the young man's fleeting part in launching the missile "was virtually identical with the role of male animals in the reproductive process," even a million years in the future.

Guayaquil goes dark. Siegfried improvises yet again, threading the bus toward the wharf where he knows the *Darwin* sat waiting. There is a figure up on its deck greeting them. Is it Leon Trout, the ghost said by locals to haunt the vessel? "Welcome to the Nature Cruise of the Century!" Captain Adolf von Kleist cries out in inebriated hilarity.

His work done, his will to go on spent, Siegfried implores his brother to figure out a way to rescue his passengers. Adolf is not up to the task, but Mary Hepburn assumes leadership in the vacuum. A revitalized and resourceful warrior, she organizes a human chain to get everyone safely on board.

A second explosion rocks the harbor. Another Peruvian missile had "mated with a radar dish," thought to be on the *Darwin*. Instead it took out the freighter with the Colombian drug lords—an "honest mistake," all too common in big-brain times. Siegfried perishes in the ensuing tidal wave and the ship's umbilical cord snaps. Adolf ascends to the bridge and switches on the diesel engines. The Ark heads out to its destiny.

The ghost of Leon Trotsky Trout, the headless marine deserter and only son of a not-so-famous science-fiction writer, is along for the ride. He watches as his host pursues a zigzag route to avoid the shooting stars he imagines to be more incoming rocks from space.

Mary Hepburn spends the first night at sea pleasantly unstuck in time, reliving her first encounter with the man who would become her husband. She and Roy met on a bird-watching trip, and their feelings of tenderness for each other were evident at first sight. "They don't make memories like that anymore," Leon Trout comments wistfully, conceding that the capacity for such bittersweet joy was one big-brain quality whose passing is to be mourned.

Mary is brought back to the present by the delirious, dying man she still believes to be Willard Flemming. "I love you so much," James Wait tells her. "Please marry me. I'm so lonesome. I'm so scared." She feels a familiar, irrational tug of compassion.

Nobody in the distant future, Leon Trout observes, has a romantic life as unpredictable and complicated as these two strangers.

> Any human love story of today would have for its crisis the simplest of questions: whether the persons involved were in heat or not. Men and women now become helplessly interested in each other and the nubbins on their flippers and so on only twice a year—or, in times of fish shortages, only once a year. So much depends on fish.

Astonishing, too, is the lust for acquisition of human beings back in 1986. On the deck of the *Darwin,* Wait declares there will be riches beyond her wildest imagination if Mary agrees to his proposal. Wait's ill-gotten gains will be hard to retrieve, scattered as they are under assumed names and backed by currencies that have already melted down. But it is an impressive fortune. Leon marvels at its sheer unsustainability:

> If his wealth had continued to grow at the rate it was growing then, the James Wait estate would now encompass the whole universe— galaxies, black holes, comets, clouds of asteroids and meteors and the Captain's meteorites and interstellar matter of every sort—simply everything.
>
> What impossible dreams of increase human beings used to have only yesterday, only a million years ago!

The captain overhears the conversation, and, looking for a victory somewhere, intervenes to exercise his authority to make the woman's promise of betrothal a reality. Moments later, Willard Flemming dies, taking all his many secrets with him.

Mary and Adolf von Kleist take turns steering the ship as day turns to night and back again. When the sun rises in the west it becomes clear they have no idea where they are headed. Not that there are promising destinations. After the *Darwin*'s exit from the mainland, big-brained pyrotechnics spread rapidly, followed by global drought and famine. Meanwhile, a contagion of unknown origin is rendering females everywhere sterile. There will be no healing of the species by the usual methods after this catastrophe, no massive production of babies, as with previous wars. "As far as humanity was concerned," Leon Trout tells us, "all wounds were about to become very permanent."

The passengers are getting hungry. The Kanaka-bono orphans, no strangers to this problem, take things into their own hands, killing and eating Selena's seeing-eye dog, Kazakh. ("Oh, well," Leon interjects, borrowing a gallows phrase from the trenches of World War I. "She wasn't going to write Beethoven's Ninth Symphony anyway.")

Captain von Kleist "[fires] his brain," turning the ship this way and that now as intuition dictates. Mary uses the impossible standard of her second husband to reproach him. "If only Willard were still alive," she sighs in frustration, "he would know exactly what to do." Von Kleist is yet another of Vonnegut's buffoonish men, overmatched and intimidated by the power of women.

Mary suggests using Mandarax to radio for help, but in response to the captain's repeated shouts of "Mayday," it displays on its screen only a *Bartlett's*-style sequence of literary quotations. The repository of so much big-brained information, the little machine is worse than useless in this situation.

Ghostly Leon spies a ball of energy off the stern of the *Darwin*. It is "the blue tunnel to the Afterlife" stalking him again. Inside is his father, asking if his curiosity about life has been satisfied yet. It is reminiscent of the author's encounter with his dead parents in *Breakfast of Champions*, and Wilbur's conversation with Eliza at the end of *Slapstick*. The question in each case is whether life is worth it—is there a point to carrying on? Vonnegut is there on both sides of the argument, young and old, hopeful and despairing. We wonder where he will end up.

"Had enough of the ship of fools, my boy?" Kilgore Trout inquires, clear about which way he thinks it should go. "You come to Papa right now. Turn me down this time, and you won't see me again for a million years." He presents his case for giving up.

The more you learn about people, the more disgusted you'll become. I would have thought that your being sent by the wisest men in your country, supposedly, to fight a nearly endless, thankless, horrifying, and, finally, pointless war, would have given you sufficient insight into the nature of humanity to last you throughout all eternity!

Haggard and chain-smoking, as he had been in life, Trout Sr. insists that the dominant species of the planet have already destroyed any chance for a future. "Like the people on this accursed ship, my boy, they are led by captains who have no charts or compasses, and who deal from minute to minute with no problem more substantial than how to protect their self-esteem."

It is all true, but Leon hesitates. Just as he seems ready to take the step, something pulls him back. "Land ho!" comes the cries from the crow's nest. The optimist wins again over the pessimist, but barely. Curiosity, empathy, maybe even *hope* commits him to staying on this side of the void awhile longer.

Von Kleist runs his vessel aground, on a lava shoal close to the fictional island of Santa Rosalia. He wades ashore with Mary to gather up all the food they can plunder—blue-footed boobies and the other protein-rich animals who, in their isolation, never developed a fear of predators. The passengers feast on meat and eggs in style, and ready themselves for the journey back to the mainland. But the engines will not restart.

Thus does the human race reduce itself to a tiny, saving remnant, a colony marooned where the idea of evolution was first born—a controlled experiment in natural selection. A decade later, in 1996, the waterlogged *Darwin* slips unceremoniously to the bottom of the ocean. Leon Trout remains an otherworldly voyeur as the group settles into its routines and cliques. Hisako gives birth to a daughter, Akiko, whose skin, to the envy of the others on cold nights, is covered by a silky pelt, a mutation with obvious advantages, inherited from her grandmother, a Hiroshima survivor.

By default, Adolf and Mary, known to all as Mrs. Flemming, set up housekeeping together. They engage in occasional sexual congress as a way to pass the time. Ever the inquisitive science teacher, Mary begins to entertain an idea for a new project. It would redeem the honorific her students had given her in the farewell edition of the Ilium High yearbook: "Mother Nature Personified." Beyond childbearing age herself, Mary wonders if it might be possible to artificially impregnate the teenaged Kanka-bonos with the captain's seed—neglecting to mention the plan to the man involved. Again Vonnegut hammers home the theme of the disparity in the sexes in reproduction, humbling to the male ego.

Mary's curiosity will not go away. "Her big brain would make her life a hell," Leon observes, "until she had actually performed that experiment." In the history of the race this has opened the door to the most grievous crimes, and considering the damage done by the unchecked human imagination Leon was surprised that Mandarax does not have in its arsenal of axioms the following warning: "In this era of big brains, anything which can be done will be done—so hunker down." But in this instance, acting on the thought proves to be humanity's salvation.

Self-absorbed as ever, the captain finds out only later that the first male born on the island, Kamikaze, was his son. He retreats into the life of a hermit, pretending to guard the colony's natural spring—his harmless, if not very effective, defense against the disease of uselessness. Adolf lacks the grace of Malachi Constant in his last years on Titan. Like the mass of men of his era, according to the Thoreau adage dutifully recited by Mandarax, the crotchety recluse endures his days in a kind of sleepy "quiet desperation."

"The mass of men was quietly desperate a million years ago," Leon Trout tells us, "because the infernal computers inside their skulls were incapable of restraint or idleness; were forever demanding more challenging problems which life could not provide." Thanks to natural selection, people now had dramatically streamlined brains. To facilitate diving and fishing, their hands—which required those baroque nervous systems to control them—had long ago receded into flippers. Low self-esteem, boredom, lack of purpose were no longer issues.

Thirty years after their arrival on Santa Rosalia, Mary Hepburn—toothless, stooped, but still self-sufficient—pays the captain a visit as he lies on his deathbed. Adolf's body is robust, but his brain has been ravaged by what Mandarax guesses to be Alzheimer's. "Thanks to sharks and killer whales, problems connected with aging are unimaginable in the present day," we are assured. Humans in the future rarely live past thirty.

The captain reacts with agitation when he sees the device Mary has kept as a companion—the Mandarax. "I hate this little son of a bitch more than anything in the whole world," he yells as he snatches it from her and heads down to the shore. He flings the Mandarax—the accursed apple of knowledge—into the shallow water. It is another rare, momentary victory in the war of men against machines that runs back to *Player Piano*'s chess-playing computer. Mary dives in after the Mandarax only to be consumed by a shark. Buffeted by a flock of vampire finches, the captain jumps in soon after and meets the same fate. The author has resolved with a flourish one of the novelist's biggest problems—how to end his tale.

In time the rest of Santa Rosalia's founding generation would die off as well. Despite its chance beginnings, it developed into a Vonnegutian folk society, held together by "a common language and a common religion and some common jokes and songs and dances and so on, almost everything Kanka-bono." There are echoes here of the survivors who carry on at the conclusion of *Cat's Cradle*. In their maturity Kamikaze and Akiko would be venerated, as the captain and Mary never were, as wise, dignified elders. "It went very fast—that formation from such random genetic materials of a perfectly cohesive human family," the author concludes through his narrator, sounding like a biochemist examining a petri dish. The human race would avoid extinction in the late twentieth century, and—with "certain modifications in design," to be sure—continue into the indefinite future.

The famously self-critical Vonnegut rated *Galápagos* one of his best books—he gave it an A+ grade, primarily for his ability to solve the dilemma of spanning a million years. "Who's going to observe it" is always a crucial decision, he knew, "because the reader is going to insist upon knowing who the hell is watching this"—and here the challenge was especially tricky. Leon Trout, the ghost of the *Darwin* who writes his observations on air—an allusion to the precariousness of words—was the inspired solution.[8]

Most critics were effusive in their praise of the book. A writer for the *New York Times Book Review* felt that *Galápagos* sealed Vonnegut's status as a "postmodern Mark Twain," and a reviewer for the *Times Literary Sup-*

plement in London found him to be "the same droll, disingenuous, utterly middle-American, if now high-middle-aged Huck Finn" readers had fallen in love with in the 1960s. The book succeeded, too, on a scientific level, something the author, who had done his homework, cared deeply about. Vonnegut's friend Stephen J. Gould, the eminent zoologist, appreciated its illustration of how suddenly mutations can operate with random circumstances in the logic of evolution. Gould assigned *Galápagos* to students in his science courses at Harvard. "In Vonnegut's novel, the pathways of history may be broadly constrained by such principles as natural selection," he observed,

> but contingency has so much maneuvering room within these boundaries that any particular outcome owes more to a quirky set of antecedent events than to channels set by nature's laws.
>
> The lunkish, furry sea creatures of the future were, it turns out, entirely plausible.[9]

Even in a book soaked in determinism, what is most memorable about *Galápagos* are the moments of innovation and *free will* we observe in its cast of not-so-exceptional characters. We are touched by the selflessness of Siegfried von Kleist and smile at the inept vulnerability of his brother Adolf, for whom we can't help rooting. Then there is James Wait's eleventh-hour turn as a healer, and Mary Hepburn's journey back from the brink—a trip that refracts the author's experience—to become the goddess of fertility, "Mother Nature Personified."

The sadness in the end is that survival involves reducing humans to such simple, *storyless* beings. There is a loss in that exchange—we will have no more Beethovens or Thoreaus, no one will live to wizened old age. Is there a less drastic remedy, can we figure out another way to manage our self-destructive thoughts and impulses? We join with Leon, and with the reborn Kurt Vonnegut, in our nostalgia for people as they once were, "big brains and all."

TWELVE

Bluebeard

An Armenian in America is a strange thing indeed.
—Arshile Gorky (1905–1948)

*Nowhere has the number zero been more of philosophical
value than in the United States.*
—Rabo Karabekian

We're dancing now.
—Circe Berman

Kurt Vonnegut continued his late-period mastery with *Bluebeard* (1987), a latticework of stories, asides, and subplots unusually tender in tone, linked by familiar questions about identity in a world where so much is determined by blind accident. America, land of second chances, is also a place of dislocation and "counterfeits," and we weigh the costs as well as the benefits of relentless reinvention, always having to start over again from zero.[1]

The author is, as usual, working on a number of different levels here. *Bluebeard* is an exploration of creativity and the possibilities of realism versus abstraction in communicating the human experience. It is a familiar subject for the author, who came from a family of artists and devoted himself increasingly to drawing and painting in his later years. It relates to the poles of his writing method, journalistic detail on the one end, experimental language, comedy, and sci-fi effects on the other, both approaches evident from his earliest fiction.

The idea for this project began with an essay on Jackson Pollock that Vonnegut wrote for *Esquire's* special fiftieth-anniversary issue in 1983. A prodigy from the Wyoming frontier, Pollock deserved his reputation as "the foremost adventurer" of the New York School, Vonnegut concluded, the man most responsible for making that city the capital of the art world.[2]

Though his own aesthetic preferences were on the "realist" side of the fence, the author admired the abstract expressionists for their assault on narrative—the only way to go after death camps and atomic bombs. This is what united the little community of dribblers and lovers of color who so suddenly began to attract interest in the late 1940s. "Its members were unanimous as to where inspiration should come from," Vonnegut explained, "the unconscious, that part of the mind which was lively, but which caught no likenesses, had no morals or politics, and had no tired old stories to tell yet again."[3]

Bluebeard is, too, another retrospective on the challenges the author's generation of child-warriors faced in adapting back to civilian life. Especially daunting were the women to whom they returned: as many other Vonnegut protagonists could attest, they wielded powers to destroy as well as to nurture and heal. Even in the face of these difficulties, however, what emerges here is Vonnegut's most accomplished love story. It is something he has avoided in the past, but now achieves with a consummation both surprising and completely satisfying.

Finally, like *Galápagos*, this is a Lazarus parable, the reflections of a man back from the dead, pondering his mistakes, coming to terms with rejection and loss, trying to find meaning in his unlikely journey. Now approaching sixty-five, Vonnegut was tentative as always about his place in the world—"birth and death were always there," all around him. He reveled in his young daughter, Lily, and the arrival of each new grandchild, even as first wife, Jane, succumbed to cancer in late 1986. Grief over her departure hangs over *Bluebeard*. He worried about old friends wrestling, without much success, against their demons, and did what he could to help members of his "family" from the Iowa Writers' Workshop days like Nelson Algren and Richard Yates. He knew their legacies were endangered, their works might be forgotten. "This is an era of short and jittery attention spans and empty memory banks," he wrote to Loree Rackstraw, another Workshop friend. An artist's output now had an ever-briefer shelf life.[4]

And what of his own work? Did it amount to anything, really? Did Kurt Vonnegut have the ideas, the talent, the soul, he wondered, to be worthy of lasting attention?

The narrator of *Bluebeard* is Rabo Karabekian, the abstract painter we met in *Breakfast of Champions.* As with Celia Hoover in *Deadeye Dick,* Vonnegut fleshes out into three dimensions a minor character from a previous book, giving us plenty of surprises. In *Bluebeard*'s Rabo we find a considerably more sympathetic figure than the braggart we encountered in Midland City's Tally-Ho Room. Chastened by age and a deep recognition of his own limitations and failures, Rabo has gone through a period of self-imposed isolation since the death of his second wife, Edith, spending his days wandering the East Hamptons oceanfront estate she left him, staring vacantly out to sea. He imagines the horror of her Anglo-Saxon forebears, who never expected their land to be in the possession of someone with a name as exotic as his. "Blame the Statue of Liberty," he plans to say if he runs into one of their ghosts. Vonnegut kept a summer home in the Hamptons, and he, like Rabo, was "a drop of spray from one of the waves which swamped the American Atlantis," as he put it in *Palm Sunday.* He must have had the same ruminations during his solitary walks on the beach.[5]

Rabo's lone companion is the novelist Paul Slazinger, "a wounded World War Two geezer like myself," he tells us, afflicted with a bad case of writer's block. Slazinger comes and goes as he pleases, helping himself to the refrigerator and "hiding from everybody and everything." These men represent different aspects of Vonnegut, the damaged veteran. Rabo is the more functional of the two, the romantic who keeps coming back to the world, sustained by moments of fierce pride, demonstrating, almost against his will, a kind of "grace in defeat." Paul is the Kilgore Trout–like cynic, more darkly ferocious in his judgments, barely hanging on.

In the servants' quarters, the cook lives with her teenaged daughter, Celeste, who entertains her loud and willfully ignorant teenaged friends around the pool and tennis courts. Rabo is estranged from his own children and grandchildren (who bear anglicized names), so Celeste and her crowd are his only window onto the preoccupations of 1980s youth. They dismiss him, perhaps with good reason, as "a senile veteran from some forgotten war, daydreaming away what little remains of his life as a museum guard."

Rabo is deep into the epilogue of his life, sustained by proceeds from selling the obscenely valuable paintings that fill the house. "About absolutely nothing but themselves," they are a legacy from his days as a fellow traveler with Pollock, Mark Rothko, and the fictional Terry Kitchen in Greenwich Village after the war. "I may have been a lousy painter," Rabo concedes, "but what a *collector* I turned out to be!"

Now he is writing his memoirs. "I am the erstwhile American painter Rabo Karabekian, a one-eyed man, born of immigrant parents in San Ignacio, California, in 1916." As a soldier in World War II he led a unit of army engineers specializing in camouflage. "What hallucinations we gave the Germans," he remembers with satisfaction. The fun ended, though, in the snowstorms of the Bulge. Rabo lost his left eye in the chaos and spent the balance of the war as a POW.

Like Vonnegut, Rabo went into battle carrying earlier, deeper burdens, inheriting the pain of parents who saw the world they knew destroyed. His ancestors perished in the century's first genocide, the murder of one million Armenians by the Ottoman Empire during the First World War. Vonnegut seems to draw here on the life of Arshile Gorky, the refugee artist whose works are haunted by nostalgia for his native land.

Rabo's mother survived the carnage by playing dead in a pile of corpses. Facing her was the body of an old woman whose mouth overflowed with diamonds and rubies. It was "birth and death together"—the jewels would make passage to America possible. Rabo's father, a schoolteacher, saved himself by hiding in a privy as the marauders swept through. "For him, the stillness of the village, of which he was the only inhabitant at nightfall, was his most terrible memory." In common with Vonnegut's Dresden tale, it is a war story with a hole in the middle.

Rabo's mother was a resilient survivor, able to move on and "daydream about a family future" in the New World. "My father *never* did," he concludes with some anger. "He welcomed all proofs that the planet he had known and loved during his boyhood had disappeared entirely. That was *his* way of honoring all the friends and relatives he had lost in the massacre." In America he took up the family tradition, working with his hands as a cobbler. Rabo recalls his bitter curses, in the native language, against the swindler who steered them to their isolation in California.

What has prompted Rabo Karabekian to open up his life this way? *"Cherchez la femme!"* Circe Berman, a fortyish widow (her name evokes the mythological sorceress who turned men into swine) strayed onto his beach one day early in the summer. "Tell mama how your parents died," she demanded when he greeted her, bypassing his casual hello. She is blunt and direct, and he has been off-balance ever since their first meeting.

With a single question Circe stirred up feelings in Rabo he thought long extinguished. "I am in a frenzy of adolescent resentment against a father who was buried almost fifty years ago!" he writes. "Let me off this hellish time machine!" Circe urges forgiveness, and he is trying. "I find myself doing whatever she says I must do," Rabo says of the interloper he gallantly calls "Mrs. Berman."

> Is this woman a friend? . . . All I know is that she isn't going to leave again until she's good and ready, and that she scares the *pants* off me.
> Help.

Rabo admits that he invited Circe into his world—on some level he likes her provocations. She presents herself as an amateur writer, working on a biography of her recently deceased husband. Soon it comes out that she is the author of a wildly popular series of youth novels under the pseudonym "Polly Madison." They are the kind of books Paul Slazinger, in his insecurity, would denounce as beneath contempt, but they attract a loyal audience because they engage real concerns—abortion, premarital sex—with what Rabo considers "shockingly frank" candor.

At dinner Mrs. Berman continued to assert her dominance, sparring with Paul about writing and Rabo about art, and exhibiting what they both agree is an appalling lack of taste. "She was outrageous!" Rabo tells us, recalling her scorn for a Pollock hanging in the dining room. Her preference ran to Victorian chromos of little girls on swings—kitsch, in his eyes. At least they told a story one could understand, she insisted, unlike the splatters and color fields lining the severe white walls of the mansion, with pretentiously obscure names like *Opus Nine* and *Blue and Burnt Orange.* "What's the point of being alive," Circe asks, "if you're not going to *communicate?*"

As we know from *Breakfast of Champions,* Rabo Karabekian was once himself a painter of some repute, known for works like Midland City's *Temptation of Saint Anthony* and the monumental *Windsor Blue Number Seventeen,* selected to adorn the lobby of GEFFCo headquarters on Park Avenue. They are minimalist in the extreme, in the manner of Barnett Newman.

Rabo became synonymous with folly in art appreciation classes when, due to "unforeseen chemical reactions" his pieces started to disintegrate, one by one. In each case the paint he had used—"Sateen Dura-Luxe, straight from the can"—congealed and heaved and buckled, leaving blank patches and "what looked like moldy Rice Krispies on the floor."

"It was a postwar miracle that did me in," Rabo laments. Vonnegut uses his character's humiliation to comment on the ephemerality of art (compare Leon Trout in *Galápagos,* writing his thoughts in the air) and also to reflect again on the failed promise of his generation's faith in science. "I had better explain to my young readers, if any, that the Second World War had many of the promised characteristics of Armageddon, a final war between good and evil, so that nothing would do but that it be followed by miracles," Rabo writes.

> During that war we had a word for extreme man-made disorder which was *fubar,* an acronym for "fucked up beyond all recognition." Well—the whole planet is now fubar with postwar miracles, but, back in the early 1960s, I was one of the first persons to be totally wrecked by one—an acrylic wall-paint, whose colors, according to advertisements of the day, would "... outlive the smile on the Mona Lisa."

Circe settles in, and no detail of domestic life is left undisturbed, no secret eludes her inquisitive eye. She knows, for example, that young Celeste (an avid fan of Polly Madison books) is using birth control pills. One mystery remains sacrosanct, however: the contents of the padlocked potato barn out back, once Rabo's studio. Like the villainous Bluebeard of the French folktale, who hides the bodies of former wives he has murdered in a secret room, he has forbidden his guest from investigating. "There is no lame joke in there," he assures us, relishing the tease—no painting of potatoes or "the Virgin Mary wearing a derby and holding a watermelon." She will have to wait to find out what is inside with everyone else, "when I have gone to the big art auction in the sky."

Circe Berman seems modeled in part on Vonnegut's second wife, Jill Krementz, the talented artist with whom he had been living since the early 1970s. "Xanthippe," he wrote of Jill on the occasion of her fiftieth birthday, "continues to empty chamber pots on my head from time to time." For all of the challenges of their partnership, he felt that she kept him on the side of going forward, remaining engaged with the world.

> If it weren't for her I think I probably would have died of too much sleep long ago. I would have napped myself to death. At the very least I would have stopped seeing movies and plays, and reading books and magazines, and going outside, things like that. She is what George Bernard Shaw called "a life force woman."[6]

"When I was a two-eyed boy, I was the best draughtsman they had ever seen in the rinky-dink public school system of San Ignacio," Rabo remembers of his early years. His father (like Vonnegut's) wanted to veto the idea of an artistic career, insisting that his son develop a useful trade, as a shoemaker. But Rabo's mother encouraged him to write to Dan Gregory, the famed New York illustrator and fellow Armenian who, she read in a magazine, "made as much money as many movie stars and tycoons." For all of his success, Gregory might be open to an overture. "My mother was shrewd about the United States, as my father was not," Rabo acknowledges. "She had figured out that the most pervasive American disease was loneliness, and that even people at the top often suffered from it."

Over the objections of his father, who stormed that "Gregorian" had surrendered his claim to being Armenian when he changed his name," Rabo went fishing, mailing off a carefully composed introduction. He was eager to try to make his mother's impossible dreams come true.

"And what a terrific bite my letter got!" The handwritten reply was the first in what would become an extensive correspondence from Marilee Kemp, a young woman also skilled at the art of reinvention. The daughter of a West Virginia coal miner, then a Ziegfeld Follies showgirl, she was now Dan Gregory's assistant (or, as Rabo's father suggested, in Armenian, ". . . maybe his cleaning woman, maybe his cook, maybe his whore").

Marilee sent expensive art supplies to San Ignacio, along with elegantly bound texts illustrated by Gregory, classics that would have been on Kurt Vonnegut's childhood bookshelf, like *Treasure Island, Robinson Crusoe,* and *Tales from Shakespeare.* "Reading matter for young people before the Second World War," Rabo editorializes, "was a dozen universes removed from the unwanted pregnancies and incest and minimum-wage slavery and treacherous high school friendships and so on in the novels of Polly Madison."

Rabo's after-school job as a cartoonist for the local paper brought in a little money to support his now-widowed father, who had lost everything with the closing of the county savings and loan. The elder Karabekian, like Vonnegut's father, retreated from the world when things got bad. He spent hours alone in his workshop making fanciful hand-tooled cowboy boots, "scintillating with gold and silver stars and eagles and flowers and bucking broncos cut from flattened tin cans and bottle caps"—similar in craftsmanship to Kurt Sr.'s creations as a potter down in the hills of southern Indiana. But when the son looked into the old man's eyes, "there wasn't anybody home anymore."

One day a telegram arrived, inviting Rabo to become Dan Gregory's apprentice. There was no hesitation about what to do. "It was and remains easy for most Americans to go somewhere else to start anew," Rabo observes.

> I wasn't like my parents. I didn't have any supposedly sacred piece of land or shoals of friends and relatives to leave behind. Nowhere has the number *zero* been of more philosophical value than in the United States. . . . "Here goes nothing," says the American as he goes off the high diving board.

Here, again, we have the Vonnegut narrative of a boy from the provinces heading out to seek his fortune in the wider world. Even with success he is forever adrift, without secure coordinates to guide him. As Felix told his brother Rudy in *Deadeye Dick,* "any city in any country was to me just another place where I might live or might not live." From his plush train compartment on the cross-continent trip to New York, Rabo took in scenes of Dust Bowl misery, displaced families with all their possessions strapped to dilapidated trucks. Then he passed though a "birth canal" of tunnels, arriving finally in the labyrinth of Grand Central Station.

No one was there to greet Rabo as he stood on the platform, carrying a cardboard valise and a portfolio of his drawings. "It would have made a great Dan Gregory illustration," he reflects now, "for a story about a yokel finding himself all alone in a big city he has never seen before." With his dark complexion he was not hard to pick out in the crowd. Still no friendly faces appeared.

The reception did not improve at the Gregory brownstone. The butler, a one-time World War I aviator named Fred Jones, familiar as a model in many of his boss's illustrations, was expressionless as he escorted the visitor through a baroque entrance hall. The rooms of the big house were like Gregory's portraits, extreme in their pretensions to realism (a cousin to the Americana of Norman Rockwell) but *counterfeit* to the core. "Nobody could counterfeit plant diseases like Dan Gregory," Rabo tells us, recalling the wreath on the front door, used as background detail for a *Liberty* magazine cover. "Nobody could counterfeit images in dusty mirrors like Dan Gregory." "Nobody could paint black people"—whom the artist detested—"like Dan Gregory."

Rabo was escorted up a spiral staircase, to a "Dan Gregory counterfeit" of the bedroom of Napoleon's Empress Josephine. As he prepared to sleep on the floor, Jones warned him not to touch anything. "One might have thought they were trying to get rid of me."

"I was never welcome anywhere either," Gregory told Rabo in his studio the next morning. "It was very good for me to be so unwelcome, so unappreciated by my own master, because look what I have become." Gregory's parents escaped a massacre by fleeing to Moscow, where as a boy he served a brutal apprenticeship under the Czar's engraver. Now it was Rabo's turn to prove himself: he was to draw everything in Gregory's studio, "*indistinguishable* from a photograph."

After months of labor Rabo presented his first effort, a "meticulously accurate" rendering. The leak dripping from a skylight contained "the wettest water you ever saw," he remembers proudly, each droplet reflecting the entire room. Gregory tossed it into the fireplace. "No *soul*," he told his stricken charge.

Rabo's master had a darkly romantic streak that led him into sympathy for the fascist movements of the day. The attention he paid to the clipper ship on the mantle and the collection of antique guns for which he had a fetish carried a "spiritual lesson," he insisted, a protest against the degeneracy of modern art, which refused to enlist in the struggles of men. "Painters—and storytellers, including poets and playwrights and historians," were supposed to take sides, he told his student. "They are the justices of the Supreme Court of Good and Evil," and admission to their ranks, he warned, was not easy. "How was that for delusions of moral grandeur?" asks Rabo.

His reservations echo Vonnegut's concern about the stories people imposed on structureless reality. We get another dose of Tralfamadorian philosophy here: the teacher's works showed material things well enough, but "they lied about time." Gregory was a gifted taxidermist and nothing more, Rabo concludes. "He stuffed and mounted and varnished and mothproofed" moments in life that, as soon as they were finished, became "depressing dust-catchers." We are reminded of Rabo's eloquence in the Tally-Ho Room as he continues:

> Life, by definition, is never still. Where is it going? From birth to death, with no stops on the way. Even a picture of a bowl of pears on a checkered tablecloth is liquid, if laid on canvas by the brush of a master. Yes, and by some miracle I was surely never able to achieve as a painter, nor was Dan Gregory, but which was achieved by the best of the Abstract Expressionists, in the paintings which have greatness birth and death are always there.

Gregory barely acknowledged Marilee when she came home from the hospital. He had pushed her down a flight of stairs when he found out she had been subsidizing a stranger in California. He soon forgot about his apprentice as well. Like Rabo's father crafting his cowboy boots, or Pollock engaged in a drip painting—like Kurt Vonnegut at his writing table—when he made art "the whole rest of the world dropped away."

Rabo would become like that, too, when he made his big abstract pieces. It sabotaged his attempt to be a husband and a father after the war. "I had a very hard time getting the hang of civilian life," he recalls, "and then I discovered something as powerful and irresponsible as shooting up with heroin."

These images bring to mind the words of Sidney Slotkin, Vonnegut's academic advisor at Chicago. A wise and tragic figure, he encouraged his student to pursue an unorthodox master's thesis project comparing the Ghost Dance plains Indians with the early-twentieth-century Cubist painters. The author closed *Palm Sunday* with a testament to the influence of Slotkin, who in time would be another suicide in his life.

"What is it an artist does—a painter, a writer, a sculptor—?" he once asked in a summer classroom filled with war veterans. "The artist says, 'I can do very little about the chaos around me, but at least I can reduce to perfect order this square of canvas, this piece of paper, this chunk of stone.'"[7]

Vonnegut often remarked on the isolation of his craft, the toll his immersion in it exacted on his marriages and his relationships with his children. The "very limited activity" of bringing order to words on sheets of paper "allowed me to ignore many a storm," he admitted, but "it has also caused many of the worst storms I ignored. Sometimes I don't consider myself very good at life, so I hide in my profession."[8]

In *Just Like Someone with Mental Illness Only More So* Mark Vonnegut gives us a revealing look into the good and bad of being his father's son. In West Barnstable, before money and fame arrived, there was plenty of freedom for a boy growing up, along with a modeling of love and high standards. "Do you want to be average?" he recalls as one of his dad's signature phrases. "Not world class" was another, expressing disapproval of unacceptable effort or judgment.[9]

But there was an absence, too. While not exactly "raised by wolves"—"I just had beautiful, slightly broken, self-absorbed parents like a lot of people," Mark insists—the patriarch was often less than fully engaged, a sporadic mentor on the journey to adulthood.[10]

It could have been the war, or simply the wages of the artistic temperament. "At this time in my life," Mark Vonnegut remembers, "my father was a proudly antisocial man who spent most of his time at a typewriter, reflecting negatively on his neighbors and society, throwing in things like 'Goddamn it, you've got to be kind.' The emphasis was on the *Goddamn it.* He was proud of the fact that I had no friends." Kurt and Jane were in many ways fish out of water on Cape Cod, "over-educated Midwestern liberals a long way from home with hopes and ambitions that would have perplexed and mystified their neighbors."

It was not at all clear what my father did for a living. He was a tall, dark-eyed, gawky, hunched-over guy you wouldn't just go up to and get to know or talk to about baseball.

Kurt Vonnegut was difficult to read, torn between propriety —he "went stiff and red whenever there was a hint of public humiliation," Mark recalls—and playful rebellion, waltzing spontaneously with his wife in the aisle of the local supermarket.[11]

In Dan Gregory's household, Rabo recalls, he was at first uncomfortable in the presence of Marilee's movie-star looks. "I have always been leery of women, possibly because, as Circe Berman suggested at breakfast this morning, I considered my mother faithless, since she had up and died on me." But together the pair forged a flirtatious sibling friendship, the female, older and more experienced, firmly in charge. They were shielded from hard times by their master's wealth. Unlike Nora in Ibsen's *A Doll's House* (a new edition of which, illustrated by Dan Gregory, arrived one day in the mail), Marilee did not consider leaving in pursuit of some kind of freedom. "There was nothing waiting for her outside the door of Gregory's very comfortable dwelling except hunger and humiliation, no matter how meanly he might treat her."

Fred Jones, the butler, was also an imprisoned Nora. "His life had been all downhill since World War One," Rabo now understands, "when he had discovered a gift for flying rattletrap kites which were machine-gun platforms." Seeing "arcs and spirals and splotches in the atmosphere," he experienced the same happiness the abstract expressionists enjoyed when they applied paint to canvas. Jones seems based on Vonnegut's agent Kenneth Littauer, one of the most important of his early mentors. Colonel Littauer was a larger-than-life figure, said to be the first man to strafe a trench from an airplane when he flew with the Lafayette Escadrille.

"Pst—you, the cocky little Armenian kid," Rabo imagines upbraiding his younger self. "You think Fred Jones is funny and sad at the same time?" Jones lost an eye and was expelled from his family in the Air Corps, condemned thereafter to a long, somnolent epilogue. "That's what you'll be someday too: a one-eyed soldier, afraid of women and with no talent for civilian life."

Dan Gregory imposed a single nonnegotiable demand on his guests: that they stay away from that den of iniquity, the Museum of Modern Art, his *Bluebeard*-like forbidden chamber. But Marilee and Rabo engaged in brazen violations of the edict, and one afternoon, inevitably, he caught them leaving the building, laughing and holding hands. "You parasites! You rotten-spoiled little kids!" Gregory shouted, as choked with pain as *Jailbird*'s Alexander McCone was when he discovered Walter's betrayal at Harvard. Adam and Eve had eaten of the Tree of Knowledge, and they were to be summarily expelled from the Garden of Eden.

The young pair slouched home, where they fell into a further transgression—the one "sexual masterpiece" of Rabo's lifetime. "Our brainless lovemaking anticipated Abstract Expressionism in a way, since it was about absolutely nothing but itself." And then, he adds with sadness, it "vanished from the Earth even more quickly than the paintings which made me a footnote in Art History." Marilee rebuffed Rabo's professions of eternal love. "This never happened," she said coldly, declining his invitation to go out into the world together to freeze to death. Rabo left, alone, dedicated to proving himself to her, like a knight in a Dan Gregory–illustrated romance.

Vonnegut notoriously downplayed romantic love in his fiction. It was, to some degree, he insisted, a technical matter. "The problem is once you set that story in motion, the mating story . . ." he explained in a 1987 interview, "this is such an absorbing subject to all human beings that you can't talk about anything else." In *Bluebeard* he would demonstrate that, finally, in his middle-sixties, he had figured out to his satisfaction a way to integrate eros into his repertoire without eclipsing the other messages he wanted to convey.[12]

Reduced to soup kitchens, Rabo Karabekian tried, with his mother's dogged determination, to preserve his American Dream.

> I improved myself in libraries while keeping warm, reading histories and novels and poems said to be great—and encyclopedias and dictionaries, and the latest self-help books about how to get ahead in the United States of America, how to learn from failures, how to make strangers like you and trust you immediately, how to start your own business, how to sell anybody anything, how to put yourself into the hands of God and stop wasting so much time and precious energy worrying. How to eat right.

He even took on an accent "as synthetic as Gregory's"—not British exactly, but blandly "trans-Atlantic," like the one perfected by Marilee. It was all for naught.

Rabo's diary of his Summer of the Widow Berman is a record of exasperation. Circe monitors his writing progress and imposes an atmosphere of "Polly Madison" brashness into every recess of his existence. She is a pushy, demanding muse, and he isn't sure how he feels about it.

"The young people of today seem to be trying to get through life with as little information as possible," he complains in a typical dinner table conversation. They know nothing about history, nothing about the Empress Josephine. Circe dismisses it all as the ranting of an out-of-touch old man. "They have more interesting ways of learning about vanity and the power of sex" than studying dead people, she declares. But what about the famous axiom of Armenian American George Santayana, Slazinger asks, unwisely. "We're doomed to repeat the past no matter what," Circe replies, without hesitation. "That's what it is to be alive."

Since the days that Kurt Vonnegut first became an accidental "guru" to the counterculture, unsure how to deal with the hippies who showed up at his door in West Barnstable looking for words of wisdom, he had been of a mixed mind about the prospects of the younger generation, as reflected in the voices of his characters here. Even as he worried about their naïvety and anti-intellectualism, he admired those who in the 1960s and early 1970s challenged authority and tried to reinvent community. They were doing their job, striving to create something new. He regretted the decline in experimentation he observed once the Vietnam War receded as a galvanizing issue.

Vonnegut always resented ivory tower dismissals of those who (like himself) had not been exposed to classical educations or Grand Tours of Europe. In 1987 he spoke of his reaction to a *New York Times* piece in which his City College colleague Anthony Burgess complained that his students knew no Greek or Latin. "I was thinking of what all these kids who grow up in New York—black, Hispanic, whatever—know that Burgess didn't know." But civic and historical illiteracy, memory holes, and a loss of common reference points presented a troubling challenge. "It's very helpful if you're painting or telling a story to assume your readers know something,"

Vonnegut lamented. "If you can't count on the churchgoers knowing that then how do you begin the sermon?"[13]

The problem seemed to get worse with each passing year as he visited college campuses. It was more than a lack of information—it was the absence of curiosity many young people displayed about things beyond their everyday lives, their limited horizons and blinkered imaginations. In 1985 he invited an audience at MIT to draft a code of ethics for scientists, foreswearing work on Star Wars and other military projects he considered wasteful and dangerous. Despite polite applause, no one took up the challenge—maybe they thought he was kidding. "What makes the students of today so unresponsive?" Vonnegut asked with disgust in 1991's *Fates Worse Than Death*. "They know what I will never get through my head: that life is *unserious*."[14]

Vonnegut periodically threatened to end his spring and fall speaking tours—he no longer needed the money as he did in the alimony-ridden years of the 1970s, and the regimen of airports and hotel rooms was exhausting, time spent away from his family and his typewriter. "I lived and behaved like the great Willy [sic] Nelson, a dazed traveler when between manic exhibitions," he wrote in a typical newsy letter to Loree Rackstraw in 1983. But he was good at it, his timing remained sharp and it was an outlet for the drive to be a performer that coexisted with his native shyness. "I have an exhibitionist side, and it's just like shifting into overdrive," he said in a 1987 interview. "And the audience feeds you, and you can feel it." As with Mark Twain, the sustenance he got from his road shows kept him young.[15]

Circe rejects the insinuation by her dinner companions that her books are dumbing down her readers. "They're about life right now," she insists to Rabo, now in full retreat. "You and your ex-pal here never got past the Great Depression and World War Two."

There is truth to the claim. Paul, it turns out, won a Silver Star by lying down on a live Japanese hand grenade to protect his squad mates, an act that left him with a scar "like a map of the Mississippi Valley running from his sternum to his crotch." The psychic damage was even worse. He and Rabo bicker constantly, but they retain an unbreakable bond, built upon "loneliness and wounds" that had never healed, and were "quite grave." They are a dialogue between different aspects of Vonnegut the survivor.

Rabo returns from a trip to the city (mandated by Mrs. Berman) to find the foyer of his house completely redecorated with wallpaper featuring "red roses as big as cabbages." The modernist pieces had all been moved, replaced by chromos of little girls on swings, encased in heavy, gilded frames. In shock, Rabo's eye patch drops to the floor.

Mrs. Berman has no time to argue about the changes—she is getting ready to go out for the evening with a Ferrari-driving psychiatrist she had met that day on the beach. Circe was "overwhelmingly erotic" in her cocktail dress, her "voluptuous figure exaggerated and cocked this way and that way as she teetered on high-heeled, golden dancing shoes." Rabo is jealous. "What a sexual bully she could be!"

As usual Circe gets in the last word as she leaves, insisting that the chromos be considered in their human context. They communicated stories, familiar and heartbreaking, as abstraction never could—Rabo just had to use his imagination.

> Try thinking what the Victorians thought when they looked at them, which was how sick or unhappy so many of these happy, innocent little girls would be in just a little while—diphtheria, pneumonia, smallpox, miscarriages, violent husbands, poverty, widowhood, prostitution—death and burial in potter's field.

There is more to this woman than met the eye.

Rabo is downstairs sleeping in a chair when Mrs. Berman gets home. They "made some kind of contract that night," he now understands. He wants her to stay, knows he needs someone as "vivid" as she is to keep him alive.

Their arrangement deepens as the weeks passed. Rabo keeps on writing, having earned privacy privileges now that he has reached the halfway point of his manuscript. He makes no objection when Circe installs a pool table in the living room. It is a pastime she had taken up as a young woman, she explains to him, to maintain sanity after her father's suicide. She has long been adept at managing losses.

Rabo remains stubborn, however, about the contents of the barn. He is not ready, yet, to be that familiar.

The sense of common cause grows with the visit one day of two German businessmen. Posing as art enthusiasts, Rabo knows they are really looking for bargain beachfront property. Circe, "child of a Jewish pants manufacturer, said to me, the child of an Armenian shoemaker, '*We* are the Indians now,'" Rabo remembers. The place is not for sale—maybe they should try to buy the Statue of Liberty instead.

Rabo revisits the moment when a fellow Armenian rescued him from his life on the streets decades earlier. A job as an illustrator with an ad agency allowed him to take lessons at the Art Students League until a teacher there rejected him as brutally as Dan Gregory once did. "Here is a man without passion," the instructor remarked, paging through Rabo's portfolio. "Why should I teach him the language of painting, since there seems to be absolutely nothing which he is desperate to talk about?"

This recurring theme of the artist who discovers he has no talent, is unmasked as a fraud—Otto and Rudy Waltz in *Deadeye Dick* come to mind—reflects Vonnegut's perpetual lack of confidence in his creative powers. Like a true child of the Great Depression, "he worried that every good idea he got might be his last and that any apparent success he had had would dry up and blow away," son Mark observed in an introduction to *Armageddon in Retrospect*. Maybe the well would run dry, as it had for Paul Slazinger, maybe the critics were right—he might not have the soul others admired in him.[16]

"To make a long story short: Germany invaded Austria and then Czechoslovakia and then Poland and then France, and I was a pipsqueak casualty in faraway New York City." Rabo lost his job at the ad agency and enlisted in the army. A Corps of Engineers general wanted a portrait of himself by a painter "with a foreign-sounding name," and Rabo seized the opportunity, plying him with flattery "in what surely must have been the manner of powerless Armenian advisors in Turkish courts" back in the days of the Ottoman Empire. He planted in his boss the idea of a camouflage unit, an experiment soon launched under the supervision of Master Sergeant Rabo Karabekian.

Rabo led his free-spirited band of artists through North Africa, Sicily, England, and France. Then came the Bulge. "There was this white flash," he recalls, followed by six months of imprisonment. One day in spring the guards marched Rabo and his companions out into the countryside and abandoned them. "We awoke the next morning on the rim of a great green valley on what is now the border between East Germany and Czechoslovakia," Rabo remembers. "There may have been as many as ten thousand people below us."

"What a *sight!*" he exclaims, still in awe. This was not a vision cooked up in Kurt Vonnegut's imagination. "It was real. O'Hare and I were there," he wrote in *Fates Worse Than Death.*[17]

"Was I bitter?" Rabo asks, reflecting on his return to New York. "No, I was simply blank, which I came to realize was what Fred Jones used to be. Neither one of us had anything to come home to." We remember Eliot Rosewater's words in the same circumstances: "The war was over, and there I was, crossing Times Square with a Purple Heart on." Rabo married his nurse, Dorothy, and together they had two sons. Why, despite his manifest lack of promise in this area, did he make the effort at family building? Another epitaph for his generation: "That's the way the postwar movie goes."

Rabo enrolled in business courses at NYU, but his heart was not in it. He played hooky in the nearby Cedar Tavern, spending evenings in the company of the then-obscure artists who congregated there. With his GI allowance he picked up checks and made loans to them. In turn, "they treated me as though I were a painter too," Rabo remembers fondly. "Here was another big family to replace my lost platoon." Its members, including his closest pals, Jackson Pollock and Terry Kitchen (together they were known as the "Three Musketeers"), repaid him with "pictures nobody wanted."

"Bulletin from the present." (The abrupt, rhythmic shifts in time and place remind us of Billy Pilgrim's spastic travels.) Paul, on a trip abroad with the writers' group PEN, is delivered home late one night after a psychotic episode. Returning from one of her dancing sessions, Mrs. Berman is upset by the scene, "almost catatonic." This is a side of the confident Circe that Rabo has never seen so clearly. "There must be a story there," he thinks to himself, grasping the fragility beneath her bluster.

The tranquility of only a few months earlier is a distant memory, but Rabo likes the ruckus, enjoys having people in his care. "Which patient needed me most now in the dead of night?" he wonders, purposeful and excited. He sits at Paul's bedside, listening to his friend's fevered ravings.

Rabo never forgets that Paul had been "a mere stripling" when he threw himself on that Japanese grenade. He understood Paul's suffering.

In 1950 Rabo traveled to Italy, all expenses paid, to testify in a lawsuit about the paintings his platoon had catalogued at the end of the war. On his last day in Florence an envelope appeared in his hotel mailbox, with an invitation on elegant stationery signed by "Marilee, Countess Portomaggiore (the coal miner's daughter)."

Rabo went to the palazzo that was her residence, expecting a triumphant reunion. He was now "a war hero, roué, and seasoned cosmopolite!" After being led down a corridor by the female attendant—all of the Contessa's servants seemed to be women—Rabo saw Marilee standing in a black gown, her face and hair ivory in the light. "So, my faithless little Armenian protégé," she said in a familiar, mocking tone, "we meet again. Thought you were going to get laid again, I'll bet."

Rabo protests his undying love, but Marilee is another Vonnegut woman victimized by her beauty, and with him we learn the sources of her cynicism on the subject.

> My father loved me so much he beat me every day. The football team at the high school loved me so much they raped me all night after the Junior Prom. The stage manager at the Ziegfeld Follies loved me so much he told me that I had to be part of his stable of whores or he'd fire me and have somebody throw acid in my face. Dan Gregory loved me so much he threw me down the stairs because I'd sent you some expensive art materials.

Marilee was not impressed by Rabo's medals, or his earlier boasts on the phone about his sexual adventures as a soldier. "I guessed that wherever you went," she said, "there were women who would do anything for food or protection for themselves and the children and the old people, since the young men were dead or gone away. The whole point of war is to put women everywhere in that condition. It's always men against women, with the men only pretending to fight among themselves." She had found her survivor mission in Italy, converting the palazzo into an asylum for her sisters disabled by the war.

The Contessa softened as she explained to Rabo how she had come to live in such lavish circumstances, her *Cinderella* story. She and Fred Jones followed Dan Gregory to Europe, as recruits for Mussolini's New Order. The two men died as heroes, and Marilee became the "toast of Rome," escorted to society events by the Count Portomaggiore, fascist Minister of Culture and a closeted homosexual. To avert scandal they were ordered to wed. She consented, at the behest of a deep-cover operative not unlike Howard W. Campbell Jr.'s "Blue Fairy Godmother," and served as a valuable asset for Allied espionage.

Rabo did not have a war story to match Marilee's. "She had had a life, I had accumulated anecdotes," he confesses. All he could offer was the chaotic panorama he remembered from VE Day, on the rim of a green valley. She grasped immediately the power of the image. Rabo described his friends in the avant garde of the New York art scene, creating works that would make Dan Gregory spin in his grave. "Leave it to Americans," Marilee said with approval, "to write, 'The End.'" She ordered ten canvases to fill the bare walls of her palazzo rotunda.

Rabo returned home with the good news, but his long-suffering Dorothy expressed only careworn skepticism. She was concerned about feeding the babies. We are transported back to the early years of Vonnegut's writing career, when success must have seemed at times like a pipe dream. "The war is *over*, Rabo!" Dorothy cried. "You don't have to do wild things, great big things, dangerous things that don't have a chance." He headed to the Cedar Tavern.

At his rented barn in what was then still the wilderness of Long Island, Rabo talked to Terry Kitchen about the things they had missed because of their time in uniform. "I should have started a family and settled down years ago," he said with regret. "There went my youth, and God, I still want it."

Dorothy finally left with their sons in 1956—Rabo's feelings of guilt toward her may reflect Vonnegut's regrets with Jane's passing. Soon Rabo's booby-trapped paintings started coming apart, and the other "Musketeers" died in quick succession. In his *Esquire* piece, Vonnegut attributed Pollock's recklessness at the end of his life to the dilemma of the artist who finds himself at an impasse, overwhelmed by the expectations of his audience.

"He was rendered unmaneuverable . . ." the author told an interviewer in 1987, "by the response of society, which was, 'Hey, these things are extremely valuable. You've got to keep doing this.'" Vonnegut knew the feeling. Everything changes when play is no longer a private affair, a child's dialogue with the universe. *"Three's a crowd."*[8]

The wave of losses left Rabo feeling as his father must have felt back in Armenia, a stunned survivor "all alone in his village after the massacre." Vonnegut was in the same spot, watching friends like Algren and Yates— his "Musketeers"—go through their death struggles. For a long time Rabo retreated into his barn, until being adopted, like a "tamed raccoon," by his landlady, Edith.

Rabo's memoir ends with the news that Mrs. Berman is back now at her home in Baltimore. He misses her, but is glad to return to the peace she had so determinedly disrupted. Paul Slazinger is gone too, in the care of the local VA hospital. "Better he should be looked after by his Uncle Sam."

On her last night in the Hamptons Circe asked Rabo to take her dancing, but he agreed only to a quiet dinner at a restaurant. Despite their months together, and the pleasantries exchanged that evening, he still thought of her as an acquaintance. The final barrier between them was, of course, the potato barn and its contents. Circe's gambit this time was cunningly indirect, challenging his ego with a question familiar to all of his now-deceased abstract expressionist brothers. Could he really draw?

Rabo took the bait, disclosing that along the center of the barn were a series of panels joined into a surface eight feet high and sixty-four feet long. They had been the source of his greatest embarrassment—the mammoth *Windsor Blue Number Seventeen* that once hung in GEFFCo headquarters, sabotaged by Sateen Dura-Luxe.

Rabo had the canvases stripped and primed until they were "dazzling white in their restored virginity" under the floodlights of the barn. As a final black joke he instructed his wife, Edith, to hold his wake there, against the backdrop of nothingness. She would announce to those in attendance the title of his farewell piece: "I Tried and Failed and Cleaned Up Afterwards, So It's *Your* Turn Now."

But Edith died first. During her memorial service Rabo unlocked the barn, stared at the empty canvases, and drove into town to buy painting supplies. For months he worked in seclusion, turning his grief into art, and then he sealed away the results—until now.

With courtly grace he invited Mrs. Berman to join him for a tour. "Out in the dark we went, a flashlight beam dancing before us," he remembers. "I was elated, high as a kite and absolutely petrified." Soon they were standing together on the rim of a beautiful green valley.

"It wasn't imaginary. It was real. O'Hare and I were there."

Rabo jokes now that the "whatchamacallit in the potato barn" is the last stop for the crowds who roam his grounds, on an itinerary that begins with Circe's "doomed little girls" and winds past the abstract expressionist pieces hanging in the other parts of the mansion. "There is a war story to go with every figure in the picture, no matter how small," Rabo explains to them of his masterpiece. "I made up a story, and then made up the person it happened to." As the visitors have grown in number, the happy "museum guard" now simply directs them out to the barn to see for it for themselves. "Make up your own war stories."

To his first audience Rabo was glad to describe what was going on in detail. Circe's reading of the chromos had obviously left a deep impression, unlocking the realist spirit of his youth he had abandoned. At the bottom of the vista, the largest figure, the size of a cigarette—"the only one of the thousands with his back to the camera, so to speak"—was himself. "The crack between the fourth and fifth panels ran up my spine and parted my hair, and might be taken for the soul of Rabo Karabekian." This was a document of witness, conveying something he cared deeply about—no mere exercise in taxidermy. The self-portrait mirrors Vonnegut's decision, from *Slaughterhouse-Five* forward, to insert himself overtly into his works. Who is the man hanging onto his leg, Mrs. Berman asked, "looking up at you as though you were God?" "He is a Canadian bombardier who was shot down over an oil field in Hungary. He doesn't know who I am. He can't even see my face. All he can see is a thick fog which isn't there, and he's asking me if we are home yet." Rabo gave him the most humane answer he could muster.

Circe was swept off her feet as they moved in tandem around the barn, her partner firmly in the lead, weaving a tapestry of stories to accompany his epic. The refugees in the painting came from all points of the compass, representing in the rawest disorder the madness of the war. There were soldiers, concentration camp survivors, prisoners of various armies, asylum inmates, local farmers—all 5,219 rendered precisely, milling about as they waited for the Russian army. Here was an SS guard who had just ditched his uniform for a scarecrow's outfit, in a futile effort at disguise. Over there were Yugoslav partisans, a Moroccan cavalryman, a Scottish glider pilot, a Nepalese Gurkha, a New Zealand artillery corporal. There was even a Japanese soldier, still fierce and holding on to his sword—a bit of license in the interest of a complete statement. And, as in a Diego Rivera mural, Rabo inserted faces of celebrities and the people in his life. A pair of Estonians looked like Laurel and Hardy, a French collaborator was Charlie Chaplin, two Polish laborers were Pollock and Kitchen.

Females were hard to identify, since almost everyone—with the exception of a few civilians hiding in a cellar—bore the ravages of starvation. The one woman who appeared to be obese had been dead for three days. "Dying is the only way to get fat in Happy Valley," Rabo comments. "Or 'Peacetime' or 'Heaven' or 'the Garden of Eden' or 'Springtime' or whatever you want to call it." Circe asked about the contents of the corpse's mouth. It was rubies and diamonds, just as Rabo's mother had encountered during the Armenian genocide. In a way the entire project was a tribute to her, and to all those innocents who, as Marilee the Contessa so convincingly reminded him, were damaged by the male instinct for violence. His last proposed title acknowledged their regenerative power: "Now It's the Women's Turn."

As his friend Slazinger once predicted, Rabo Karabekian had saved his best for last. He proved to everyone, most of all himself, that he did, indeed, have soul. Mrs. Berman took his hand as they walked back to the house, feeling with him a kind of postcoital satisfaction. "We're dancing now," she told him. Circe admits that she, too, had been dealing with grief, over her husband's death. Her approach was to throw herself into activity, too, "talking loud and brassy, telling everybody when they're right and wrong, giving orders to everybody: Wake up! Cheer up! Get to work!" Now she was free to drop her guard.

They were friends at last.

Rabo's canvases would go to his sons after he died, he told Circe as they said goodnight. There was only one thing he would ask of them, an homage to his ancestors, another closing of the circle—that they change their names, and those of his grandchildren, back to "Karabekian."

As with all of his books, Vonnegut felt mostly relief when he completed *Bluebeard*. He had solved another set of problems, passed another test, and it was the last installment due in his current contract. "I'm not mad. I just didn't want to be sold to Germans," he quipped acidly to Loree Rackstraw as Dell was being acquired by foreign investors. But he was not about to retire. "Writing was as much a survival behavior for him as breathing," his old friend knew, as he signed on for future projects with Putnam Press.[19]

Reviews for his twelfth novel were mixed. A critic for the *Village Voice* was particularly harsh, decrying "a final scene of revolting sentimentality," but the author was undaunted. "What makes them so mad," Vonnegut wrote of his detractors, "is that I say art is child's play, and can be discussed in plain, simple language." He would remain true to his heart, and to the principles of clarity he had learned as a young journalist—and it was too late now to change.[20]

Vonnegut was proud of his generation of veterans who became writers, especially those who, like himself, experienced the event as foot soldiers without rank or privileged perspective. "I think we've produced quite a literature" he said of Joseph Heller, Norman Mailer, James Jones, Irwin Shaw, and the others who returned to tell their war stories, ordinary Americans thrust into extraordinary circumstances. "I think we've written so well about the Second World War, better than almost anybody in any other country, because we were on the edge of it." (We recall Finnerty's credo from *Player Piano*: "Out on the edge you can see all kinds of things you can't see from the center.") Clear-eyed, "no longer needing a Hemingway to say what war was like," their best work endures.[21]

Bluebeard is the closest thing we have to a sequel to *Slaughterhouse-Five*, its final pages giving us the rest of the story of Vonnegut's wartime captivity. In its dexterity and cumulative power, it is another survivor's mission, admirably accomplished.

THIRTEEN

Hocus Pocus

While there is a lower class I am in it. While there is a criminal element
I am of it. While there is a soul in prison I am not free.
—Eugene Victor Debs (1855–1926)

Vietnam!
—Gene Hartke

Kurt Vonnegut remained active on a number of fronts in the late 1980s, showing no signs of slowing down. He worked on another play (*Make Up Your Mind*) and, in the summer of 1989, made his second humanitarian trip to Africa. At the invitation of CARE he traveled with a group of journalists to the former Portuguese colony of Mozambique, to observe up close the ravages of its civil war. In *Parade* magazine he described the ruthless bands of armed marauders (celebrated as "freedom fighters" by some on the American right) who plagued the country, and conveyed the human misery of the refugee camps he visited. He had seen this kind of disease and hunger before, during World War II and again in Biafra in 1970. It left him numb.[1]

In April 1990, as he was wrapping up revisions of his new novel, *Hocus Pocus*, Vonnegut telegraphed his frame of mind in a piece for the *New York Times Book Review* titled "Notes from My Bed of Gloom: Or, Why the

Joking Had to Stop." He feared that late-life pessimism was overtaking his more hopeful impulses, as it had for Mark Twain. Each day it was harder to laugh at a world so filled with suffering, hurtling fast toward self-destruction. But the book released later that year showed that his absurdist side was still intact. Even if we were doomed—and in an era of globalization there was no longer any unspoiled frontier, real or mythic, to which to escape—the sharp eye of satire still had its empowering effect, and his audience was glad to get it.[2]

In *Hocus Pocus* we have the jailhouse reflections of another "epilogue" man, Gene Hartke, a generation younger than the author and a veteran of the Vietnam War. He scribbles his thoughts on odd bits of paper, a method that accounts for the especially episodic, nonlinear tempo. Some scraps contain only one word. Gene is the familiar Vonnegut victim of chain reactions and "booby traps," mixed, to be sure, with a few character flaws and regrettable choices. Survivor guilt, PTSD, and suicide have been his companions along the way.

Gene faces trial for masterminding the largest prison break in American history. He will own up to many sins—drinking, drugs, womanizing, and some of the violent things he did as a soldier—but protests his innocence of the crime for which he is now charged. Like Howard W. Campbell Jr., Gene is an accomplished actor, so we take his version of events with caution. Some of the lies he has told in his life—the "hocus pocus" he learned to conjure at an early age—are the opposite of *foma*, the "harmless untruths" of *Cat's Cradle*.

The prisoner writes to us from the near future, the year 2001, and there are "idiosyncrasies" in the memoir besides its fragmented composition. To taunt his critics Vonnegut has the narrator studiously avoid profanity, even when discussing the most disturbing subjects. Readers will not be able to use dirty language to dismiss the story. Also, in a reversal from *Jailbird*, numbers are left in their Arabic form. Converting them to words, an anonymous editor explains in the introduction, would dilute their impact. These are all devices intended by the author to dislodge our big brains from rote thinking.

Born in 1940, Eugene Debs Hartke acquired his name at the insistence of his grandfather, Benjamin Wills, a groundskeeper at Butler University in

Indianapolis and a self-taught philosopher. To the day he died, Wills was a proudly unreconstructed socialist and an ardent admirer of the original Debs, the union leader involved in the Pullman Palace Car Company strike of 1894. Gene was required to commit to memory his namesake's famous declaration of solidarity with the incarcerated—for Vonnegut, a modern distillation of the Sermon on the Mount.

The lessons didn't take. Gene was never much interested in politics, and can't be accused of being some kind of "bleeding heart." As an officer in Vietnam he always did his duty without hesitation, however unpleasant at times. "I would have killed Jesus Christ Himself or Herself or Itself or Whatever if ordered to do so," he insists. Subordinates marveled at his cool under fire.

Gene's ability to project a true believer's faith regardless of circumstances allowed him to sell even the most fanciful lies, the most lethal "hocus pocus," to his men and to the press. His nickname in the field was "The Preacher." "Somebody had to speak," he explains, "or we couldn't have had a war."

But Gene emerged from his war no less haunted than Eliot Rosewater or Rabo Karabekian did from theirs. Allusions to Vietnam, an experience which now seems to him like "1 big hallucination," leak onto almost every page. Gene was the last American standing during the rooftop evacuation at the end of that national misadventure, center stage and full of adrenaline when "the excrement hit the air-conditioning."

Gene's prison is the campus of what, until two years ago, had been Tarkington College, an academy overlooking the village of Scipio in the Mohiga Valley, on New York's picturesque Finger Lakes. Tarkington boasted a tradition of educating children of monied families who, due to impairments of mind or temperament, could not succeed at more conventional institutions of learning. Gene was on its faculty for almost a quarter of a century after he got out of the service, and he is even today the custodian of its history— the rituals and myths, the scandals and unsolved mysteries. What he doesn't know, he can look up, thanks to the holdings in the library—never used much, even when the place was a college.

Scipio's patriarch was Aaron Tarkington, who started the Mohiga Wagon Company there in 1830, in "more optimistic times" of empire building and homesteading. Its products made him a millionaire, despite the challenges of his illiteracy—he suffered from the genetic defect now known as dyslexia. Aaron's wife read to him every evening, and he was able to deliver lectures to his employees leavened with inspirational quotations memorized from Homer, Shakespeare, and the Bible.

In time Aaron's son Elias took over the business, adding a brewery and a steam-powered carpet factory. These enterprises flourished, Gene underscores, thanks to "inventiveness and high standards of workmanship"—the same quaint virtues that built the Vonnegut Hardware business in Indianapolis. Elias was wounded in the Civil War, shot while observing the Battle of Gettysburg by a Rebel soldier who mistook him, with his beard and stovepipe hat, for Abraham Lincoln. He returned to Scipio, keeping himself busy by tinkering with perpetual-motion machines. Gene discovered some of the old gadgets in storage, and was moved by the ingenuity of their design. They were works of art, testimony to skills that would never again be practiced in the valley.

Elias oversaw the conversion of the family estate into the Mohiga Valley Free Institute, an outpost of open-admissions education intended as a model of social uplift. Its doors opened in 1869, with a freshman class that included a wounded Union veteran and a former slave. The instructors were drawn from the clergymen and artisans of the surrounding community. André Lutz, a Belgian immigrant and the chief engineer of the wagon company, expressed his faith in the endeavor by forging a set of bells from ordinance gathered up at Gettysburg, an attempt to transform death into beauty. A generation later, in 1899, Lutz's gift finally had a proper home, in a belfry erected above the academy's new library.

"Accident after accident" conspired to keep the academy on the hill going over the decades, even as the town below boomed, busted, and withered into permanent decline. When Gene Hartke arrived in the mid-1970s, Tarkington was upgrading to keep up with the times. To the dismay of traditionalists, automation hit even the Lutz Carillon—its bells now tolled by means of an electronic keyboard.

But enrollment at the college was still limited to three hundred—in stark contrast to the institution across the lake, also conceived on bygone utopian principles. In 1875, overlooking the hamlet of Athena, a prison work camp was built, a place where wayward youngsters from the city could experience fresh air and discipline, en route to a life of good citizenship. By the time

Gene got to the valley its founding mission had long been abandoned. The camp had grown into "a brutal fortress of iron and masonry," a maximum-security warehouse for thousands of adult men. This was no country club prison, like the one filled with Ivy Leaguers in *Jailbird.* Some of the inmates were hardened criminals, others had been swept up in the Reagan-era War on Drugs.

Conditions at the campus and the penitentiary were microcosms of the betrayal of the American Dream, but nobody paid much attention to the inequities. What went on behind the walls and razor wire above Athena was invisible to the residents over in Scipio, a kind of "pornography" far removed from their consciousness. The two worlds existed in mutual isolation—until, "1 cold winter's night," the prison witnessed its first big security breach.

Gene mixes history with an account of his own life, as much a Rube Goldberg contraption as Elias Tarkington's perpetual-motion machines. Growing up in suburban Midland City, Ohio, who could have imagined the destiny that lay before him—as a soldier, teacher, and now, a jailbird, "so despised" that only a saint like Debs himself could have felt any sympathy for him.

Gene's father was a chemist at Barrytron, the sprawling defense contractor known for developing indestructible plastics. His son would see its products in use in Vietnam. As a youngster Gene was embarrassed by his parents, especially his mother, a woman so obese she never left the house. He learned to cook and do housework like another Midland City boy, Rudy Waltz from *Deadeye Dick,* welcoming the chores as time spent "accomplishing something undeniably good."

In high school Gene found other ways to amuse himself, playing piano in a jazz combo, where he honed the skills that would later qualify him to be carillonneur at Tarkington. With his friends he imitated the creative freedom of the black musicians they admired, and indulged in the sex, alcohol, and drugs that went with their status as town bohemians. He might have thrived at the University of Michigan, where, with his buddies, he had already been admitted as graduation approached. "Who knows?" he wonders now. "We might have become so popular that we went on world tours and made great fortunes, and been superstars at peace rallies and love-ins when the Vietnam War came along."

But events would derail those dreams. Gene's dad became a laughingstock when a clumsy infidelity went public and, desperate to restore the family honor, he began meddling in his son's life, convinced that an eleventh-hour entry in the school science fair would make everything right again. The boy would heal the damaged parent, an archetypal Vonnegut motif.

With the covert but obvious help of Barrytron chemists and graphic designers, Gene's exhibit ("something about crystals and how they grew and why") easily vanquished the competition. He was a winner! No one denounced the fraud—"Nobody in the county gave much of a darn about science anyway," he points out, and maybe his entry would do Midland City proud in the state finals up in Cleveland. He went along with the deception, despite a foreboding that things would not turn out well.

It all now seems a metaphor for the Vietnam War, where, on a much larger scale, a mixture of untruths, vanity, and silent complicity abetted what everyone had to know was a catastrophe in the making. In both cases, Gene writes, "I remained philosophical, thanks to marijuana and alcohol."

His worst fears came to pass in the big auditorium in Cleveland. As the exhibits went up his father remained oblivious to the certainty of being exposed. From body language alone—Gene stood to the side as his dad did all the work—it was clear that the prime directive of the competition had been violated. Taunts from the gathering crowd recall Rudy Waltz's ordeal in the basement of the police station.

"If we had folded up and vanished quietly right there," Gene laments, perhaps the damage could have been contained. There was still time for a strategic withdrawal. The father, though, would have none of his son's defeatism. "He said we had nothing to be ashamed of, and that we certainly weren't going to go home with our tails between our legs." Again, it is a preview of things to come:

"Vietnam!"

Gene tried to slip out on his own through the nearest exit, but his path was blocked by Sam Wakefield, a man who would play a pivotal role in his life on more than one occasion. Impressive in his dress uniform, he was there to recruit scientists for the U.S. Military Academy. "What's the hurry, Son?" he asked, and before Gene knew what was happening his father was there shaking hands with Wakefield, beaming with the news that his son was going to West Point. That would impress the folks back in Midland City.

This tale of feckless youth and a family plagued by humiliating circumstances mirrors Vonnegut's sense of the early chapters of his life, which also ended abruptly with enlistment in the army. Gene's military career was considerably longer and more distinguished than the author's, but it would unfold in similarly bizarre fashion.

> Seventeen years later, in 1975, I was a Lieutenant Colonel on the roof of the American Embassy in Saigon, keeping everybody but Americans off helicopters that were ferrying badly rattled people out to ships offshore. We had lost a war!

"Losers!"

Gene recalls Jack Patton, his best friend as a cadet, a character who might have come from the Wyoming hometown of *Slaughterhouse-Five*'s "Wild Bob." Patton was memorable for his flat affect and his habit of declaring the urge to "laugh like hell" when confronted with absurdity. Pathologically numbed, Jack represents an extreme in Vonnegut's gallows humor.

There may be in this character also a bit of the author's longtime friend and war buddy, Bernard V. O'Hare, the Pennsylvania lawyer known for his gruff, "feisty" demeanor, who died in 1990, the same year *Hocus Pocus* was published. Kurt and Bernie met during training at Camp Atterbury, south of Indianapolis, and, thanks to the army's "buddy system," they stayed together through the Bulge, the months of imprisonment, all the way through the experience of repatriation and the trip home from the war. They kept in touch over the years and revisited Germany as civilians when Vonnegut was gathering information for what would become *Slaughterhouse-Five*. "It was uncomfortable being there the first time," O'Hare observed at the author's sixtieth birthday party, "and it was uncomfortable being there the second time." He continued:

> Except in generalities, we never presently talk about Dresden or the war. This is probably because when together we laugh too much.

We laughed excessively on our return to Dresden, hysterical laughter, I believe.

Both of us agreed that we could still smell the smoke and some other things.

"I am glad Kurt and I did not die," O'Hare declared, his words eloquent in their unvarnished directness, "and I would go back to Dresden with him again." Their bond had endured for decades, and now another link to the author's past was gone.[3]

Jack Patton adapted readily to the fighting in Vietnam until a sniper's bullet killed him during the Tet Offensive in early 1968. Gene performed comparable acts of bravery, but insists, "I was worried sick most of the time. Jack never worried. He told me so." He was lucky, at least in the sense that he never knew what hit him. This was not the fate of many of the wounded GIs Gene cradled in his arms as they died in the field. One youngster asked to be "turned off like a light bulb" after stepping on a landmine. Like the Canadian bombardier clutching Rabo's leg in *Bluebeard*'s "Happy Valley," he needed help going home, and Gene obliged with the only thing he had, the gift of reassurance, a bit of benign hocus pocus.

For all of his madness, Jack Patton possessed a rare clarity of vision. He never wanted children, he told his buddy just before he died, because he wished no part in contributing to the survival of a species "about 1,000 times dumber and meaner than they think they are." He was conveying in his unschooled way the wisdom of Shakespeare, whose insights on human conceit embellish Gene's memoir.

It was for Patton whom Gene rang Tarkington's bells every morning and evening. "Laugh, Jack, laugh!" he shouted amid the reverberations. It was both a prayer and a form of therapy. His friend surely would have wanted to laugh if he had seen the final moments of the war they fought in together. Atop the U.S. Embassy, Gene watched North Vietnamese tanks enter Saigon unopposed. As he struggled to keep former allies from deliverance, enemy troops below held their fire. "All they had ever wanted from us was that we go home," he observes. Gene's description of what happened next evokes a forgotten race from a remote time:

The helicopter carrying the last American to leave Vietnam joined a swarm of helicopters over the South China Sea, driven from their roosts on land and running out of gasoline. How was that for Natural History in the 20th Century: the sky filled with chattering, man-made pterodactyls, suddenly homeless, unable to swim a stroke, about to drown or starve to death.

At thirty-five, Gene came home from the war "again as dissolute with respect to alcohol and marijuana and loose women" as he had been in high school. His lawyers now approve when he begins assembling a "body count" of the females he has "made love to" over the years, accompanied by a parallel list of the deaths he caused in wartime. Maybe this will establish a pattern useful to an insanity defense.

Gene admits remorse for the women he treated so carelessly in his life, but points out that many of them were "booby-trapped," not unlike the devices he encountered on recon missions in Vietnam. This was certainly true of his wife, Margaret, Jack Patton's sister, who inherited the family's genetic predisposition to insanity. Here again is the shadow of biological determinism, the dread of mental illness, that hovers over so many Vonnegut novels. Gene wound up caretaking for his wife and mother-in-law, cooking and cleaning for them every day, just as he had done for his parents back in Midland City. It was a source of irritation that his efforts were not appreciated, and he used the grievance to justify serial violations of his wedding vows.

It was strange how Gene landed on his feet after the war. He remembers being harassed as he walked down the street in Cambridge, Massachusetts. "This was how ridiculous men in uniform had become in academic communities," he insists with some anger, despite the open secret that institutions like Harvard and MIT had profited handsomely from their contracts in military research.

The sanctimony of the hecklers, combined with the fact that he had just failed an admissions test for graduate studies in physics, brought Gene to the breaking point even before he joined his family one evening in a restaurant. Gene's companions barely acknowledged him as they babbled on about their sightseeing adventures of the day. Margaret and her mother, along with the children, had effectively buried him while he was away, he now realizes. "Nobody asked me what it was like to be home from the war."

Vonnegut identified, of course, with the difficulties of a soldier's return, regardless of the time or circumstances. The home front has changed, friends and loved ones have gone on with their lives, and the expectations civilians carry are often insensitive and based on clichés. "When I came home to Indianapolis," Vonnegut remembered of his summer of 1945, "an uncle of mine said to me, 'By golly—you look like a man now.' I wanted to strangle him. If I had, he would have been the first German I'd killed."[4]

But at least in World War II all Americans felt connected to the men on the battle lines. "I would have given anything," Gene tells us, "to die in a war that meaningful."

> But the Vietnam War belongs exclusively to those of us who fought in it. Nobody else had anything to do with it, supposedly. Everybody else is as pure as the driven snow. We alone are stupid and dirty.

"What makes the Vietnam veterans so somehow spooky?" Vonnegut asked in *Fates Worse Than Death*. "We could describe them almost as being 'unwholesomely mature.'" They carried wounds, he knew, from a conflict that resisted romantic framing: the story lacked a satisfactory resolution, theirs was not a "Good War," and Americans were not interested in "*losers.*"[5]

Many came back bitter, feeling used and betrayed by their country. Vonnegut empathized. On assignment in Miami Beach for *Harpers* at the Republican National Convention in 1972, where President Nixon was being nominated for reelection, he saluted the courage and dignity of a group of Vietnam Veterans Against the War he saw parade in silent protest past the luxury hotels.

> They marched silently, in the slope-shouldered route step of tired, hungry veterans—which they were. Their hair was often long, which gave them the cavalier beauty of Indian killers from another time.

Some were in wheelchairs. Many had wounds. John Wayne, the gunfighter's gunfighter, was in Miami Beach somewhere. But he was nowhere to be seen when these real gunfighters came to town. Here was Billy the Kid, multiplied by a thousand—not even whispering, and formed into platoons before the Fontainebleau. . . .

How many nice people came out of the hotel or came to hotel windows to watch them? None—almost none.[6]

At dinner Gene learned for the first time about his wife's hereditary insanity. It was not a good day. As he took in the shock of this latest booby trap, a young man walking by the table took the liberty of touching his bristly haircut, and Gene exploded. "Everybody and everything was my enemy. I was back in Vietnam!"

As Gene ran past overturned trays and out the door, a Christlike figure stood blocking his exit. "What's the hurry, Son?" asked Sam Wakefield, without missing a beat—just as he had done years earlier, at the science fair in Cleveland. In terms of storytelling, the author treats himself to another coincidence to advance the action. Wakefield had resigned his commission late in the war, and was now president of a small liberal arts college in upstate New York. Flashing "eyes full of love and pity," he was able to calm Gene down with the promise of a teaching job.

Gene's years as an instructor at Tarkington—drawn from Vonnegut's experiences in the academy, from teaching at the Hopefield School for disturbed children on Cape Cod in the 1950s, to his residencies later at Iowa and Harvard and City College—were pleasant enough. He was a dedicated teacher, in spite of the fact that the curriculum was not very demanding—grades had been phased out, and polo, tennis, and sailing loomed larger on campus than academics. In truth the students awarded associate degrees in the arts and sciences could not read or write any better than the convicts he would later encounter on the other side of the lake.

Twice a day Gene rang the Lutz Carillon to honor his friend Jack, "sending thunderbolts down the hillside and through the industrial ruins of Scipio." For those few minutes he was a god, a winner, as the echoes bounced off abandoned buildings and across Lake Mohiga. The ritual did for him what Sateen Dura-Luxe did for Rabo Karabekian, causing the complications of the rest of the world to drop away. Gene sometimes imagined being back in the war, when the big guns lobbed their payloads on his radioed command, "at who knows what in some jungle."

Life behind the drawn shades of his house below campus was, in contrast, not very fulfilling. The Hartke children were long gone, blaming their father for the prospect of insanity that hung over them like a black cloud. Gene was left alone to manage two childishly uncooperative "hags."

There were plenty of other females around for diversion, however. Gene had a nose in particular for "shopworn," middle-aged women in trouble. The most reckless of his indiscretions was with Zuzu Johnson, wife of the man who replaced Sam Wakefield as Tarkington's president after his suicide. One of the few women on campus Gene did not approach with an erotic agenda was Marilyn Shaw, head of life sciences. Marilyn had been a nurse in Vietnam, and, like him, carried with her the odor of death. Perhaps they avoided each other because of an unconscious "incest taboo."

There was male companionship on campus too. Daniel Stern, a history professor, got away with scathing indictments of his country's shortcomings by couching his lectures, à la Vonnegut, in the language of operatic farce. Stern coated his bitter pills with sugar, earning laughs and applause from overflow audiences, which often included Gene. Another pal was the refreshingly bawdy Paul Slazinger, last seen in the mental ward of a VA hospital in *Bluebeard*. Slazinger treated his sinecure as Tarkington writer-in-residence—an honor apparently reserved for out-of-print authors—as a joke, and was a model of alcoholic irresponsibility during his months in the valley.

Fellow veterans, Gene and Paul became fast friends. In the evening they could be seen playing eight-ball in the lavish new student building, Pahlavi Pavilion. But Slazinger left before the term ended, rescued from the boondocks by a MacArthur "Genius Grant." Before decamping to Key West he delivered a scorched-earth diatribe in the school's chapel on the topic of how easy it was for the wealthy to exploit the poor in America. Grandfather Wills would have loved it. Slazinger relished the shock of his listeners—and then he was gone.

Gene assumed that he would remain a member-in-good-standing of the Tarkington family until retirement, realizing too late that his status came with conditions. It turns out he was never anything more than a member of the "servant class," to use the lexicon of his grandfather. His reflexes, so acute in wartime, had been dulled by comfort, causing him to miss a series of traps directly in his path.

Jason Wilder, a conservative talk-show host the author based on William F. Buckley Jr., targeted Gene for a surveillance operation, hoping to use him as an example of university professors "who secretly hated their country." Wilder deployed his own dull-witted daughter, a student at Tarkington, to shadow Gene for months with a Nixonesque hidden tape recorder.

Vonnegut reserved special scorn for Buckley and his Eastern prep school–bred "neocon" admirers. In *Fates Worse Than Death* he identified the "myth" at the core of this political clan, smug in its sense of entitlement, enthusiastic about trickle-down economics, cheerleaders for a newly muscular foreign policy. "They are British aristocrats," Vonnegut concluded, "graduates of Oxford or Cambridge, living in the world as it was one hundred years ago."[7]

On graduation day Gene saw no reason for concern when he was summoned from his duties at Lutz Tower to the administration building, Samoza Hall. If there was trouble, surely "The Preacher" could talk his way out of it. But once he entered the conference room it was clear he might be in over his head. Around the table sat the Board of Trustees, a rogue's gallery of figures from the go-go Reagan age of greed, with Jason Wilder as their special invited guest.

After a perfunctory (and obviously insincere) nod to Gene's military service, Wilder played back the tapes of every damning comment his daughter had gathered, raw and out-of-context—ribald jokes with Slazinger, approving reactions to Daniel Stern's lectures, socialist axioms remembered from childhood. Attempts to explain the words away were batted down by Wilder, flashing his "supercilious, vulpine, patronizing, silky debater's grin" as he closed in for the kill.

Most damaging of all were excerpts from a tirade Gene delivered in the student lounge one night. Repressed memories about his experiences as a soldier spilled forth loud and unfiltered, his tongue loosened by alcohol. "If I were a fighter plane instead of a human being," he announced tearfully to a group of mystified coeds, "there would be little pictures of people painted all over me." This was his real crime: sharing "ugly, personal knowledge of the disgrace that was the Vietnam War." In a culture of amnesia, he had crossed a line that had to be defended.

For the coup de grâce, Wilder slid a folder across the table containing an investigator's log of the amorous liaisons of the accused, including those with the president's wife. Gene surrendered, tendering his resignation. Again he was in full retreat, but this time Sam Wakefield was not around to bail him out.

Shell-shocked, Gene walked across a campus festooned with graduation regalia. Andrea Wakefield, Sam's widow, passed him as she was heading to the faculty procession. She saw the strain on Gene's face and thought of her husband. "Don't let the war kill you, too," she warned softly.

A thunderous spectacle now shook the valley, a "doomsday chorus" of high-powered motorcycles. It was not Hell's Angels, but another kind of marauder, a pack of "highly successful Americans" led by Arthur Clarke, the famous "fun-loving billionaire" in town to pick up his honorary degree. Vonnegut is parodying the people-collector Malcolm Forbes, icon of shameless 1980s ostentation. His entourage included a Liz Taylor look-alike and Gene's old boss from the Vietnam War days, Henry Kissinger.

Gene's sleepwalk continued. He stepped right into an ambush by Pamela Ford Hall, Tarkington's failed performance-artist-in-residence. Sitting at the foot of Musket Mountain imbibing brandy, Pamela bemoaned having fallen for Gene's hocus pocus. Any woman foolish enough to get involved with him, she remarked acidly, should be forewarned: "Welcome to Vietnam."

As with all of Vonnegut's protagonists, Gene's guilt here draws in some measure from the author's own sense of having failed the women in his life, beginning with his mother. In marriage his faithlessness took the form of emotional withdrawal, a remoteness typical of soldiers who suffered from PTSD. Maybe his wives should have been told in advance: "Welcome to Dresden!"

It is time now for a break, a sci-fi interlude to give the reader relief from the series of defeats we have just witnessed. Gene made it down to his house just as a parcel was being delivered, a curious time capsule—his old footlocker from the war. Among its contents was a copy of *Black Garterbelt*, a soft-core skin rag that was his final birthday present from Jack Patton. Gene scanned its pages, and like Dwayne Hoover in *Breakfast of Champions* he was ready for any message that might explain the contradictions of his life.

We recognize "The Protocols of the Elders of Tralfamadore" as the work of Kilgore Trout, a parable about "intelligent threads of energy trillions of light years long" that wanted to breed germs capable of space flight. The Elders chose to experiment with Earthlings because their freakish "extralarge brains" could be counted on to devise tests that only the strongest of organisms would endure. As in *Sirens of Titan*, human history turns out to have been the plaything of a remote extragalactic alien civilization, and only in that context can it be made to make sense.

Flattery was the means of manipulation, and it was predictably effective. A founding myth was implanted, the story of Adam and Eve, to assure the subjects of the trial that they had been given "dominion" over the planet. "So the people on Earth thought they had instructions from the Creator of the Universe to wreck the joint," Vonnegut says through his narrator. Added to this dangerous arrogance was scientific knowledge. Nations soon devised ever more deadly weapons and used them against each other, leaving a byproduct of superresilient microbes. From the perspective of the Tralfamadorians, the exercise was a rousing success.

"What a relief it was, somehow, to have somebody else confirm what I had come to suspect toward the end of the Vietnam War," Gene thought to himself as he put down the magazine.

Just as human beings in Trout's story had been reduced to "germ hotels," so Gene Hartke had been "busted down to Townie" that afternoon. He headed over to the Black Cat Café, a local watering hole, needing a drink and hoping for job leads. At the bar he pondered why the Black Cat was the lone successful enterprise in this desolate part of Scipio. It wasn't just the cocktails and the ambience that kept business booming. The parking lot was the valley's center for prostitution, a widely known fact the owner, Lyle Hooper, denied all the way to his death in the prison break two years later. Like so many others, Hooper had a boundless capacity to believe his own hocus pocus, to rationalize away anything that might disturb his fragile self-image.

Gene found a ride to the only place in the valley hiring at the time. Hiroshi Matsumoto, the CEO at Athena prison, was a Japanese businessman sent to manage the American concerns his company had been acquiring in recent years. Gene worried about how to explain his time in Asia during the interview, but when he mentioned service in Vietnam, Matsumoto considered it a bond of brotherhood. "So we both know what it is," the warden said as he came around the desk to shake hands, "to be shipped to an alien land on a dangerous mission of vainglorious lunacy!"

Jack Patton and Hiroshi Matsumoto, an odd coupling if there ever was one, are the moral lynchpins of *Hocus Pocus*. (Gene is too passive to serve that function.) From an early age, each came to understand the human capacity for brutality, and each was inoculated against lying to themselves about it. The warden got his baptism as a schoolboy in Hiroshima at the end of World War II. During recess one morning he chased a soccer ball into a culvert. "There was a flash and wind. When he straightened up, his city was gone." It is a familiar image for Vonnegut readers, more testimony from the holy fraternity of bombing survivors. "He was alone on a desert, with little spirals of dust dancing here and there."

At Harvard Business School in the 1960s, Matsumoto would participate in antiwar rallies. Now he used, word for word, the rhetoric from those days to describe his country's present predicament. "We were a quagmire," Gene remembers him saying. "There was no light at the end of the tunnel over here, and on and on." In short, "America was Japan's Vietnam."

As a cost-saving measure Matsumoto recruited mercenaries, farm boys from the rural northern reaches of his homeland, for six-month "tours of duty" as guards at the prison. His bosses focused on the bottom line just as Gene's wartime superiors had obsessed about the arithmetic of "body counts." Despite its initial prospects, the "Army of Occupation in Business Suits" had proven a disaster. "What a clever trap your Ruling Class set for us," Matsumoto remarked to Gene one day. "First the atomic bomb. Now this." Those responsible had already absconded with their loot, leaving it to foreigners to clean up the mess. They were like the B-52 pilots Gene knew in Vietnam, unconcerned about the devastation they left below them.

The central "character" in *Hocus Pocus*, Vonnegut explained in *Fates Worse Than Death*—"excluding myself, of course"—was imperialism. It was approaching an end-stage as the wealthiest citizens around the world erected fortifications and detached themselves ever more completely from all the "complicated property" they owned, "in need of skilled management and exceedingly boring and appallingly expensive maintenance." In America everything was for sale, with the vendors no more "patriotic" in feeling than the British who occupied Rhodesia or the Belgians who had once ruled in the Congo. The trip to Mozambique was on the author's mind. "When the Portuguese were departing . . ." he discovered, "they poured cement down the sewer lines of toilets in office buildings and hotels and hospitals and so on which weren't going to belong to them anymore."[8]

The United States, Vonnegut warned, was "the last big colony to be abandoned by its conquerors," and the process now might be irreversible. "After they are gone, taking most of our money with them (maybe to Europe, maybe to compounds right here in the former colony, such as the Hamptons or Palm Beach or Palm Springs), we will be like Nigeria, a sort of improbable Dr. Seuss–like nation composed of several tribes." Institutions like the one at Athena were symptomatic of the new order.[9]

Used to starting over from zero, in classic American style, Gene embraced his new opportunity across the lake and moved his family to a guest house provided by the warden, his next-door neighbor. Teaching at the prison was not that different from being an instructor at the college, he soon concluded. The inmates, all African Americans by an order of the Supreme Court segregating the nation's burgeoning jail population, actually proved better equipped than the privileged Tarkington undergrads to deal with certain subjects. Many had been entrepreneurs in the narcotics trade, so for them the metric system Gene talked about in his math classes was not a challenge. They joked that he was a flying saucer visitor to their world. "I was in the food business," a drug dealer told him.

Just because people on one planet eat a certain kind of food they're hungry for, that makes them feel better after they eat it, that doesn't mean people on other planets shouldn't eat something else. On some planets I'm sure there are people who eat stones, and then feel wonderful for a little while afterwards. Then it's time to eat stones again.

Gene succeeded in expanding literacy among his students at the prison, but this led to disturbing unintended consequences. The most popular read at Athena was a booklet of anti-Semitic hate literature. Printed in Libya, it was circulated by the ruling class of the cell blocks, the "Black Brothers of Islam." Gene could provide the tools to communicate, but he had no control over how they might be used.

After two years in the new job Gene awakened one night to the sound of an explosion above his house. It was the opening salvo in a military-style assault on the prison, executed with sledgehammer effectiveness by a Jamaican drug cartel seeking to liberate its leader. Like most residents in the valley, Gene was slow to grasp the urgency of the situation, interpreting lulls in the shooting to mean that the crisis had subsided. Here again was the big-brained complacency Vonnegut described in *Galápagos*. Many said later "they had just pulled the covers over their heads and gone to sleep again" when they heard the noises. "What could be more human?" Only when he spied "100s of men" crossing the icy lake did he understand the scale of the emergency. In its stealth the advance reminded him of operations he had led in Vietnam.

The Battle of Scipio, based on the suppression of the uprising at Attica State Prison in September 1971, lasted for five days. The ground assault by the Athena prisoners, slowed only by token resistance, was spearheaded by Alton Darwin, a convict Gene knew well from his classes. Darwin proved to be as psychotically fearless as Jack Patton, and his delusional sense of mission—he spoke of converting the Mohiga Valley into an independent Black Republic—transformed him into a charismatic, self-styled Man of Destiny. He knew where he was going and others followed, even though things were doomed from the start. Most of Athena's inmates stayed in their cells, aware that "color coding" gave them little chance of survival outside the prison walls. "There was nothing but White people all the way to Rochester's city-limits sign," Gene explained, and a "Free Fire Zone" of black targets would be a dream come true for area gun enthusiasts.

The occupiers insisted on being called Freedom Fighters. "We are not against America," Alton Darwin declared. "We *are* America." It was a white xenophobe's nightmare. The justice dispensed by the guerrillas was random and extreme. Gene appreciated the irony that getting fired from Tarkington probably saved his life.

The prize trophies in the insurrection were the college trustees, assembled and held at gunpoint in the belfry of Lutz Tower. Darwin calculated correctly that Jason Wilder, the celebrity among them, would serve as a shield for his charges, analogous in its protective magic to Reagan's Star Wars space defense program. Authorities shelved plans to end the occupation with massive force as soon as they learned the identity of the hostages. Planes, helicopters, and shock troops proceeded with surgical restraint after this band of "nobodies" made it clear that they had a "somebody" in their custody.

Gene operated during the siege as a kind of neutral observer. Like Vonnegut, he was used to being a wanderer between worlds, not really at home in any of them. The escapees respected him as "The Preacher" for his knowledge of military strategy and "The Professor" for his familiarity with the layout of the campus and the town below. His freedom of movement gave Wilder and the other board members the impression that he had orchestrated the assault. The attack had a diabolical complexity they assumed beyond the skills of a group of black convicts. The narrator is defensive about his actual role:

> As at Athena Prison, I tried to give the most honest answer I could to any question anyone might care to put to me.... I simply described the truth of the inquirer's situation in the context of the world outside as best I could. What he did next was up to him. I call that being a teacher. I don't call that being a mastermind of a treasonous enterprise. All I ever wanted to overthrow was ignorance and self-serving fantasies.

"Don't blame the messenger," the author seems to be saying to his readers.

Alton Darwin was felled by a sniper's bullet while skating on the ice of Lake Mohiga. The remaining Freedom Fighters were quickly outmaneuvered, their hostages airlifted to safety. Gene watched the drama unfold from the bell tower, and it reminded him of the exit scene back in Saigon—only this time the press framed it as a happy ending. "Several nobodies tried to get onto a helicopter," he remembered, but they were thwarted as easily as he had once repelled uninvited passengers on an embassy rooftop.

Vonnegut used similar theatrical language to describe the "indisciminate butchery of bit-part players" that ended the real-life standoff at Attica in 1971. He blamed storytellers for the ruthlessness of the climactic assault. "All leading characters were elsewhere, so State Police with automatic shotguns blazing could be sent in without harming the play." The narrative focus moved on once order was restored. The scene reminds us of the Cuyahoga Massacre Vonnegut conjured for *Jailbird*.[10]

In the epilogue we learn that the Japanese Army of Occupation has been withdrawn, its architects concluding that upkeep was too expensive in a colony "in such an advanced state of physical and intellectual dilapidation." The thirst for empire receded, as it always did, when it became apparent that too many "unhappy and increasingly lawless people of all races, who don't own anything, turn out to come along with the properties."

After the siege was lifted there were more rapid-fire reinventions and reversals of fortune for Gene Hartke. The colonel who led the Scipio rescue operation recognized him amid the onlookers. "My Lord, it's The Preacher!" he said, just before appointing him brigadier general in charge of the valley under martial law. Gene accepted the job, with the vanity of Jonah in *Cat's Cradle*, agreeing to be president of troubled San Lorenzo. "I had always wanted to be a General," Gene explains, and he took all available measures to repair the damage and restore calm. Gene recalls with particular pride his decision to assign troops to firefighting details. The trucks needed for the task were unmolested, their fuel tanks full. Here was a ray of hope, something, perhaps, to build on. "Every so often, in the midst of chaos, you come across an amazing, inexplicable instance of civic responsibility," Gene observes with wonder. "Maybe the last shred of faith people have is in their firemen." Eliot Rosewater would have agreed.

"Hello, Warden Hartke," Gene's boss greeted him two weeks later. He was now handed the responsibility of converting Tarkington College into a prison. Gene wants it known that he performed the duties with diligence during his brief administration, which ended with his arrest. Why was he being held responsible for the jailbreak? It was more showbiz. "Some ambitious young Prosecutor," the officer in charge confided to him, "thinks you'll make good TV."

Interrupted by a tubercular cough he picked up at Athena, Gene ends his reflections by recalling the curiously sweet visit he received from the son he had never met, the product of a liaison in the Philippines en route home from Vietnam. He is glad that he was still wearing his general's stars when the young man dropped by. Gene also describes the shock he felt when told of the suicide of Hiroshi Matsumoto back in Hiroshima. It had to have been a delayed reaction to the atomic bomb. "I wish I had been born a bird instead," the warden once remarked to Gene. "I wish we had all been born birds instead." We hear the aching *Poo-tee-weet* Vonnegut used to conclude *Slaughterhouse-Five*.

Looking back, Gene admits to a life more reckless than Matsumoto's, with real things to feel guilty about. He ends his memoir with the twin columns he has been compiling in his cell, one listing his sexual conquests and the other his "100-percent-legal military kills" in Vietnam. The reader is put through a series of arithmetic problems to arrive at totals for each—which prove to be identical. This will be the epitaph on his tombstone.

The body count exercise burlesques the American obsession with numbers. It is also a metaphor for the kind of stock-taking that now preoccupied Vonnegut, not unusual for a man at his stage in life. As the toll of deceased friends and family grew year by year, and as he faced his own approaching mortality, it was natural to ask himself who he had disappointed, misused— even, symbolically, murdered. What trail of wreckage was he leaving behind? Why not reduce it to a list?

Jack Patton would have wanted to "laugh like hell" at his friend's story, and he certainly would have agreed with the moral Gene draws from it, a final practical joke: "Just because some of us can read and write and do a little math, that doesn't mean we deserve to conquer the Universe."

With *God Bless You, Mr. Rosewater* and *Jailbird,* we can read *Hocus Pocus* as the last installment in a trilogy addressing "the savage and stupid and entirely inappropriate American class system" that eclipsed the utopia dreamt of by the author's immigrant ancestors. Gene Hartke is our Virgil as we are reminded that the news is bad and getting worse. Vonnegut described it this way:

> In my very first book, *Player Piano* . . . I asked a question which is even harder to answer nowadays: "What are people for?" My own answer is: "Maintenance." In *Hocus Pocus* . . . I acknowledged that everybody wanted to build and nobody wanted to do maintenance. So there goes the ball game.[11]

But the gloom is relieved by outrageous situations and razor-sharp jokes, inducing that most human of reflexes, the belly laugh. Vonnegut deconstructs lies, moralizes about injustice, indulges in despair at times—all the while keeping in mind his advice to young writers: "Be sure to sound user-friendly and not all that serious when doing it." As we put aside the book we are amazed at Vonnegut's skill in anchoring dark truths to a campus comedy of manners, seasoned with a dollop of sci-fi speculation just to keep things in perspective. Maybe it is all just a matter of "intelligent threads of energy" conducting an experiment.[12]

FOURTEEN

Timequake

You were sick, but now you're well again,
and there's work to do.
—Kilgore Trout

Timequake (1997) is a heroic, magnificent ruin, erected on a story that would not allow itself to be finished. At the beginning of the 1990s Vonnegut complained about critics insisting that "I am not the promising writer I used to be," and the fact that he was able, after long struggle, to get this second book for Putnam into shape is testament to his spirit of healthy defiance. He started it over multiple times in the course of five years, and wondered in any case if there would be anyone interested in reading it. "A raccoon with a lump of sugar washes and washes it until it disappears," he wrote to his friend Loree Rackstraw in the middle of the frustrating process. "The same thing keeps happening to my novel *Timequake*, which has to do with the disappearance of the America I tried to write for." But what emerged from the struggle, the culmination of his ventures into "autobiographical collage," is in some ways the author's most audacious experiment in demolishing the boundaries between life and art. In the prologue he compares himself to Hemingway's dogged protagonist in *The Old Man and the Sea*. "Fillet the fish," Vonnegut concludes, looking for a way to preserve the best of his catch from the sharks. "Throw the rest away."[1]

It didn't help that during this period Vonnegut's private life was unsettled again. Jill's papers for divorce in 1991 (later withdrawn) were a symptom of the estrangement that would limit his time with daughter Lily and exile him to long, bleak winters alone at the East Hamptons house in Sagaponack. There would be no quick resolution to the difficulties.

He found relief from these professional and personal pressures in new creative ventures. These included a partnership with silkscreen artist Joe Petro III from Kentucky, to produce and market prints of his India ink doodles, and collaboration with California filmmaker Bob Weide on a cinematic version of *Mother Night* and a documentary about his early life in Indiana. Vonnegut was grateful for interaction with younger people like these, which kept him energetic even as he ruminated about mortality. In life, as he said in *Bluebeard*, "birth and death are always there."

Back now for one last campaign in *Timequake* is Vonnegut's warhorse, Kilgore Trout, with his hobo's satchel of disposable sci-fi parables. Revisiting the mysteries of agency versus determinism, things unfold here in a conversational voice long past any need for artifice. Even more than usual, the premise and characters are an excuse for Vonnegut to expound on human folly, on the bittersweet ironies of love and loss. Through Trout, he defends his method once again:

> If I'd wasted my time creating characters, I would never have gotten around to things that really matter: irresistible forces in nature, and cruel inventions, and cockamamie ideas and governments and economies that make heroes and heroines alike feel like something the cat drug in.

Vonnegut fills this valedictory with references to his body of work as it coalesces into wholeness. "I don't see it as a freestanding novel," he said when *Timequake* was finished, "but as the last chapter in one long book." It is a diary of elegiac personal reflections, laments about a fin de siècle culture of mindless speed and forgetting, and last goodbyes to the signposts and loved ones who, we know, have been the real characters in his life.

A reworking of the notion of being unstuck in time—the nonlinearity of experience—*Timequake* started with the idea of a "hiccup" in the workings of the universe, a passing crisis of confidence in its outward momentum. "Should it go on expanding indefinitely? What was the point?" We wonder if the cosmos is contemplating suicide as we consider the phenomenon, "a cosmic charley horse in the sinews of Destiny."

On Earth this seizing-up thrusts everyone back a decade, from February 13, 2001 (the Dresden anniversary), to February 17, 1991. What follows from there is a "rerun" in which people are forced to negotiate "obstacle courses of their own construction" until "free will kicked in again." The only way back to the present is "the hard way, minute by minute, hour by hour, year by year, betting on the wrong horse again, marrying the wrong person again, getting the clap again. You name it!"

Trout would record it all in the "never-to-be-finished" memoir *My Ten Years on Automatic Pilot.* After a lifetime of dead-end jobs he has landed, finally, on the streets, loitering on Christmas Eve in front of the American Academy of Arts and Letters, "way-the-hell-up-and-gone" in upper Manhattan. Now in his eighties, Trout has been swept up from the New York Public Library with other "sacred cattle" and delivered to a homeless shelter adjacent to the academy, in what was once the Museum of the American Indian. He registers under the name "Vincent van Gogh," another artist ignored and scorned when he was alive.

We find Trout placing something in a trash bin as he carries on an animated conversation with himself. To passersby he looks like a member of Mary Kathleen O'Looney's army of bag ladies, in his thermal underwear, navy surplus coat and "babushka, fashioned from a crib blanket printed with red balloons and blue teddy bears." He is another Vonnegut holy fool, an aged counterpart to Billy Pilgrim in his Cinderella costume.

The Trout alter ego embodies the author's truth, sacrilege in the affirmative gospel of the American Dream, that the world is often a hostile place, that virtue is not always rewarded, and that losing is a far more common experience than winning. The most we can hope for—and, in the end, it is enough—are the consolations of friendship, the dignity of "grace in defeat." Recalling his mother and sister, Vonnegut concludes that a lot of people simply don't like life very much. The same theme pervades the last works of "the funniest American of his time," Mark Twain. The cruelty of life is also central to the Sermon on the Mount, the dramas of Shakespeare, and Thoreau's *Walden*. It runs, too, through the "artificial timequakes" of the theater that helped shape Vonnegut's imagination, "emotional and ethical landmarks" performed live before "rapt congregations" when he was young. *Our Town*, *Death of a Salesman*, *A Streetcar Named Desire*—all speak to the longing for community in our culture of loneliness and dislocation. Like the poems he spoke of in *Palm Sunday*, they chart "the queer shapes which the massive indifference of America gives to lives."[2]

Vonnegut feels like Thornton Wilder's dead Emily when he looks back to the abundant Indianapolis of his youth,

> a place as seemingly safe and simple, as learnable, as acceptable as Grover's Corners at the turn of the century, with ticking clocks and Mama and Papa and hot baths and new-ironed clothes and all the rest of it, to which I've already said good-by, good-by, one hell of a long time ago now.

The author is far along now in his reconciliation with his hometown, lampooned in earlier works as the spiritually arid Midland City. In a 1996 commencement speech at Butler University he recalled the miracle of its schools and libraries, the cross section of humanity—the intimate, stable "folk society"—provided by his family and neighbors when he was a boy. "It was all here for me, just as it has all been here for you," he told the graduates, "the best and the worst of Western Civilization, if you cared to pay attention." In his own backyard were all the role models he would ever need. "People so smart you can't believe it, and people so dumb you can't believe it. People so nice you can't believe it, and people so mean you can't believe it." We can hear Otto Waltz from *Deadeye Dick*, insisting "this is as much Shangri-La as anywhere."

And the hard times were part of the package. "I wouldn't have missed the Great Depression or my part in World War Two for anything," Vonnegut declares in *Timequake*. He can smile now at the struggles he and his wife Jane endured raising six children on a shoestring in Barnstable Village. His eldest son put those years in perspective in response to a query about what it was like to have a celebrity in the house. "When I was growing up," Mark Vonnegut replied, "my father was a car salesman who couldn't get a job teaching at Cape Cod Junior College."

Kilgore Trout is throwing away the latest of his thousands of stories in the trash bin. Not even *Black Garterbelt* is going to get this one. "Easy come, easy go" is his philosophy. Vonnegut had for decades channeled his profligate short story reflexes into Trout fables, meant to be tossed aside before the ink dried. In *Timequake* they include "The Sisters B-36," about a planet in the Crab Nebula where computers made imaginations obsolete. In "No Laughing Matter," a plane carrying a third atomic bomb turns around over Japan without dropping its payload. "That," the pilot explains at his court martial, "is what his mother would have wanted him to do." "Dog's Breakfast" is another consideration of the human brain, which, for all its capacity for mischief, was a singularly unimpressive-looking organ. And then there is Trout's revision of the Book of Genesis. Satan introduces ideas about "sin"—gambling, intoxicants, singing, and dancing—with benevolent intent, to make human existence more bearable. She understands, as God did not, that "to be alive was to be either bored or scared stiff."

The American Academy of Arts and Letters was an anachronism, a symbol of the best and worst features of Victorian Age high culture. Vonnegut had been admitted to the club, but had his usual mixed feelings about being on the inside. He admired the guild's dedication to "making old-fashioned art in old-fashioned ways," but disliked the elitism of its selection process. It offended him that so many worthy candidates, like James Jones and Irwin Shaw, were overlooked. Nelson Algren, a friend from the Iowa Writers' Workshop days, felt snubbed when he was awarded a Medal for Literature but not membership. He rebuffed a phone call from Vonnegut urging him to come to New York to accept the prize anyway. The clerical oversight was corrected just weeks before his death, too late to undo the hurt.[3]

In 1972 Vonnegut was asked by *Newsweek* what he thought about being elected with Allen Ginsberg to the Academy's Institute of Arts and Letters. "If we aren't the establishment, I don't know who is," he quipped. In his acceptance speech Vonnegut called its headquarters a "tomb" and flaunted his unorthodox credentials, championing the insights of anthropology, biochemistry, and physics over the more conventional literary pedigrees of most of those in his audience.[4]

In the lobby of the *Timequake*'s academy is Monica Pepper, the executive secretary, a lanky middle-aged woman modeled on Vonnegut's sister, Alice. To deter vandals Monica has done everything possible "to make the place look as abandoned and looted as the ruins of Columbia University" two miles to the south. Bars fortify its windows and graffiti covers the facade, the message "FUCK ART" spray-painted across the massive front door. Alice would have loved the symbolism.

Guard Dudley Prince, part of the skeleton crew on duty that Christmas Eve, spies Trout dumping "The Sisters B-36" into the trash. Curious about the strange dance that accompanies the act, Prince retrieves the manuscript and shares its contents with his coworkers. Over the following weeks there would be more deposits, more stories to decipher from this apparent bag lady. Vonnegut has set up a typically fractured dialogue here, with the readers free to form their own conclusions about the message.

Trout has contempt for the institution on the other side of the wall, its members as blind to the precincts he walked as the arts festival philistines in *Breakfast of Champions*. They only want "literature" over there, he snarls to the man in the next bunk, works with fancy prose and elaborate protagonists—not the quickly drawn caricatures that are his bread and butter. Indeed, the only "living, breathing, three-dimensional character" he has ever created is his son, Leon, whose ghost we recall from *Galápagos*.

Prince takes the orphaned stories to be communications from God. He had become a devout Christian during his years at the penitentiary upstate in Athena, where he was incarcerated for a crime he did not commit. DNA evidence secured his release, but the timequake would make him a jailbird again, reliving the tedious horror of maximum security incarceration. A person never really leaves prison.

The author does not begrudge Prince the comforts of his beliefs. People needed all the help they could get, even if it was based upon what some would consider superstition, the *foma* of *Cat's Cradle*. Bernard V. O'Hare,

Vonnegut's late army buddy, had given up his Catholic faith under the stresses of World War II. "I didn't like that," his old friend confesses. "I thought that was too much to lose." Thoughts arise of Vonnegut's first wife, Jane, whose embrace of "anything that made being alive seem full of white magic" helped her endure a long journey with cancer. "She died believing in the Trinity and Heaven and Hell and the rest of it. I'm so glad," the author tells us. "Why? Because I loved her."

The challenges of family remain, even as he looks back on his life with the compassionate eyes of old age. Like *Bluebeard*'s Rabo Karabekian, Vonnegut thinks he failed at the task in important ways. Maybe he didn't have that much potential in the first place. World War II was "a time of panic for unmarried women," Vonnegut writes, and Jane ended up with "a guy who came home a PFC, who had been flunking all his courses at Cornell when he went off to war, and who didn't have a clue as to what to do next, now that free will had kicked in again." Half a century later he was still trying to figure out how to be husband and a father.

"After the relentless reprise of their mistakes and bad luck and hollow victories during the past ten years," many people suffered from Post-Timequake Apathy, or PTA, leading to all manner of accidents. Most were harmless pratfalls of the kind that would have had sister Alice doubled over in laughter. But it was a more serious matter for anyone involved with heavy machines, who often realized, too late, that they needed directing again.

Trout is on his cot during the hiccup, "operating nothing more dangerous or headstrong than a ballpoint pen." A crash outside brings him to his feet to investigate. For want of "sincere steering," a fire truck has careened into the front of the academy, and dead and injured people now lie scattered in the street along its path. Trout steps through a gaping hole where the door had been and awakens the people inside. "You were sick, but now you're well again," he called out instinctively, "and there's work to do." Soon Dudley Prince joins him in pronouncing the words to everyone within earshot.

> They went into the former Museum of the American Indian, and said them to the catatonic bums in there. A goodly number of the aroused sacred cattle, maybe a third of them, became anti-PTA evangelists in turn. Armed with nothing more than Kilgore's Creed,

these ragged veterans of unemployability fanned out through the neighborhood to convert more living statues to lives of usefulness.

Old Trout has risen to the occasion, mobilizing those around him with a call to action that surprises even himself in its hopefulness. He organizes the shelter into a field hospital until more help can arrive, and is recognized and rewarded for his heroics. With his new friends he is whisked from the disaster area, courtesy of an academy patron, to Xanadu, an exclusive writer's retreat on the Rhode Island shore. Trout's days as a bag lady are over.

Vonnegut addresses us directly as we near the end of this salvaged project, pecked out, Luddite-style, on his typewriter. He has taken plenty of breaks in the work, strolling his neighborhood to buy manila envelopes and flirt with the pretty clerk at the post office. These excursions are joyful in their everydayness, opportunities for human contact and the lost art of conversation. Digital distractions and cell phones had not yet completely colonized the streets in the mid-1990s.

Bernard Vonnegut, the last member of the author's Indianapolis family, has been diagnosed with cancer, adding for us another layer of poignancy. So many friends have been "put to bed" lately, so many reference points irretrievably lost. Again, *Timequake* is, at its deepest level, a set of reflections by the author on "the disappearance of the America I tried to write for." Even books, those vehicles for spiritual adventure so beguiling for the human hands and eyes, might be extinct soon for youngsters the age of his teenaged daughter, Lily. Vonnegut has been expressing reservations about the cyber-revolution since *Player Piano*, and the latest stages of that process, a long way from the vacuum-tubed behemoths of the early 1950s, still gave him pause. "I hate the idea of the Information Superhighway," he wrote to Loree Rackstraw, "which will almost certainly turn out to be a narrow thoroughfare with lots of cops and tollgates."[5]

No one remembers the labor battles of Debs and Hapgood, he laments, no one cares anymore about the dreams of social justice so ennobling during the Depression and the war against fascism. It is all being erased—by garish virtual realities and the simple passage of time. Meanwhile robber barons keep winning, the "losers" fall farther behind, the world burns. "Many members of my generation are disappointed," he tells us.

The author catches himself at the brink of despair, and like Trout, brings us back to the work we need to do. "Still and all, why bother?" he asks. Why keep putting words to paper and making art, why dwell on the distant past? As the universe wondered in its moment of existential doubt, "What was the point?" Vonnegut gives his answer, the message of companionship so many are desperate to receive: "I feel and think much as you do, care about many of the things you care about, although most people don't care about them. You are not alone."

Six months after the cosmic shudder Kilgore Trout is still ensconced in the Hemingway suite at Xanadu. The local Mask and Wig Club is putting on its own "man-made timequake," a production of *Abe Lincoln in Illinois* with a mixed-race descendent of John Wilkes Booth in the lead role. From backstage, as the play winds down, Trout provides the sound effect of an old-fashioned steam whistle, signaling that the train from Springfield to the nation's besieged capital is about to depart.

Trout is moved to tears by Lincoln's farewell to his well-wishers, the prayer of a son of the Midwest to the resilient possibilities of the American Dream. "It is a grave duty which I now face," the president-elect said as the country was coming apart. The experiment in democracy is dying. "And yet—let us believe that it is not true!"

> Let us live to prove that we can cultivate the natural world that is about us, and the intellectual and moral world that is within us, so that we may secure an individual, social and political prosperity, whose course shall be forward, and which, while the earth endures, shall not pass away.

At the clambake afterward Trout is the life of the party, "as witty as Oscar Wilde." His Creator is with him on the beach, along with Monica Pepper and Dudley Prince. They mingle with people who have been important in Kurt Vonnegut's life—his parents; his big brother and sister; Ida Young; Phoebe Hurty; "nine of my teachers at Shortridge High School"; Bernard V. O'Hare; Jane Cox Vonnegut; and his mentors, Knox

Burger, Kenneth Littauer, and Sam Lawrence, to whom he dedicates *Time-quake*. (Wife Jill is there, too, but the children and grandchildren, all in the prime of life, are absent. "That was OK, perfectly understandable," he reassures us. "It wasn't my birthday, and I wasn't a guest of honor.") Two "luckless fishermen" languish in a rowboat offshore, "dead ringers for the saints Stanley Laurel and Oliver Hardy."

As the cast party winds down, Trout makes a theatrical exit, summoning a volunteer to help him with a magic trick. His Creator steps forward. Looking at the points of light in the sky, Trout declares that he embodies a new force in the cold physics of the universe, the quality of awareness that makes human beings so beautiful sometimes. We are reminded of Rabo's "bands of light" speech in *Breakfast of Champions*.

In the epilogue we learn that Bernard Vonnegut has died, at age eighty-two. He was "courtly" and "elegant" to the end, a woman who knew him in hospice care reports. The author celebrates his brother's experimental spirit, his stoicism and integrity, his sense of humor. "I was honored that he found me funny too," he adds, newly adrift. "Now I don't have anybody to show off for anymore."

Vonnegut felt relief that this project, his self-declared last novel, was done. Now he could really leave behind the burdens of this particular channel of activity. "With *Timequake* finished, I feel as though I've been fired from a job I needed but didn't like very much," he wrote to Loree Rackstraw. "I sure don't want to start another book. What next? Nothing."[6]

But the author was cheered and surprised by the response of critics who took this "anti-novel" for the radically unorthodox summing-up exercise that it was intended to be. Acknowledging its heartfelt power, Brad Stone of *Newsweek* called it Vonnegut's "funniest book since *Breakfast of Champions*." "The real pleasure lies in Vonnegut's transforming his continuing interest in the highly suspicious relationship between fact and fiction into the neatest trick yet played on a publishing world consumed with the furor over novel versus memoir," Valerie Sayers wrote in her enthusiastic review for the *New York Times*.[7]

Readers similarly embraced the book. The launch event at Barnes and Noble's flagship store in Manhattan was the biggest in the chain's history.

"By six o'clock the place was full," observed James Atlas in the *New Yorker*'s "Talk of the Town." "Hundreds of disappointed fans, some of whom had traveled from other states, were being turned away." Nearly half a century after his first novel, the audience was not ready to let Kurt Vonnegut leave the stage.[8]

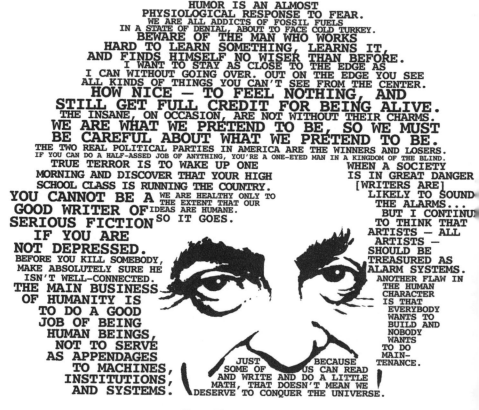

HUMOR IS AN ALMOST
PHYSIOLOGICAL RESPONSE TO FEAR.
WE ARE ALL ADDICTS OF FOSSIL FUELS
IN A STATE OF DENIAL, ABOUT TO FACE COLD TURKEY.
BEWARE OF THE MAN WHO WORKS
HARD TO LEARN SOMETHING, LEARNS IT,
AND FINDS HIMSELF NO WISER THAN BEFORE.
I WANT TO STAY AS CLOSE TO THE EDGE AS
I CAN WITHOUT GOING OVER. OUT ON THE EDGE YOU SEE
ALL KINDS OF THINGS YOU CAN'T SEE FROM THE CENTER.
HOW NICE — TO FEEL NOTHING, AND
STILL GET FULL CREDIT FOR BEING ALIVE.
THE INSANE, ON OCCASION, ARE NOT WITHOUT THEIR CHARMS.
WE ARE WHAT WE PRETEND TO BE, SO WE MUST
BE CAREFUL ABOUT WHAT WE PRETEND TO BE.
THE TWO REAL POLITICAL PARTIES IN AMERICA ARE THE WINNERS AND LOSERS.
IF YOU CAN DO A HALF-ASSED JOB OF ANYTHING, YOU'RE A ONE-EYED MAN IN A KINGDOM OF THE BLIND.
TRUE TERROR IS TO WAKE UP ONE   WHEN A SOCIETY
MORNING AND DISCOVER THAT YOUR HIGH   IS IN GREAT DANGER
SCHOOL CLASS IS RUNNING THE COUNTRY.   [WRITERS ARE]
YOU CANNOT BE A WE ARE HEALTHY ONLY TO   LIKELY TO SOUND
                 THE EXTENT THAT OUR   THE ALARMS...
GOOD WRITER OF IDEAS ARE HUMANE.   BUT I CONTINU
SERIOUS FICTION SO IT GOES.   TO THINK THAT
  IF YOU ARE   ARTISTS — ALL
                                                ARTISTS —
NOT DEPRESSED.   SHOULD BE
BEFORE YOU KILL SOMEBODY,   TREASURED AS
MAKE ABSOLUTELY SURE HE   ALARM SYSTEMS.
ISN'T WELL-CONNECTED.   ANOTHER FLAW IN
THE MAIN BUSINESS   THE HUMAN
OF HUMANITY IS   CHARACTER
TO DO A GOOD   IS THAT
JOB OF BEING   EVERYBODY
HUMAN BEINGS,   WANTS TO
                                                BUILD AND
NOT TO SERVE   NOBODY
AS APPENDAGES   WANTS
  TO MACHINES,   TO DO
                       JUST   BECAUSE   MAIN-
  INSTITUTIONS,   SOME OF   US CAN READ   TENANCE.
  AND SYSTEMS.   AND WRITE AND DO A LITTLE
                 MATH, THAT DOESN'T MEAN WE
                 DESERVE TO CONQUER THE UNIVERSE.

Kurt Vonnegut
1922 – 2007

A Man without a Country, a "Planetary Citizen"

When he finished *Slaughterhouse-Five* Kurt Vonnegut observed that he felt like a flower that had blossomed, as programmed by nature. He wasn't sure what, if anything, would come next. After *Timequake*, despite repeated protests about his desire to stop ("Can I go home now?" was a favorite phrase in his last decade), Vonnegut found himself still driven to communicate, through writing, speeches, and his visual art. There was, too, an urgent need to speak up as he watched his country and indeed the entire planet continue down a fool's path to destruction. As a citizen and an elder, it was his duty to keep on telling the truth, to protest against unjust wars and environmental degradation, to decry ever more brazen examples of greed and corruption. Almost against his will, Vonnegut produced some beautiful, vivid blooms in the epilogue of his long life.[1]

His public activities included a conversation in front of a bookstore audience with Lee Stringer, whose account of life on the streets, *Grand Central Winter* (1998), Vonnegut liked and strongly championed. That lively and profound October 1998 evening, along with a subsequent dialogue, is preserved in the volume *Like Shaking Hands with God* (2000).[2]

Vonnegut hit the fiction shelves again with *Bagombo Snuff Box* (1999), a collection of previously unreleased short stories from early in his career, as well as *God Bless You, Dr. Kevorkian* (1999), a series of ninety-second "interviews" he conducted for New York public radio (WYNC) across the void with figures like Isaac Newton, Clarence Darrow, James Earl Ray, and—inevitably—Kilgore Trout. Vonnegut had trouble keeping his promises to quit. Work on a fifteenth novel, to be titled *If God Were Alive Today*, did not advance much beyond the exploratory stages, however.

Meanwhile the Kurt Vonnegut road show continued. In October 1999 he made a pilgrimage to Dresden, going back down into the cellar where he and his fellow prisoners had ridden out the storm nearly fifty-five years earlier. "Only then did I realize that we had seen an Atlantis—before it sank forever beneath the waves," he wrote to Loree Rackstraw. "I have seen Dresden," he thought to himself as he lectured to an audience there, "and you have not."[3]

Back home Vonnegut shared with overflow college audiences calculatedly rambling observations about "How to Get a Job Like Mine," a talk that quickly became a YouTube favorite. His cachet among younger fans explains how the text of a fake MIT commencement address, urging the use of sunscreen and other "Vonnegutian" life lessons, went "viral" on the internet at about the same time.[4]

Pushing hard as he approached eighty, Vonnegut's energy ebbed and flowed. In January 2000, he almost perished in his Manhattan townhouse, in a fire caused by an errant cigarette. Relocating to Northampton, Massachusetts, to be near his daughter Nanny, Vonnegut's recovery from smoke inhalation was slow, but by April he was able to return to New York to speak at a memorial tribute for Joseph Heller. In the fall he was back in the classroom, teaching a course in creative writing at Smith College.

On January 22, 2001, Kurt Vonnegut was honored at an official ceremony in Albany with the Edith Wharton Citation of Merit by the New York State Writers Institute, which came with a two-year appointment as state author. He was introduced to the standing-room crowd by his East Hamptons friend and neighbor George Plimpton and novelist William Kennedy. Vonnegut's "questioning of our values, our sense of progress, even our existence," Kennedy said, served as a touchstone for millions of readers. "His wry satire and cosmic wit keep us sane." The guest of honor then entertained everyone with his chalkboard analysis of Shakespeare's *Hamlet*. "He tells the truth," Vonnegut said of the Bard, "and the truth is we don't know enough about life to know what the good news is and what the bad news is."[5]

Vonnegut was in Manhattan during the trauma of 9/11, and joined his Turtle Bay neighbors later that September in a candlelight ceremony to remember the dead. In his remarks he warned against resorting to violence and blind revenge, advocating as always for future bombing victims, and he recalled how local firefighters had saved his life less than two years earlier. He read aloud the names of those from the firehouse, Engine Company 8, Ladder Company 2, Battalion 8, lost in the Twin Towers.[6]

Vonnegut's signature work in his last years, and the book that confirmed his status with a new generation of readers, was *A Man without a Country* (2005), edited by Daniel Simon for Seven Stories Press. It is a collage of poems, aphorisms, and silkscreen drawings, whimsical reflections on the author's Midwestern roots and his smoking, tutorials on the mechanics of storytelling, and testimonials to the beauty of African American jazz and the healing power of making art. Ever the Luddite, Vonnegut took a dim view of advances in cyber-technology. "Bill Gates says, 'Wait till you can see what your computer can become.' But it's you who should be doing the becoming, not the damn fool computer." He expressed similar skepticism toward the burgeoning realm of social networking. Interaction by way of push buttons and screens was no substitute for the nourishment of face-to-face contact. "Electronic communities build nothing," Vonnegut insisted. "We are dancing animals."[7]

A Man without a Country served also as a vehicle for the author's Twain-like jeremiads about politics in the new century, drawn from essays he had written for the Chicago-based progressive journal, *In These Times*. Describing himself as a member of a dying species—"a lifelong Northern Democrat in the Franklin Delano Roosevelt tradition, a friend of the working stiffs"—Vonnegut charged that George W. Bush had come into office by means of "the sleaziest, low-comedy, Keystone Cops style coup d'état imaginable," and with fellow "psychopathic personalities" Cheney and Rumsfeld, had proceeded to "[disconnect] all the burglar alarms prescribed by the Constitution" in their consolidation of executive power. With the invasion of Iraq the president treated American soldiers "as I never was," Vonnegut concluded with disgust, "like toys a rich kid got for Christmas."[8]

Complicity was not limited to those at the top, however. In our addiction to fossil fuels, Vonnegut insisted, too many in the developed world were content to sit back while their leaders commit "violent crimes to get what little is left of what we're hooked on." He did not soft-peddle his fears about the future. "The biggest truth to face now," he declared, "what is probably making me unfunny now for the remainder of my life—is that I don't think people give a damn whether the planet goes on or not. . . . I know of very few people who are dreaming of a world for their grandchildren."[9]

The success of *A Man without a Country* prompted a wave of critical reevaluation of Kurt Vonnegut and his career. Historian Douglas Brinkley celebrated him in a feature article for *Rolling Stone,* and A. O. Scott used the opportunity to issue his own highly personal appreciation in the *New York Times.* "This book's publication causes me to realize that, over the years, I've taken Vonnegut somewhat for granted, and perhaps not taken him as seriously as I should have," Scott wrote. He lauded the novels from the author's long years in obscurity, "planting seeds of allegory in the pulpy loam of 50's genre publishing," and argued that despite Vonnegut's experimental style he "never really belonged among the hothouse practitioners" of postmodernism like John Barth and Thomas Pynchon with whom he was later classified. Vonnegut's politics defied prevailing categories as well. "His liberalism grows out of some principles that can only be called conservative," Scott concluded, "like the belief in community and extended family that has become one of the big themes of his later work. He remains unimpressed by technology or the other trappings of progress, and he remains one of America's leading critics of evolution—not of the theory, mind you, but of the practice, which has left us far too clever and vain for our own good."[10]

George W. Bush's victory in November 2004 was another blow to Vonnegut's flagging hopes for his country, and he did not live to see the turn of political fortunes in the next election cycle. How would "our sage and chain-smoking truth-teller" have reacted to the ascension of Barack Obama, asked another admirer, Dave Eggers, in his 2009 review of *Look at the Birdie,* a collection of unpublished short stories released after Vonnegut's death. "Most likely he'd have been momentarily heartened," Eggers speculated, "then exasperated once again witnessing the lunatic-strewn town halls, the Afghanistan quagmire, the triumph of volume over reason, of machinery over humanity."[11]

Kurt Vonnegut "vanished from our table of organization" on April 11, 2007, weeks after a fall outside his brownstone that caused severe brain injuries. "He didn't wake up," remembered Mark Vonnegut, who, with other family members, was there at the bedside, playing music, telling jokes, and serving as medical proxy. "So I took care of my father like my father had cut through the crap and taken care of me thirty-six years earlier in British Columbia," Mark said, referring to the breakdown he described in his own book *The Eden Express*. I was glad to be able to repay the favor. He took responsibility for hospitalizing me, and I took responsibility for letting him go."[12]

After a small memorial service at New York's Algonquin Hotel, Mark traveled to Indianapolis to deliver the typically irreverent, digression-filled speech his father had prepared as the keynote for "The Year of Kurt Vonnegut," the city's celebration of its most famous native son. I remember the emotion of that spring evening, the mix of laughter and tears in the audience that packed into Butler University's Clowes Hall. The absent guest of honor would have found it an appropriate send-off. "And I thank you for your attention, and I'm out of here," were the last words Mark read in his name from the podium.[13]

Meanwhile, tributes poured forth from around the globe, expressing loss and gratitude for the icon millions had come to regard as a friend. The Internet, toward which Vonnegut was so ambivalent, came alive with idiosyncratic testimonies from people of all ages and backgrounds about the impact of his books on their lives. One of my college students admitted that she cried when she heard the news of her hero's death. Another told me of a cousin stationed in a bunker in Afghanistan, who had a line from *Slaughterhouse-Five* tattooed on his arm: "Everything was Beautiful and Nothing Hurt." Perhaps the gesture Vonnegut would have most appreciated was the decision by the Alplaus, New York, volunteer fire department, where he had served after the war, to lower the flag and ring its alarm bell with a 5-5-5 cadence—the traditional salute to a fallen brother.

Vonnegut would no doubt be amused and gratified to see how his career has boomed even after his death. In addition to the posthumous publication of

Armageddon in Retrospect, Look at the Birdie, and other anthologies of previously unreleased works, all of his novels remain in print and are being reissued in new editions. The Kurt Vonnegut Society, a group dedicated to promoting scholarship about the author, was founded by Marc Leeds in May 2008, and the Kurt Vonnegut Memorial Library opened its doors to great fanfare in Indianapolis in November 2010. The prestigious Library of America launched its first volume of Vonnegut novels the following June. And Vonnegut's work continues to inspire controversy, as evidenced by the storm over a decision by the board of education of Republic, Missouri, to remove *Slaughterhouse-Five* and other allegedly "age-inappropriate" texts from its high school library and curriculum. His legacy is secure.[14]

Who stands as the successor? While the author's influence is everywhere, there is no one who can take his place, as an artist and as a moral voice. Business manager Donald Farber spoke to the uniqueness of his longtime friend in an interview with Joshua Chaplinsky in January 2011. "I have people approaching me all the time asking me to represent them because, they say, I write the way Vonnegut wrote," Farber observed, "but that's a load of crap."

> Nobody writes the way Kurt wrote. And why would we need anybody who writes the way Kurt wrote? Kurt wrote the way Kurt wrote.[15]

A Man without a Country contains a "Requiem" Kurt Vonnegut wrote as a reflection of his late-life pessimism about the future. It concludes:

> *When the last living thing*
> *has died on account of us,*
> *how poetical it would be*
> *if Earth could say,*
> *in a voice floating up*
> *perhaps*
> *from the floor*
> *of the Grand Canyon,*
> *"It is done."*
> *People did not like it here.*

Vonnegut's gloom about the human race and its prospects was nothing new, of course. "I can see maybe forty years' more hope," he prophesied in an interview on *Sixty Minutes* in 1969. We are now past that doomsday deadline, and as we move forward without him we should keep in mind the author's other side, his curiously resilient faith in people. His optimism, if we can call it that, rested on the legions of the young who were always so drawn to him. For them Kurt Vonnegut is a man unstuck in time, a prophet for the twenty-first century—an exemplar of "planetary citizenship," his own highest ideal. It is to them that his most urgent messages were always directed, and for them, his grandchildren and great-grandchildren, that he continued to dream.[16]

Scientific and technological innovations could help, but the real answers to our predicament were less glamorous, embedded already in our everyday experience. "This promising of great secrets which are beyond our grasp— I don't think they exist," Vonnegut observed in 1973. "The mysteries which remain to be solved have to do with relating to each other."[17]

"It may be that Eden is this planet," he said a year later, in an essay reprinted in *Palm Sunday*. "If that is so, then we are still in it. It may be that we, poisoned by all our knowledge, are still crawling toward the gate." What to do?

> We had better make the best of a bad situation, which is a wonderful human skill. We had better make use of what has poisoned us.
>
> Why don't we use it to devise realistic methods for preventing us from crawling out the gate of the Garden of Eden? We're such wonderful mechanics. Maybe we can lock that gate with us inside.[18]

Notes

EPIGRAPHS

1. Quoted in Kurt Vonnegut, *Palm Sunday: An Autobiographical Collage* (New York: Delta, 1999), 152.
2. William Rodney Allen, ed., *Conversations with Kurt Vonnegut* (Jackson: University Press of Mississippi, 1988), 64.

PREFACE

1. Kurt Vonnegut to Gregory Sumner, April 5, 1997; Vonnegut to Sumner, February 14, 1998.

INTRODUCTION

1. Vonnegut, *Palm Sunday*, 64, 152–53; Kurt Vonnegut, *Fates Worse Than Death: An Autobiographical Collage of the 1980s* (New York: Putnam's, 1991), 35.
2. Kurt Vonnegut and Lee Stringer, *Like Shaking Hands with God: A Conversation about Writing* (New York: Seven Stories Press, 2010), 70.
3. Michael Walzer, *The Company of Critics: Social Criticism and Political Commitment in the Twentieth Century* (New York: Basic Books, 1988); Richard Rorty, *Achieving Our Country: Leftist Thought in Twentieth-Century America* (Cambridge, Mass.: Harvard University Press, 1998).

PROLOGUE

1. Vonnegut and Stringer, *Like Shaking Hands with God*, 51.
2. Vonnegut, *Palm Sunday*, 41.
3. Ibid., 46–48.
4. Ibid., 19–21.
5. Allen, ed., *Conversations*, 172.
6. Vonnegut, *Fates Worse Than Death*, 23; Vonnegut, *Palm Sunday*, 143.
7. Vonnegut, *Fates Worse Than Death*, 22.
8. Ibid., 24–25.
9. Vonnegut, *Palm Sunday*, 86.
10. Vonnegut, *Fates Worse Than Death*, 28, 33–34.
11. Vonnegut, *Palm Sunday*, 53–54; Allen, ed., *Conversations*, 89, 245.
12. Allen, ed., *Conversations*, 103.
13. Kurt Vonnegut, *God Bless You, Dr. Kevorkian* (New York: Seven Stories Press, 1999), 14.
14. Allen, ed., *Conversations*, 72.
15. Vonnegut, *Palm Sunday*, 89; Vonnegut, *Fates Worse Than Death*, 54–55; Allen, ed., *Conversations*, 5, 120, 157.
16. Robert Jay Lifton, *Witness to an Extreme Century: A Memoir* (New York: Free Press, 2011), 19.
17. Vonnegut, *Fates Worse Than Death*, 95; Vonnegut, *Palm Sunday*, 75–77.
18. Vonnegut, *Fates Worse Than Death*, 95–96.
19. Vonnegut, *Fates Worse Than Death*, 96; Vonnegut, *Palm Sunday*, 77.
20. Vonnegut, *Palm Sunday*, 79.
21. Kurt Vonnegut, *Armageddon in Retrospect: And Other New and Unpublished Writings on War and Peace* (New York: Putnam's, 2008), 11–13.
22. Vonnegut, *Palm Sunday*, 79; Vonnegut, *Fates Worse Than Death*, 100.

23. Vonnegut, *Armageddon in Retrospect*, 12.
24. Ibid., 34.
25. Ibid., 13.
26. Allen, ed., *Conversations*, 94–95.
27. Vonnegut, *Fates Worse Than Death*, 108.
28. Vonnegut, *Palm Sunday*, 90; Kurt Vonnegut, *Wampeters, Foma & Granfalloons (Opinions)* (New York: Delacorte Press/Seymour Lawrence, 1974), 176–78; Vonnegut, *Fates Worse Than Death*, 34–35.
29. Vonnegut, *Fates Worse Than Death*, 26.

ONE: *Player Piano*

1. Preface to Kurt Vonnegut, *Between Time and Timbuktu; or Prometheus-5: A Space Fantasy: Based on Materials by Kurt Vonnegut* (New York: Delacorte Press/Seymour Lawrence, 1972), xv.
2. Jerome Klinkowitz and John Somer, eds., *The Vonnegut Statement* (New York: Delacorte Press, 1973), 144; Danielle Furfaro, "Inspiration for Unfettered Imagination," *Albany Times Union* (April 13, 2007).
3. Allen, ed., *Conversations*, 93.
4. Ibid.
5. Ibid.
6. Klinkowitz and Somer, eds., *Vonnegut Statement*, 58.
7. Vonnegut, *Fates Worse Than Death*, 23–24.
8. Jerome Klinkowitz, *Kurt Vonnegut* (London: Methuen, 1982), 32.
9. Jerome Klinkowitz and Donald L. Lawler, eds., *Vonnegut in America: An Introduction to the Life and Work of Kurt Vonnegut* (New York: Delacorte Press/Seymour Lawrence, 1977), 18.
10. Allen, ed., *Conversations*, 74.
11. Ibid., 158–59.
12. Ibid., 113.
13. Vonnegut, *Palm Sunday*, 1; Allen, ed., *Conversations*, 294; Klinkowitz and Somer, eds., *Vonnegut Statement*, 8.
14. Allen, ed., *Conversations*, 157.
15. Ibid., 247.
16. Ibid., 199.

TWO: *The Sirens of Titan*

1. Klinkowitz, *Kurt Vonnegut*, 44.
2. Joseph Campbell, *The Hero with a Thousand Faces* (New York: Pantheon Press, 1949).
3. Mark Vonnegut, *Just Like Someone Without Mental Illness Only More So: A Memoir* (New York: Delacorte Press, 2010), 15; Kurt Vonnegut, *A Man Without a Country* (New York: Seven Stories Press, 2005), 125.
4. Allen, ed., *Conversations*, 159.
5. Vonnegut, *Wampeters*, 77; Allen, ed., *Conversations*, 98.
6. Allen, ed., *Conversations*, 98; Klinkowitz and Lawler, eds., *Vonnegut in America*, 21–22.
7. Allen, ed., *Conversations*, 99; Vonnegut, *Palm Sunday*, 184.
8. Allen, ed., *Conversations*, 104, 181.
9. Vonnegut, *Palm Sunday*, 172–73.
10. Ibid., 50.
11. Allen, ed., *Conversations*, 160.
12. Ibid., 35.

THREE: *Mother Night*

1. Kurt Vonnegut, *Mother Night* (New York: Dell, 1996), v.

2. Ibid., vii.
3. Ibid.
4. Ibid., v.
5. Allen, ed., *Conversations*, 69; Klinkowitz and Somer, eds., *Vonnegut Statement*, 161.
6. Allen, ed., *Conversations*, 49–51.
7. Klinkowitz and Lawler, eds., *Vonnegut in America*, 205.
8. Allen, ed., *Conversations*, 204.
9. I thank Dan Simon for drawing the connection here between spies and novel writers.

FOUR: *Cat's Cradle*

1. Peter Freese, *The Clown of Armageddon: The Novels of Kurt Vonnegut* (Heidelberg, Ger.: Universitatsverlag, 2009), 187.
2. Ibid., 209.
3. Allen, ed., *Conversations*, 182.
4. Peter Reed quoted in Klinkowitz and Lawler, eds., *Vonnegut in America*, 170.
5. Allen, ed., *Conversations*, 182.
6. Ibid., 232.
7. Ibid., 233.
8. Loree Rackstraw, *Love as Always, Kurt: Vonnegut as I Knew Him* (Cambridge, Mass.: Da Capo Press, 2009), 124.
9. Allen, ed., *Conversations*, 204–5.
10. John Updike, "All's Well in Skyscraper National Park," *The New Yorker* (October 25, 1976), reprinted in John Updike, *Hugging the Shore: Essays and Criticism* (New York: Penguin, 1985), 263–73, 270.
11. Allen, ed., *Conversations*, 234–35.
12. Freese, *Clown of Armageddon*, 183–84; Allen, ed., *Conversations*, 57.
13. Freese, *Clown of Armageddon*, 209.

FIVE: *God Bless You, Mr. Rosewater*

1. "Snippets Remembering Kurt Vonnegut," comp. Cliff Hayes, http://www.alplaus.org/In%20memorium/Kurt%20Vonnegut.html; Allen, ed., *Conversations*, 4.
2. Vonnegut, M., *Just Like Someone Without Mental Illness*, 15.
3. Freese, *Clown of Armageddon*, 273–74.
4. Allen, ed., *Conversations*, 160.
5. Dan Simon alerted me to this double entendre, which he said the author's friend and fellow war veteran, Howard Zinn, found particularly clever and amusing.
6. Allen, ed., *Conversations*, 3.
7. Freese, *Clown of Armageddon*, 251–52.
8. Ibid., 253.
9. Vonnegut, M., *Just Like Someone Without Mental Illness*, 23; Jane Vonnegut Yarmolinsky, *Angels Without Wings: A Courageous Family's Triumph over Tragedy* (New York: Fawcett, 1988).
10. Allen, ed., *Conversations*, 243.
11. Ibid., 89.
12. Ibid., 225.

SIX: *Slaughterhouse-Five*

1. Vonnegut, *Armageddon in Retrospect*, 12.
2. Allen, ed., *Conversations*, 275; Vonnegut, *Palm Sunday*, 273. Dan Simon, who was with the author during interviews for *A Man Without a Country*, shared with me Vonnegut's habit of bringing up Dresden after declaring it a taboo subject.
3. Klinkowitz and Lawler, eds., *Vonnegut in America*, 25.

4. Klinkowitz and Somer, eds., *Vonnegut Statement,* 64.
5. Allen, ed., *Conversations,* 91.
6. Ibid., 163.
7. Primo Levi, *Survival in Auschwitz: The Nazi Assault on Humanity* (New York: Touchstone, 1996).
8. Vonnegut, *Palm Sunday,* 83.
9. Gregory Sumner, "*Slaughterhouse* at Forty," *In These Times,* December 23, 2009, http://www.inthe-setimes.com/article/5348/slaughterhouse-five_at_forty. Billy Pilgrim was based in part on Edward Crone, a fellow POW from Rochester, New York who did not survive the war. See Grant Holcomb, vonnegutlibrary.org (June 8, 2010).
10. Allen, ed., *Conversations,* 163.
11. Vonnegut, *Palm Sunday,* 77.
12. Ibid., 78.
13. Allen, ed., *Conversations,* 94.
14. Ibid., 214.
15. Vonnegut, *Armageddon in Retrospect,* 12.
16. Vonnegut, *Palm Sunday,* 81.
17. Vonnegut, *Fates Worse Than Death,* 108; Vonnegut, *Palm Sunday,* 84; Vonnegut, *Fates Worse Than Death,* 222.
18. Vonnegut, *Palm Sunday,* 81.

SEVEN: *Breakfast of Champions*

1. Allen, ed., *Conversations,* 142; Ibid., 105.
2. Vonnegut, M. *Just Like Someone with Mental Illness,* 15–17, 46.
3. Rackstraw, *Love as Always,* 38; Vonnegut, *Palm Sunday,* 172.
4. Vonnegut, *Wampeters,* 139–58; Vonnegut, M. *Just Like Someone with Mental Illness,* 46; Rackstraw, *Love as Always,* 37–38.
5. Allen, ed., *Conversations,* 107.
6. Ibid., 86–87.
7. Ibid., 202.
8. Vonnegut, *Palm Sunday,* 203, 206–7.
9. Allen, ed., *Conversations,* 87.
10. Ibid., 108.
11. Ibid., 9.
12. Vonnegut, *Wampeters,* 25–30.
13. Allen, ed., *Conversations,* 49; Freese, *Clown of Armageddon,* 356.
14. Allen, ed., *Conversations,* 65–66, 69–70; Freese, *Clown of Armageddon,* 362.
15. Ibid., 110.

EIGHT: *Slapstick*

1. Allen, ed., *Conversations,* 186.
2. Ibid., 124; Vonnegut, *Palm Sunday,* 127–29.
3. John Updike, "All's Well in Skyscraper National Park," *The New Yorker,* October 25, 1976, reprinted in Updike, *Hugging the Shore,* 265.
4. Vonnegut, *Palm Sunday,* 294.
5. Allen, ed., *Conversations,* 83.
6. Ibid., 102–3.
7. Vonnegut, *Wampeters,* 147–48.
8. Allen, ed., *Conversations,* 85.
9. Vonnegut, *Fates Worse Than Death,* 151.
10. Rackstraw, *Love as Always,* 59.
11. Updike, *Hugging the Shore,* 271–72.
12. Allen, ed., *Conversations,* 80.

NINE: *Jailbird*

1. Vonnegut, *Wampeters*, xxi.
2. Vonnegut, *Palm Sunday*, 102–3.
3. Allen, ed., *Conversations*, 183–84.
4. Freese, *Clown of Armageddon*, 480-81; Allen, ed., *Conversations*, 101, 27.
5. Ibid., 227–28.
6. Ibid., 220.
7. Vonnegut, *Palm Sunday*, 1.
8. Ibid., 117–123, 121.
9. Ibid., 110.
10. Allen, ed., *Conversations*, 219.
11. Freese, *Clown of Armageddon*, 484–85.
12. Vonnegut, *Palm Sunday*, 110–14.
13. Ibid., xiii.
14. Allen, ed., *Conversations*, 222.
15. Freese, *Clown of Armageddon*, 490.
16. Allen, ed., *Conversations*, 217–18.
17. Peter J. Reed, "A Conversation with Kurt Vonnegut, 1982," in *The Vonnegut Chronicles*, ed. Peter J. Reed and Marc Leeds (Westwood, Conn.: Greenwood Press), 10.

TEN: *Deadeye Dick*

1. Vonnegut, *Palm Sunday*, 284.
2. Ibid., 68–72, 289.
3. Ibid., 70.
4. Ibid., 39.
5. Ibid., 33–36, 42–45.
6. Allen, ed., *Conversations*, 275.
7. Freese, *Clown of Armageddon*, 547.
8. Vonnegut, *Wampeters*, xxiv–xxv.
9. Reed, *Vonnegut Chronicles*, 9.
10. Ibid.
11. Vonnegut, *Fates Worse Than Death*, 38.
12. Freese, *Clown of Armageddon*, 528.
13. Dan Wakefield, *New York in the Fifties* (Boston: Houghton Mifflin/Seymour Lawrence, 1992), 277.
14. Rackstraw, *Love as Always*, 100.
15. Allen, ed., *Conversations*, 295.
16. Vonnegut, *Palm Sunday*, 104–5.
17. Vonnegut, *Fates Worse Than Death*, 97.
18. Vonnegut, *Palm Sunday*, 53.

ELEVEN: *Galápagos*

1. Reed, *Vonnegut Chronicles*, 13; Vonnegut, *Fates Worse Than Death*, 142, 145.
2. Vonnegut, *Armageddon in Retrospect*, 7.
3. Vonnegut, *Fates Worse Than Death*, 181.
4. Vonnegut, *Palm Sunday*, 299.
5. Allen, ed., *Conversations*, 76.
6. Vonnegut, *Armageddon in Retrospect*, 71.
7. Allen, ed., *Conversations*, 252–53.
8. Ibid., 259, 251.
9. Freese, *Clown of Armageddon*, 555–57, 581–82.

TWELVE: *Bluebeard*

1. Harry Rand, *Arshile Gorky: The Implications of Symbols* (Berkeley: University of California Press, 1991), 242.
2. Vonnegut, *Fates Worse Than Death*, 41–48.
3. Ibid., 43.
4. Rackstraw, *Love as Always*, 118.
5. Vonnegut, *Palm Sunday*, 195.
6. Vonnegut, *Fates Worse Than Death*, 188–89.
7. Vonnegut, *Palm Sunday*, 291–93.
8. Ibid., 293.
9. Vonnegut, M., *Just Like Someone with Mental Illness*, 24.
10. Ibid., 9–17, 10.
11. Ibid., 23, 26–27.
12. Allen, ed., *Conversations*, 242.
13. Ibid., 283–84.
14. Vonnegut, *Fates Worse Than Death*, 117–121.
15. Rackstraw, *Love as Always*, 104; Allen, ed., *Conversations*, 273.
16. Vonnegut, *Armageddon in Retrospect*, 3.
17. Vonnegut, *Fates Worse Than Death*, 171.
18. Allen, ed., *Conversations*, 265.
19. Rackstraw, *Love as Always*, 131.
20. Ibid., 133.
21. Allen, ed., *Conversations*, 299–300.

THIRTEEN: *Hocus Pocus*

1. Vonnegut, *Fates Worse Than Death*, 166–75.
2. Kurt Vonnegut, "Notes from My Bed of Gloom: Or, Why the Joking Had to Stop," *New York Times Book Review*, April 22, 1990, 14.
3. Vonnegut, *Fates Worse Than Death*, 216.
4. Vonnegut, *Palm Sunday*, 162.
5. Vonnegut, *Fates Worse Than Death*, 146.
6. Vonnegut, *Wampeters*, 190.
7. Vonnegut, *Fates Worse Than Death*, 127.
8. Ibid., 130, 174.
9. Ibid., 131.
10. Vonnegut, *Wampeters*, 215.
11. Vonnegut, *Fates Worse Than Death*, 201.
12. Ibid., 195.

FOURTEEN: *Timequake*

1. Vonnegut, *Fates Worse Than Death*, 196; Rackstraw, *Love as Always*, 182.
2. Vonnegut, *Palm Sunday*, 138.
3. Rackstraw, *Love as Always*, 125.
4. Vonnegut, *Wampeters*, 173–81.
5. Rackstraw, *Love as Always*, 181.
6. Ibid., 193.
7. Brad Stone, "Vonnegut's Last Stand," *Newsweek*, September 29, 1997; Valerie Sayers, "Vonnegut Stew," *New York Times*, September 28, 1997.
8. Rackstraw, *Love as Always*, 196–97.

EPILOGUE

1. Allen, ed., *Conversations,* 107; Douglas Brinkley, "Vonnegut's Apocalypse," *Rolling Stone,* August 24, 2006.
2. Kurt Vonnegut, *God Bless You, Dr. Kevorkian* (New York: Seven Stories Press, 1999).
3. Rackstraw, *Love as Always,* 201.
4. Ibid., 209–10.
5. "John Ashbery & Kurt Vonnegut Transcript: State Author/Poet Reading/Presentations—January 22, 2001," *New York State Writers Institute Online Magazine* 5, no. 3 (Summer 2001), http://www.albany.edu/writers-inst/webpages4/archives/olv5n3.html#vonnegut.
6. Ibid., 225; see also Gregory Sumner, "Vonnegut's Firefighters," Vonnegutlibrary.org (September 11, 2011).
7. Vonnegut, *A Man without a Country,* 56, 61.
8. Ibid., 105, 99, 110, 72.
9. Ibid., 42, 70–71.
10. Brinkley, "Vonnegut's Apocalypse"; A. O. Scott, "God Bless You, Mr. Vonnegut," *New York Times,* October 9, 2005.
11. Dave Eggers, "One for the Good Guys," *New York Times,* November 1, 2009.
12. Vonnegut, M., *Just Like Someone with Mental Illness,* 189–93.
13. Vonnegut, *Armageddon in Retrospect,* 10.
14. Ken Paulson, "'Slaughterhouse Five' ban should make school blush," *USA Today,* August 16, 2011.
15. Joshua Chaplinsky, "Donald Farber on the Legacy of Kurt Vonnegut," February 8, 2011, *The Cult: The Official Chuck Palahniuk Website,* http://chuckpalahniuk.net/interviews/authors/donald-farber-on-the-legacy-of-kurt-vonnegut.
16. Allen, ed., *Conversations,* 17.
17. Ibid., 74.
18. Vonnegut, *Palm Sunday,* 182.

Kurt Vonnegut's Novels

Player Piano. New York: Delacorte Press, 1952.

Sirens of Titan. New York: Delacorte Press, 1959.

Mother Night. New York: Harper & Row, 1961.

Cat's Cradle. New York: Delacorte Press, 1963.

God Bless You, Mr. Rosewater. New York: Holt, Rinehart & Winston, 1965.

Slaughterhouse-Five. New York: Delacorte Press, 1969.

Breakfast of Champions. New York: Delacorte Press, 1973.

Slapstick. New York: Delacorte Press/Seymour Lawrence, 1976.

Jailbird. New York: Delacorte Press/Seymour Lawrence, 1979.

Deadeye Dick. New York: Delacorte Press/Seymour Lawrence, 1982.

Galápagos. New York: Delacorte Press/Seymour Lawrence, 1985.

Bluebeard. New York: Delacorte Press, 1987.

Hocus Pocus. New York: Putnam's, 1990.

Timequake. New York: Putnam's, 1997.

Acknowledgments

"Find a subject you care about and which you in your heart feel others should care about." This was Kurt Vonnegut's first rule for writers, and it is one I followed with great care in committing to this project. I had plenty of help along the way, and would like here to offer my regards to at least some of those whose support sustained and nourished me.

First, I am grateful to Random House, Seven Stories Press, and Penguin, for permission to quote from Kurt Vonnegut's books.

I would like also to thank the National Endowment for the Humanities and the William J. Fulbright program for fellowship assistance during various stages of work on this book. I appreciate deeply the interest and feedback I received from Professor Roy Finkenbine and my colleagues and students at the University of Detroit Mercy. Thanks also to my students at Roma Tre in 2001 and 2010, who helped me to understand, from an Italian perspective, Vonnegut and the uniqueness of his American Dream.

I want to express my gratitude to Julia Whitehead of the Kurt Vonnegut Memorial Library in Indianapolis, and to the folks I met at the annual meeting of the Kurt Vonnegut Society in Boston in May 2011. I look forward to future collaborations. Thank you to Kurt Vonnegut's friend and executor Donald Farber for his assistance in the final stages of this project.

I am grateful to my agent, Robert Thixton, who, along with his partner Dick Duane, saw potential in my early manuscript and have ever since been staunch allies in guiding me to where I needed to go. I think of Bob in Vonnegutian terms, as a kind of "Blue Fairy Godmother" who came along at just the right time to help make my Cinderella story come true.

Vonnegut believed that people were "programmed" to express things as they did, like the big old computers of *Player Piano*. His job with each student in his writing classes involved, he said, "reaching into the mouth, taking hold of the piece of tape, pulling gently to see if I could read what was printed on it." The process sounds inelegant, but it is effective, and nobody does it better than Daniel Simon, my editor, another "Blue Fairy Godmother" in my journey. I am forever in debt to Dan for his acuity, patience, and passion in helping me to find my voice, to build and rebuild this house, "brick-by-brick." Dan has been an exemplary advocate for the reader and the subject alike, and I was privileged to work with him and his colleagues at Seven Stories Press. Special thanks to copyeditor extraordinaire Sarah McBride. Any errors or mistakes in judgment in this book are, of course, mine alone.

Another lesson Vonnegut taught writers was to "begin as close to the end as possible," so I will conclude with a gesture of gratitude to all of my friends and family who have been at my side, they know what their love and support means to me. I will single out a few who deserve special mention in relation to this project: Professor Casey Blake, Donald Kroger, Professor James Madison, Dr. Uday Desai, Joe Froslie and the Lockslie gang, Eric Mesko and Dan Rosbury, Chad Hickox, Battle Captain Robert Rouse, Captain Fred Moeller, Gerry Doelle, Rob Pernick, and my Wednesday night musical companions at A.J.'s Café. My thanks also to Greg Schroeder, whose enthusiasm for all things Vonnegut infected me back in 1992. Best wishes to my friends at Still Point Detroit, especially Koho, who reminded me of the Buddhist proverb that "a bucket of a water is filled one drop at a time." And warm thanks to Professor Rita Barrios for her technical help, and her abiding encouragement, laughter, and moral support.

Finally, let me acknowledge three men who have been a special inspiration to me as I wrote this book: my great-uncle, Lieutenant Colonel Robert O. Gregory (1915–2004); my father, Fredric Dean Sumner (1934–1973); and Kurt Vonnegut himself (1922–2007). Each is a presence in my life, an unwavering band of light.

NOTES ON PERMISSIONS

Hocus Pocus by Kurt Vonnegut, © 1990 by Kurt Vonnegut. *Timequake* by Kurt Vonnegut, © 1997 by Kurt Vonnegut. Excerpts used by permission of G.P. Putnam's Sons, a division of Penguin Group (USA) Inc.

Index

About the Author

Gregory Sumner, JD, PhD, is professor and chair of the department of history at the University of Detroit Mercy, where he has taught since 1993. He is the author of *Dwight Macdonald and the Politics Circle* (1996). Dr. Sumner has been a Fellow with the National Endowment for the Humanities, and has twice served as William J. Fulbright Lecturer at the Università di Roma Tre. He grew up in Indianapolis, Indiana.

Sumner, Gregory D.
Unstuck in time.

DATE			